MW00717336

Making Economic Sense

2nd Edition

Making Economic Sense

2nd Edition

Murray N. Rothbard

Ludwig von Mises Institute
Auburn, Alabama

Copyright © 1995, 2006, 2008 by the Ludwig von Mises Institute

All rights reserved. No part of this book may be reproduced in any manner whatsoever without written permission except in the case of reprints in the context of reviews. For information write the Ludwig von Mises Institute, 518 West Magnolia Avenue, Auburn, Alabama 36832.

ISBN: 978-0-945466-46-8

CONTENTS

THE SOCIALISM OF WELFARE

POLITICS AS ECONOMIC VIOLENCE

ENTERPRISE UNDER ATTACK

FISCAL MYSTERIES REVEALED

ECONOMICS BEYOND THE BORDERS

THE END OF COLLECTIVISM

PREFACE

The academic contributions of Murray N. Rothbard (1926–1995) are legion, but he also had a passion for public persuasion. A free society can only be sustained if the general public is aware of the vital importance of the market and the terrible consequences of statism. That's why Rothbard hoped to convince everyone about the virtues of the free economy. For Rothbard, educating the public was strategically necessary and morally obligatory. It was also lots of fun.

From 1982 to 1995, the *Free Market* was home to Rothbard's monthly explanation of economic events. He presented theory and policy in clear, sprightly prose while never sacrificing intellectual rigor. Keeping with Mencken's rule, Rothbard's clear writing was a product of his clear thought. Even when discussing subjects like interest rates and excise taxes—subjects economists typically take pains to make unbearably boring—Rothbard teaches and entertains at the same time.

The *Free Market* essays are a crucial part of the legacy he has left us. As he skewers both parties in all branches of government, and all their connected interests, we see a principled Austrian School economist at work.

The Second Edition is expanded to include "Protectionism and the Destruction of Prosperity," a monograph printed by the Mises Institute in 1986; "Taking Money Back," a piece crafted in 1991 to make a populist case for radical monetary reform, and a brief but moving obituary of Mises published in 1973.

No matter how specialized and distant from reality the economic profession becomes, Rothbard proves it is always possible to communicate truth more broadly. In this area, as in so much else, Rothbard shows us the way.

Llewellyn H. Rockwell, Jr.
Auburn, Alabama
January 2006

INTRODUCTION TO THE SECOND EDITION

Murray Newton Rothbard (1926–1995) was one of the most important thinkers of the twentieth century. I choose the somewhat vague term thinker because Rothbard's interests were so diverse that they defy conventional classification. Yes, Rothbard was an economic theorist in the "Austrian" tradition of Ludwig von Mises and Friedrich Hayek. But Rothbard also wrote a detailed history of the Great Depression, two volumes on the history of economic thought, several methodological articles, as well as an incredibly lucid text on economic principles. With the specialization of the modern economics profession, these feats alone would be unusual: You do either economic theory, economic history, history of economic thought (if you don't care about getting a job, at any rate), or—if you're one of the few economists who can actually produce prose that students and the lay public find comprehensible—you go ahead and write an introductory textbook. Except for freaks like Paul Samuelson (and Murray Rothbard), you don't do all of these things, just as a surgeon specializes in the heart or the brain, but never both.

And yet we can't stop there. In addition to his contributions to all areas of economics, Rothbard wrote four (provocative) volumes on the history of colonial America. He also drew on philosophy, political science, and legal theory to synthesize a 357-page deductive treatise on the nature and content of the legal code in a just and free society. Oh yes, I almost forgot:

Rothbard virtually single-handedly created the modern libertarian movement through his ceaseless agitation and two books, one explaining the terrible consequences of all government intervention and the other giving the virtual blueprints for a society with no government.

"An impressive fellow," you may say, "who was no doubt a genius. Yet surely he was a humorless robot of a man, spewing forth lonely and bitter critiques of all those lesser mortals with whom he could not identify."

Now this relates to the really surprising aspect of Murray Rothbard—the guy was funny, and he was a real person. You will see this immediately as you read the essays, but I fear that if the present volume is your only sampling of Rothbard's work, it may give the impression that his writing was remarkably entertaining in light of how, well, stuffy the topics were. But what do you expect? Most of these essays were originally published in the *Free Market*, a newsletter obviously devoted to economic and political issues, subjects that can at times (despite their tremendous importance) be a bit dry. If this is indeed your reaction, you absolutely must go on to read *The Irrepressible Rothbard*, a collection of some of his lighter essays. There you will see the same impeccable logic, brutal honesty, and wonderful wit, but in the context of antiwar polemics, politically incorrect musings on various racial and sexual conflicts, surprisingly plausible conspiracy theories, insensitive *ad hominem* (yet undeniably funny) attacks on people Rothbard can't stand, good old Clinton bashing, and, believe it or not, movie reviews that are far more insightful than what you will likely get in your local newspaper.

As I mentioned above, most of the essays in the present volume originally ran in the the *Free Market*, a monthly newsletter put out by the Ludwig von Mises Institute, which was founded in 1982 to promote and advance the legacy of Rothbard's beloved mentor. Ludwig von Mises (1881–1973) was the undisputed champion of the Austrian School of economics during his lifetime. (The term "Austrian" refers to the nationality of the

School's pioneers; Austrian economists do not study the unemployment rate of Vienna.) Among his theoretical achievements was the incorporation, in the early twentieth century, of money prices into the subjectivist, marginalist framework that other economists of that day had used only to explain prices in a barter economy. Mises also drew on the work of his own mentor, Eugen von Böhm-Bawerk, as well as Knut Wicksell, to elaborate a theory of the business cycle that laid the blame not on capitalism but rather on the central government's manipulations of the banking system. (It was for his elaboration of the Misesian cycle theory that Friedrich Hayek won the Nobel Prize in economics in 1974.)

Another major contribution was Mises's work on methodology, in which he argued that economic laws were a subset of "praxeology"—the logic or science of human action—and were not comparable to the physical laws of the natural sciences. In the natural sciences, we observe the actual outcome—the trajectory of a cannonball, let us say—and then we must come up with hypotheses to explain the causal forces at work. In contrast, in the social sciences (whether criminology, sociology, psychology, or economics) we presumably know the motivating forces at work, at least at a certain level of generality: When a man robs a bank, we do not study the physical forces on the atoms in his body, but rather ask, "What drove him to this desperate act? Didn't he have a strong role model to teach him right from wrong?" and so on. (It's not so much that we couldn't use the methods of the physicist or chemist, but just that they wouldn't take us very far. They certainly wouldn't help detectives recover the loot! For that task, we need to "get inside the head" of the thief.) Mises looked at the growing body of economic analysis (at least in the early twentieth century) and crystallized its essence as logical deductions from the fact that people act; in other words, Mises felt all valid economic laws were implied by the fact that people are rational (though fallible) beings who choose means to (attempt to) achieve desired ends. I bring this point up because there is a tendency among certain people to lump all "free market" economists together, so that Milton

Friedman and Ludwig von Mises (or Murray Rothbard) are "basically saying the same thing." This issue of the proper foundation of economic science is one major example of the error of such careless grouping; in exact contradiction to the view of Mises and Rothbard, Milton Friedman is famous for his defense of positivism in economics, i.e., the application of the methods of the physical sciences to the social sciences.

There is another difference between Mises (and Rothbard) and such popular advocates of laissez-faire as Milton Friedman or, more recently, heroes of American political "conservatives" such as Lawrence Kudlow or Alan Greenspan. It is true that all of these economists would agree, say, that a cut in the capital gains tax would be good for the American economy, or that raising the minimum wage to $10 per hour would hurt inner city minorities. In that sense they are all "anti-government." But Mises (and even more so, Rothbard) were far more consistent in their promotion of individual liberty and free enterprise, and their condemnation of government intervention in the economy. Thus Friedman could advocate a "negative income tax"— i.e., a welfare program that is novel only in the method by which the amounts of the checks are calculated—and Greenspan and Kudlow certainly do not feel "government is the problem" when it comes to the Federal Reserve.

Of course, some may feel that these last remarks are both unfair and politically naïve. Indeed, one of the biggest complaints against Mises, and especially Rothbard, is that they were stubborn, "dogmatic" ideologues, who couldn't support a move in the right direction because of their unrealistic principles. Although I don't subscribe to this objection, this Introduction is hardly the place for me to answer it. Let me mention, though, that another popular objection is that Rothbard was a sellout who would ally with various communists, Democrats, protectionist Republicans, etc. based on the shifting political winds. Now say what you will about his strategic vision—and the huge growth of the extremely radical "anarcho-capitalist" movement is a point in his favor—but Rothbard can't be both a dogmatic purist and an opportunistic sellout at the same time!

I wish I could include some of my personal anecdotes of Rothbard to give you a sense of the man, but unfortunately I never met him. As many say of John F. Kennedy, I can truly remember exactly where I was when I learned the news. I was an economics major at Hillsdale College, and another student mentioned to me that "some big free market economist" had died. With a sinking stomach I asked, "It's not Murray Rothbard, is it?" to which my friend replied, "Yeah, that was his name." I was extremely disappointed because, in many respects, Rothbard's work (in both economics proper and political philosophy) had been the standard by which I would judge my own. On those issues where we disagreed—and there were many—I wanted to hear him reply to my critiques, and now that would be impossible. (Yes, I was as self-absorbed as any other American undergrad.) But on those issues where we agreed—where Rothbard really nailed the issue on the head, in my mind—wow did he do it beautifully.

You will see this in the present collection. In addition to being correct, Rothbard's prose is also precise and direct. (In contrast, Hayek's points are often valid and extremely precise, but might involve seven clauses and three semicolons.) You will also get a sense of Rothbard's extreme breadth of knowledge. To paraphrase Mark Twain: the older I get, the smarter Murray Rothbard becomes. I realized this when I first taught an advanced class in Austrian economics, and one of the readings was Rothbard's famous (1956) essay, "Toward a Reconstruction of Utility and Welfare Economics." Having just graduated from a fairly highly ranked doctoral program in mathematical economics, I considered myself quite knowledgeable about abstract concepts such as von Neumann-Morgenstern utility functions. I was quite surprised, then, to see that Rothbard was perfectly adept with the mathematical sophistication in these demonstrations, and could point out their underlying (false) assumptions. I was surprised yet again when rereading the present collection, and came across Rothbard's essay on chaos theory. Because of an honors seminar on "spontaneous order" (i.e., the emergence of orderly macro phenomena from simple micro foundations) I had just read an entire book on the history and current applications of chaos theory—and that's how I knew that Rothbard had apparently done the same, because his essay contains references to names and subtle points that suggest a deep understanding. What's particularly ironic is that I had read this essay years earlier, when *Making Economic Sense* first appeared, and must have skimmed over these subtleties because at the time I didn't quite know what Rothbard was talking about.

The one other anecdote I can share concerns a roadtrip that I was taking with my mother and her friend. I had taken my (first edition) copy of *Making Economic Sense* even though I had read it cover to cover before. At some point in the trip, my mother's friend became bored and asked if she could look at it. I agreed with hesitation; even though I knew Rothbard was great, surely a "real person" would find him boring and/or crazy! But as it turns out, she was chuckling after a few pages, and even began discussing the book with my mother. She particularly liked Rothbard's observation that new houses can't be built to last as long as older ones, because, "Oh, we couldn't afford to build it that way today." In short, although I can't remember exactly what drove my insecurity—hey, I think I was still a teenager—it was completely unfounded.

Although many of us younger libertarians were shocked and disillusioned with the Republican Party over George W. Bush's unprecedented deficits and propensity to conquer other countries, some of the enclosed essays show us that this is nothing new. Of Ronald Reagan Rothbard writes,

> It is no accident that the same administration that manages to combine the rhetoric of 'getting government off our back' with the reality of enormously escalating Big Government, should also have brought back a failed and statist Keynesianism in the name of prosperity and free enterprise.

In a later essay he continues:

> Since the beginning of the Reagan administration, the much heralded "cuts" in the officially dubbed "income-tax"

segment of our payroll taxes have been more than offset by the rise in the "Social-Security" portion. But since the public has been conditioned into thinking that the Social Security tax is somehow not a tax, the Reagan-Bush administrations have been able to get away with their pose as heroic champions of tax cuts and resisters against the tax-raising inclinations of the evil Democrats.

As far as the Middle East, Rothbard's essay "Why the Intervention in Arabia?" is cogent reading for today. (A similar phenomenon occurs if one listens to the stand-up rantings of the late comedian Bill Hicks. Even though he died before the invasion of Iraq, one could listen to his criticism of "Bush's" justifications for war, as well as his hypocritical demonization of Saddam, for several minutes without realizing that Hicks is referring to George Herbert Walker Bush.)

I began this Introduction by stating that Murray Rothbard was one of the most important thinkers of the twentieth century. Largely through the efforts of the Mises Institute, his work, of which the present collection is just a morsel, continues to reach ever wider audiences. Although it's much too soon to be confident, perhaps future writers will refer to Murray Rothbard as one of the most influential thinkers of the twenty-first century.

Robert P. Murphy
Hillsdale College
December 2005

Making Economic Sense

I

IS IT THE "ECONOMY, STUPID"?

One of the persistent Clintonian themes of the 1992 campaign still endures: if "it's the economy, stupid," then why hasn't President Clinton received the credit among the public for our glorious economic recovery? Hence the Clintonian conclusion that the resounding Democratic defeat in November, 1994, was due to their failure to "get the message out" to the public, the message being the good news of our current economic prosperity.

Some of the brighter Clintonians realized that the President and his minions had been repeating this very message endlessly all over America; so they fell back on the implausible alternative explanation that the minds of the voting public had been temporarily addled by listening to Rush Limbaugh and his colleagues.

So what went wrong with this popular line of reasoning? As usual, there are many layers of fallacy contained in this political analysis. In the first place, it's crude economic determinism, what is often called "vulgar Marxism." While the state of the economy is certainly important in shaping the public's political attitudes, there are many non-economic reasons for public protest.

First published in February 1995.

The public is particularly exercised, for example, about crime, gun control, the flood of immigration, and the continuing wholesale assault by government and the dominant liberal culture upon religion and upon "bourgeois" as well as traditional ethical principles.

Other non-economic reasons: a growing pervasive skepticism about politicians keeping their pledges to the voters, a skepticism born of hard-won experience rather than of some infection by a bacillus of "cynicism." *A fortiori* removed from economics is an intense revulsion for the president, his wife, and their personal traits ("the character question"), a visceral response that made a powerful impact on the election.

But even apart from the numerous non-economic motivations for political attitudes and actions by the public, the common "it's the economy" argument even leaves out some of the important features of economic-based motivation in politics. For the famous Clintonian slogan does not even begin to focus on all the relevant features of the economy.

Instead, to capture the Clintonian meaning, the sentiment should be rephrased as "it's the business cycle, stupid." For what the Clintonians and the media are really advocating is "vulgar business-cycle determinism": if the economy is booming, the ins will be reelected: if we're in recession, the public will oust the ruling party.

The "Business cycle" may at first appear to be equivalent to "the economy," but in fact it is not. There are vital aspects of the economy felt by the voters that are not cyclical, not part of a boom-bust process, but that rather reflect "secular" (long-run) trends. What's happening to taxes and to secular living standards, and among such standards the intangible, unmeasurable but vital concept of the "quality of life," is extremely important, often more so than whether we are technically in the expansion or contraction phase of the cycle.

Indeed, the major economic grievance agitating the public has little or nothing to do with the cycle, with boom or recession: it is secular and seemingly permanent, specifically a slow, inexorable, debilitating decline in the standard of living that grinds down the people's spirit as well as their pocketbooks. Taxes, and the tax bite into their earnings, keep going up, on the federal, state, county, and local levels of government. Semantic disguises don't work any more: call them "fees," or "contributions," or "insurance premiums," they are taxes nevertheless, and they are increasingly draining the people's substance.

And while Establishment economists, statisticians, and financial experts keep proclaiming that "inflation has been licked," that "structural economic factors preclude a return to inflation," and all the rest of the blather, all consumers *know* in their hearts and wallets that the prices they pay at the supermarket, at the store, in tuition, in insurance, in magazine subscriptions, keep going up and up, and that the dollar's value keeps going down and down.

The contemptuous charge by economic "scientists" that all this experience by consumers is merely "anecdotal," that hard quantitative data and their statistical manipulations demonstrate that economic growth is lively, that the economy is doing splendidly, that inflation is over, and all the rest, doesn't cut any ice either. In the end, all this "science" has only succeeded in convincing the public that economic and statistical experts rank up there with lawyers and politicians as a bunch of—how shall we put it?—"disinformation specialists."

If everything is going so well, the public increasingly wants to know, how come young married couples today can no longer afford the standard of living enjoyed by their parents when they were newlyweds? How come they can't afford to buy a home of their own? One of the glorious staples of the American experience has always been that each generation expects its children to be better off than they have been. This expectation was never the result of mindless "optimism"; it was rooted in the experience of each preceding generation, which indeed had been more prosperous than their parents.

But now the reality is quite the opposite. People know they are worse off than their parents, and therefore they rationally expect their children to be in still worse shape. Everywhere you turn you get a similar answer: "Why couldn't you construct a new building with the same sturdy qualities as this (50-year old) house? . . . Oh, we couldn't *afford* to build it that way today."

Even official statistics bear out this point, if you know where to look. For example, the median real income in dollars, (that is, corrected for inflation) of American families is lower than it was in 1973. Then, if we disaggregate households, we get a far gloomier picture. Family income has not only been slightly reduced; it has collapsed in the last 20 years because of the phenomenal increase of the proportion of married women in the workforce.

This massive shift from motherhood and the domestic arts to the tedium of offices and time clocks has been interpreted by our dominant liberal culture as a glorious triumph of feminism in liberating women from the drudgery of being housewives so that they can develop their personalities in a fulfilling career. While this may be true for some occupations, one still hears on every side, once again, that the "reason I went to work is because we could no longer afford to live on one salary."

Again, since there is no way to quantify subjective motivations, we can't measure this factor, but I suspect that the great bulk of working women, i.e., those in non-glamorous careers, are only working to keep the family income from falling steeply. Given their druthers, I suspect they would happily return to the much-maligned "Ozzie and Harriet" family of the Neanderthal era.

Of course, there are some sectors of the economy that are indeed growing rapidly, where prices are falling instead of rising; notably the computer industry, and whatever emerges from the much-hyped "information superhighway," when, at some wonderful point in the near or mid-future, Americans can drown their increasing miseries in the glories of 500 interactive, digital, cybernetic channels, each offering another subvariant of mindless pap.

This is a future that may satisfy techno-futurist gurus like Alvin Toffler and Newt Gingrich, but the rest of us, I bet, will become increasingly unhappy and ready to lash out at the political system that—through massive taxation, cheap money and credit, social insurance schemes, mandates, and government regulation—has brought us this secular deterioration, and has laid waste to the American dream. ▶

2
TEN GREAT ECONOMIC MYTHS

Our country is beset by a large number of economic myths that distort public thinking on important problems and lead us to accept unsound and dangerous government policies. Here are ten of the most dangerous of these myths and an analysis of what is wrong with them.

Myth 1: *Deficits are the cause of inflation; deficits have nothing to do with inflation.*

In recent decades we always have had federal deficits. The invariable response of the party *out* of power, whichever it may be, is to denounce those deficits as being the cause of perpetual inflation. And the invariable response of whatever party is *in* power has been to claim that deficits have nothing to do with inflation. *Both* opposing statements are myths.

Deficits mean that the federal government is spending more than it is taking in in taxes. Those deficits can be financed in two ways. If they are financed by selling Treasury bonds to the public, then the deficits are not inflationary. No new money is created; people and institutions simply draw down their bank deposits to pay for the bonds, and the Treasury spends that money. Money has simply been transferred from the public to

First published in April 1984.

the Treasury, and then the money is spent on other members of the public.

On the other hand, the deficit may be financed by selling bonds to the banking system. If that occurs, the banks create new money by creating new bank deposits and using them to buy the bonds. The new money, in the form of bank deposits, is then spent by the Treasury, and thereby enters permanently into the spending stream of the economy, raising prices and causing inflation. By a complex process, the Federal Reserve enables the banks to create the new money by generating bank reserves of one-tenth that amount. Thus, if banks are to buy $100 billion of new bonds to finance the deficit, the Fed buys approximately $10 billion of *old* Treasury bonds. This purchase increases bank reserves by $10 billion, allowing the banks to pyramid the creation of new bank deposits or money by ten times that amount. In short, the government and the banking system it controls in effect "print" new money to pay for the federal deficit.

Thus, deficits are inflationary to the extent that they are financed by the banking system; they are *not* inflationary to the extent they are underwritten by the public.

Some policymakers point to the 1982–83 period, when deficits were accelerating and inflation was abating, as a statistical "proof" that deficits and inflation have no relation to each other. This is no proof at all. General price changes are determined by two factors: the supply of, and the demand for, money. During 1982–83 the Fed created new money at a very high rate, approximately at 15 percent per annum. Much of this went to finance the expanding deficit. But on the other hand, the severe depression of those two years increased the demand for money (i.e., lowered the desire to spend money on goods) in response to the severe business losses. This temporarily compensating increase in the demand for money does not make deficits any less inflationary. In fact, as recovery proceeds, spending picked up and the demand for money fell, and the spending of the new money accelerated inflation.

Myth 2: *Deficits do not have a crowding-out effect on private investment.*

In recent years there has been an understandable worry over the low rate of saving and investment in the United States. One worry is that the enormous federal deficits will divert savings to unproductive government spending and thereby crowd out productive investment, generating ever-greater long-run problems in advancing or even maintaining the living standards of the public.

Some policymakers once again attempted to rebut this charge by statistics. In 1982–83, they declare deficits were high and increasing while interest rates fell, thereby indicating that deficits have no crowding-out effect.

This argument once again shows the fallacy of trying to refute logic with statistics. Interest rates fell because of the drop of business borrowing in a recession. "Real" interest rates (interest rates minus the inflation rate) stayed unprecedentedly high, however—partly because most of us expect renewed inflation, partly because of the crowding-out effect. In any case, statistics cannot refute logic; and logic tells us that if savings go into government bonds, there will necessarily be less savings available for productive investment than there would have been, and interest rates will be higher than they would have been without the deficits. If deficits are financed by the public, then this diversion of savings into government projects is direct and palpable. If the deficits are financed by bank inflation, then the diversion is indirect, the crowding-out now taking place by the new money "printed" by the government competing for resources with old money saved by the public.

Milton Friedman tries to rebut the crowding-out effect of deficits by claiming that *all* government spending, not just deficits, equally crowds out private savings and investment. It is true that money siphoned off by taxes could also have gone into private savings and investment. But deficits have a far greater crowding-out effect than overall spending, since deficits financed by the public obviously tap savings and savings alone, whereas taxes reduce the public's consumption as well as savings.

Thus, deficits, whichever way you look at them, cause grave economic problems. If they are financed by the banking system, they are inflationary. But even if they are financed by the public, they will still cause severe crowding-out effects, diverting much-needed savings from productive private investment to wasteful government projects. And, furthermore, the greater the deficits the greater the permanent income tax burden on the American people to pay for the mounting interest payments, a problem aggravated by the high interest rates brought about by inflationary deficits.

Myth 3: *Tax increases are a cure for deficits.*

Those people who are properly worried about the deficit unfortunately offer an unacceptable solution: increasing taxes. Curing deficits by raising taxes is equivalent to curing someone's bronchitis by shooting him. The "cure" is far worse than the disease.

One reason, as many critics have pointed out, raising taxes simply gives the government more money, and so the politicians and bureaucrats are likely to react by raising expenditures still further. Parkinson said it all in his famous "Law": "Expenditures rise to meet income." If the government is willing to have, say, a 20 percent deficit, it will handle high revenues by raising spending still more to maintain the same proportion of deficit.

But even apart from this shrewd judgment in political psychology, why should anyone believe that a *tax* is better than a higher price? It is true that inflation is a form of taxation, in which the government and other early receivers of new money are able to expropriate the members of the public whose income rises later in the process of inflation. But, at least with inflation, people are still reaping some of the benefits of exchange. If bread rises to $10 a loaf, this is unfortunate, but *at least* you can still eat the bread. But if taxes go up, your money is expropriated for the benefit of politicians and bureaucrats, and you are left with no service or benefit. The only result is that the producers' money is confiscated for the benefit of a bureaucracy that adds insult to injury by using part of that confiscated money to push the public around.

No, the only sound cure for deficits is a simple but virtually unmentioned one: cut the federal budget. How and where? Anywhere and everywhere.

Myth 4: *Every time the Fed tightens the money supply, interest rates rise (or fall); every time the Fed expands the money supply, interest rates rise (or fall).*

The financial press now knows enough economics to watch weekly money supply figures like hawks; but they inevitably interpret these figures in a chaotic fashion. If the money supply rises, this is interpreted as lowering interest rates and inflationary; it is *also* interpreted, often in the very same article, as raising interest rates. And vice versa. If the Fed tightens the growth of money, it is interpreted as both raising interest rates and lowering them. Sometimes it seems that *all* Fed actions, no matter how contradictory, must result in raising interest rates. Clearly something is very wrong here.

The problem is that, as in the case of price levels, there are several causal factors operating on interest rates and in different directions. If the Fed expands the money supply, it does so by generating more bank reserves and thereby expanding the supply of bank credit and bank deposits. The expansion of credit necessarily means an increased supply in the credit market and hence a lowering of the price of credit, or the rate of interest. On the other hand, if the Fed restricts the supply of credit and the growth of the money supply, this means that the supply in the credit market declines, and this should mean a rise in interest rates.

And this is precisely what happens in the first decade or two of chronic inflation. Fed expansion lowers interest rates; Fed tightening raises them. But after this period, the public and the market begin to catch on to what is happening. They begin to realize that inflation is chronic because of the systemic expansion of the money supply. When they realize this fact of life, they will also realize that inflation wipes out the creditor for the benefit of the debtor. Thus, if someone grants a loan at 5 percent for one year, and there is 7 percent inflation for that year, the creditor loses, not gains. He loses 3 percent, since he gets paid back in dollars that are now worth 7 percent less in purchasing power. Correspondingly, the debtor gains by inflation. As creditors begin to catch on, they place an inflation premium on the interest rate, and debtors will be willing to pay it. Hence, in the long-run anything which fuels the expectations of inflation will raise inflation premiums on interest rates; and anything which dampens those expectations will lower those premiums. Therefore, a Fed tightening will now tend to dampen inflationary expectations and *lower* interest rates; a Fed expansion will whip up those expectations again and *raise* them. There are two, opposite causal chains at work. And so Fed expansion or contraction can either raise or lower interest rates, depending on which causal chain is stronger.

Which will be stronger? There is no way to know for sure. In the early decades of inflation, there is no inflation premium; in the later decades, such as we are now in, there is. The relative strength and reaction times depend on the subjective expectations of the public, and these cannot be forecast with certainty. And this is one reason why economic forecasts can never be made with certainty.

Myth 5: *Economists, using charts or high speed computer models, can accurately forecast the future.*

The problem of forecasting interest rates illustrates the pitfalls of forecasting in general. People are contrary cusses whose behavior, thank goodness, cannot be forecast precisely in advance. Their values, ideas, expectations, and knowledge change all the time, and change in an unpredictable manner. What economist, for example, could have forecast (or did forecast) the Cabbage Patch Kid craze of the Christmas season of 1983? Every economic quantity, every price, purchase, or income figure is the embodiment of thousands, even millions, of unpredictable choices by individuals.

Many studies, formal and informal, have been made of the record of forecasting by economists, and it has been consistently abysmal. Forecasters often complain that they can do well enough as long as current trends continue; what they have difficulty in doing is catching changes in trend. But of course there is no trick in extrapolating current trends into the near future. You don't need sophisticated computer models for that; you can do it better and far more cheaply by using a ruler. The real trick is precisely to forecast when and how trends will change, and forecasters have been notoriously bad at that. No economist forecast the depth of the 1981–82 depression, and none predicted the strength of the 1983 boom.

The next time you are swayed by the jargon or seeming expertise of the economic forecaster, ask yourself this question: If he can really predict the future so well, *why* is he wasting his time putting out newsletters or doing consulting when he himself could be making trillions of dollars in the stock and commodity markets?

Myth 6: *There is a tradeoff between unemployment and inflation.*

Every time someone calls for the government to abandon its inflationary policies, establishment economists and politicians warn that the result can only be severe unemployment. We are trapped, therefore, into playing off inflation against high unemployment, and become persuaded that we must therefore accept some of both.

This doctrine is the fallback position for Keynesians. Originally, the Keynesians promised us that by manipulating and fine-tuning deficits and government spending, they could and would bring us permanent prosperity and full employment without inflation. Then, when inflation became chronic and ever-greater, they changed their tune to warn of the alleged tradeoff, so as to weaken any possible pressure upon the government to stop its inflationary creation of new money.

The tradeoff doctrine is based on the alleged "Phillips curve," a curve invented many years ago by the British economist A.W. Phillips. Phillips correlated wage rate increases with unemployment, and claimed that the two move inversely: the higher the increases in wage rates, the lower the unemployment. On its face, this is a peculiar doctrine, since it flies in the face of logical, commonsense theory. Theory tells us that the higher the wage rates, the *greater* the unemployment, and *vice versa*. If everyone went to their employer tomorrow and insisted on double or triple the wage rate, many of us would be promptly out of a job. Yet this bizarre finding was accepted as gospel by the Keynesian economic Establishment.

By now, it should be clear that this statistical finding violates the facts as well as logical theory. For during the 1950s, inflation was only about one to two percent per year, and unemployment hovered around three or four percent, whereas later unemployment ranged between eight and 11 percent, and inflation between five and 13 percent. In the last two or three decades, in short, *both* inflation *and* unemployment have increased sharply and severely. If anything, we have had a *reverse* Phillips curve. There has been anything but an inflation-unemployment tradeoff.

But ideologues seldom give way to the facts, even as they continually claim to "test" their theories by facts. To save the concept, they have simply concluded that the Phillips curve still remains as an inflation-unemployment tradeoff, except that the curve has unaccountably "shifted" to a new set of alleged tradeoffs. On this sort of mind-set, of course, no one could ever refute any theory.

In fact, current inflation, even if it reduces unemployment in the shortrun by inducing prices to spurt ahead of wage rates (thereby reducing *real* wage rates), will only create more unemployment in the long run. Eventually, wage rates catch up with inflation, and inflation brings recession and unemployment inevitably in its wake. After more than two decades of inflation, we are now living in that "long run."

Myth 7: *Deflation—falling prices—is unthinkable, and would cause a catastrophic depression.*

The public memory is short. We forget that, from the beginning of the Industrial Revolution in the mid-eighteenth century until the beginning of World War II, prices generally went down, year after year. That's because continually increasing productivity and output of goods generated by free markets caused prices to fall. There was no depression, however, because costs fell along with selling prices. Usually, wage rates remained constant while the cost of living fell, so that "real" wages, or everyone's standard of living, rose steadily.

Virtually the only time when prices rose over those two centuries were periods of war (War of 1812, Civil War, World War I), when the warring governments inflated the money supply so heavily to pay for the war as to more than offset continuing gains in productivity.

We can see how free-market capitalism, unburdened by governmental or central bank inflation, works if we look at what has happened in the last few years to the prices of computers. Even a simple computer used to be enormous, costing millions of dollars. Now, in a remarkable surge of productivity brought about by the microchip revolution, computers are falling in price even as I write. Computer firms are successful despite the falling prices because their costs have been falling, and productivity rising. In fact, these falling costs and prices have enabled them to tap a mass market characteristic of the dynamic growth of free-market capitalism. "Deflation" has brought no disaster to this industry.

The same is true of other high-growth industries, such a electronic calculators, plastics, TV sets, and VCRs. Deflation, far from bringing catastrophe, is the hallmark of sound and dynamic economic growth.

Myth 8: *The best tax is a "flat" income tax, proportionate to income across the board, with no exemptions or deductions.*

It is usually added by flat-tax proponents, that eliminating such exemptions would enable the federal government to cut the current tax rate substantially.

But this view assumes, for one thing, that present deductions from the income tax are immoral subsidies or "loopholes" that should be closed for the benefit of all. A deduction or exemption is only a "loophole" if you assume that the government owns 100 percent of everyone's income and that allowing some of that income to remain untaxed constitutes an irritating "loophole." Allowing someone to keep some of his own income is neither a loophole nor a subsidy. Lowering the overall tax by abolishing deductions for medical care, for interest payments, or for uninsured losses, is simply lowering the taxes of one set of people (those that have little interest to pay, or medical expenses, or uninsured losses) at the expense of raising them for those who have incurred such expenses.

There is furthermore neither any guarantee nor even likelihood that, once the exemptions and deductions are safely out of the way, the government would keep its tax rate at the lower level. Looking at the record of governments, past and present, there is every reason to assume that more of our money would be taken by the government as it raised the tax rate backup (at least) to the old level, with a consequently greater overall drain from the producers to the bureaucracy.

It is supposed that the tax system should be analogous to roughly that of pricing or incomes on the market. But market pricing is not proportional to incomes. It would be a peculiar world, for example, if Rockefeller were forced to pay $1,000 for a loaf of bread—that is, a payment proportionate to his income relative to the average man. That would mean a world in which equality of incomes was enforced in a particularly bizarre and inefficient manner. If a tax were levied like a market price, it would be *equal* to every "customer," not proportionate to each customer's income.

Myth 9: *An income tax cut helps everyone; not only the taxpayer but also the government will benefit, since tax revenues will rise when the rate is cut.*

This is the so-called "Laffer curve," set forth by California economist Arthur Laffer. It was advanced as a means of allowing politicians to square the circle; to come out for tax cuts, keeping spending at the current level, and balance the budget all at the same time. In that way, the public would enjoy its tax cut, be happy at the balanced budget, and still receive the same level of subsidies from the government.

It is true that if tax rates are 99 percent, and they are cut to 95 percent, tax revenue will go up. But there is no reason to assume such simple connections at any other time. In fact, this relationship works much better for a local excise tax than for a national income tax. A few years ago, the government of the District of Columbia decided to procure some revenue by sharply raising the District's gasoline tax. But, then, drivers could simply nip over the border to Virginia or Maryland and fill up at a much cheaper price. D.C. gasoline tax revenues fell, and much to the chagrin and confusion of D.C. bureaucrats, they had to repeal the tax.

But this is not likely to happen with the income tax. People are not going to stop working or leave the country because of a relatively small tax hike, or do the reverse because of a tax cut.

There are some other problems with the Laffer curve. The amount of time it is supposed to take for the Laffer effect to work is never specified. But still more important: Laffer assumes that what all of us want is to maximize tax revenue to the government. If—a big if—we are really at the upper half of the Laffer curve, we should then all want to set tax rates at that "optimum" point. But why? *Why* should it be the objective of every one of us to maximize government revenue? To push to the maximum, in short, the share of private product that gets siphoned off to the activities of government? I should think we would be more interested in *minimizing* government revenue by pushing tax rates far, far below whatever the Laffer Optimum might happen to be.

Myth 10: *Imports from countries where labor is cheap cause unemployment in the United States.*

One of the many problems with this doctrine is that it ignores the question: why are wages low in a foreign country and high in the United States? It starts with these wage rates as ultimate givens, and doesn't pursue the question why they are what they are. Basically, they are high in the United States because labor productivity is high—because workers here are aided by large amounts of technologically advanced capital equipment. Wage rates are low in many foreign countries because capital equipment is small and technologically primitive. Unaided by much capital, worker productivity is far lower than in the United States. Wage rates in every country are determined by the productivity of the workers in that country. Hence, high wages in the United States are not a standing threat to American prosperity; they are the result of that prosperity.

But what of certain industries in the U.S. that complain loudly and chronically about the "unfair" competition of products from low-wage countries? Here, we must realize that wages in each country are interconnected from one industry and occupation and region to another. All workers compete with each other, and if wages in industry A are far lower than in other industries, workers—spearheaded by young workers starting their careers—would leave or refuse to enter industry A and move to other firms or industries where the wage rate is higher.

Wages in the complaining industries, then, are high because they have been bid high by all industries in the United States. If the steel or textile industries in the United States find it difficult to compete with their counterparts abroad, it is not because foreign firms are paying low wages, but because other American industries have bid up American wage rates to such a high level that steel and textile cannot afford to pay. In short, what's really happening is that steel, textile, and other such firms are using labor inefficiently as compared to other American industries. Tariffs or import quotas to keep inefficient firms or industries in operation hurt everyone, in every country, who is not in that industry. They injure all American consumers by keeping up prices, keeping down quality and competition, and distorting production. A tariff or an import quota is equivalent to chopping up a railroad or destroying an airline—for its point is to make international transportation artificially expensive.

Tariffs and import quotas also injure other, efficient American industries by tying up resources that would otherwise move to more efficient uses. And, in the long run, the tariffs and quotas, like any sort of monopoly privilege conferred by government, are no bonanza even for the firms being protected and subsidized. For, as we have seen in the cases of railroads and airlines, industries enjoying government monopoly (whether through tariffs or regulation) eventually become so inefficient that they lose money anyway, and can only call for more and more bailouts, for a perpetual expanding privileged shelter from free competition. ▶

3
DISCUSSING THE "ISSUES"

Depending on your temperament, a presidential election year is a time for either depression or amusement. One befuddling aspect of campaign time is the way the Respectable Media redefine our language. Orwell wrote a half-century ago that he who controls the language wields the power, and the media have certainly shown that they have learned this lesson. For example, the Respectable Media have presumed to declare what "the issues" are in any campaign. If Candidate X finds his

First published in February 1992.

Opponent Y's hand in the till, the media rush up to exclaim: "That's irrelevant. Why don't you talk about The Issues?"

In the Bush-Dukakis race, the media anointed The Economy as the only worthwhile topic; anything else was only a smokescreen designed to "detract" from the "real issues." One would think that such a focus would gladden the heart of any economist, but if you thought so, you're not reckoning with the semantics experts in the Establishment media. For the Economy can only be approached in certain, narrow, allowable grooves. Any other approach is brusquely read out of court.

The media focus, quite legitimately, on The Recession, but again, only in certain narrowly permissible ways. Because of the recession, Unemployment has soared (a "lack of jobs"); Affordable Housing has dwindled (the Homeless); Affordable Health Care is diminishing because of increased health costs, and, in addition to these particular sectors, deficits have soared to $400 billion a year.

In short: there is a lack of jobs, health care, housing and other goodies, and it follows, either implicitly or explicitly, that the federal government must expand its spending by an enormous amount, as part of its alleged Responsibility to supply such goods and services, or to see to it that they are supplied. Anyone who may presume to rise up and say, "Whoa, it is not the responsibility of the federal government to supply these goodies," is, of course, accused by the ever-vigilant Respectable Media of Evading and not discussing The Issues.

In media lingo, in short, "discussing" the issues means accepting the media's statist premises, and solemnly haggling over minute technicalities within those premises. If, for example, you say that national health insurance is tantamount to socialized medicine you are accused of using "scare words" and of not discussing The Issues. Anyone who thinks that socialism or collectivism *is* an important issue is quickly swept aside.

But how then is the federal government to spend hundreds of billions more and yet Do Something about the deficit? Ahh, the cure-all, of course: huge increases in taxation. It is only a myth that anyone who proposes tax cuts is lionized while those who urge tax increases are ostracized. While the general public may still feel a vestigial admiration for tax cuts, they are usually overwhelmed by the intellectual and media elites who trumpet the precise opposite message: that proposing big tax increases "faces The Issues," is courageous and responsible, and on and on.

Narrow-gauge discussions also have the advantage of bringing in the ubiquitous Washington "policy wonks," the supposedly value-free "experts" who are ready to trot out computerized analyses of the alleged quantitative results of every proposed tax increase or of any other program. And so we have this unedifying spectacle: Candidate A proposes a tax increase; his opponent B charges that A's plan will cost middle-income taxpayers X-hundred billion dollars; A accuses B of "lying," while B does the same to A's different proposal for tax increases.

Most irritating of all is the media's current penchant for making their alleged "correction," in which a paper or network's own policy wonk claims that the "facts are" that B's increase will cost taxpayers Y-hundred billion instead. The media's "correction" is most annoying because everyone realizes that each candidate and his supporters will put the best possible spin on his own programs and the worst on his opponents'; but the media's *own* bias masquerades as objective truth and expertise.

For the point is that no one actually knows how much is going to be paid by which group under any of these programs. The numbers that are tossed around as gospel truth, as "facts," in an America that has always worshiped numbers, all depend on various fallacious assumptions. They all assume, for example, that quantitative relations between different variables in the economy will continue to be what they have been in the last several years. But the whole point is that these relations change and in unpredictable ways.

How is it that not a single computerized economist or policy wonk predicted the current recession? That not a single one predicted its great length and depth? Precisely because this recession, like all recessions, is quantitatively unique; if there hadn't been some sudden change in the various numbers, there wouldn't have *been* a recession, and we'd still be enjoying a seemingly untroubled boom. As former German banker Kurt Richebacher pointed out in his *Currency and Credit Markets* newsletter, in contrast to the 1920s and 1930s, economists don't think anymore; they just plug in obsolescent numbers, and then wonder why their forecasts all go blooey.

Here is a suggested Discussion of The Issues that will never make the media hit parade: Yes, the deficit is a grave problem, but the way to cut it is never to increase taxes (certainly not during a recession!) but instead to slash government expenditures. In contrast to the conventional media wisdom, increasing taxes is *not*, except strictly arithmetically, equivalent to cutting expenditures. Increasing taxes *or* expenditures aggravates the dangerous parasitic burden of the unproductive public sector and its clients, upon the increasingly impoverished but productive private sector; while cutting taxes or expenditures serves to lighten the chains of the productive private sector.

In the long run, as we have seen under communism, the parasitic sector destroys the private productive sector and harms even the parasites in the process. But it is ironic that left-liberals who affect to be so concerned about the state of "the environment" or of Mother Earth 5,000 years from now, should adopt such a short-sighted perspective on the economy that only immediate problems count, and who cares about savers, investors, and entrepreneurs?

Where to cut the government budget? The simplest way is the best: just pass a law, overriding all existing ones, that no agency of the federal government is allowed to spend more, next year, that it did in some previous year—the earlier the year the better, but for openers how about the penultimate Carter year of 1979, when the federal government spent $504 billion? Just decree that no agency can spend more than whatever it spent in 1979; agencies that didn't exist in 1979 could just subsist from then on, if they so desire, on zero funding.

But of course, this proposal would be both too simple and too radical for the Establishment policy wonks. By definition, it cannot come under the official rubric of "discussing The Issues." ▶

4

CREATIVE ECONOMIC SEMANTICS

If the federal government's economists have been good for nothing else in recent years, they have made great strides in what might be called "creative economic semantics." First they're defined the seemingly simple term "budget cut." In the old days, a "budget cut" was a reduction of next year's budget below this year's. In that old-fashioned sense, Dwight Eisenhower's first two years in office actually cut the budget substantially, though not dramatically, below the previous year. Now we have "budget cuts" which are not cuts, but rather substantial increases over the previous year's expenditures.

"Cut" became subtly but crucially redefined as reducing something else. What the something else might be didn't seem to matter, so long as the focus was taken off actual dollar expenditures. Sometimes it was a cut "in the rate of increase," other times it was a cut in "real" spending, at still others it was a percentage of GNP, and at yet other times it was a cut in the sense of being below past projections for that year.

The result of a series of such "cuts" has been to raise spending sharply and dramatically not only in old-fashioned terms, but even in all other categories. Government spending has gone up considerably any way you slice it. As a result, even the idea of a creatively semantic budget cut has not gone the way of the nickel fare and the Constitution of the United States.

Another example of creative semantics was the "tax cut" of 1981–1982, a tax cut so allegedly fearsome that it had to be offset

---

First published in September 1984.

by outright tax increases late in 1982, in 1983, in 1984,and on
and on into the future. Again in the old days, a cut in income
taxes meant that the average person would find less of a slice
taken out of his paycheck. But while the 1981–82 tax changes did
that for some people, the average person found that the piddling
cuts were more than offset by the continuing rise in the Social
Security tax, and by "bracket creep"—a colorful term for the
process by which inflation (generated by the federal government's expansion of the money supply) wafts everyone into
higher money income (even though a price rise might leave
them no better off) and therefore into a higher tax bracket. So
that even though the official schedule of tax rates might remain
the same, the average man is paying a higher chunk of his
income.

The much-vaunted and much-denounced "tax cut" turns
out, in old-fashioned semantics, to be no cut at all but rather a
substantial increase. In return for the dubious pleasure of this
non-cut, the American public will have to suffer by paying
through the nose for years to come in the form of "offsetting,"
though unfortunately all-too-genuine, tax increases.

Of course, government economists have been doing their
part as well to try to sugar-coat the pill of tax increases. They
never refer to these changes as "increases." They have not been
increases at all; they were "revenue enhancement" and "closing
loopholes." The best comment on the concept of "loopholes"
was that of Ludwig von Mises. Mises remarked that the very
concept of "loopholes" implies that the government rightly
owns all of the money you earn, and that it becomes necessary
to correct the slipup of the government's not having gotten its
hands on that money long since.

Despite promises of a balanced budget by 1984, we found
that several years of semantically massaged "budget cuts" and
"tax cuts" as well as "enhancements" resulted in an enormous,
seemingly permanent, and unprecedented deficit. Once again,
creative semantics have come to the rescue. One route is to use
time-honored methods to redefine the deficit out of existence.

The Keynesians used to redefine it by claiming that in something called a "full employment budget" there was no deficit, that is, that if one subtracts the spending necessary to achieve full employment, there would be no deficit, perhaps even a surplus. But while such a sleight-of-hand might work with a deficit of $20 billion, it is a puny way to wish away a gap of $200 billion. Still, the government's economists are trying.

They have already redefined the "deficits" as a "real increase" in debt, that is, a deficit discounted by inflation. The more inflation generated by the government, then, the more it looks as if the deficit is washed away. On the very same semantic magic, the apologists for the disastrous runaway German inflation of 1923 claimed that there was no inflation at all, since in terms of gold, German prices were actually falling! And similarly, they claimed, that since in real terms the supply of German marks was falling, that the real trouble in Germany was that there was too little money being printed rather than too much.

There is no general acceptance for the idea that, based on some legerdemain, the deficit doesn't really exist. But there is acceptance of the view that a tax increase constitutes a "down payment" on the deficit. Again, in the old days, a "down payment" on a debt meant that part of the debt was being paid off. Washington's creative economists have managed to redefine the term to mean a hoped-for reduction of next years's increase in the debt—a very different story indeed. ▸

5
CHAOS THEORY: DESTROYING MATHEMATICAL ECONOMICS FROM WITHIN?

The hottest new topic in mathematics, physics, and allied sciences is "chaos theory." It is radical in its implications,

First published in March 1988.

but no one can accuse its practitioners of being anti-mathematical, since its highly complex math, including advanced computer graphics, is on the cutting edge of mathematical theory. In a deep sense, chaos theory is a reaction against the effort, hype, and funding that have, for many decades, been poured into such fashionable topics as going ever deeper inside the nucleus of the atom, or ever further out in astronomical speculation. Chaos theory returns scientific focus, at long last, to the real "microscopic" world with which we are all familiar.

It is fitting that chaos theory got its start in the humble but frustrating field of meteorology. Why does it seem impossible for all our hot-shot meteorologists, armed as they are with ever more efficient computers and ever greater masses of data, to predict the weather? Two decades ago, Edward Lorenz, a meteorologist at MIT stumbled onto chaos theory by making the discovery that ever so tiny changes in climate could bring about enormous and volatile changes in weather. Calling it the Butterfly Effect, he pointed out that if a butterfly flapped its wings in Brazil, it could well produce a tornado in Texas. Since then, the discovery that small, unpredictable causes could have dramatic and turbulent effects has been expanded into other, seemingly unconnected, realms of science.

The conclusion, for the weather and for many other aspects of the world, is that the weather, in principle, cannot be predicted successfully, no matter how much data is accumulated for our computers. This is not *really* "chaos" since the Butterfly Effect does have its own causal patterns, albeit very complex. (Many of these causal patterns follow what is known as "Feigenbaum's Number.") But even if these patterns become known, who in the world can predict the arrival of a flapping butterfly?

The upshot of chaos theory is *not* that the real world is chaotic or *in principle* unpredictable or undetermined, but that in practice much of it is unpredictable. And in particular that mathematical tools such as the calculus, which assumes smooth surfaces and infinitesimally small steps, is deeply flawed in dealing with much of the real world. (Thus, Benoit Mandelbroit's "fractals" indicate that smooth curves are inappropriate and misleading for modeling coastlines or geographic surfaces.)

Chaos theory is even more challenging when applied to human events such as the workings of the stock market. Here the chaos theorists have directly challenged orthodox neoclassical theory of the stock market, which assumes that the expectations of the market are "rational," that is, are omniscient about the future. If all stock or commodity market prices perfectly discount and incorporate perfect knowledge of the future, then the patterns of stock-market prices must be purely accidental, meaningless, and random ("random walk"), since all the underlying basic knowledge is already known and incorporated into the price.

The absurdity of believing that the market is omniscient about the future, or that it has perfect knowledge of all "probability distributions" of the future, is matched by the equal folly of assuming that all happenings on the real stock market are "random," that is, that no one stock price is related to any other price, past or future. And yet a crucial fact of human history is that all historical events are interconnected, that cause and effect patterns permeate human events, that very little is homogeneous, and that nothing is random.

With their enormous prestige, the chaos theorists have done important work in denouncing these assumptions, and in rebuking any attempt to abstract statistically from the actual concrete events of the real world. Thus, the chaos theorists are opposed to the common statistical technique of "smoothing out" the data by taking twelve-month moving averages of monthly data—whether of prices, production, or employment. In attempting to eliminate jagged "random elements" and separate them out from alleged underlying patterns, orthodox statisticians have been unwittingly getting rid of the very real-world data that need to be examined.

These are but a few of the subversive implications that chaos science offers for orthodox mathematical economics. For if rational expectations theory violates the real world, then so too does general equilibrium, the use of the calculus in assuming infinitesimally small steps, perfect knowledge, and all the rest of the elaborate neoclassical apparatus. The neoclassicals have for a long while employed their knowledge of math and their use of advanced mathematical techniques as a bludgeon to discredit Austrians; now comes the most advanced mathematical theorists to replicate, unwittingly, some of the searching Austrian critiques of the unreality and distortions of orthodox neoclassical economics. In the current mathematical pecking order, fractals, nonlinear thermodynamics, the Feigenbaum number, and all the rest rank far higher than the old-fashioned techniques of the neo-classicals.

This does not mean that all the philosophical claims for chaos theory must be swallowed whole—in particular, the assertions of some of the theorists that nature is undetermined, or even that atoms or molecules possess "free will." But Austrians can hail the chaos theorists in their invigorating assault on orthodox mathematical economics from within. ▶

6
STATISTICS: DESTROYED FROM WITHIN?

As improbable as this may seem now, I was at one time in college a statistics major. After taking all the undergraduate courses in statistics, I enrolled in a graduate course in mathematical statistics at Columbia with the eminent Harold Hotelling, one of the founders of modern mathematical economics. After listening to several lectures of Hotelling, I experienced an epiphany: the sudden realization that the entire "science" of statistical inference rests on one crucial assumption,

---

First published in February 1989.

and that that assumption is utterly groundless. I walked out of the Hotelling course, and out of the world of statistics, never to return.

Statistics, of course, is far more than the mere collection of data. Statistical *inference* is the conclusions one can draw from that data. In particular, since—apart from the decennial U.S. census of population—we never know all the data, our conclusions must rest on very small samples drawn from the population. After taking our sample or samples, we have to find a way to make statements about the population as a whole. For example, suppose we wish to conclude something about the average height of the American male population. Since there is no way that we can mobilize every male American and measure everyone's height, we take samples of a small number, say 500 people, selected in various ways, from which we presume to say what the average American's height may be.

In the science of statistics, the way we move from our known samples to the unknown population is to make one crucial assumption: that the samples will, in any and all cases, whether we are dealing with height or unemployment or who is going to vote for this or that candidate, be distributed around the population figure according to the so-called "normal curve."

The normal curve is a symmetrical, bell-shaped curve familiar to all statistics textbooks. Because all samples are assumed to fall around the population figure according to this curve, the statistician feels justified in asserting, from his one or more limited samples, that the height of the American population, or the unemployment rate, or whatever, *is* definitely XYZ within a "confidence level" of 90 or 95 percent. In short, if, for example, a sample height for the average male is 5 feet 9 inches, 90 or 95 out of every 100 such samples will be within a certain definite range of 5 feet 9 inches. These precise figures are arrived at simply by assuming that all samples are distributed around the population according to this normal curve.

It is because of the properties of the normal curve, for example, that the election pollsters could assert, with overwhelming confidence, that Bush was favored by a certain percentage of voters, and Dukakis by another percentage, all within "three percentage points" or "five percentage points" of "error." It is the normal curve that permits statisticians not to claim absolute knowledge of all population figures precisely but instead to claim such knowledge within a few percentage points.

Well, what is the evidence for this vital assumption of distribution around a normal curve? None whatever. It is a purely mystical act of faith. In my old statistics text, the only "evidence" for the universal truth of the normal curve was the statement that if good riflemen shoot to hit a bullseye, the shots will tend to be distributed around the target in something like a normal curve. On this incredibly flimsy basis rests an assumption vital to the validity of all statistical inference.

Unfortunately, the social sciences tend to follow the same law that the late Dr. Robert Mendelsohn has shown is adopted in medicine: never drop any procedure, no matter how faulty, until a better one is offered in its place. And now it seems that the entire fallacious structure of inference built on the normal curve has been rendered obsolete by high-tech.

Ten years ago, Stanford statistician Bradley Efron used high-speed computers to generate "artificial data sets" based on an original sample, and to make the millions of numerical calculations necessary to arrive at a population estimate without using the normal curve, or any other arbitrary, mathematical assumption of how samples are distributed about the unknown population figure. After a decade of discussion and tinkering, statisticians have agreed on methods of practical use of this "bootstrap." method, and it is now beginning to take over the profession. Stanford statistician Jerome H. Friedman, one of the pioneers of the new method, calls it "the most important new idea in statistics in the last 20 years, and probably the last 50."

At this point, statisticians are finally willing to let the cat out of the bag. Friedman now concedes that "data don't always follow bell-shaped curves, and when they don't, you make a mistake" with the standard methods. In fact, he added that "the data frequently are distributed quite differently than in bell-shaped curves." So that's it; now we find that the normal curve Emperor has no clothes after all. The old mystical faith can now be abandoned; the Normal Curve god is dead at long last. ▶

7
THE CONSEQUENCES OF HUMAN ACTION: INTENDED OR UNINTENDED?

Some economists are given to insisting that Austrian economics studies only the *un*intended consequences of human action, or, in the favorite phrase (from the 18th-century Scottish sociologist Adam Ferguson as filtered down to F.A. Hayek), "the consequences of human action, not human design."

At first glance, there is some plausibility to this oft-repeated slogan. As Adam Smith pointed out, it is a good thing that we don't rely on the benevolence of the butcher or baker for our daily bread, but rather on their self-interested drive for income and profit. They may intend to achieve a profit, but the efficient production for consumer wants and the advancement of the prosperity of all is the unintended consequence of their actions.

But this slogan can be shown to be faulty on further analysis. For example, how do we *know* what the intentions of the butcher, the baker, or indeed any businessman, are? We cannot look inside their heads and tell for sure. Suppose, for example, that the butcher and baker, out to maximize their profits, read free-market economics and see that maximizing profit also benefits their fellow-man and society as a whole.

As they go about their business, they now *intend* the consequence of efficient satisfaction of consumer wants as well as their own monetary profit. So if, as some indicate, economic theory only studies unintended consequences of human action,

---

First published in May 1987.

does the learning of some economic theory by businessmen invalidate that theory because now these consequences are consciously intended by the participants on the market?

Furthermore, the learning of sound economic theory can actually *change* the actions of businessmen on the market. Many businessmen, influenced by anti-capitalist propaganda, have been consumed by guilt, and may consciously restrict their pursuit of profit in the mistaken idea that they are helping their fellow man. Reading and absorbing sound economic analysis may relieve them of guilt and lead them to seek the maximization of their own profit. In short, now that they are fully cognizant of economics, the *intended* consequences of their actions will lead to higher profits for themselves as well as greater prosperity for society.

So what is so great about unintended consequences, and why may no intended consequences be studied as well? And doesn't the accumulation of knowledge in society change consequences from unintended to intended?

Not only that: the Misesian discipline of praxeology explicitly states that individual men consciously pursue goals, and choose means to try to attain them. And if men pursue goals, surely it is only common sense to conclude that a good deal of the time they will attain them, in others words they will intend, and attain, the consequences of their actions. Mises's emphasis on conscious choice treats men and women as rational, conscious actors in the market and the world; the other tradition often falls into the trap of treating people as if they were robots or amoebae blindly responding to stimuli.

Arcane matters of methodology often have surprising political consequences. Perhaps, then, it is not an accident that those who believe in unintended and not intended consequences, will also tend to whitewash the growth of government in the twentieth century. For if actions are largely always unintended, this means that government just grew like Topsy, and that no person or group ever willed the pernicious consequences of that growth. Stressing the Ferguson-Hayek formula cloaks the self-interested actions of the power elite in seeking and obtaining special privileges from government, and thereby impelling its continuing growth.

There are two ways to advance the message of Austrian economics. One is to fearlessly hold high the banner of Misesian theory to which the wise and honest can repair—a banner which requires calling a spade a spade and pointing out the special interests all too consciously at work behind the government's glittering facade of the "public interest" and the "general welfare."

The other path is to seek acceptance and respectability by watering down the Misesian message beyond repair, and carefully avoiding anything remotely "controversial" in your offering. Even to the point of taking the "free" out of "free market." Such a path only entrenches big government. ▶

8
THE INTEREST RATE QUESTION

The Marxists call it "impressionism": taking social or economic trends of the last few weeks or months and assuming that they will last forever. The problem is not realizing that there are underlying economic laws at work. Impressionism has always been rampant; and never more so than in public discussion of interest rates. For most of 1987, interest rates were inexorably high; for a short while after Black Monday, interest rates fell, and financial opinion turned around 180 degrees, and started talking as if interest rates were on a permanent downward trend.

No group is more prone to this day-to-day blowin' with the wind than the financial press. This syndrome comes from lack

---

First published in February 1988.

of understanding of economics and hence being reduced to reacting blindly to rapidly changing events. Sometimes this basic confusion is reflected within the same article. Thus, in the not-so-long ago days of double-digit inflation, the same article would predict that interest rates would fall because the Fed was buying securities in the open market, and *also* say that rates would be going *up* because the market would be expecting increased inflation.

Nowadays, too, we read that fixed exchange rates are bad because interest rates will have to rise to keep foreign capital in the U.S., but also that *falling* exchange rates are bad because interest rates will have to rise for the same reason. If financial writers are mired in hopeless confusion, how can we expect the public to make any sense of what is going on?

In truth, interest rates, like any important price, are complex phenomena that are determined by several factors, each of which can change in varying, or even contradictory, ways. As in the case of other prices, interest rates move inversely with the supply, but directly with the demand, for credit. If the Fed enters the open market to buy securities, it thereby increases the supply of credit, which will tend to lower interest rates; and since this same act will increase bank reserves by the same extent, the banks will now inflate money and credit out of thin air by a multiple of the initial jolt, nowadays about ten to one. So if the Fed buys $1 billion of securities, bank reserves will rise by the same amount, and bank loans and the money supply will then increase by $10 billion. The supply of credit has thereby increased further, and interest rates will fall some more.

But it would be folly to conclude, impressionistically, that interest rates are destined to fall indefinitely. In the first place, the supply and demand for credit are themselves determined by deeper economic forces, in particular the amount of their income that people in the economy wish to save and invest, as opposed to the amount they decide to consume. The more they save, the lower the interest rate; the more they consume, the higher. Increased bank loans may mimic an increase in genuine savings, yet they are very far from the same thing.

Inflationary bank credit is artificial, created out of thin air; it does not reflect the underlying saving or consumption preferences of the public. Some earlier economists referred to this phenomenon as "forced" savings; more importantly, they are only temporary. As the increased money supply works its way through the system, prices and all values in money terms rise, and interest rates will then bounce back to something like their original level. Only *a repeated* injection of inflationary bank credit by the Fed will keep interest rates artificially low, and thereby keep the artificial and unsound economic boom going; and this is precisely the hallmark of the boom phase of the boom-bust business cycle.

But something else happens, too. As prices rise, and as people begin to anticipate further price increases, an inflation premium is placed on interest rates. Creditors tack an inflation premium onto rates because they don't propose to continue being wiped out by a fall in the value of the dollar; and debtors will be willing to pay the premium because they too realize that they have been enjoying a windfall.

And this is why, when the public comes to expect further inflation, Fed increases in reserves will *raise*, rather than lower, the rate of interest. And when the acceleration of inflationary credit finally stops, the higher interest rate puts a sharp end to the boom in the capital markets (stocks and bonds), and an inevitable recession liquidates the unsound investments of the inflationary boom.

An extra twist to the interest rate problem is the international aspect. As a long-run tendency, capital moves from low-return investments (whether profit rates or interest rates) toward high-return investments until rates of return are equal. This is true within every country and also throughout the world. Internationally, capital will tend to flow from low-interest- to high-interest-rate countries, raising interest rates in the former and lowering them in the latter.

In the days of the international gold standard, the process was simple. Nowadays, under fiat money, the process continues, but results in a series of alleged crises. When governments try to fix exchange rates (as they did from the Louvre agreement of February 1987 until Black Monday), then interest rates cannot fall in the United States without losing capital or savings to foreign countries.

In the current era of a huge balance of trade deficit in the U.S., the U.S. cannot maintain a fixed dollar if foreign capital flows outward; the pressure for the dollar to fall would then be enormous. Hence, after Black Monday, the Fed decided to allow the dollar to resume its market tendency to fall, so that the Fed could then inflate credit and lower interest rates.

But it should be clear that that interest rate fall could only be ephemeral and strictly temporary, and indeed interest rates resumed their inexorable upward march. Price inflation is the consequence of the monetary inflation pumped in by the Federal Reserve for several years before the spring of 1987, and interest rates were therefore bound to rise as well.

Moreover, the Fed, as in many other matters, is caught in a trap of its own making; for the long-run trend to equalize interest rates throughout the world is a drive to equalize not simply money, or nominal, returns, but *real* returns corrected for inflation. But if foreign creditors and investors begin to receive dollars worth less and less in value, they will require higher money interest rates to compensate—and we will be back again, very shortly, with a redoubled reason for interest rates to rise.

In trying to explain the complexities of interest rates, inflation, money and banking, exchange rates and business cycles to my students, I leave them with this comforting thought: Don't blame me for all this, blame the government. Without the interference of government, the entire topic would be duck soup. ◗

9
ARE SAVINGS TOO LOW?

One strong recent trend among economists, businessmen, and politicians, has been to lament the amount of savings and investment in the United States as being far too low. It is pointed out that the American percentage of savings to national income is far lower than among the West Germans, or among our feared competitors, the Japanese. Recently, Secretary of the Treasury Nicholas Brady sternly warned of the low savings and investment levels in the United States.

This sort of argument should be considered on many levels. First, and least important, the statistics are usually manipulated to exaggerate the extent of the problem. Thus, the scariest figures (e.g., U.S. savings as only 1.5 percent of national income) only mention *personal* savings, and omit business savings; also, capital gains are almost always omitted as a source of savings and investment.

But these are minor matters. The most vital question is: even conceding that U.S. savings are 1.5 percent of national income and Japanese savings are 15 percent, *what*, if anything, is the proper amount or percentage of savings?

Consumers voluntarily decide to divide their income into spending on consumer goods, as against saving and investment for future income. If Mr. Jones invests X percent of his income for future use, by what standard, either moral or economic, does some outside person come along and denounce him for being wrong or immoral for not investing X+1 percent? Everyone knows that if they consume less now, and save and invest more, they will be able to earn a higher income at some point in the future. But which they choose depends on the rate of their time preferences: how much they prefer consuming now to consuming later. Since everyone makes this decision on the basis of his

First published in November 1989.

own life, his particular situation, and his own value-scales, to denounce his decision requires some extraindividual criterion, some criterion outside the person with which to override his preferences.

That criterion cannot be economic, since what is efficient and economic can only be decided within a framework of voluntary decisions made by individuals. For the criterion to be moral would be extraordinarily shaky, since moral truths, like economic laws, are not quantitative but qualitative. Moral laws, such as "thou shalt not kill" or "thou shalt not steal," are qualitative; there is no moral law which says that "thou shalt not steal more than 62 percent of the time." So, if people are being exhorted to save more and consume less as a moral doctrine, the moralist is required to come up with some quantitative optimum, such as: when specifically, is saving too low, and when is it too high? Vague exhortations to save more make little moral or economic sense.

But the lamenters do have an important point. For there are an enormous number of government measures which cripple and greatly lower savings, and add to consumption in society. In many ways, government steps in, employs many instruments of coercion, and skews the voluntary choices of society away from saving and investment and toward consumption.

Our complainers about saving don't always say what, beyond exhortation, they think should be done about the situation. Left-liberals call for more governmental "investment" or higher taxes so as to reduce the government deficit, which they assert is "dissaving." But one thing which the government can legitimately do is simply get rid of its own coercive influence in favor of consumption and against saving and investment. In this way, the voluntary time preferences and choices of individuals would be liberated, instead of overridden, by government.

The Bush administration began eliminating some of the coercive anti-saving measures that had been imposed by the so-called Tax Reform Act of 1986. One was the abolition of tax-deduction for IRAs, which wiped out an important category of middle-class saving and investment; another was the steep increase in the capital gains tax, which is a confiscation of savings, and—to the extent that capital gains are not indexed for inflation—a direct confiscation of accumulated wealth.

But this is only the tip of the iceberg. To say that only government deficits are "dis-saving" is to imply that higher taxes increase social savings and investment. Actually, while the national income statistics assume that all government spending except welfare payments are "investment," the truth is precisely the opposite.

All business spending is investment because it goes toward increasing the production of goods that will eventually be sold to consumers. But government spending is simply consumer spending for the benefit of the income, and for the whims and values, of government's politicians and bureaucrats. Taxation and government spending siphon social resources away from productive consumers who earn the money they receive, and away from their private consumption and saving, and toward consumption expenditure by unproductive politicians, bureaucrats, and their followers and subsidies.

Yes, there is certainly too little saving and investment in the United States, as a result of which the U.S. standard of living per person is scarcely higher than it was in the early 1970s. But the problem is not that individuals and families are somehow failing their responsibilities by consuming too much and saving too little, as most of the complainers contend. The problem is not in ourselves the American public, but in our overlords.

All government taxation and spending diminishes saving and consumption by genuine producers, for the benefit of a parasitic burden of consumption spending by non-producers. Restoring tax deductions and repealing—not just lowering—the capital gains tax, would be most welcome, but they would only scratch the surface.

What is really needed is a drastic reduction of all government taxation and spending, state, local, and federal, across the board. The lifting of that enormous parasitic burden would bring about great increases in the standard of living of all productive Americans, in the short-run as well as in the future. ▶

10

A WALK ON THE SUPPLY SIDE

Establishment historians of economic thought—they of the Smith-Marx-Marshall variety—have a compelling need to end their saga with a chapter on the latest Great Man, the latest savior and final culmination of economic science. The last consensus choice was, of course, John Maynard Keynes, but his *General Theory* is now a half-century old, and economists have for some time been looking around for a new candidate for that final chapter.

For a while, Joseph Schumpeter had a brief run, but his problem was that his work was largely written before the *General Theory*. Milton Friedman and monetarism lasted a bit longer, but suffered from two grave defects: (1) the lack of anything resembling a great, integrative work; and (2) the fact that monetarism and Chicago School Economics is really only a gloss on theories that had been hammered out before the Keynesian Era by Irving Fisher and by Frank Knight and his colleagues at the University of Chicago.

Was there nothing new to write about since Keynes?

Since the mid-1970s, a school of thought has made its mark that at least gives the impression of something brand new. And since economists, like the Supreme Court, follow the election returns, "supply-side economics" has become noteworthy.

Supply-side economics has been hampered among students of contemporary economics in lacking anything like a grand treatise, or even a single major leader, and there is scarcely unanimity among its practitioners. But it has been able to take

---

First published in October 1984.

shrewd advantage of highly placed converts in the media and easy access to politicians and think tanks. Already it has begun to make its way into last chapters of works on economic thought.

A central theme of the supply-side school is that a sharp cut in marginal income-tax rates will increase incentives to work and save, and therefore investment and production. That way, few people could take exception. But there are other problems involved. For, at least in the land of the famous Laffer Curve, income tax cuts were treated as the panacea for deficits; drastic cuts would so increase stated revenue as allegedly to yield a balanced budget.

Yet there was no evidence whatever for this claim, and indeed, the likelihood is quite the other way. It is true that if income-tax rates were 98 percent and were cut to 90 percent, there would probably be an increase in revenue; but at the far lower tax levels we have been at, there is no warrant for this assumption. In fact, historically, increases in tax rates have been followed by increases in revenue and vice versa.

But there is a deeper problem with supply-side than the inflated claims of the Laffer Curve. Common to all supply-siders is nonchalance about total government spending and therefore deficits. The supply-siders do not care that tight government spending takes resources that would have gone into the private sector and diverts them to the public sector.

They care only about taxes. Indeed, their attitude toward deficits approaches the old Keynesian "we only owe it to ourselves." Worse than that: the supply-siders want to maintain the current swollen levels of federal spending. As professed "populists," their basic argument is that the people want the current level of spending and the people should not be denied.

Even more curious than the supply-sider attitude toward spending is their viewpoint on money. On the one hand, they say they are for hard money and an end to inflation by going back to the "gold standard." On the other hand, they have consistently attacked the Paul Volcker Federal Reserve, not for being too inflationist, but for imposing "too tight" money and thereby "crippling economic growth."

In short, these self-styled "conservative populists" begin to sound like old-fashioned populists in their devotion to inflation and cheap money. But how square that with their championing of the gold standard?

In the answer to this question lies the key to the heart of the seeming contradictions of the new supply-side economics. For the "gold standard" they want provides only the illusion of a gold standard without the substance. The banks would not have to redeem in gold coin, and the Fed would have the right to change the definition of the gold dollar at will, as a device to fine-tune the economy. In short, what the supply-siders want is not the old hard-money gold standard, but the phony "gold standard" of the Bretton Woods era, which collapsed under the bows of inflation and money management by the Fed.

The heart of supply-side doctrine is revealed in its best-selling philosophic manifesto, *The Way the World Works*, by Jude Wanniski. Wanniski's view is that the people, the masses, are always right, and have always been right through history.

In economics, he claims, the masses want a massive welfare state, drastic income-tax cuts, and a balanced budget. How can these contradictory aims be achieved? By the legerdemain of the Laffer Curve. And in the monetary sphere, we might add, what the masses seem to want is inflation and cheap money along with a return to the gold standard. Hence, fueled by the axiom that the public is always right, the supply-siders propose to give the public what they want by giving them an inflationary, cheap-money Fed plus the illusion of stability through a phony gold standard.

The supply-side aim is therefore "democratically" to give the public what they want, and in this case the best definition of "democracy" is that of H.L. Mencken: "Democracy is the view that the people know what they want, and deserve to get it good and hard." ▸

11
KEYNESIAN MYTHS

The Keynesians have been caught short again. In the early and the late 1970s, the wind was taken out of their sails by the arrival of inflationary recession, a phenomenon which they not only failed to predict, but whose very existence violates the fundamental tenets of the Keynesian system. Since then, the Keynesians have lost their old invincible arrogance, though they still constitute a large part of the economics profession.

In the last few years, the Keynesians have been assuring us with more than a touch of their old *hauteur*, that inflation would not and could not arrive soon, despite the fact that "tight-money" hero Paul Volcker had been consistently pouring in money at double-digit rates. Chiding hard-money advocates, the Keynesians declared that, despite the monetary inflation, American industry still suffered from "excess" or "idle" capacity, functioning at an overall rate of something like 80 percent. Thus, they pointed out, expanded monetary demand could not result in inflation.

As we all know, despite Keynesian assurances that inflation could not reignite, it *did* despite the idle capacity, leaving them with something else to puzzle over. Inflation rose from approximately 1 percent in 1986 to 6 percent, interest rates the next year rose again, the falling dollar raised import prices, and gold prices went up. Once again, the hard-money economists and investment advisors have proved far sounder than the Establishment-blessed Keynesians.

Along with that the best way to explain where the Keynesians went wrong is to turn against them their own common reply to their critics: that anti-Keynesians, who worry about the waste of inflation or government programs, are "assuming full

---

First published in September 1987.

employment" of resources. Eliminate this assumption, they say, and Keynesianism becomes correct in the through-the-looking glass world of unemployment and idle resources. But the charge should be turned around, and the Keynesians should be asked: why should there be unemployment (of labor or of machinery) at all? Unemployment is not a given that descends from heaven. Of course, it often exists, but what can account for it?

The Keynesians themselves create the problem by leaving out the price system. The hallmark of crackpot economics is an analysis that somehow leaves out prices, and talks only about such aggregates as income, spending, and employment.

We know from "microeconomic" analysis that if there is a "surplus" of something on the market, if something cannot be sold, the only reason is that its price is somehow being kept too high. The way to cure a surplus or unemployment of anything, is to lower the asking price, whether it be wage rates for labor, prices of machinery or plant, or of the inventory of a retailer.

In short, as Professor William H. Hutt pointed out brilliantly in the 1930s, when his message was lost amid the fervor of the Keynesian Revolution: idleness or unemployment of a resource can only occur because the owner of that resource is deliberately withholding it from the market and refusing to sell it at the offered price. In a profound sense, therefore, all unemployment and idleness is voluntary.

Why should a resource owner deliberately withhold it from the market? Usually, because he is holding out for a higher price, or wage rate. In a free and unhampered market economy, the owners will find out their error soon enough, and when they get tired of making no returns from their labor or machinery or products, they will lower their asking price sufficiently to sell them.

In the case of machinery and other capital goods, of course, the owners might have made a severe malinvestment, often due to artificial booms created by bank credit and central banks. In that case, the lower market clearing price for the machinery or plant might be so low as to not be worth the laborer's giving up his leisure—but then the unemployment is purely voluntary and the worker holds out permanently for a higher wage.

A worse problem is that, since the 1930s, government and its privileged unions have intervened massively in the labor market to keep wage rates above the market-clearing wage, thereby insuring ever higher unemployment among workers with the lowest skills and productivity. Government interference, in the form of minimum wage laws and compulsory unionism, creates compulsory unemployment, while welfare payments and unemployment "insurance" subsidize unemployment and make sure that it will be permanently high. We can have as much unemployment as we pay for.

It follows from this analysis that monetary inflation and greater spending will not necessarily reduce unemployment or idle capacity. It will *only* do so if workers or machine owners are induced to think that they are getting a higher return and at least some of their holdout demands are being met. And this can only be accomplished if the price paid for the resource (the wage rate or the price of machinery) *goes up*. In other words, greater supply or use of capacity will only be called forth by wage and price increases, i.e., by *price inflation*.

As usual, the Keynesians have the entire causal process bollixed up. And so, as the facts now poignantly demonstrate, we can and do have inflation along with idle resources. ▶

12

KEYNESIANISM REDUX

One of the ironic but unfortunately enduring legacies of eight years of Reaganism has been the resurrection of Keynesianism. From the late 1930s until the early 1970s, Keynesianism rode high in the economics profession and in the corridors of power in Washington, promising that, so long as

First published in January 1989.

Keynesian economists continued at the helm, the blessings of modern macroeconomics would surely bring us permanent prosperity without inflation. Then something happened on the way to Eden: the mighty inflationary recession of 1973–74.

Keynesian doctrine is, despite its algebraic and geometric jargon, breathtakingly simple at its core: recessions are caused by underspending in the economy, inflation is caused by overspending. Of the two major categories of spending, consumption is passive and determined, almost robotically, by income; hopes for the proper amount of spending, therefore, rest on investment, but private investors, while active and decidedly non-robotic, are erratic and volatile, unreliably dependent on fluctuations in what Keynes called their "animal spirits."

Fortunately for all of us, there is another group in the economy that is just as active and decisive as investors, but who are also—if guided by Keynesian economists—scientific and rational, able to act in the interests of all: Big Daddy government. When investors and consumers underspend, government can and should step in and increase social spending via deficits, thereby lifting the economy out of recession. When private animal spirits get too wild, government is supposed to step in and reduce private spending by what the Keynesians revealingly call "sopping up excess purchasing power" (that's ours).

In strict theory, by the way, the Keynesians could just as well have called for lowering government spending during inflationary booms rather than sopping up our spending. But the very idea of cutting government budgets (and I mean actual cut-cuts, not cuts in the rate of increase) is nowadays just as unthinkable, as, for example, adhering to a Jeffersonian strict construction of the Constitution of the United States, and for similar reasons.

Originally, Keynesians vowed that they, too, were in favor of a "balanced budget," just as much as the fuddy-duddy reactionaries who opposed them. It's just that they were not, like the fuddy-duddies, tied to the *year* as an accounting period; they would balance the budget, too, but over the business cycle. Thus, if there are four years of recession followed by four years of boom, the federal deficits during the recession would be compensated for by the surpluses piled up during the boom; over the eight years of cycle, it would all balance out.

Evidently, the "cyclically balanced budget" was the first Keynesian concept to be poured down the Orwellian memory hole, as it became clear that there weren't going to be any surpluses, just smaller or larger deficits. A subtle but important corrective came into Keynesianism: *larger* deficits during recessions, *smaller* ones during booms.

But the real slayer of Keynesianism came with the double-digit inflationary recession of 1973–74, followed soon by the even more intense inflationary recessions of 1979–80 and 1981–82. For if the government was supposed to step on the spending accelerator during recessions, and step on the brakes during booms, what in blazes is it going to do if there is a steep recession (with unemployment and bankruptcies) and a sharp inflation *at the same time*? What can Keynesianism say? Step on both accelerator and brake at the same time? The stark fact of inflationary recession violates the fundamental assumptions of Keynesian theory and the crucial program of Keynesian policy. Since 1973–74, Keynesianism has been intellectually finished, dead from the neck up.

But very often the corpse refuses to lie down, particularly one made up of an elite which would have to give up their power positions in the academy and in government. One crucial law of politics or sociology is: no one ever resigns. And so, the Keynesians have clung to their power positions as tightly as possible, never resigning, although a bit less addicted to grandiose promises.

A bit chastened, they now only promise to do the best they can, and to keep the system going. Essentially, then, shorn of its intellectual groundwork, Keynesianism has become the pure economics of power, committed only to keeping the Establishment-system going, making marginal adjustments, babying things along through yet one more election, and hoping that by tinkering with the controls, shifting rapidly back and forth between accelerator and brake, something will work, at least to preserve their cushy positions for a few more years.

Amidst the intellectual confusion, however, a few dominant tendencies, legacies from their glory days, remain among Keynesians: (1) a penchant for continuing deficits, (2) a devotion to fiat paper money and at least moderate inflation, (3) adherence to increased government spending, and (4) an eternal fondness for higher taxes, to lower deficits a wee bit, but more importantly, to inflict some bracing pain on the greedy, selfish, and short-sighted American public.

The Reagan administration managed to institutionalize these goodies, seemingly permanently on the American scene. Deficits are far greater and apparently forever; the difference now is that formerly free-market Reaganomists are out-Keynesianing their liberal forebears in coming up with ever more ingenious apologetics for huge deficits. The only dispute now is within the Keynesian camp, with the allegedly "conservative" supply-siders enthusiastically joining Keynesians in devotion to inflation and cheap money, and differing only on their call for moderate tax cuts as against tax increases.

The triumph of Keynesianism within the Reagan administration stems from the rapid demise of the monetarists, the main competitors to the Keynesians within respectable academia. Having made a series of disastrously bad predictions, they who kept trumpeting that "science is prediction," the monetarists have retreated in confusion, trying desperately to figure out what went wrong and which of the many "M"s they should fasten on as being the money supply. The collapse of monetarism was symbolized by Keynesian James Baker's takeover as Secretary of the Treasury from monetarist-sympathizer Donald Regan. With Keynesians dominant during the second Reagan term, the transition to a Keynesian Bush team—Bush having always had strong Keynesian leanings—was so smooth as to be almost invisible.

Perhaps it is understandable that an administration and a campaign that reduced important issues to sound bites and TV images should also be responsible for the restoration to dominance of an intellectually bankrupt economic creed, the very same creed that brought us the political economics of every administration since the second term of Franklin D. Roosevelt.

It is no accident that the same administration that managed to combine the rhetoric of "getting government off our back" with the reality of enormously escalating Big Government, should also have brought back a failed and statist Keynesianism in the name of prosperity and free enterprise. ▶

The Socialism of Welfare

13
ECONOMIC INCENTIVES AND WELFARE

Most people disagree with economists, who point out the important impact that monetary incentives can have on even seemingly "non-economic" behavior. When, for example, coffee prices rise due to a killing frost of the coffee crop in Brazil, or when New York subway fares go up, most people believe that the quantity purchased will not be affected, since people are "addicted" to coffee, and people "have to get to work" by subway.

What they don't realize, and what economists are particularly equipped to point out, is that individual consumers vary in their behavior. Some, indeed, are hard core, and will only cut their purchases a little bit should the cost of a product or service rise. But others are "marginal" buyers, who will cut their coffee purchases, or shift to tea or cocoa. And subway rides consist, not only of "getting to work," but also short, "marginal" rides which can and will be cut down. Thus, subway fares are now 25 times what they were in World War II, and as a result, the number of annual subway rides have fallen by more than half.

People are shocked, too, when economists assert that monetary incentives can affect even such seemingly totally non-economic activity as producing babies. Economists are accused of

---

First published in October 1994.

being mechanistic and soulless, devoid of humanity, for even mentioning such a connection. And yet, while some people may have babies with little or no regard to economic incentive, I am willing to bet that if the government, for example, should offer a bounty of $100,000 for each new baby, considerably more babies would be produced.

Liberals are particularly shocked that economists, or anyone else, could believe that a close connection exists between the level of welfare payments, and the number of welfare mothers with children. Babymaking, they declare, is solely the result of "love" (if that's the correct word), and not of any crass monetary considerations. And yet, if welfare payments are far higher than any sum that a single teenager can make on the market, who can deny the powerful extra tug from the prospects of tax-subsidized moolah without any need to work?

The conservative organization Change-NY has recently issued a study of the economic incentives for going on, and staying on, welfare in New York. The "typical" welfare recipient is a single mother with two children. This typical welfare "client" receives, in city, state, and federal benefits, the whopping annual sum of $32,500, which includes approximately $3,000 in cash, $14,000 in Medicaid, $10,000 in housing assistance, and $5,000 in food assistance. Since these benefits are non-taxable, this sum is equivalent to a $45,000 annual salary before taxes.

Furthermore, this incredibly high figure for welfare aid is "extremely conservative," says Change-NY, because it excludes the value of other benefits, including Head Start (also known as pre-school day care), job training (often consisting of such hard-nosed subjects as "conversational skills"), child care, and the Special Supplemental Food program for Women, Infants, and Children (or WIC). Surely, including all this would push up the annual benefit close to $50,000. This also presumes that the mother is not cheating by getting more welfare than she is entitled to, which is often the case.

Not only is this far above any job available to our hypothetical teenaged single mother, it is even far higher than a typical entry level job in the New York City government. Thus, the *New York Post*, (Aug. 2) noted the following starting salaries at various municipal jobs: $18,000 for an office aid; $23,000 for a sanitation worker; $27,000 for a teacher; $27,000 for a police officer or firefighter; $18,000 for a word processor—all of these with far more work skills than possessed by your typical welfare client. And all of these salaries, of course, are fully taxable.

Given this enormous disparity in benefits, is it any wonder that 1.3 million mothers and children in New York are on welfare, and that welfare dependence is happily passed on from one generation of girls to the next? As Change-NY puts it, "why accept a job that requires 40 hours of work a week when you can remain at home and make the equivalent" of $45,000 a year?

Economists, then, are particularly alert to the fact that, the more any product, service, or condition is subsidized, the more of it we are going to get. We can have as many people on welfare as we are willing to pay for. If the state of being a single mother with kids is the fastest route to getting on welfare, that social condition is going to multiply.

Not, of course, that *every* woman will fall for the blandishments of welfare, but the more intense those subsidies and the greater the benefit compared to working, the more women and illegitimate children on welfare we are going to be stuck with.

Moreover, the longer this system remains in place, the worse will be the erosion in society of the work ethic and of the reluctance to be on the dole that used to be dominant in the United States. Once that ethical shift takes place, the welfare system will only snowball.

Change-NY wryly points out that it would be cheaper for the taxpayer to send welfare recipients to Harvard than to maintain the current system. In view of the decline of educational standards generally and Harvard's Political Correctness in particular, Harvard would probably be happy to enroll them. ▸

14
WELFARE AS WE DON'T KNOW IT

The welfare system has become an open scandal, and has given rise to justified indignation throughout the middle and working classes. Unfortunately, as too often happens when the public has no articulate leadership, the focus of its wrath against welfare has become misplaced.

The public's rage focuses on having to pay taxes to keep welfare receivers in idleness; but what people should zero in on is their having to pay these people taxes, period. The concentration on idleness vs. the "work ethic," however, has given the trickster Bill Clinton the loophole he always covets: seeming to pursue conservative goals while actually doing just the opposite. Unfortunately, the welfare "reform" scam seems to be working.

The President's pledge to end "welfare as we know it," therefore, turns out not to be dumping welfare parasites off the backs of the taxpayers. On the contrary, the plan is to load even more taxpayer subsidies and privileges into their eager pockets. The welfarees will become even more parasitic and just as unproductive as before, but at least they will not be "idle." Big deal.

The outline of the Clintonian plan is as follows: Welfarees will be given two years to "find a job." Since nothing prevents them from "finding a job" now except their own lack of interest, there is no reason for expecting much from job-finding. At that point, "reform" kicks in. The federal government will either pay private employers to hire these people or, if no employers can be found, will itself "employ" the welfarees in various "community service" jobs. The latter, of course, are unproductive boondoggles, jobs which no one will pay for in the private sector, what used to be called "leaf-raking" in the Federal Works Progress Administration of the 1930s New Deal.

First published in April 1994.

Welfarees will now be paid at minimum wage scale by tax-payers to shuffle papers from one desk to another or to engage in some other unproductive or counter-productive activity. As for subsidizing private jobs, the employers' businesses will be hampered by unproductive or surly or incompetent workers. In the private jobs, furthermore, the taxpayers will wholly subsidize wages not only at minimum wage scale (which we can expect to keep rising), but also at whatever pay may be set between employer and government. The taxpayer picks up the full tab.

But this is scarcely all. In addition to the actual job subsidies, Clinton proposes that the federal government also pay the following to the welfare parasites: free medical care for all (courtesy the Clinton health "reform"); plenty of food stamps for free food; free child care for the myriad of welfare children; free public housing; free transportation to and from their jobs; free child "nutrition" programs; and lavish "training programs" to train these people for productive labor.

If these training programs are anything like current models, they will be lengthy and worthless, including "training" in "conversational skills." If a free and lavishly funded public school system can't seem to manage teaching these characters to read, why should anyone think government qualified to "train" them in any other skills? In addition to the huge cost of direct payments to the welfarees, an expensive government bureaucracy will have to be developed to supervise the training, job finding, and job supervision. In addition, welfare mothers with young children will be exempt from the workfare requirements altogether.

Even the supporters of the Clinton welfare plan concede that the plan will greatly increase the welfare cost to the taxpayers. The Clintonians of course, as usual with government, try to underestimate the cost to get a foot in the door, but even moderate observers estimate the annual extra cost to be no less than $20 billion. And that's probably a gross underestimate. And while the White House claims that only 600,000 people will need the workfare, internal Health and Human Services memoranda estimate the number at no less than 2.3 million, and that's from Clintonian sources.

Of course, the Clintonian claim is that these huge increases are "only in the short-run"; in the long run, the alleged improvement in the moral climate is supposed to lower costs to the taxpayers. Sure.

Forcing taxpayers to subsidize employers or to provide busy-work for unproductive "jobs" is worse than keeping welfare recipients idle. There is no point to activity or work unless it is productive, and enacting a taxpayer subsidy is a sure way to keep the welfarees unproductive. Subsidizing the idle is immoral and counterproductive; paying people to work and creating jobs for them is also crazy, as well as being more expensive.

But paying people to work is worse than that. For it removes low-income recipients of subsidy from the status of an exotic, marginal, and generally despised group, and brings the subsidized into the mainstream of the workforce. The change from welfare to workfare thereby accelerates the malignant socialist and egalitarian goal of coerced redistribution of income. It is, in other words, simply another part of the twentieth century's Long March toward socialism. ▶

15
THE INFANT MORTALITY "CRISIS"

I first heard of the Infant Mortality Question last summer, when I had the misfortune to spend an evening with an obnoxious leftist who claimed that, despite any other considerations, U.S. capitalism had failed and the Soviet Union had succeeded, because of the high "infant mortality" rate here. She must have been ahead of the left-wing learning curve, for since

---

First published in June 1991.

then the press has been filled with articles proclaiming the self-same doctrine.

First, on the Soviet Union, I learned from Soviet economist Dr. Yuri Maltsev that the Soviets had achieved low infant mortality rates by a simple but effective device, one that is considerably easier than medical advances, nutritional improvement, or behavioral reform for pregnant women. Namely: by holding up the statistical reporting of a death until the mortality is beyond "infant" status. No one, apparently, pays much attention to the death rate of post-infants.

But what of the U.S. infant mortality record? Well, in 1915, 100 infants died for every 1,000 live births in the U.S. Since then, the mortality rate has fallen spectacularly: to 47 for every 1,000 in 1940, 20 by 1970, and down to 10 per 1,000 by 1988. A 90 percent drop in the infant mortality rate since 1915 does not seem to be a record calculated to induce an orgy of breast-beating and collective guilt among the American people.

So why should Dr. Louis W. Sullivan, our official scourge as Secretary of Health and Human Services, denounce the U.S. record as "shameful and unconscionable?" And why should a proposal by President Bush for an additional federal prenatal care program of $171 million be denounced by some Congress-men as amounting only to a net increase of $121 million, since $50 million would be deducted from existing programs? Why is it assumed on all sides that more federal spending is necessary?

The problem seems to be that many countries have lowered their infant mortality rates even faster, so that the U.S. now ranks 22nd in infant mortality; rates in Japan and in Scandinavia are less than half that in the U.S.

As in economic statistics, it helps our understanding to dis-aggregate; and we then find that black infant mortality has long been far higher than white; specifically, the 1988 U.S. rate was 17.6 for blacks and 8.5 for whites.

Apparently, the key to infant mortality is low birth-weight, and low birth-weight rates in the U.S. have long been far greater for black than for white infants. The white rate has remained at about 7 percent of live births since 1950, while the black rate has hovered around 10 to 14 percent of births. Starting at 14 percent in 1969—the first year black birthrate figures were kept separately—black low-weight births fell after abortion was legalized, only to go back up since the mid-1980s to over 13 percent.

So central is the birth-weight problem that Christine Layton of the Children's Defense Fund, a left-liberal "health advocacy group" (is anyone opposed to health?) in Washington, welcomed the recent news that infant mortality rates fell to 9.1 deaths per 1,000 live births in 1990 only grudgingly. She pointed out that this decline since 1988 is due only to new medical advances in drugs for treating lungs of premature babies; apparently this decline doesn't really count, since it will not "have the kind of lasting effect we need to see on the problems of being born too soon or too small."

But how come the low birthrate problem among blacks has persisted for decades even though, with its usual energy in spending taxpayer money, the federal government has been tackling the problem since 1972 by its immensely popular WIC (Special Supplemental Food Program for Women, Infants, and Children) program? WIC costs the federal government $2.5 billion a year, in addition to federal subsidies to states administering the program.

In the left liberal worldview, every social problem can be cured by federal spending, and so the government assumed that low birth-weight among black babies was due to malnutrition, which was in turn due to poverty. WIC, therefore, has been providing poor American women with vast amounts of milk, cheese, eggs, cereal, and peanut butter. WIC has been supplying all this food to half of the eight million pregnant women, infants, mothers, and children eligible—family incomes must be below 185 percent of the official poverty line and the family must be officially judged to be at "nutritional risk."

So why is it that impoverished black mothers, despite the intake of all this federally sponsored nutrition, have not seen the low birth-weight or the mortality problem reduced over these two decades? Why has the only accomplishment of WIC been to provide massive subsidies to dairy and peanut farmers? (We set aside the rising obesity and cholesterol rates among poor blacks.)

The answer is that, remarkably enough, nutrition, and therefore low incomes, is not the problem. It turns out, according to an article by prominent nutritionist and pediatrician Dr. George Graham of Johns Hopkins Medical School (*Wall Street Journal*, April 2, 1991), that the key cause of low birth-weight, and especially of very low birth-weight, in the U.S. is premature birth, and that malnutrition plays virtually no role in causing premature birth. In Third World countries, on the contrary, low birth-weight is caused by malnutrition and poverty, but premature birth in those countries is not a particular problem.

Unlike Third World countries, low birth-weight, and therefore high mortality rates, in the U.S. are a problem of prematurity and not malnutrition. In fact, the infant mortality rate on the island of Jamaica, almost all of whose population is poor and black, is substantially lower than in Washington, D.C., whose blacks enjoy a far higher income than in Jamaica, and two-thirds of whom were beneficiaries of the WIC program.

The cause of premature births, in fact, is not nutritional but behavioral, that is the behavior of the pregnant mother. In particular tobacco smoking, ingestion of cocaine and crack, previous abortions, and infections of the genital tract and of the membranes surrounding the fetus, which often are the consequence of sexual promiscuity. And there we have it.

These are not facts that left-liberalism likes to hear, and obviously no federal mulcting of taxpayers is going to improve the situation. Left-liberals might try to evade the truth by charging that this is the old conservative tack of "blaming the victim." They're wrong. No one is blaming the babies. ▶

16
THE HOMELESS AND THE HUNGRY

W inter is here, and for the last few years this seasonal event has meant the sudden discovery of a brand-new category of the pitiable: the "homeless."

A vast propaganda effort has discovered the homeless and adjured us to do something about it—inevitably to pour millions of tax-dollars into the problem. There is now even a union of homeless lobbying for federal aid. Not so long ago there was another, apparently entirely different category: the "hungry," for whom rock stars were making records and we were all clasping hands across America. And what has now happened to the Hungry? Have they all become well fed, and so rest content, while the Homeless are held up for our titillation? Or have they too organized a union of the Hungry?

And what of next year? Are we to be confronted with a new category, the "unclothed," or perhaps the "ill-shod"? And how about the "thirsty"? Or the candy-deprived? How many more millions are standing in line, waiting to be trotted out for consideration?

Do the Establishment liberals engaged in this operation really believe, by the way, that these are all ironclad separate categories? Do they envision, for example, a mass of hungry living in plush houses, or a legion of the homeless who are living it up every night at Lutece?

Surely not; surely there are not a half-dozen or so different sets of the ill-served. Doesn't the Establishment realize that all these seemingly unconnected problems: housing, food, clothing, transportation, etc. are all wrapped up in One Big Problem: lack of money? If this were recognized, the problem would be

---

First published in February 1987.

simplified, the causal connections would be far clearer, and the number of afflicted millions greatly reduced: to poverty, period.

Why aren't these connections recognized, as even Franklin Roosevelt did in the famous passage of his second inaugural where he saw "one-third of a nation ill-housed, ill-clad, and ill-nourished?" Presumably, FDR saw considerable overlap between these three deprivations. I think the Establishment treats these problems separately for several reasons, none of them admirable. For one reason, it magnifies the hardship, making it appear like many sets of people suffering from grave economic ailments. Which means that more taxpayer money is supposed to be funneled into a far greater number of liberal social workers.

But there is more. By stressing particular, specific problems, the inference comes that the taxpayer must quickly provide each of a number of goodies: food, housing, clothing, counseling, et al. in turn. And this means far greater subsidies to different sets of bureaucrats and special economic interests: e.g., construction companies, building trade unions, farmers, food distributors, clothing firms, etc. Food stamps, housing vouchers, public housing follow with seemingly crystal-clear logic.

It is also far easier to sentimentalize the issues and get the public's juices worked up by sobbing about the homeless, the foodless, etc. and calling for specific provision of these wants— far easier than talking about the "moneyless" and calling upon the public merely to supply do-re-mi to the poor. Money does not have nearly the sentimental value of home and hearth and Christmas dinner.

Not only that: but focusing on money is likely to lead the public to begin asking embarrassing questions. Such as: WHY are these people without money? And isn't there a danger that taxing A to supply B with money will greatly reduce the incentive for both A and B to continue working hard in order to acquire it ? Doesn't parasitism gravely weaken the incentives to work among both the producer and the parasite class?

Further, if the poor are without money because they don't feel like working, won't automatic taxpayer provision of a permanent supply of funds weaken their willingness to work all the more, and create an ever greater supply of the idle looking for handouts? Or, if the poor are without money because they are disabled, won't a permanent dole reduce their incentive to invest in their own vocational rehabilitation and training, so that they will once again be productive members of society? And, in general, isn't it far better for all concerned (except, of course, the social workers) to have limited private funds for charity instead of imposing an unlimited burden on the hapless taxpayer?

Focusing on money, instead of searching for an ever-greater variety of people to be pitied and cosseted, would itself tend to clear the air and the mind and go a long way toward a solution of the problem. ▶

17
RIOTING FOR RAGE, FUN, AND PROFIT

The little word "but" is the great weasel word of our time, enabling one to subscribe to standard pieties while getting one's *real* contrary message across. "Of course, I deplore communism, but . . ."; "Of course, I approve of the free market, but . . ." have been all too familiar refrains in recent decades. The standard reaction of our pundits, and across the entire respectable political spectrum, to the great Los Angeles et al. riots of April 29–May 2 went: "Of course, I can't condone violence, but . . . ." In every instance, the first clause is slid over rapidly and ritualistically, to get to the real diametrically opposed message after the "but" is disposed of.

The point, of course, is precisely to condone violence, by rushing to get to the alleged "real structural causes" of riots and

First published in July 1992.

the violence. While the "causes" of any human action are imprecise and complex, none of that is attended to, for everyone knows what the "solution" is supposed to be: to tax the American people, including the victims of the massive looting, burning, beating, killing rampage, to "assuage the rage of the inner cities" by paying off the rampaging "community" so handsomely that they supposedly won't do it again.

Before we rush past the riots themselves, the whole point of government, of an institution with a monopoly, or preponderance, of violence, is to use it to defend persons and property against violent assault. That role is not as obvious as it may seem, since the Los Angeles, state, and federal forces most conspicuously did *not* perform that function. Sending in police and troops late and depriving them of bullets, cannot do the job.

There is only one way to fulfill the vital police function, the only way that works: the public announcement—backed by willingness to enforce it—made by the late Mayor Richard Daley in the Chicago riots of the 1960s—ordering the police to shoot to kill any looters, rioters, arsonists, or muggers they might find. That very announcement was enough to induce the rioters to pocket their "rage" and go back to their peaceful pursuits.

Who knows the hearts of men? Who knows all the causes, the motivations, of action? But one thing is clear: regardless of the murky "causes," would-be looters and muggers would get such a message loud and clear.

But the federal government, and most state and local governments, decided to deal with the great riots of Watts and other inner cities of the 1960s in a very different way: the now accepted practice of a massive buyout, a vast system of bribes in the form of welfare, setasides, affirmative action, etc. The amount spent on such purposes by federal, state, and local governments since the Great Society of the 1960s totals the staggering sum of $7 trillion.

And what is the result? The plight of the inner cities is clearly worse than ever: more welfare, more crime, more dysfunction, more fatherless families, fewer kids being "educated" in any sense, more despair and degradation. And now, bigger riots than ever before. It should be clear, in the starkest terms, that throwing taxpayer money and privileges at the inner cities is starkly counterproductive. And yet: this is the only "solution" that liberals can ever come up with, and without any argument—as if this "solution" were self-evident. How long is this nonsense supposed to go on?

If that is the absurd liberal solution, conservatives are not much better. Even liberals are praising—always a bad sign—Jack Kemp for being a "good" conservative who cares, and who is coming up with innovative solutions trumpeted by Kemp himself and his neoconservative fuglemen. These are supposed to be "non-welfare" solutions, but welfare is precisely what they are: "public housing "owned" by tenants, but only under massive subsidy and strict regulation—with no diminution of the public housing stock; "enterprise zones" which are not free enterprise zones at all, but simply zones for more welfare subsidy and privileges to the inner city.

Various left-libertarians focus on removal of minimum wage laws and licensing requirements as the cure for the disaster of the inner cities. Well, repeal of minimum wages would certainly be helpful, but they are largely irrelevant to the riots: after all, minimum wage laws exist all across the country, in areas just as poor as the inner cities—such as Appalachia. How come there are no riots in Appalachia? The abolition of licensing laws would also be welcome, but just as irrelevant.

Some claim the underlying cause is racial discrimination. And yet, the problem seems worse, rather than better, after three decades of aggressive civil rights measures. Moreover, the Koreans are undoubtedly at least equal victims of racial discrimination—and they also have the problem of English being their second, and often a distant second, language. So how is it that

Korean-Americans never riot, indeed that they were the major single group of *victims* of the Los Angeles riot?

The Moynihan thesis of the cause of the problem is closer to the mark: the famous insight of three decades ago that the black family was increasingly fatherless, and that therefore such values as respect for person and property were in danger of disappearing. Three decades later, the black family is in far worse shape, and the white family isn't doing too well, either. But even if the Moynihan thesis is part of the problem, what can be done about it? Families cannot be forced together.

A greater part of the cause of the rot is the moral and esthetic nihilism created by many decades of cultural liberalism. But what can be done about it? Surely, at best it would take many decades to take back the culture from liberalism and to instill sound doctrine, if it can be done at all. The rot cannot be stopped, or even slowed down, by such excruciatingly slow and problematic measures.

Before we can set about curing a disease we must have some idea of what that disease is. Are we really sure that "rage" is the operative problem? For the most part, the young rioters caught on television mostly did not look angry at all. One memorable exchange took place as the TV camera caught a happy, grinning young lad hauling off a TV set from a looted store and putting it in his car. Asked the dimwit reporter: "Why are you taking that TV set?" The memorable answer: "Because it's free!" It is no accident, too, that the arsonists took care to loot thoroughly the 10,000 stores before they burned them to the ground.

The crucial point is that whether the motivation or the goal is rage, kicks, or loot, the rioters, with a devotion to present gratification as against future concerns, engaged in the joys of beating, robbing, and burning, and of massive theft, because they saw they could get away with it. Devotion to the sanctity of person and property is not part of their value-system. That's why, in the short term, all we can do is shoot the looters and incarcerate the rioters. ▶

18
THE SOCIAL SECURITY SWINDLE

Senator Daniel P. Moynihan (D-NY) has performed a signal service for all Americans by calling into question, for the first time since the early 1980s, the soundness of the nation's beloved Social Security System. A decade ago, the public was beginning to learn of the imminent bankruptcy of Social Security, only to be sent back into their half-century slumber in 1983 by the bipartisan Greenspan commission, which "saved" Social Security by installing a whopping and ever-rising set of increases in the Social Security tax. Any government program, of course, can be bailed out by levying more taxes to pay the tab.

Since the beginning of the Reagan administration, the much heralded "cuts" in the officially dubbed "income-tax" segment of our payroll taxes have been more than offset by the rise in the "Social-Security" portion. But since the public has been conditioned into thinking that the Social Security tax is somehow not a tax, the Reagan-Bush administrations have been able to get away with their pose as heroic champions of tax cuts and resisters against the tax raising inclinations of the evil Democrats.

For the Social Security System is the biggest single racket in the entire panoply of welfare-state measures that have been fastened upon us by the New Deal and its successors. The American public has been conned into thinking that the Social Security tax is not a tax at all, but a benevolent national "insurance" scheme into which everyone pays premiums from the beginning of their working lives, finally "collecting" benefits when they get to be 65. The system is held to be analogous to a private insurance firm, which collects premiums over the years, invests them in productive ways that yield interest, and then later pays old-age annuities to the lucky beneficiaries.

First published in April 1990.

So much for the facade. The reality, however, is the exact opposite. The federal government taxes the youth and adult working population, takes the money, and spends it on the boondoggles that make up the annual federal budget. Then, when the long-taxed person gets to be 65, the government taxes someone else—that is, the still-working population, to pay the so-called benefits.

Be assured, the executives of any private insurance company that tried this stunt would be spending the rest of their lives in much-merited retirement in the local hoosegow. The whole system is a vast Ponzi scheme, with the difference that Ponzi's notorious swindle at least rested solely on his ability to con his victims, whereas the government swindlers, of course, rely also on a vast apparatus of tax-coercion.

But this covers only one dimension of the Social Security racket. The "benefits," of course, are puny compared to a genuine private annuity, which makes productive investments. The purchasers of a private annuity receive, at the age, say of 65, a principal sum which they can obtain and which can also earn them further interest. The person on Social Security gets only the annual benefits, void of any capital sum. How could he, when the Social Security "fund" doesn't exist?

The notion that a fund really exists rests on a "creative" accounting fiction; yes, the fund does exist on paper, but the Social Security System actually grabs the money as it comes in and purchases bonds from the Treasury, which spends the money on its usual boondoggles.

But that's not all. The Social Security System is a "welfare" program that levies high and continually increasing taxes (a) only on wages, and on no other investment or interest income; and (b) is steeply regressive, hitting lower wage earners far more heavily than people in the upper brackets. Thus, income earners up to $51,300 per year are forced to pay, at this moment, 7.65 percent of their income to Social Security; but there the tax stops, so that, for example a person who earns $200,000 a year pays the same absolute amount ($3,924), which works out as only 2 percent of income. That's a welfare state!?

Over the years, the government has vastly increased the tax bite in two ways: by increasing the percentage, and by raising the maximum income level at which the tax ceases. As a result, since the start of the Reagan administration, the rate has gone up from 5.80 percent to 7.65 percent, and the maximum tax from $1,502 to $3,924 per year. And that's only the beginning.

The final aspect of the swindle was contributed by Reagan-Greenspan & Co. in 1983. Observing the high and mounting federal deficits, our bipartisan rulers decided to raise taxes and pile up a huge "surplus" in the non-existent Social Security fund, thereby "lowering" the embarrassing deficit on paper, while continuing the same stratospheric deficit in reality. Thus, the projected federal deficit for fiscal 1990 is $206 billion; but the estimated $65 billion "surplus" in the Social Security account officially reduces the deficit to $141 billion, thereby appeasing the ghosts of Gramm-Rudman. But of course there is no surplus; the $65 billion are promptly spent on Treasury bonds, and the Treasury adds that to the stream of general expenditures on $20,000 coffeemakers, bailouts for S&L crooks, and the rest of its worthy causes.

But Senator Moynihan, one of the authors of the current swindle as part of the Greenspan Commission, has blown at least part of the lid off the scam. At which point, the Republicans happily took up the traditional Democratic count that their opposition has set out, cruelly and heartlessly, to throw the nation's much revered elderly into the gutter.

Senator Moynihan's proposal for a small rollback of the Social Security tax to 6.55 percent at least opens the entire matter for public debate. Moynihan's motives have been called into question, but after we recover from our shock at a politician possibly acting for political motives, we must realize that we owe him a considerable debt. The problem is that, while many writers and journalists understand the truth and tell it in print, they generally do so in subdued and decorous tones, drenching the reader in reams of statistics.

The public will never be roused to rise up and get rid of this monstrous system until they are told the truth in no uncertain terms: in other words, until a swindle is called a swindle. ▶

19
ROOTS OF THE INSURANCE CRISIS

The latest large-scale assault upon property rights and the free market comes from the insurance industry and its associated incurrers of liability: particularly groups of manufacturers and the organized medical profession. They charge that runaway juries have been awarding skyrocketing increases in liability payments, thereby threatening to bankrupt the insurance industry as well as impose higher costs upon, or deprive of liability insurance, those industries and occupations that juries have adjudged to be guilty.

In response, the insurance and allied industries have demanded legal caps, or maxima, on jury awards, as well as maximum limits on or even elimination of, legal fees, especially contingency fees paid to lawyers by plaintiffs out of their awarded damages.

Before analyzing these measures, it must be pointed out that there may well be no crisis. Critics of the insurance industry have pointed out that insurance companies have refused to reveal the figures on verdicts and settlements from year to year, or to break them down by industry or occupation. Instead, the insurance industry has relied solely on colorful anecdotes about bizarre individual awards—something they would scarcely do in running their own business.

Also, the critics have demonstrated that average insurance payments have not advanced, in the last 25 years, much beyond

---

Previously unpublished.

the rate of inflation. So there may well be no insurance crisis at all, and the entire hysteria may be trumped-up to gain benefits for the insurance industry at the expense of victims of injury to person or property who are entitled to just compensation.

But let us assume for the sake of argument that the insurance crisis is every bit as dramatic as the industry says it is. Why are the rest of us supposed to bail them out? Insurance companies, like other business firms, are entrepreneurial. As entrepreneurs, they take risks; when they do well and forecast correctly, they properly make profits; when they forecast badly, they make losses. That is the way it should be. They should be honored when they make profits, and suffer the consequences when they make losses. In the case of insurance, companies charge premiums so as to cover, with a profit, the liabilities they expect to pay. If they suffer losses because their entrepreneurship is poor, and payments are higher than premiums, they should expect no sympathy, let alone bailout, from the long-suffering consuming and taxpaying public.

It is particularly outrageous that the insurance companies are trying to place maximum limits on jury awards and on legal fees. It is everyone's right as a free person to hire lawyers for whatever fee they both agree upon, and it is no one's right to interfere with private property and the freedom to make such contracts. Lawyers, after all, are our shield and buckler against unjust laws and torts committed against us, and we must not be deprived of the right to hire them.

Furthermore, the much abused contingency fee is actually a marvelous instrument which enables the poorest among us to hire able lawyers. And the fact that the attorney depends for his fee on his "investment" in the case, gives him the incentive to fight all the harder on behalf of his clients. Outlawing contingency fees would leave attorneys only in service to the rich, and would deprive the average person of his day in court. Is that what the insurance industry really wants?

As for jury awards, do the insurance industry and organized medicine really wish to destroy the Anglo-American jury system, which for all its faults and inefficiencies, has long been a bulwark of our liberties against the State? And if they wish to destroy it, what would they replace it with—rule by government? As long as we keep the jury system as the arbitrator of civil and criminal cases, we must not hobble its dispensing of justice—especially by senseless quantitative caps that simply proclaim that justice may only be dispensed in small, but not adequate, amounts.

None of this means that tort law itself is in no need of reform. The problem is not really quantitative but qualitative: *who* should be liable for *what* damages? In particular, we must put an end to the theory of "vicarious liability," i.e., that people or groups are liable, *not* because their actions incurred damages, but simply because they happened to be nearby and are conveniently wealthy, i.e., in the apt if inelegant legal phrase, they happily possess "deep pockets."

Thus, if we bought a product from a retailer and the product is defective, it is the *retailer* that should be liable and not the manufacturer, since we did not make a contract with the manufacturer (unless he placed an explicit warranty upon the product). It is the retailer's business to sue the wholesaler, the latter the manufacturer, etc., provided the latter really did break his contract by providing a defective product.

Similarly, if a corporate manager committed a wrong and damaged the person or property of others, there is no reason but "deep pockets" to make the stockholders pay, provided that the latter were innocent and did not order the manager to engage in these tortious actions.

To the extent, then, that cries about an insurance crisis reflect an increased propensity by juries to sock it to "soul-less corporations," i.e., to the stockholders, then the remedy is to take that right away from them by changing tort law to make liable only those actually committing wrongful acts.

Let liability, in short, be full and complete; but let it rest only upon those at fault, i.e., those actually damaging the persons and property of others. ▶

20
GOVERNMENT MEDICAL "INSURANCE"

One of Ludwig von Mises's keenest insights was on the cumulative tendency of government intervention. The government, in its wisdom, perceives a problem (and Lord knows, there are always problems!). The government then intervenes to "solve" that problem. But lo and behold! instead of solving the initial problem, the intervention creates two or three further problems, which the government feels it must intervene to heal, and so on toward socialism.

No industry provides a more dramatic illustration of this malignant process than medical care. We stand at the seemingly inexorable brink of fully socialized medicine, or what is euphemistically called "national health insurance." Physician and hospital prices are high and are always rising rapidly, far beyond general inflation. As a result, the medically uninsured can scarcely pay at all, so that those who are not certifiable claimants for charity or Medicaid are bereft. Hence, the call for national health insurance.

But why are rates high and increasing rapidly? The answer is the very existence of health care insurance, which was established or subsidized or promoted by the government to help ease the previous burden of medical care. Medicare, Blue Cross, etc., are also very peculiar forms of "insurance."

If your house burns down and you have fire insurance, you receive (if you can pry the money loose from your friendly insurance company) a compensating fixed money benefit. For this privilege, you pay in advance a fixed annual premium. Only in our system of medical insurance, does the government or Blue Cross pay, not a fixed sum, but whatever the doctor or hospital chooses to charge.

First published in August 1990.

In economic terms, this means that the demand curve for physicians and hospitals can rise without limit. In short, in a form grotesquely different from Say's Law, the suppliers can literally create their own demand through unlimited third-party payments to pick up the tab. If demand curves rise virtually without limit, so too do the prices of the service.

In order to stanch the flow of taxes or subsidies, in recent years the government and other third party insurers have felt obliged to restrict somewhat the flow of goodies: by increasing deductibles, or by putting caps on Medicare payments. All this has been met by howls of anguish from medical customers who have come to think of unlimited third-party payments as some sort of divine right, and from physicians and hospitals who charge the government with "socialistic price controls"—for trying to stem its own largesse to the health-care industry!

In addition to artificial raising of the demand curve, there is another deep flaw in the medical insurance concept. Theft is theft, and fire is fire, so that fire or theft insurance is fairly clear-cut the only problem being the "moral hazard" of insurees succumbing to the temptation of burning down their own unprofitable store or apartment house, or staging a fake theft, in order to collect the insurance.

"Medical care," however, is a vague and slippery concept. There is no way by which it can be measured or gauged or even defined. A "visit to a physician" can range all the way from a careful and lengthy investigation and discussion, and thoughtful advice, to a two-minute run-through with the doctor doing not much else than advising two aspirin and having the nurse write out the bill.

Moreover, there is no way to prevent a galloping moral hazard, as customers—their medical bills reduced to near-zero—decide to go to the doctor every week to have their blood pressure checked or their temperature taken. Hence, it is impossible, under third-party insurance, to prevent a gross decline in the quality of medical care, along with a severe shortage of the supply of such care in relation to the swelling demand. Everyone old enough to remember the good-old-days of family physicians making house calls, spending a great deal of time with and getting to know the patient, and charging low fees to boot, is deeply and properly resentful of the current assembly-line care. But all too few understand the role of the much-beloved medical insurance itself in bringing about this sorry decline in quality, as well as the astronomical rise in prices.

But the roots of the current medical crisis go back much further than the 1950s and medical insurance. Government intervention into medicine began much earlier, with a watershed in 1910 when the much celebrated Flexner Report changed the face of American medicine.

Abraham Flexner, an unemployed former owner of a prep school in Kentucky, and sporting neither a medical degree nor any other advanced degree, was commissioned by the Carnegie Foundation to write a study of American medical education. Flexner's only qualification for this job was to be the brother of the powerful Dr. Simon Flexner, indeed a physician and head of the Rockefeller Institute for Medical Research. Flexner's report was virtually written in advance by high officials of the American Medical Association, and its advice was quickly taken by every state in the Union.

The result: every medical school and hospital was subjected to licensing by the state, which would turn the power to appoint licensing boards over to the state AMA. The state was supposed to, and did, put out of business all medical schools that were proprietary and profit-making, that admitted blacks and women, and that did not specialize in orthodox, "allopathic" medicine: particularly homeopaths, who were then a substantial part of the medical profession, and a respectable alternative to orthodox allopathy.

Thus through the Flexner Report, the AMA was able to use government to cartelize the medical profession: to push the supply curve drastically to the left (literally half the medical schools in the country were put out of business by post-Flexner state governments), and thereby to raise medical and hospital prices and doctors' incomes.

In all cases of cartels, the producers are able to replace consumers in their seats of power, and accordingly the medical establishment was now able to put competing therapies (e.g., homeopathy) out of business; to remove disliked competing groups from the supply of physicians (blacks, women, Jews); and to replace proprietary medical schools financed by student fees with university-based schools run by the faculty, and subsidized by foundations and wealthy donors.

When managers such as trustees take over from owners financed by customers (students of patients), the managers become governed by the perks they can achieve rather than by service of consumers. Hence: a skewing of the entire medical profession away from patient care toward high-tech, high-capital investment in rare and glamorous diseases, which rebound far more to the prestige of the hospital and its medical staff than is actually useful for the patient-consumers.

And so, our very real medical crisis has been the product of massive government intervention, state and federal, throughout the century; in particular, an artificial boosting of demand coupled with an artificial restriction of supply. The result has been accelerating high prices and deterioration of patient care. And next, socialized medicine could easily bring us to the vaunted medical status of the Soviet Union: everyone has the right to free medical care, but there is, in effect, no medicine and no care. ▶

21
THE NEOCON WELFARE STATE

Ever since its inception in the 1930s, the welfare state has proceeded in the following way. First, liberals discover

---

First published in September 1992.

social and economic problems. Not a difficult task: the human race has always had such problems and will continue to, short of the Garden of Eden. Liberals, however, usually need scores of millions in foundation grants and taxpayer-financed commissions to come up with the startling revelations of disease, poverty, ignorance, homelessness, *et al.*

Having identified "problems" to the accompaniment of much coordinated fanfare, the liberals proceed to invoke "solutions," to be supplied, of course, by the federal government, which we all know and love as the Great Problem-Solving Machine.

Whatever the problem or its complexity, we all know that the Solution is always the same: a huge amount of taxpayer money to be trundled out by local, state, and especially the federal government, and spent on building up an ever-growing giant bureaucracy swarming with bureaucrats dedicated to spending their lives combatting the particular problem in view. The money is supplied, of course, by the taxpayer, and by a burgeoning debt to be financed either by inflation or by future taxpayers.

From the beginning, each new creative Leap Forward in the welfare state is launched by liberals in the Democratic Party. That, since the 1930s, has been the Democrats' historical function. The Republicans' function, on the other hand, has been to complain about the welfare state and then, when in power, to fasten their yoke upon the public by not only retaining the Democratic "advances" but also by expanding them.

The best that we have been able to hope for under Republican administrations is a slight slowing down of the rate of expansion of the welfare state, and a relative absence of new, "innovative" proposals.

The result of each of the Great Leaps Forward of the welfare state (The New Deal–Fair Deal of the '30s and '40s, and the Great Society of the '60s), has clearly *not* been to "solve" the problems the welfare state has addressed. On the contrary, each of these problems is demonstrably far worse two or three decades after the innovation and expansion. At the same time, the government Problem Solving Machine: taxes, deficits, spending, regulations, and bureaucracy, has gotten far bigger, stronger, and hungrier for taxpayer loot.

Now, in the Nineties, we are at another crossroads. The results are now in on the Great Society and its Nixonian codicils. A massive and expensive attempt to stamp out poverty, inner-city problems, racism, and disease, has only resulted in all of these problems being far worse, along with a far-greater machinery for federal control, spending, and bureaucracy.

Liberal Democrats, who now call themselves "moderates" because of the perceived failures of liberalism, have come up with the usual "solutions": redoubled and massive federal spending to "help" the inner cities, "rebuilding" the decaying infrastructure, helping to make declining industries "competitive," *et al*. But whereas Republican administrations in the 1950s and 1970s were in the hands of avowed "moderates" or "liberals," the Republican administration is now run, or at least guided by, conservatives.

What is the "conservative" (read: neoconservative) Republican response to the welfare state and to the Democratic proposals for yet another great Leap Forward?

The good news is that the neoconservative alternative is not just another "me-too" proposal for slightly less of what the Democratic liberals are proposing. The bad news, however, is that the proposed "conservative welfare state"—in the words of neocon godfather Irving Kristol—is a lot worse. For once, under the aegis of the neocons, the Republicans are coming up with genuinely innovative proposals.

But that's the trouble: the result is far more power and more resources to the Leviathan State in Washington, all camouflaged in pseudoconservative rhetoric. Since the conservative public always tends to put more emphasis on rhetoric than on substance, this makes the looming Alternative Welfare State of the Republicans all the more dangerous.

The dimensions of the Neocon Welfare State in embryo may be seen in the Bush-endorsed proposals of Education Secretary Lamar Alexander, aided and guided by neocon educationists Chester Finn and Diane Ravitch. The education disaster in this country has been largely created by the massive federal funds and controls that have already fastened a gigantic educational bureaucracy on the American people, and have gone a long way toward taking control of our children out of the hands of parents and putting it into the maw of the State.

The Neocon Welfare State would finish the job: expanding budgets, nationalizing teachers and curricula, and seizing total control of children on behalf of the State's malignant educational bureaucracy.

The housing and urban dimensions of the Alternative Welfare State have been worked out by the neocon's favorite politician, HUD secretary Jack Kemp. While Kemp's vision was kept at arm's length by the Bush administration, the L.A. riots have brought it a virtual Republican endorsement, in the wake of President Bush's deficiency in the "vision thing," and of the liberals' chorus of adulation for Jack Kemp's "caring and compassion" for the inner cities.

As Jeff Tucker has pointed out in the *Free Market*, Kemp's proposed "enterprise zones" and "empowerment" turn out to be still more of the welfare state. The "enterprise zone" concept, originally meant to be islands of genuine free enterprise in a statist morass, have been cunningly turned into yet more welfare, and affirmative-action-type subsidies. The Thatcherite idea of selling public housing to tenants has merely turned into another method of *expanding* public housing, of subsidizing inner cities, and of keeping the tenants dependent on the federal bureaucracy and on Big Massa in the White House.

How would the greater Neocon Welfare State be financed? Neocons are the most enthusiastic fans of the federal deficit since the Left-Keynesians of the 1930s. We can expect, then, much bigger deficits, accompanied by a large and innovative battery of excuses. Statistics will be dredged up to the effect that the deficit and the debt "really aren't so bad," compared, say, with some year during World War II, or, that on deep and murky philosophic grounds, they *really* don't exist.

On taxes, we can probably trust neocons to keep marginal income tax rates on upper brackets down, as well as to cut capital gains taxes, but the sky's the limit on everything else. We can look forward to a lot more of the "loophole closing" that helped send the real estate market into a long and continuing tailspin after the Tax Reform Act of 1986. We can also look forward to increases in excise taxes, and perhaps a national sales or value-added tax.

Harry Hopkins is supposed to have outlined the basic New Deal Strategy: "We shall tax and tax, spend and spend, elect and elect." He might have added: control and control. Over the decades, the outer forms, the glittering trappings, have changed in order to entice new generations of suckers. But the essence of the ever-expanding Leviathan has remained the same. ▶

22
BY THEIR FRUITS...

One of the most horrifying features of the New Deal was its agricultural policy: in the name of "curing the depression," the federal government organized a giant cartel of America's farmers. In the middle of the worst depression in American history, the federal government forced farmers to plow under every third acre of wheat and to kill one-third of their little pigs, all to drive up food prices by forcing the supply of each product downward. Leftists blamed "American capitalism" for the government's forcing deep cuts in farm supply while urban Americans were starving; but the problem was not "capitalism," it was organized pressure groups—in this case agribusiness—using the

_____

First published in October 1992.

federal government as the organizer and mighty enforcer of farm cartel policy. And all this in the name of helping the "one-third of a nation" that Franklin D. Roosevelt saw "ill-nourished" as well as "ill-clad" and "ill-housed."

Since 1933, New Deal farm policy has continued and expanded, pursuing its grisly logic at the expense of the nation's consumers, year in and year out, in Democrat or Republican regimes, in good times and in bad. But there is something about government brutally destroying food during recessions that rightfully raises one's hackles—if the media bother to deal with it at all. The latest outrage is now occurring in the central valleys of California, a state in deep recession.

The particular problem is fruit, slightly "undersized" peaches and nectarines grown in California. Since the 1930s, the Secretary of Agriculture has been setting minimum size standards for peaches and nectarines. Any fruit even microscopically below the minimum size and weight set by the government is illegal and must be destroyed by the farmer, under pain of severe penalties.

It's not that these slightly smaller peaches and nectarines are unsaleable to the consumer. On the contrary: most people, including trained fruit pickers, can't tell the difference visually, so they are forced to use expensive weighing and sorting machines. It is estimated that, during the 1992 growing season in California, fruit growers will be forced to destroy no less than 500 million pounds of this undersized fruit.

Thus, Gerawan Farming, the largest peach, nectarine, and plum grower in the world, has been accused of violating federal law because, instead of destroying all of its small fruit, it dared to sell some to a wholesaler in Los Angeles, who in turn resold it to mom-and-pop grocery stores who catered to poorer consumers eager to buy the cheaper, if smaller fruit.

The cheapness, of course, is the key. The Secretary of Agriculture does not dream up these vicious regulations out of his own noodle. By law, these minimum sizes are determined by farmers' committees growing the particular product. The farmers are permitted to use the government to enforce cartels, in which larger and more expensive fruit is protected from smaller and cheaper competition. It's as if Cadillacs and Lincoln Town Cars were able to enforce minimum size car standards that would outlaw every smaller-size car on the market.

Perhaps the most repellent aspect of this system is the rationale by the farm committee leaders that they are doing all of this in pursuit of the welfare of consumers. Thus, Tad Kozuki, member of the eight-man Nectarines Administrative Committee, opines that "smaller fruit isn't as appealing to the eye, so the committees tried to please the consumer, thinking the demand for our fruit would rise."

To top this whopper about "pleasing the consumer," John Tos, chairman of the ten-man Peach Commodity Committee, solemnly states that "we eliminate those small sizes because of what the focus groups tell us," adding that these two committees are now spending $50,000 on a more detailed study into consumer fruit preferences.

Save your money, fellas. I can predict the result every time: consumers will always prefer larger peaches to smaller ones, just as given the choice, they would prefer a Cadillac to a Geo. Given the choice of receiving a gift, that is, without having to pay for the difference. And price, of course, is the point of the whole deal. Smaller peaches will be cheaper, just as Geos will be cheaper, and consumers should be able to choose among these various grades, sizes, and prices.

Eric Forman, deputy director of the Fruit and Vegetable Division of the Agricultural Marketing Service of the U.S. Department of Agriculture, was a little more candid than the cartelist farmers. "Consumers are prepared to spend more money for larger fruit than smaller fruit," said Forman, "so why undermine the higher-profit item for the grower?" That is, why allow growers to "undermine" the high profit items by what is also called "competition," apparently a Concept that Dare Not Speak Its Name in agricultural circles.

Sound on the fruit question are consumer groups and the beleaguered Gerawan Farming. Scott Pattison, executive director of Consumer Alert, correctly declared that the whole policy is "outrageous." "Why are bureaucrats and growers telling us there's no market?" asked Pattison. "If consumers really won't buy the small fruit, then the growers will give up trying to ship them. But I think low-income mothers would welcome a smaller fruit that they could afford to buy and put in their kids' lunches." And Dan Gerawan, head of Gerawan Farming, held up a nectarine, and declared sardonically: "This is evil, illegal fruit." Gerawan added that the government "is sanctioning the destruction of fruit meant for the poor."

Here is the essence of the "welfare state" in action: The government cartelizing and restricting competition, cutting production, raising prices, and particularly injuring low-income consumers, all with the aid of mendacious disinformation provided by technocrats hired by the government to administer the welfare state, all meanwhile bleating hypocritically about how the policy is all done for the sake of the consumers. ▶

23
THE POLITICS OF FAMINE

The media focuses primarily on the horrifying shots of starving children, and secondarily on the charges and countercharges about which governments—the Western, the Ethiopian, or whatever—are responsible for relief not getting to the starving thousands on time. In the midst of the media blitz, the important and basic questions get lost in the shuffle. For example, why does Nature seem to frown only on socialist countries? If the problem is drought, why do the rains only elude countries that are socialist or heavily statist? Why does

---

First published in April 1985.

the United States never suffer from poor climates, which threaten famine?

The root of famine lies not in the gods or in the stars but in the actions of man. Climate is not the reason that Russia before Communism was a heavy exporter of grain, while now the Soviet Union is a grain importer. Nature is not responsible for the fact that, of all the countries of East Africa, the Marxist-Leninist nations of Ethiopia and Mozambique are now the major sufferers from mass famine and starvation. Given causes yield given effects, and it is an ineluctable law of nature and of man that if agriculture is systematically crippled and exploited, food production will collapse, and famine will be the result.

The root of the problem is the Third World, where (a) agriculture is overwhelmingly the most important industry, and (b) the people are not affluent enough, in any crisis, to purchase foods from abroad. Hence, to Third World people, agriculture is the most precious activity, and it becomes particularly important that it not be hobbled or discouraged in any way. Yet, wherever there is production, there are also parasitic classes living off the producers. The Third World in our century has been the favorite arena for applied Marxism, for revolutions, coups, or domination by Marxist intellectuals. Whenever such new ruling classes have taken over, and have imposed statist or full socialist rule, the class most looted, exploited, and oppressed have been the major productive class: the farmers or peasantry. Literally tens of millions of the most productive farmers were slaughtered by the Russian and Chinese Communist regimes, and the remainder were forced off their private lands and onto cooperative or state farms, where their productivity plummeted, and foods production gravely declined.

And even in those countries where land was not directly nationalized, the new burgeoning State apparatus flourished on the backs of the peasantry, by levying heavy taxes and by forcing peasants to sell grain to the State at far below market price. The artificially cheap food was then used to subsidize food supplies for the urban population which formed the major base of support for the new bureaucratic class.

The standard paradigm in African and in Asian countries has been as follows: British, French, Portuguese, or whatever imperialism carved out artificial boundaries of what they dubbed "colonies" and established capital cities to administer and rule over the mass of peasantry. Then the new class of higher and lower bureaucrats lived off the peasants by taxing them and forcing them to sell their produce artificially cheaply to the State. When the imperial powers pulled out, they turned over these new nations to the tender mercies of Marxist intellectuals, generally trained in London, Paris, or Lisbon, who imposed socialism or far greater statism, thereby aggravating the problem enormously.

Furthermore, a vicious spiral was set up, similar to the one that brought the Roman Empire to its knees. The oppressed and exploited peasantry, tired of being looted for the sake of the urban sector, decided to leave the farm and go sign up in the welfare state provided in the capital city. This makes the farmer's lot still worse, and hence more of them leave the farm, despite brutal measures trying to prevent them from leaving. The result of this spiral is famine.

Thus, most African governments force farmers to sell all their crops to the State at only a half or even a third of market value. Ethiopia, as a Marxist-Leninist government, also forced the farmers onto highly inefficient state farms, and tried to keep them working there by brutal oppression.

The answer to famine in Ethiopia or elsewhere is not international food relief. Since relief is invariably under the control of the recipient government, the food generally gets diverted from the farms to line the pockets of government officials to subsidize the already well-fed urban population. The answer to famine is to liberate the peasantry of the Third World from the brutality and exploitation of the State ruling class. The answers to famine are private property and free markets. ▶

24
GOVERNMENT VS. NATURAL RESOURCES

It is a common myth that the near-disappearance of the whale and of various species of fish was caused by "capitalist greed," which, in a shortsighted grab for profits, despoiled the natural resources—the geese that laid the golden eggs—from which those profits used to flow. Hence, the call for government to step in and either seize the ownership of these resources, or at least to regulate strictly their use and development.

It is private enterprise, however, not government, that we can rely on to take the long and not the short view. For example, if a private investor or business firm owns a natural resource, say a forest, it knows that every tree cut down and sold for short-run profits will have to be balanced by a decline in the capital value of the forest remaining. Every firm, then, must balance short-run returns as against the loss of capital assets. Therefore, private owners have every economic incentive to be farsighted, to replant trees for every tree cut down, to increase the productivity and to maintain the resource, etc. It is precisely government—or firms allowed to rent resources from government but not own them—whose every incentive is to be short-run. Since government bureaucrats control but do not own the resource "owned" by government, they have no incentive to maximize or even consider the long-run value of the resource. Their every incentive is to loot the resource as quickly as possible.

And, so, it should not be surprising that every instance of "overuse" and destruction of a natural resource has been caused, not by private property rights in natural resources, but by government. Destruction of the grass cover in the West in the late nineteenth-century was caused by the Federal government's failure to recognize homesteading of land in large-enough technological units to be feasible. The 160-acre legal maximum for

---

First published in December 1986.

private homesteading imposed during the Civil War made sense for the wet agriculture of the East; but it made no sense in the dry area of the West, where no farm of less than one or two thousand acres was feasible.

As a result, grassland and cattle ranches became land owned by the federal government but used by or leased to private firms. The private firms had no incentive to develop the land resource, since it could be invaded by other firms or revert to the government. In fact, their incentive was to use up the land resource quickly to destroy the grass cover, because they were prevented from owning it.

Water, rivers, parts of oceans, have been in far worse shape than land, since private individuals and firms have been almost universally prevented from owning parts of that water, from owning schools of fish, etc. In short, since homesteading private property rights has generally not been permitted in parts of the ocean, the oceans and other water resources have remained in a primitive state, much as land had been in the days before private property in land was permitted and recognized. Then, land was only in a hunting-and-gathering stage, where people were permitted to own or transform the land itself. Only private ownership in the land itself can permit the emergence of agriculture— the transformation and cultivation of the land itself—bringing about an enormous growth in productivity and increase in everyone's standard of living.

The world has accepted private agriculture, and the marvelous fruits of such ownership and cultivation. It is high time to expand the dominion of man to one of the last frontiers on earth: aquaculture. Already, private property rights are being developed in water and ocean resources, and we are just beginning to glimpse the wonders in store. More and more, in oceans and rivers, fish are being "farmed" instead of relying on random supply by nature. Whereas only 3 percent of all seafood produced in the United States in 1975 came from fish-farms, this proportion quadrupled to 12 percent by 1984.

In Buhl, Idaho, the Clear Spring Trout Company, a fish-farm, has become the single largest trout producer in the world, expanding its trout production from 10 million pounds per year in 1981 to 14 million pounds this year. Furthermore, Clear Springs is not content to follow nature blindly; as all farmers try to do, it improves on nature by breeding better and more productive trout. Thus, two years ago Clear Springs trout converted two pounds of food into one pound of edible flesh; Clear Springs scientists have developed trout that will convert only 1.3 pounds of food into one pound of flesh. And Clear Springs researchers are in the process of developing that long-desired paradise for consumers: a boneless trout.

At this point, indeed, all rainbow trout sold commercially in the United States are produced in farms, as well as 40 percent of the nation's oysters, and 95 percent of commercial catfish.

Aquaculture, the wave of the future, is already here to stay, not only in fishery but also in such activities as off-shore oil drilling and the mining of manganese nodules on the ocean floor. What aquaculture needs above all is the expansion of private property rights and ownership to all useful parts of the oceans and other water resources.

Fortunately, the Reagan administration rejected the Law of the Sea Treaty, which would have permanently subjected the world's ocean resources to ownership and control by a world-government body under the aegis of the United Nations. With that threat over, it is high time to seize the opportunity to allow the expansion of private property in one of its last frontiers. ▶

25
ENVIRONMENTALISTS CLOBBER TEXAS

We all know how the environmentalists, seemingly determined at all costs to save the spotted owl, delivered a

First published in April 1993.

crippling blow to the logging industry in the Northwest. But this slap at the economy may be trivial compared to what might happen to the lovely city of San Antonio, Texas, endangered by the deadly and despotic combination of the environmentalist movement and the federal judiciary.

The sole source of water for the 900,000-resident city, as well as the large surrounding area, is the giant Edwards Aquifer, an underground river or lake (the question is controversial) that spans five counties. Competing for the water, along with San Antonio and the farms and ranches of the area, are two springs, the Comal and the Aquarena on the San Marcos River, which are becoming tourist attractions. In May 1991, the Sierra Club, along with the Guadalupe-Blanco River Authority which controls the two springs, filed a suit in federal court, invoking the Endangered Species Act. It seems that, in case of a drought, any cessation of water flow to the two springs would endanger four obscure species of vegetables or animals fed by the springs: the Texas blind salamander; Texas wild rice; and two tiny brands of fish: the fountain darter, and the San Marcos gambusia.

On February 1, 1993, federal district judge Lucius Bunton, in Midland, Texas, handed down his ruling in favor of the Sierra Club; in case of drought, no matter the shortage of water hitting San Antonio, there will have to be enough water flowing from the aquifer to the two springs to preserve these four species. Judge Bunton admitted that, in a drought, San Antonio, to obey the ruling, might have to have its water pumped from the aquifer cut by as much as 60 percent. This would clobber both the citizens of San Antonio, and the farmers and ranchers of the area; man would have to suffer, because human beings are always last in line in the environmentalist universe, certainly far below wild rice and the fountain darter.

San Antonio Mayor Nelson Wolff was properly incensed at the judge's ruling. "Think about a world where you are only allowed to take a bath twice a week," exclaimed the mayor. "Think about a world where you have to get a judge's permission to irrigate your crops." John W. Jones, president of the

Texas and Southwestern Cattle Raisers Association, graphically complained that the judge's decision "puts the protection of Texas bugs before Texas babies."

How did the federal courts horn into the act anyway?

Apparently, if the Edwards Aquifer were ruled a "river," then it would come under the jurisdiction of the Texas Water Commission rather than of the federal courts. But last year, a federal judge in Austin ruled that the aquifer is a "lake," bringing it under federal control.

Environmentalists oppose production and use of natural resources. Federal judges seek to expand federal power. And there is another outfit whose interest in the proceedings needs scrutinizing: the governmental Guadalupe-Blanco River Authority. In addition to the tourist income it wishes to sustain, there is another, hidden and more abundant source of revenue that may be animating the Authority.

This point was raised by Cliff Morton, chairman of the San Antonio Water System. Morton said that he believed that the Authority would, during a drought, direct the increased spring flow into a reservoir, and then sell to beleaguered San Antonio at a high price the water the city would have gotten far more cheaply from the aquifer. Is the Authority capable of such Machiavellian maneuvering? Mr. Morton thinks so. "That's what this is all about," he warned bitterly. "It's not about fountain darters."

Wolff, Jones, and other protesters are calling upon Congress to relax the Draconian provisions of the Endangered Species Act, but there seems to be little chance of that in a Clinton-Gore administration.

A longer-run solution, of course, is to privatize the entire system of water and water rights in this country. All resources, indeed all goods and services, are scarce, and they are all subject to competition for their use. That's why there is a system of private property and free market exchange. If all resources are privatized, they will be allocated to the most important uses by means of a free-price system, as the bidders able to satisfy the consumer demands in the most efficient ways are able to out-compete less able bidders for these resources.

Since rivers, aquifers, and water in general, have been largely socialized in this country, the result is a tangled and terribly inefficient web of irrational pricing, massive subsidies, overuse in some areas and underuse in others, and widespread controls and rationing. The entire water system is a mess, and only privatization and free markets can cure it.

In the meanwhile, it would be nice to see the Endangered Species Act modified or even—horrors!—repealed. If the Sierra Club or other environmentalists are anxious to preserve critters of various shapes or sizes, vegetable, animal, or mineral, let them use their own funds and those of their bedazzled donors to buy some land or streams and preserve them.

New York City has recently decided to abolish the good old word "zoo" and substitute the Politically Correct euphemism: Wildlife Preservation Park. Let the Sierra Club and kindred outfits preserve the species in these parks, instead of spending their funds to control the lives of the American people. ▶

26

GOVERNMENT AND HURRICANE HUGO: A DEADLY COMBINATION

Natural disasters, such as hurricanes, tornadoes, and volcanic eruptions, occur from time to time, and many victims of such disasters have an unfortunate tendency to seek out someone to blame. Or rather, to pay for their aid and rehabilitation. These days, Papa Government (a stand-in for the hapless taxpayer) is called on loudly to shell out. The latest incident followed the ravages of Hurricane Hugo, when many South

---

First published in December 1989.

Carolinians turned their wrath from the mischievous hurricane to the federal government and its FEMA (Federal Emergency Management Agency) for not sending far more aid more quickly.

But why must taxpayers A and B be forced to pay for natural disasters that strike C? Why can't C—and his private insurance carriers—foot the bill? What is the ethical principle that insists that South Carolinians, whether insured or non-insured, poor or wealthy, must be subsidized at the expense of those of us, wealthy or poor, who don't live on the southern Atlantic Coast, a notorious hurricane spot in the autumn? Indeed, the witty actor who regularly impersonates President Bush on *Saturday Night Live* was perhaps more correct than he realized when he pontificated: "Hurricane Hugo—not my fault." But in that case, of course, the federal government should get out of the disaster aid business, and FEMA should be abolished forthwith.

If the federal government is not the culprit as portrayed, however, other government forces have actually weighed in on Hugo's side, and have escalated the devastation that Hugo has wreaked. Consider the approach taken by local government. When Hurricane Hugo arrived, government imposed compulsory evacuation upon many of the coastal areas of South Carolina. Then, for nearly a week after Hugo struck the coast, the mayor of one of the hardest-hit towns in South Carolina, the Isle of Palms near Charleston, used force to prevent residents from returning to their homes to assess and try to repair the damage.

How dare the mayor prevent people from returning to their own homes? When she finally relented, six days after Hugo, she continued to impose a 7:00 p.m. curfew in the town. The theory behind this outrage is that the local officials were "fearful for the homeowners' safety and worried that there would be looting." But the oppressed residents of the Isle of Palms had a different reaction. Most of them were angered; typical was Mrs. Pauline Bennett, who lamented that "if we could have gotten here sooner, we could have saved more."

But this was scarcely the only case of a "welfare state" intervening and making matters worse for the victims of Hugo. As a result of the devastation, the city of Charleston was of course short of many commodities. Responding to this sudden scarcity, the market acted quickly to clear supply and demand by raising prices accordingly: providing smooth, voluntary, and effective rationing of the suddenly scarce goods. The Charleston government, however, swiftly leaped in to prevent "gouging"— grotesquely passing emergency legislation making the charging of higher prices post-Hugo than pre-Hugo a crime, punishable by a maximum fine of $200 and 30 days in jail.

Unerringly, the Charleston welfare state converted higher prices into a crippling shortage of scarce goods. Resources were distorted and misallocated, long lines developed as in Eastern Europe, all so that the people of Charleston could have the warm glow of knowing that if they could ever find the goods in short supply, they could pay for them at pre-Hugo bargain rates.

Thus, the local authorities did the work of Hurricane Hugo—intensifying its destruction by preventing people from staying at or returning to their homes, and aggravating the shortages by rushing to impose maximum price controls. But that was not all. Perhaps the worst blow to the coastal residents was the intervention of those professional foes of humanity— the environmentalists.

Last year, reacting to environmentalist complaints about development of beach property and worry about "beach erosion" (do beaches have "rights", too?), South Carolina passed a law severely restricting any new construction on the beachfront, or any replacement of damaged buildings. Enter Hurricane Hugo, which apparently provided a heaven-sent opportunity for the South Carolina Coastal Council to sweep the beachfronts clear of any human beings. Geology professor Michael Katuna, a Coastal Council consultant, saw only poetic justice, smugly declaring that "Homes just shouldn't be right on the beach where Mother Nature wants to bring a storm ashore."

And if Mother Nature wanted us to fly, She would have supplied us with wings?

Other environmentalists went so far as to praise Hurricane Hugo. Professor Orrin H. Pilkey, geologist at Duke who is one of the main theoreticians of the beach-suppression movement, had attacked development on Pawleys Island, northeast of Charleston, and its rebuilding after destruction by Hurricane Hazel in 1954. "The area is an example of a high-risk zone that should never have been developed, and certainly not redeveloped after the storm." Pilkey now calls Hugo "a very timely hurricane," demonstrating that beachfronts must return to Nature.

Gered Lennon, geologist with the Coastal Council, put it succinctly: "However disastrous the hurricane was, it may have had one healthy result. It hopefully will rein in some of the unwise development we have had along the coast."

The Olympian attitude of the environmentalist rulers contrasted sharply with the views of the blown-out residents themselves. Mrs. Bennett expressed the views of the residents of the Isle of Palms. Determined to rebuild on the spot, she pointed out: "We have no choice. This is all we have. We have to stay here. Who is going to buy it?" Certainly not the South Carolina environmental elite. Tom Browne, of Folly Beach, S.C., found his house destroyed by Hurricane Hugo. "I don't know whether I'll be able to rebuild it or if the state would even let me," complained Browne. The law, he pointed out, is taking a property without compensation. "It's got to be unconstitutional."

Precisely. Just before Hugo hit, David Lucas, a property owner on the Isle of Palms, was awarded $1.2 million in a South Carolina court after he sued the state over the law. The court ruled that the state could not deprive him of his right to build on the land he owned without due compensation. And the South Carolina environmentalists are not going to be able to force the state's taxpayers to pay the enormous compensation for not being allowed to rebuild all of the destruction wrought by Hurricane Hugo.

Skip Johnson, an environmental consultant in South Carolina, worries that "it's just going to be a real nightmare. People are going to want to rebuild and get on with their lives." The Coastal Council and its staff, Johnson lamented, "are going to have their hands full." Let's hope so. ▶

27
THE WATER IS *NOT* RUNNING

Most people agree that government is generally less efficient than private enterprise, but it is little realized that the difference goes far beyond efficiency. For one thing, there is a crucial difference in attitude toward the consumer. Private business firms are constantly courting the consumer, always eager to increase the sales of their products. So insistent is that courtship that business advertising is often criticized by liberal aesthetes and intellectuals as strident and unmannerly.

But government, unlike private enterprise, is not in the business of seeking profits or trying to avoid losses. Far from eager to court the consumer, government officials invariably regard consumers as an annoying intrusion and as "wasteful" users of "their" (government's) scarce resources. Governments are invariably at war with their consumers.

This contempt and hostility toward consumers reaches its apogee in socialist states, where government's power is at its maximum. But a similar attitude appears in areas of government activity in all countries. Until a few decades ago, for example, water supplies to consumers in the United States were furnished by private companies. These were almost all socialized over time, so that government has come to monopolize water services.

In New York City, which shifted to a monopoly of government water several decades ago, there was never, in previous

---

First published in September 1985.

decades, any wailing about a "water shortage." But, recently, in a climate that is not conspicuously dry, a water shortage has reappeared every few years. In July 1985 water levels in the reservoirs supplying New York City were down to an unprecedented 55 percent of capacity, in contrast to the normal 94 percent. But surely, nature is not solely to blame, since neighboring New Jersey's water levels are still at a respectable 80 percent. It seems that the New York water bureaucrats must have carefully sought our nearby spots that particularly suffer from chronic drought. It also turns out that the New York pipelines were constructed too narrowly to increase water flow from wetter regions.

More important is New York's typical bureaucratic response to this, as well as to other periodic water crises. Water, as usual with government, is priced in an economically irrational manner. Apartment buildings, for example, pay a fixed water fee per apartment to the government. Since tenants pay nothing for water, they have no incentive to use it economically; and since landlords pay a fixed fee, regardless of use, they too couldn't care less.

Whereas private firms try to price their goods or services to achieve the highest profit—i.e, to supply consumer needs most fully and at least cost—government has no incentive to price for highest profit or to keep down costs. Quite the contrary. Government's incentive is to subsidize favored pressure groups or voting blocs; for government is pressured by its basic situation to price politically rather than economically.

Since government services are almost never priced so as to clear the market, i.e., equate supply and demand, it tends to price far below the market, and therefore bring about an artificial "shortage." Since the shortage is manifest in people not being able to find the product, government's natural despotic bent leads it invariably to treat the shortage by turning to coercive restraints and rationing.

Morally, government can then have its cake and eat it too: have the fun of pushing people around, while wrapping itself in the cloak of solidarity and universal "sacrifice" in the face of the great new emergency. In short, when the supply of water drops, governments almost never respond the way a business firm would: raise the price in order to clear the market. Instead, the price stays low, and restraints are then placed on watering one's lawn, washing one's car, and even taking showers. In this way, everyone is exhorted to sacrifice, except that priorities of sacrifice are worked out and imposed by the government, which happily decides how much lawn watering, or showering, may be permitted on what days in the face of the great crisis.

Several years ago, California water officials were loudly complaining about a water shortage and imposing local rationing, when suddenly an embarrassing event occurred: torrential rains all over the drought areas of the state. After lamely insisting that no one should be misled by the seeming end of the drought, the authorities finally had to end that line of attack, and then the title of the Emergency Office of Water Shortage was hastily changed to the Office of Flood Control.

In New York, this summer, Mayor Edward Koch has already levied strict controls on water use, including a ban on washing cars, and imposition of a minimum of 78 degrees for air conditioners in commercial buildings, plus the turning off of the conditioners for two hours during each working day (virtually all of these air conditioners are water-cooled). This 78-degree rule is, of course, tantamount to no air-conditioning at all, and will wreak great hardship on office workers, as well as patrons of movies and restaurants.

Air-conditioning has always been a favorite target for puritanical government officials; during the trumped-up "energy shortage" of the late 1970s, President Carter's executive order putting a floor of 78 degrees on every commercial air conditioner was enthusiastically enforced, even though the "energy saving" was negligible. As long as misery can be imposed on the consumer, why worry about the rationale? (What is now a time-honored custom in New York of reluctance to serve water to restaurant patrons originated in a long-forgotten water "short-age" of decades ago.)

There is no need for any of these totalitarian controls. If the government wants to conserve water and lessen its use, all it need do is raise the price. It doesn't have to order an end to this or that use, set priorities, or decide who should be allowed to drink more than three glasses a day. All it has to do is clear the market, and let people conserve each in his own way and at his own pace.

In the longer run, what the government should do is privatize the water supply, and let water be supplied, like oil or Pepsi-Cola, by private firms trying to make a profit and to satisfy and court consumers, and not to gain power by making them suffer. ▶

Politics as Economic Violence

28
RETHINKING THE '80S

Since the first presidential election of the new decade coincided with the longest recession since World War II, both parties wrestled with the problem of interpreting the 1980s. For the Democrats the issue was clear: the recession was reaped the wages of sin sowed by the "decade of greed," greed stimulated by Reaganomic deregulation, tax cuts, and massive deficits, culminating in the unconscionable amounts of money made by archvillain Michael Milken.

For Bush Republicans, the President was only unlucky: the current recession is worldwide (the same line unconvincingly offered by Herbert Hoover during *his* term in office), and has no causal relation to the Reagan boom. For the growing number of anti-Bush Republicans, the Reagan boom was wonderful and was only turned around by the Bush tax increases and massive new regulation upon American business.

Unpacking all the fallacies and half-truths in these positions is a daunting task. In the first place, Americans were no more nor less "greedy" in the 1980s than they were before or since. Second, Michael Milken was no villain; his large monetary earnings reflected, as free-market analysis shows, his tremendous

First published in May 1992.

productivity in helping stockholders get out from under the Williams Act of 1967, which crippled takeover bids and thereby fastened the rule of inefficient, old-line corporate managers and financial interests upon the backs of the stockholders.

To stop effective competition from brash newcomers from Texas and California, the Bush administration carried out the bidding of the Rockefeller-allied Old Guard from the Rust Belt to destroy Milken and stop this competitive threat to their control.

Third, Ronald Reagan did *not*, despite the propaganda, "cut taxes"; instead, the 1981 cuts in upper-income taxes were more than offset, for the average American, by rises in the Social Security tax. The "boll weevil" conservative Democrats had insisted on indexing tax rates for inflation, but unfortunately, personal exemption totals were never indexed, and continue to wither away in real terms. Every year after 1981, the Reagan administration agreed to continuing tax *increases*, apparently to punish us all for the non-existent tax cut. The topper was the bipartisan Jacobinical Tax Reform Act of 1986, which lowered upper income rates some more, but again clobbered the middle class by wiping out a large number of tax deductions, in the name of "closing the loopholes."

One of those "loopholes" was the real estate market, which lost most of its tax deductions for mortgages and tax shelters, and which helped put real estate a few years later into perhaps its deepest depression since the 1930s.

Indeed, from 1980, before Reagan's advent, until 1991, federal government revenues increased by 103.1 percent. Whatever that is, that is *not* a "tax cut." It is a massive tax increase. But why then did deficits become far more massive? Because federal expenditures went up even faster, during this period, by 117.1 percent. In short, the problem is that both taxes and expenditures have been increasing at a frenetic pace, with expenditures going up faster: hence the deficit problem.

And while it is certainly true that George Bush greatly aggravated the recession by dramatically increasing taxes, deficits, and regulations on business, the Reagan administration cannot be let off the hook. In fact, the greatest if not the only strength of the Democrat analysis is that they, at least, recognize that the boom of the 1980s *did* lead ineluctably to the deep and long recession of the early 1990s. The weakest point of the anti-Bush Republicans is the view that the 1980s were a wonderful, unalloyed boom that stored up no economic ills for the future.

But those ills were not due to greed, tax cuts, or any of the rest. The problem of the '80s was the monetary and banking system and the blame comes down squarely on the Federal Reserve masters of that system. In fact, as the German economist and former banker Kurt Richebacher has pointed out, the U.S. boom of the 1980s was uncannily similar to the boom of the 1920s. In both decades, inflationary bank credit generated by the Federal Reserve went mainly into real estate and, a bit later in the '80s into the stock market—in short, the boom came in titles to capital and in speculation, while price inflation was much lower in the "real economy," in particular in consumer goods.

Indeed, wholesale and consumer price levels remained flat in the 1920s, misleading pre-monetarist economists such as Irving Fisher into proclaiming that inflation did not exist and that there was nothing to worry about. And while price inflation was not exactly flat during the 1980s, it was low enough for the Establishment to proclaim that the inflation problem (and the business cycle) had been licked forevermore. In the 1980s, price inflation was moderated by various external factors—such as hyperinflating Third World countries using cash dollars as their informal money, and foreigners financing American deficits and permitting the U.S. to buy cheap goods from abroad.

The real estate hysteria during the 1980s fully matched that of the 1920s, and everyone adopted the unquestioned credo that housing prices are destined to rise forever. While real estate has finally gotten its comeuppance, and a more realistic attitude prevails at last, the stock market continues to levitate in a dream world, again confusing observers, and allowing them to ignore the grim reality in the "real world" down below.

The culprit then, is and was, not taxes or greed, but above all inflationary credit expansion generated by the Fed. And now that Greenspan is frantically trying to inflate to save Bush's bacon, we are storing up the seeds of another recession in a few years' time. The bank collapse, the S&L scandal, the real estate debacle, all can be laid at the door of the chairman of the Federal Reserve, who is invariably treated in the media as an all-wise monarch when he should really be sent to the showers and his throne sold for scrap. The arch-villains of the 1980s (and the '90s) are Paul Volcker and Alan Greenspan, but they will never be treated as such so long as they remain two of the most beloved figures in American public life. ▶

29
BUSH AND DUKAKIS:
IDEOLOGICALLY INSEPARABLE

George Wallace's famous adage that "there ain't a dime's worth of difference between the two parties" was never more true than in election year 1988.

This maxim is particularly true if we concentrate, as we should, on the actual and proposed *policies* of the candidates rather than the rhetoric or their media imagery. Both Bush and Dukakis are centrists ("mainstreamers") devoted to the preservation and furtherance of the Establishment status quo. Set aside the cut-and-thrust of negative campaigning, and both men meet on that broad, fuzzy, and cozy ground where "moderate conservative" meets "moderate liberal."

First published in November 1988.

Lew Rockwell has demonstrated in the *Free Market* that Bush's and Dukakis's leading economic advisors are old buddies, and students of one another, who agree on virtually everything. (How different, indeed, can a "moderate conservative Keynesian" be from a "moderate liberal Keynesian"?) Neither candidate will do a single thing to cut government spending; neither one will cut the enormous deficit that both parties and all centrists have now come to accept as a fundamental part of the American way of life.

Both candidates will, if elected, sharply increase our taxes. Both will search for creative semantics in deciding how to label a tax hike. Dukakis has promised a drastic escalation of enforcement as the first step in a tax program, and Bush will not be far behind (What is this but a tax increase?), although Bush, following the lead of the Reagan administration, may be expected to be more innovative in fancy linguistic substitutes. (The last eight years have already brought us: "increasing fees," "revenue enhancement," "plugging the loopholes," and "tax reform" in the name of "fairness.")

Both Bush and Dukakis, as dedicated Keynesians, propose to solve the deficit problem by the fatuous suggestion that the economy will "grow out of it." "Growth," indeed, will be a keyword for both prospective presidents, and "growth," it should never be forgotten, is simply a code term for "inflation."

As Keynesians, both candidates may be expected to expand the money supply mightily, and then strive, by fine-tuning and coercive policies, to try to control the resulting price inflation through manipulations by the Federal Reserve. Indeed, the Greenspan Fed has emulated its predecessors in monetary expansion; this year, the money supply (e.g., governmental counterfeiting) has been increasing at a rapid rate of 7 percent per year. Greenspan's inflationism, coupled with cautious dampening when things threaten to get out of hand, has delighted the Democrats in Congress, who report that they, and a Democratic president, would be delighted to work with a Greenspan Fed. (And, I am sure, *vice versa*.)

Either Bush or Dukakis can be relied upon to continue the expansion of government power and domination over the individual and the private sector. Thus, when "wild spender" Jimmy Carter became president, he found a federal government that was spending 28 percent of the private national product. After four years of Carter's wild spending, federal government spending was about the same: 28.3 percent of private product. Eight years of Ronald Reagan's "anti-government" and "get government off our back" policy has resulted in the federal government spending 29.9 percent of private product. We can certainly expect Bush and Dukakis to do no less.

Neither is "deregulation" an issue when we realize that the major deregulatory reforms of the last ten years (CAB, ICC) were installed by the Carter administration, and when we understand that the Reagan administration has greatly added to the weight of regulation—particularly when we focus on the savage attack that it has conducted on the non-crime of "insider trading."

Neither can we conjure up "protectionist" Democrats versus "free-trade" Republicans; the Reagan administration has been the most protectionist in American history, imposing "voluntary" as well as outright compulsory import quotas, and organizing a giant government-business computer chip cartel to battle the efficient Japanese.

The farm program has become truly monstrous, as government intervention doubles and redoubles upon itself; whatever happens, whatever the climatic conditions—whether the crops are good and therefore there is a "glut" or whether there is a drought—ever more billions of taxpayer money are ladled out to the farmers so that they may produce less for the consumer.

Bush will certainly do no less; and, furthermore, he promises to intensify federal government spending on "education" (i.e., the swollen and inefficient Department of Education that he and Reagan promised to abolish), and on "cleaning up the environment," which means further cost-raising regulations on American business. In short, we are seeing, more than ever before, a bipartisan Keynesian consensus, an economic policy to match bipartisan policies in all other spheres of politics. But the single most dangerous aspect of the economics of the next four years has gone unnoticed.

Since he replaced Donald Regan as Secretary of the Treasury, James R. Baker (a close friend of Bush and slated to be Secretary of State in a Republican administration) has been unfortunately effective in pushing the Keynesian agenda on the international economic front: that is, worldwide fiat money inflation coordinated by the world's central banks, ending in the old Keynesian goal; a world paper currency unit (whether named the "bancor" [Keynes], the "unita" [Harry Dexter White], or the "phoenix" [the *Economist*]) printed by a World Central Bank.

The World Central Bank would then be able to inflate the phoenix, and pump in reserves to all countries, so that the national central banks could pyramid their liabilities on top of the World Bank. In that way, the entire world could experience an inflation controlled and coordinated by the World Central Bank, so that no one country would suffer from its inflationary policies by losing gold (as under a gold standard), losing dollars (as under Bretton Woods), or suffering from a drop in its exchange rate (as under Friedmanite monetarism). There would be no remaining checks on any country's inflation except the wisdom and the will of the World Central Bank.

What this amounts to, of course, is economic world government, which, because of the necessity of coordination, would bring a virtual political world government in its wake. Because of his powerful international financial connections, Baker has been able to move rapidly toward this coordination, to bring European and even Japanese central bankers into line, and to help bring a new European currency unit and central bank, which would be an important prelude to a world paper currency.

Whoever Dukakis would appoint to his Cabinet would not have the powerful financial connections, or the track record of the last four years, and so the only real difference I can see in a

Dukakis victory is that it would significantly slow down, and perhaps totally derail, the menacing drive toward Keynesian economic world government. ▶

30
PEROT, THE CONSTITUTION, AND DIRECT DEMOCRACY

R oss Perot's proposal for direct democracy through "electronic town meetings" is the most fascinating and innovative proposal for fundamental political change in many decades. It has been greeted with shock and horror by the entire intellectual-technocratic-media Establishment. Arrogant pollsters, who have made a handsome living via "scientific" sampling, faulty probability theory, and often loaded questions, bluster that direct mass voting by telephone or television would not *really* be as "representative" as their own little samples.

Of course they would say that; theirs is the first profession to be rendered as obsolete in the Perotvian world of the future as the horse and buggy today. The pollsters will not get away with that argument; for if they were right, the public has enough horse sense to realize that it would then be more "representative" and "democratic" to dispense with voting altogether. And let the pollsters choose.

When we cut through the all-too-predictable shrieks of "demagogy" and "fascism," it would be nice if the opponents would favor us with some arguments against the proposal. What exactly is the argument against electronic direct democracy?

The standard argument against direct democracy goes as follows: direct democracy was fine, and wonderful in colonial town

---

First published in August 1992.

meetings, where every person could familiarize himself with the issues, go to the local town hall, and vote directly on those issues. But alas, and alack!, the country got larger and much too populous for direct voting; for technological reasons, therefore, the voter has had to forego himself going to a meeting and voting on the issues of the day; he necessarily had to entrust his vote to his "representative."

Well, technology rolls on, and direct voting has, for a long while, since the age of telephone and television, much less of the computer and emerging "interactive" television, been technologically feasible. Why, then, before Ross Perot, has no one pointed this out and advocated high-tech, electronic democracy? And why, when Perot has pointed this out, do all the elites react in dread and consternation, as if to the face of Medusa, or as vampires react to the cross?

Could it be that—for all their prattle about "democracy," for all their ritualistic denunciation of voter "apathy" and call for voter participation—that more participation is precisely what the elites *don't* want?

Could it be that what the political class: politicians, bureaucrats, and intellectual and media apologists for the system, really want is more sheep voting merely to ratify the continuance and expansion of the current system, of the Demopublican and Republicrat parties, of phony choices between Tweedledum and Tweedledumber?

For those critics who worry that somehow the American Constitution, that Constitution which has been a hollow shell and mockery for many decades, will suffer; the correct reply is the Perotvian: the vaunted "two-party" system, much less the Democratic and Republican parties, is not even mentioned, much less enshrined, in the Constitution.

The only possible argument against direct democracy, now that the technological argument is obsolete, is that the public's choices would be wrong. But in that case: it would follow directly that the public shouldn't vote *at all*, since if the public is not to be allowed to vote on issues that affect their lives, why should they be allowed to vote for the people who will make those very decisions: for the beloved President, the Congress, etc.? Perhaps this logic is the reason that the hysterical opponents of the electronic town hall confine themselves to smear terms; since to make this argument at all would condemn them to scorn and irrelevance.

In other words: if the logic be unwrapped, it is the opponents of the Perot plan who are much more liable to the charge of "fascism" than are the Perot supporters.

Furthermore, making such an argument ignores the vital point: that the decisions of the parasitic bipartisan political class that has run this country for decades have been so abysmal, and recognized to be so abysmal by the public, that almost any change from this miasma and gridlock would be an improvement. Hence—to cite a poll myself—the recent sentiment of *80 percent* of the American public that radical change in the system is necessary, and hence the willingness to embrace Ross Perot as agent of such a change.

And speaking of the Constitution, Perot has called for a Constitutional amendment that would prohibit Congress from raising taxes unless such a proposal were ratified by electronic direct voting. There are two points to be noted: first, for those of us strongly opposed to tax increases, we would be no worse off, and unquestionably better off, than we are now. And second, note the superiority of this tough proposal to the latest warmed-over Republicrat proposal of a "balanced budget" amendment to the Constitution: a proposal even phonier than Gramm-Rudman, a proposal doomed from the beginning to be nothing but an Establishment attempt to fool the public into thinking that something constructive is being done about the deficit.

For the Establishment amendment would only mandate a budget balanced *in prospect*, not in fact; would allow Congress to set aside the balanced budget as it deems necessary; and would also permit the government to make expenditures "off budget" that would not count in the amendment.

The absurdity of a budget balance in-prospect may be seen in this example: suppose that you are a spendoholic, and that your wife and your creditors set up a watchdog committee to see that you balance your budget, but not in fact, only in advance estimates that you yourself make. Clearly, *anyone* can balance one's budget under those restrictions. And if we bear in mind that government *always* underestimates its future costs and expenses, the absurdity should become evident. With schemes like these, it is no wonder that the public is turning for candor, and for genuine choice, to the billionaire from East Texas. ▶

3 I
THE FLAG FLAP

There are many curious aspects to the latest flag fracas. There is the absurdity of the proposed change in our basic constitutional framework by treating such minor specifics as a flag law. There is the proposal to outlaw "desecration" of the American flag. "Desecration" means "to divest of a sacred character or office." Is the American flag, battle emblem of the U.S. government, supposed to be "sacred"? Are we to make a religion of statolatry? What sort of grotesque religion is that?

And what is "desecrate" supposed to mean? What specific acts are to be outlawed? Burning seems to be the big problem, although the quantity of flag-burning in the United States seems to be somewhere close to zero. In fact, most flag burning occurs when patriotic groups such as the American Legion and the Veterans of Foreign Wars solemnly burn their worn-out American flags in the prescribed manner.

But if burning the flag is to be banned, are we to clap numerous American Legion or VFW people in the hoosegow? Oh,

---

Previously unpublished.

you say that intent is the crucial point, and that you want to outlaw hippie types who burn U.S. flags with a sneer and a curse. But how are the police supposed to figure out intent, and make sure that the majesty of the law falls only upon hippie-sneerers, and spares reverent, saluting Legionnaires?

But if the supporters of the proposed flag amendment are mired in absurdity, the arguments of the opponents are in almost as bad a shape. Civil libertarians have long placed their greatest stress on a sharp difference between "speech" and "action," and the claim that the First Amendment covers only speech and not actions (except, of course, for the definite action of printing and distribution of a pamphlet or book, which would come under the free press clause of the First Amendment).

But, as the flag amendment advocates point out, what kind of "speech" is burning a flag? Isn't that most emphatically an action—and one that cannot come under the free press rubric? The fallback position of the civil libertarians, as per the majority decisions in the flag cases by Mr. Justice Brennan, is that flag burning is "symbolic" speech, and therefore, although an action, comes under the free speech protection.

But "symbolic speech" is just about as inane as the "desecration" doctrine of the flag-law advocates. The speech/action distinction now disappears altogether, and every action can be excused and protected on the ground that it constitutes "symbolic speech."

Suppose, for example, that I were a white racist, and decided to get me a gun and shoot a few blacks. But then I could say, that's OK because that's only "symbolic speech," and political symbolic speech at that, because I'm trying to make a political argument against our current pro-black legislation.

Anyone who considers such an argument far-fetched should ponder a recent decision by a dotty leftist New York judge to the effect that it is "unconstitutional" for the New York subway authorities to toss beggars out of the subway stations. The jurist's argument held that begging is "symbolic speech," and expressive argument for more help to the poor. Fortunately, this argument was overturned on appeal, but still "symbolic arguers" are everywhere in New York, clogging streets, airports, and bus terminals.

There is no way, then, that flag laws can be declared unconstitutional as violations of the First Amendment. The problem with flag laws has nothing to do with free speech, and civil libertarians have gotten caught in their own trap because they do in fact try to separate speech and action, a separation that is artificial and cannot long be maintained.

As in the case of all dilemmas caused by the free speech doctrine, the entire problem can be resolved by focusing, not on a high-sounding but untenable right to freedom of speech, but on the natural and integral right to private property and its freedom of use. As even famed First Amendment absolutist Justice Hugo Black pointed out, no one has the free-speech right to burst into your home and harangue you about politics.

"The right to freedom of speech" really means the right to hire a hall and expound your views; the "right to freedom of press" (where, as we have seen, speech and action clearly cannot be separated) means the right to print a pamphlet and sell it. In short, free speech or free press rights are a subset, albeit an important one, of the rights of private property: the right to hire, to own, to sell.

Keeping our eye on property rights, the entire flag question is resolved easily and instantly. Everyone has the right to buy or weave and therefore own a piece of cloth in the shape and design of an American flag (or in any other design) and to do with it what he will: fly it, burn it, defile it, bury it, put it in the closet, wear it, etc. Flag laws are unjustifiable laws in violation of the rights of private property. (Constitutionally, there are many clauses in the Constitution from which private property rights can be derived.)

On the other hand, no one has the right to come up and burn your flag, or someone else's. That should be illegal, not because a flag is being burned, but because the arsonist is burning your property without your permission. He is violating your property rights.

Note the way in which the focus on property rights solves all recondite issues. Perhaps conservatives, who proclaim themselves defenders of property rights, will be moved to reconsider their support of its invasion. On the other hand, perhaps liberals, scorners of property rights, might be moved to consider that cleaving to them may be the only way, in the long run, to insure freedom of speech and press. ▶

32
CLINTONOMICS: THE PROSPECT

Not the least irritating aspect of the ascension of Bill Clinton to the presidency is that his name ends in "n." As a result, "omics" fits neatly to the end of his name, and we are bound to be stuck with the appellation "Clintonomics" from now until the end of his term. In contrast, "Bushonomics" or "Perotnomics" wouldn't quite make it.

The late nihilist economist Ludwig M. Lachmann liked to keep repeating that "the future is unknowable" as the key to his world-outlook. Not true. For we know with certainty that President Clinton will not, in his first set of proposals to Congress, introduce legislation to repeal the income tax or abolish the Federal Reserve. Other aspects of the Clinton presidency we do not know with quite the same degree of certainty; but we can offer credible insights into the outlines of Clintonian Democracy, based on his proposals, his advisers, and the concerns and interests they carry into office.

We know for example that a new set of hungry young Democratic sharks has descended upon Washington, scrambling and knifing each other for position, perks and influence, displacing

---

First published in January 1993.

the set of once-hungry, once-young Republican sharks that have been fattening upon the taxpayers since 1980. Those who can count themselves FOB (Friends of Bill) or, better yet, EFOB (Early Friends of Bill) can be expected to do well. Those who were friends, classmates, and fellow Rhodes Scholars at Oxford, such as left-liberal Harvard economist Robert Reich, will do very well. On the other hand, those of us who were EOB (Enemies of Bill) will not be living high off the hog in Washington.

In general, we must batten down the hatches for another one of those periodic Great Leaps Forward into statism that have afflicted us since the New Deal (actually, since the Progressive Era). The cycle works as follows: Democrats engineer a leap forward of activist government, accompanied by "progressive," "moving America forward again" rhetoric. Then, after a decade or so, the Republicans come in armed with conservative, free-market rhetoric, but in reality only slow down the rate of statist advance. After another decade or so, people become tired of the rhetoric (though not the reality) of the free market, and the time has come for another Leap Forward. The names of the players change, but the reality and the phoniness of the game remains the same, and no one seems to wake up to the shell game that is going on.

The Reagan and Bush administrations, like the Eisenhower, Nixon, and Ford administrations before them, were run by right-wing Keynesians, which is why the same people seem to pop up in all of them (Burns, Volcker, Greenspan). Right-wing Keynesians advocate high deficits, high taxes, and manipulation of the budget and of monetary policy to try to achieve full employment without inflation. The result has been permanent inflation plus periodically steep recessions.

Left-wing Keynesians, the hallmark of Democrat administrations, hold a similar macro view, except that they favor bigger inflations and higher taxes than their more conservative counterparts. The major difference comes in "micro-economic policy," where conservative Keynesians tend to favor the free market, at least in rhetoric, whereas left-Keynesians are more frankly in favor of "industrial policy," "economic strategy," and an activist "partnership of government and business."

The Clinton administration will bring the younger "activist" left-Keynesians to the fore, including the aforesaid Reich, Robert Shapiro of Washington's Progressive Policy Institute, and what might be called the "Wall Street Left," including the venerable Felix Rohatyn of Lazard Freres, Robert Rubin of Goldman, Sachs, and Roger Altman of the Blackstone Group.

We can therefore expect a raft of government measures that will further cripple and distort the market economy. From left-wing groups will come "social" affirmative action-type and environmental regulations that will impose further costs and wreck productivity, particularly of smaller business. Reich and the Wall Street Left will micro-manage the economy into further ailments and disease, while, in the macro-sphere, we can expect higher taxes on the rich in order to "reduce the deficit" while, at the same time, higher government spending will raise the deficit further.

We will receive endless assurances that the increased deficits will "only be temporary," to be eventually offset by increased production and a growing economy. There will be endless malarkey about monetary and fiscal stimulus by Clinton helping us to "grow out of our deficit." (Wanna bet?) There will be further attempts to redefine our deficit out of existence, calling government spending "investment," and insisting that we allocate most government expenses into a "capital budget" that will increase growth and productivity in the long run. All of this craftily overlooks the fact that while business investment must make a future profit, government "investment" need only receive hosannas from its paid and unpaid apologists in order to be pronounced "successful."

There will also be a further malodorous attempt to excuse increased bureaucratic jobs and salaries, as well as more billions poured into "education," on the grounds of productive investment in "human capital" (the unfortunate concept of Nobel Laureate Gary Becker). Once again, the strictures against calling government spending "investment" apply, plus the fact that outside of the economy of slavery, it is impossible to sell your "human capital," so that it cannot be used as an economic concept with a monetary value.

Finally, we will probably see another leap forward into fully socialized medicine; already a host of people, including someone who was the head of "Republicans for Clinton," are insisting that "universal medical care is a right, not a privilege." These are ominous words indeed, because the last place that insisted on the "right" of free universal medical care was the Soviet Union, which wound up with medical care establishments without medicine and without care.

The United States, heedless of the lesson of the collapse of Communism, is falling headlong into its own pit of socialism, except we won't be calling it "socialism," but rather a "caring, compassionate society enjoying the partnership of government and business." ▶

33
CLINTONOMICS REVEALED

After a campaign that stressed "the economy, stupid," a middle-class tax cut, and assurances by neoconservative pundits that Bill Clinton was a "moderate" and a "New Democrat," Clintonomics is at last being unveiled in the budget message of February 17 and in other intimations, such as "health care," of actions to come. And the news is that Bill and Hillary Clinton are only "moderates" in the sense that Brezhnev was more "moderate" than Stalin, or Göring than Himmler. Hold on to your seats, Mr. and Mrs. America: we're in for a very bumpy ride.

Each recent administration has had a far worse "nomics" than its predecessor. Reaganomics was no bargain; it was a

First published in May 1993.

melange of four clashing schools of economic thought, each professing outward loyalty to the Reagan result while trying hard to best their competitors. The four groups were the classical liberal or semi-Austrian wing, the smallest and least influential group that lasted less than a year of the first Reagan term; the Friedmanite monetarists; the supply-siders; and the conservative Keynesians. Bushonomics was solely dominated by the worst group of the four: the conservative Keynesians.

(Briefly: the classical liberals wanted drastic expenditure *and* tax cuts; the supply-siders wanted only tax cuts; the monetarists confined their desires to a steady rate of money growth; and the conservative Keynesians, as is their wont, pursued both expenditure and tax increases.)

But even conservative Keynesianism, though profoundly wrong, is at least a coherent and respectable school of economic thought, a foe worthy of intellectual combat. Such an accolade cannot be accorded to Clintonomics, which does not deserve the quasi-honorable label of "economics" at all. For Clintonomics is, Alice-in-Wonderland economics, schizoid economics, loony-tunes economics.

Why schizoid? Consider: Much propaganda is made about the horrors of the deficit, of the necessity of "sacrificing" for the future, for our children, in order to help close the deficit. That is the excuse for the vanishing of the middle-class tax cut, to be replaced by a whopping tax increase on the middle class. And yet, at the very same time, there is supposed to be a massive spending *increase*. Why? For two reasons: to "jump start the economy," which is barely out of a recession, if not still mired in one; and second, to provide "investment" for an economy that has been stagnating for 20 years, and needs more saving and investment.

The proposal is schizoid because it implicitly assumes that the economy, or the political economy, is separated into two hermetically sealed compartments, with neither influencing the other. On the one hand, tax increases help with the deficit, but have *no* unfortunate effects on the fragile, recession-bound economy; while on the other, the stimulating spending increases apparently have no effect in worsening the deficit!

Once we realize, however, that the economy is interconnected, and that one part influences the other, then the absurdity of Clintonomics becomes evident. For the huge increase in taxes will deliver a kick in the head to the economy: first, by crippling saving and investment by levying higher taxes on corporations and on upper income groups; and second, by imposing higher costs on business through the energy tax and other assorted "fees" that are really taxes in another guise. The higher costs on business will raise prices to consumers far beyond the moderate increases forecast in consumer utility bills. For higher energy costs will enter into every good produced by energy, and will particularly hit hard at manufacturing, such as the aluminum and chemical industries, and at transportation such as airlines. These are some of the very industries hit hardest by the recession.

Note that the effect of increasing energy taxes is not only to raise consumer prices. For cost increases, despite popular myth, are not simply "passed on" easily to consumers in the form of higher prices. They will make American firms less competitive abroad, and they will lead to lower profits, reduced production, and increased unemployment, as well as higher prices.

Furthermore, the huge increases in government spending proposed by Clinton will, of course, make the deficit worse. Apart from this, no tax increase in modern times has ever helped close the deficit. The Reagan tax increases of 1982 and after, and the infamous Bush tax increase of 1990, did not lower the deficit. The only practical way to lower the deficit is to cut government spending.

Neither will the government spending "stimulus" aid the economy, nor the government "investment" alleviate the long-term stagnation caused by puny saving and investment. The American economy has a twofold problem: short-run, where we are either still in a recession or in a very fragile and timid recovery; and long-run, where we are suffering stagnation caused by low saving and investment. The cure for the latter is more saving and investment; but, contrary to Keynesian nostrums, the cure for the former is precisely the same.

The recession of 1990 was the inevitable result of the bank credit expansion (not the "Greed") of the 1980s, and the adjustment process of that recession can only be speeded up by two kinds of government policy: (a) *not* interfering in the healthy process of liquidating unsound investments by bailouts or by Keynesian "stimuli"; and (b) drastically cutting the government's own budget as well as its taxation.

The supply-siders are right that tax cuts rather than tax increases are best both for getting out of recessions and for long-run growth; but they overlook the important point that government *spending* also cripples the economy, both in the short and long-run, for government spending is wasteful and parasitic upon productive private enterprise. The greater the burden on the private economy, the lower the genuine saving and investment for recovery and long-term growth.

The Clinton regime tries to get around this problem by semantic trickery: by renaming government spending as "investment," just as it dares to relabel taxation as "contributions." But regardless of such deception, government spending is wasteful spending for the benefit of the unproductive "consumers" in politics and the bureaucracy.

But what of the deficit? The Clintonians claim that the deficit is the biggest problem because government borrowing channels private savings out of productive investments. And yet the same Clintonians wish to lower interest payments by shifting from long-term to short-term debt, which will crowd out private investment far more frequently from the capital markets. In fact, the unproductive crowding out of saving comes not just from deficits but from all government spending; after all, taxes crowd out and even destroy private savings far more ruthlessly than mere borrowing. The problem is government taxation-and-spending.

Thus, Clintonomics is really Orwellian economics. It is self-contradictory Orwellian "doublethink"; to the classic Orwellian "Freedom is Slavery" and "War is Peace," Clintonomics adds "government spending is investment" and "taxes are contributions." No school of economic thought, not even the Keynesian, advocates a big tax increase while the economy has not yet recovered from a recession; and yet Clintonomics does.

But though Clintonomics be madness, "yet there is method in it." For shining through all the lies and contradictions and evasions, there is one red thread: government power increases at the expenses of the private marketplace. In short, Clintonomics is, in essence, a Great Leap Forward, American style, not toward Maoist communism but toward Democratic Socialism, toward Marxism without the Leninism.

So far, the American public, snowed by the propaganda of Clinton's Permanent Campaign, seems to be willing to accept the "sacrifices" involved, cozy in the assurance that the rich guy down the block will be forced to sacrifice even more. In the long run, however, Americans will find soaking-the-rich to be cool comfort, indeed. ◗

34
PRICE CONTROLS ARE BACK!

B ad and discredited ideas, it seems, never die. Neither do they fade away. Instead, they keep turning up, like bad pennies or Godzilla in the old Japanese movies.

Price controls, that is, the fixing of prices below the market level, have been tried since ancient Rome; in the French Revolution, in its notorious "Law of the Maximum" that was responsible for most of the victims of the guillotine; in the Soviet Union, ruthlessly trying to suppress black markets. In every age,

---

First published in June 1993.

in every culture, price controls have never worked. They have always been a disaster.

Why did Chiang-kai-Shek "lose" China? The main reason is never mentioned. Because he engaged in runaway inflation, and then tried to suppress the results through price controls. To enforce them, he wound up shooting merchants in the public squares of Shanghai to make an example of them. He thereby lost his last shreds of support to the insurgent Communist forces. A similar fate awaited the South Vietnamese regime, which began shooting merchants in the public squares of Saigon to enforce its price decrees.

Price controls didn't work in World War I, when they began as "selective"; they didn't work in World War II, when they were comprehensive and the Office of Price Administration tried to enforce them with hundreds of thousands of enforcers. They didn't work when President Nixon imposed a wage-price freeze and variants of such a freeze from the summer of 1971 until the spring of 1973 or when President Carter tried to enforce a more selective version.

The first thing I ever wrote was an unpublished memo for the New York Republican Club denouncing President Truman's price controls on meat. I was a young graduate student in economics at Columbia University, fresh from my M.A., and I wrote the piece for the Republican campaign of 1946. Price controls, I, and countless economists before and since, pointed out, never work; they don't check inflation, they only create shortages, rationing, declines in quality, black markets, and terrible economic distortions. Furthermore, they get worse as time goes on, as the economy adjusts out from under these pernicious controls.

In 1946, all federal price controls had been lifted except on meat, and as a result, meat was in increasingly short supply. It got so bad that no meat could be found, and diabetics could not even find insulin, a meat-derived product. Radio disk jockeys implored their listeners to write to their Congressmen urging them to keep price controls on meat, for if not the price would triple, quadruple, who knows, rise to infinity. (Ignored was the question: what's so great for the consumers about cheap meat that no one can find?)

Finally, in summer, President Truman went on the air in a nationwide radio address. Summing up the dire meat crisis, he said, in effect, that he had seriously considered nationalizing the Chicago meatpackers in order to commandeer hoarded meat. But then he realized that the meat-packers had no meat either. Then, in a remarkable revelation that few commented on, he disclosed that he had given serious consideration to mobilizing the National Guard and the Army, and sending troops into Midwestern farms to seize all their chickens and livestock. But then, he reluctantly added, he had decided that such a course was "impractical."

Impractical? A nice euphemism. Sending troops into the farms, Truman would have had a revolution on his hands. Every farmer would have been out there with a gun, defending his precious land and property from a despotic invader. Besides, it was a Congressional election year, and the Democrats were already in deep trouble in the farm states. As it was, the Old Right Republicans swept both houses of Congress that year in a landslide, and on the slogan: "controls, corruption, and Communism." It was the last principled stand of right-wing Republicanism, and, not coincidentally, its last political victory.

Truman reluctantly concluded that there seemed to be only one course left to him: to abolish the price controls on meat, which he proceeded to do. In a couple of days there was plenty of meat for consumers and the diabetic alike. The meat crisis was over. Prices? They did not, of course, go up to infinity. They rose by something like 20 percent from the unrealistic control level.

The most remarkable part of this affair went unremarked: that President Truman, apparently without knowing it, had conceded the crucial point: that the "shortage" was, pure and simple, an artificial creation of his own price controls. How else interpret the fact that even he admitted that the last, unfortunate resort to end the crisis was to abolish the controls? And yet, no one drew this lesson and so no one initiated impeachment proceedings.

Twenty-five years later, President Nixon imposed a price-wage freeze because inflation had reached what was then an "unacceptable" level of 4.5 percent a year. I went ballistic, denouncing the controls everywhere I could. That winter, I debated Presidential economic adviser Herbert Stein before the Metropolitan Republican Club of Washington, D.C. After I denounced price controls, Stein remarked that, in essence, the price controls were *my* fault, not his and President Nixon's.

Stein knew as well as I did that price controls were disastrous and counterproductive, but I and others like me had not done a good enough job of educating the American public, and so the Nixon administration had been "forced" by public pressure to impose the controls anyway. Needless to say, I was not convinced about my guilt. Years later, in his memoirs, Stein wrote of the heady rush of power he felt at Camp David when planning to impose price controls on everyone. Poor Stein: another "victim" amidst the victimology of American culture!

And now, Bill Clinton is in the White House, and price controls are back in a big way. The FCC has ordered a 15 percent rollback on two-thirds of the TV cable rates in this country, thereby re-regulating communications with a bang. The reasoning? Since being deregulated in 1987, cable rates have risen twice as fast as general inflation. Well: averages usually have roughly half of the data rising higher and roughly half lower; that's the nature of an average. Are we proposing to combat inflation by going after every price that rises higher than the average?

That, indeed, is the major reasoning behind the looming Clintonian program for price controls on health care. Health care prices have risen faster than inflation. The threat of controls over health care has brought forth a chorus of protests from economists, and from former price controllers, who learned about price controls the hard way. Thus, C. Jackson

Grayson, who headed Nixon's price-wage control experiment from 1971 to 1973, warns: "price" controls will make things worse. Believe me, I've been there . . . . Controls have not worked in 40 centuries. They will not work now."

Grayson warns that already 24 percent of U.S. health care is spent on administrative costs, largely imposed by government. Clintonian price control will cause regulations and bureaucrats to proliferate; it will *raise* medical costs, not lower them. Barry Bosworth, who headed price control efforts under Jimmy Carter, reacted similarly: "I can't believe they [the Clinton administration] are going to do it. I can't believe they are that stupid." He pointed out that health care, a field where there is rapid innovation in goods and services, is a particularly disastrous area to try to impose price controls.

But none of these objections is going to work. The brash young Clintonians don't mind if price controls cause shortages of health care. In fact, they welcome the prospect, because then they can impose *rationing*; they can impose priorities, and tell everyone how much of what kind of medical care they can have. And besides, as Herb Stein found out, there's that deeply satisfying rush of power. We should know by now that reasoned arguments by economists or disillusioned ex-controllers are not going to stop them: only determined and militant opposition and resistance by the long-suffering public. ▶

35
THE HEALTH PLAN'S DEVILISH PRINCIPLES

The standard media cliche about the Clinton health plan is that God, or the Devil, depending on your point of view, "is in the details." There is surprising agreement among both the supporters and all too many of the critics of the Clinton

First published in December 1993.

health "reform." The supporters say that the general principles of the plan are wonderful, but that there are a few problems in the details: e.g., how much will it cost, how exactly will it be financed, will small business get a sufficient subsidy to offset its higher costs, and on into the night.

The alleged critics of the Clinton Plan also hasten to assure us that they too accept the general principles, but that there are *lots* of problems in the details. Often the critics will present their own alternative plans, only slightly less complex than the Clinton scheme, accompanied by assertions that their plans are less coercive, less costly, and less socialistic than the Clinton effort. And since health care constitutes about one-seventh of the American output, there are enough details and variants to keep a host of policy wonks going for the rest of the their lives.

But the details of the Clintonian Plan, however diabolic, are merely petty demons compared to the general principles, where Lucifer really lurks. By accepting the principles, and fighting over the details, the Loyal Opposition only succeeds in giving away the store, and doing so before the debate over the details can even get under way. Lost in an eye-glazing thicket of minutiae, the conservative critics of Clintonian reform, by being "responsible" and working within the paradigm set by The Enemy, are performing a vital service for the Clintonians in snuffing out any clear-cut opposition to Clinton's Great Leap Forward into health collectivism.

Let us examine some of the Mephistophelean general principles in the Clintonian reform, seconded by the conservative critics.

1. GUARANTEED UNIVERSAL ACCESS. There has been a lot of talk recently about "universal access" to this or that good or service. Many "libertarian" or "free-market" proponents of education "reform," for example, advocate tax-supported voucher schemes to provide "access" to private schooling. But there is one simple entity, in any sort of free society, that provides "universal access" to every conceivable good or service, and not just to health or education or food. That entity

is not a voucher or a Clintonian ID card; it's called a "dollar." Dollars not only provide universal access to all goods and services, they provide it to each dollar-holder for each product only to the extent that the dollar-holder desires. Every other artificial accessor, be it voucher or health card or food stamp, is despotic and coercive, mulcts the taxpayer, is inefficient and egalitarian.

2. COERCIVE. "Guaranteed universal access" can only be provided by the robbery of taxation, and the essence of this extortion is not changed by calling these taxes "fees . . . premiums," or "contributions." A tax by any other named smells as rotten, and has similar consequences, even if only "employers" are forced to pay the higher "premiums."

Furthermore, for anyone to be "guaranteed" access to anything, he has to be forced to participate, both in receiving its "benefits" and in paying for them. Hence, "guaranteed universal access" means coercing not only taxpayers, but everyone as participants and contributors. All the weeping and wailing about the 37 million "uninsured" glosses over the fact that most of these uninsured have a made a rational decision that they don't *want* to be "insured," that they are willing to take the chance of paying market prices should health care become necessary. But they will not be permitted to remain free of the "benefits" of insurance; their participation will become compulsory. We will all become health draftees.

3. EGALITARIAN. Universal means egalitarian. For the dread egalitarian theme of "fairness" enters immediately into the equation. Once government becomes the boss of all health, under the Clinton Plan or the Loyal Opposition, then it seems "unfair" for a rich man to enjoy better medical care than the lowest bum. This "fairness" ploy is considered self evident and never subject to criticism. Why is "the two-tier" health system (actually it has been *multi*-tier) any more "unfair" than the multi-tier system for clothing or food or transportation? So far at least, most people don't consider it unfair that some people can afford to dine at The Four Seasons and vacation at Martha's

Vineyard, whereas others have to rest content with McDonald's and staying home. Why is medical care any different?

And yet, one of the major thrusts of the Clinton Plan is to reduce us all to "one-tier," egalitarian health care status.

4. COLLECTIVIST. To insure equality for one and all, medical care will be collectivist, under close supervision of the federal Health Care Board, with health provision and insurance dragooned by government into regional collectives and alliances. The private practice of medicine will be essentially driven out, so that these collectives and HMOs will be the only option for the consumer. Even though the Clintonians try to assure Americans that they can still "choose their own doctor," in practice this will be increasingly impossible.

5. PRICE CONTROLS. Since it is fairly well known that price controls have never worked, that they have always been a disaster, the Clinton administration always keen on semantic trickery, have stoutly denied that any price controls are contemplated. But the network of severe price controls will be all too evident and painful, even if they wear the mask of "premium caps . . . cost caps," or "spending control." They will have to be there, for it is the promise of "cost control" that permits the Clintonians to make the outrageous claim that taxes will hardly go up at all. (Except, of course, on employers.) Tight spending control will be enforced by the government, not merely on its own, but particularly on private spending.

One of the most chilling aspects of the Clinton Plan is that any attempt by us consumers to get around these price controls, e.g., to pay higher than controlled prices to doctors in private practice, will be criminalized. Thus, the Clinton Plan states that "A provider may not charge or collect from the patient a fee in excess of the fee schedule adopted by an alliance," and criminal penalties will be imposed for "payment of bribes or gratuities" (i.e., "black market prices") to "influence the delivery of health service."

In arguing for their plan, by the way, the Clintonians have added insult to injury by employing absurd nonsense in the form of argument. Their main argument for the plan is that health care is "too costly," and that thesis rests on the fact that health care spending, over recent years, has risen considerably as a percentage of the GDP But a spending rise is scarcely the same as a cost increase; if it were, then I could easily argue that, since the percentage of GDP spent on computers has risen wildly in the past ten years, that "computer costs" are therefore excessive, and severe price controls, caps, and spending controls must be imposed promptly on consumer and business purchases of computers.

6. MEDICAL RATIONING. Severe price and spending controls means, of course, that medical care will have to be strictly rationed, especially since these controls and caps come at the same time that universal and equal care is being "guaranteed." Socialists, indeed, always love rationing, since it gives the bureaucrats power over the people and makes for coercive egalitarianism.

And so this means that the government, and its medical bureaucrats and underlings, will decide who gets what service. Medical totalitarians, if not the rest of us, will be alive and well in America.

7. THE ANNOYING CONSUMER. We have to remember a crucial point about government as against business operations on the market. Businesses are always eager for consumers to buy their product or service. On the free market, the consumer is king or queen and the "providers" are always trying to make profits and gain customers by serving them well. But when government operates a service, the consumer is transmuted into a pain-in-the-neck, a "wasteful" user-up of scarce social resources. Whereas the free market is a peaceful cooperative place where everyone benefits and no one loses; when government supplies the product or service, every consumer is treated as using a resource only at the expense of his fellow-men. The "public service" arena, and not the free market, is the dog-eat-dog jungle.

So there we have the Clintonian health future: government as totalitarian rationer of health care, grudgingly doling out care on the lowest possible level equally to all, and treating each "client" as a wasteful pest. And if, God forbid, you have a serious health problem, or are elderly, or your treatment requires more scarce resources than the Health Care Board deems proper, well then Big Brother or Big Sister Rationer in Washington will decide, in the best interests of "society," of course, to give you the Kevorkian treatment.

8. THE GREAT LEAP FORWARD. There are many other ludicrous though almost universally accepted aspects of the Clinton Plan, from the gross perversion of the concept of "insurance" to the imbecilic view that an enormous expansion of government control will somehow eliminate the need for filling out health forms. But suffice it to stress the most vital point: the plan consists of one more Great Leap Forward into collectivism.

The point was put very well, albeit admiringly, by David Lauter in the *Los Angeles Times* (September 23, 1993). Every once in a while, said Lauter, "the government collectively braces itself, takes a deep breath and leaps into a largely unknown future." The first American leap was the New Deal in the 1930s, leaping into Social Security and extensive federal regulation of the economy. The second leap was the civil rights revolution of the 1960s. And now, writes Lauter, "another new President has proposed a sweeping plan" and we have been hearing again "the noises of a political system warming up once again for the big jump."

The only important point Mr. Lauter omits is leaping into *what?* Wittingly or unwittingly, his "leap" metaphor rings true, for it recalls the Great Leap Forward of Mao's worst surge into extreme Communism.

The Clinton Health Plan is not "reform" and it doesn't meet a "crisis." Cut through the fake semantics, and what we have is another Great Leap Forward into socialism. While Russia and the former Communist states are struggling to get out of socialism and the disaster of their "guaranteed universal health care" (check their vital statistics), Clinton and his bizarre Brain Trust of aging leftist grad students are proposing to wreck our economy, our freedom, and what has been, for all of the ills imposed by *previous* government intervention, the best medical system on earth.

That is why the Clinton Health Plan must be fought against root and branch, why Satan is in the general principles, and why the Ludwig von Mises Institute, instead of offering its own 500-page health plan, sticks to its principled "four-step" plan laid out by Hans-Hermann Hoppe (*Free Market*, April 1993) of dismantling existing government intervention into health.

Can we suggest nothing more "positive?" Sure: how about installing Doc Kevorkian as the Clinton family physician? ▶

36
OUTLAWING JOBS:
THE MINIMUM WAGE, ONCE MORE

There is no clearer demonstration of the essential identity of the two political parties than their position on the minimum wage. The Democrats proposed to raise the legal minimum wage from $3.35 an hour, to which it had been raised by the Reagan administration during its allegedly free-market salad days in 1981. The Republican counter was to allow a "subminimum" wage for teenagers, who, as marginal workers, are the ones who are indeed hardest hit by any legal minimum.

This stand was quickly modified by the Republicans in Congress, who proceeded to argue for a teenage subminimum that would last only a piddling 90 days, after which the rate would rise to the higher Democratic minimum (of $4.55 an hour). It was left, ironically enough, for Senator Edward Kennedy to point out the ludicrous economic effect of this proposal: to induce employers to hire teenagers and then fire them after 89 days, to rehire others the day after.

First published in December 1988.

Finally, and characteristically, George Bush got the Republicans out of this hole by throwing in the towel altogether, and plumping for a Democratic plan, period. We were left with the Democrats forthrightly proposing a big increase in the minimum wage, and the Republicans, after a series of illogical waffles, finally going along with the program.

In truth, there is only one way to regard a minimum wage law: it is *compulsory unemployment*, period. The law says: it is illegal, and therefore criminal, for anyone to hire anyone else below the level of X dollars an hour. This means, plainly and simply, that a large number of free and voluntary wage contracts are now outlawed and hence that there will be a large amount of unemployment. Remember that the minimum wage law provides no jobs; it only outlaws them; and outlawed jobs are the inevitable result.

All demand curves are falling, and the demand for hiring labor is no exception. Hence, laws that prohibit employment at any wage that is relevant to the market (a minimum wage of 10 cents an hour would have little or no impact) must result in outlawing employment and hence causing unemployment.

If the minimum wage is, in short, raised from $3.35 to $4.55 an hour, the consequence is to disemploy, permanently, those who would have been hired at rates in between these two rates. Since the demand curve for any sort of labor (as for any factor of production) is set by the perceived marginal productivity of that labor, this means that the people who will be disemployed and devastated by this prohibition will be precisely the "marginal" (lowest wage) workers, e.g., blacks and teenagers, the very workers whom the advocates of the minimum wage are claiming to foster and protect.

The advocates of the minimum wage and its periodic boosting reply that all this is scare talk and that minimum wage rates do not and never have caused any unemployment. The proper riposte is to raise them one better; all right, if the minimum wage is such a wonderful anti-poverty measure, and can have no unemployment-raising effects, why are you such pikers? Why you are helping the working poor by such piddling amounts? Why stop at $4.55 an hour? Why not $10 an hour? $1.007 $10,007?

It is obvious that the minimum wage advocates do not pursue their own logic, because if they push it to such heights, virtually the entire labor force will be disemployed. In short, *you can have as much unemployment as you want*, simply by pushing the legally minimum wage high enough.

It is conventional among economists to be polite, to assume that economic fallacy is solely the result of intellectual error. But there are times when decorousness is seriously misleading, or, as Oscar Wilde once wrote, "when speaking one's mind becomes more than a duty; it becomes a positive pleasure." For if proponents of the higher minimum wage were simply wrongheaded people of good will, they would not stop at $3 or $4 an hour, but indeed would pursue their dimwit logic into the stratosphere.

The fact is that they have always been shrewd enough to stop their minimum wage demands at the point where only marginal workers are affected, and where there is no danger of disemploying, for example, white adult male workers with union seniority. When we see that the most ardent advocates of the minimum wage law have been the AFL-CIO, and that the concrete effect of the minimum wage laws has been to cripple the low-wage competition of the marginal workers as against higher-wage workers with union seniority, the true motivation of the agitation for the minimum wage becomes apparent.

This is only one of a large number of cases where a seemingly purblind persistence in economic fallacy only serves as a mask for special privilege at the expense of those who are supposedly to be "helped."

In the current agitation, inflation—supposedly brought to a halt by the Reagan administration—has eroded the impact of the last minimum wage hike in 1981, reducing the real impact of the minimum wage by 23 percent. Partially as a result, the unemployment rate has fallen from 11 percent in 1982 to under

6 percent in 1988. Possibly chagrined by this drop, the AFL-CIO and its allies are pushing to rectify this condition, and to boost the minimum wage rate by 34 percent.

Once in a while, AFL-CIO economists and other knowledgeable liberals will drop their mask of economic fallacy and candidly admit that their actions will cause unemployment; they then proceed to justify themselves by claiming that it is more "dignified" for a worker to be on welfare than to work at a low wage. This of course, is the doctrine of many people on welfare themselves. It is truly a strange concept of "dignity" that has been fostered by the interlocking minimum wage-welfare system.

Unfortunately, this system does not give those numerous workers who still prefer to be producers rather than parasites the privilege of making their own free choice. ▶

37
THE UNION PROBLEM

Labor unions are flexing their muscles again. Last year, a strike against the *New York Daily News* succeeded in inflicting such losses upon the company that it was forced to sell cheap to British tycoon Robert Maxwell, who was willing to accept union terms. Earlier, the bus drivers' union struck Greyhound and managed to win a long and bloody strike. How were the unions able to win these strikes, even though unions have been declining in numbers and popularity since the end of World War II? The answer is simple: in both cases, management hired replacement workers and tried to keep producing. In both cases, systematic violence was employed against the product and against the replacement workers.

_____

First published in December 1991.

In the *Daily News* strike, the *Chicago Tribune Company*, which owned the *News*, apparently did not realize that the New York drivers' union had traditionally been in the hands of thugs and goons; what the union apparently did was commit continuing violence against the newsstands—injuring the newsdealers and destroying their stands, until none would carry the *News*. The police, as is typical almost everywhere outside the South, were instructed to remain "neutral" in labor disputes, that is, look the other way when unions employ gangster tactics against employers and non-striking workers. In fact, the only copies of the *News* visible during the long strike were those sold directly to the homeless, who peddled them in subways. Apparently, the union felt that beating up or killing the homeless would not do much for its public relations image. In the Greyhound strike, snipers repeatedly shot at the buses, injuring drivers and passengers. In short, the use of violence is the key to the winning of strikes.

Union history in America is filled with romanticized and overblown stories about violent strikes: the Pullman strike, the Homestead strike, and so on. Since labor historians have almost all been biased in favor of unions, they strongly imply that almost all the violence was committed by the employer's guards, wantonly beating up strikers or union organizers. The facts are quite the opposite. Almost all the violence was committed by union goon squads against the property of the employer, and in particular, against the replacement workers, invariably smeared and dehumanized with the ugly word "scabs." (Talk about demeaning language!)

The reason unions are to blame is inherent in the situation. Employers don't want violence; all they want is peace and quiet, the unhampered and peaceful production and shipment of goods. Violence is disruptive, and is bound to injure the profits of the company. But the victory of unions depends on making it impossible for the company to continue in production, and therefore they must zero in on their direct competitors, the workers who are replacing them.

Pro-union apologists often insist that workers have a "right to strike." No one denies that. Few people—except for panicky instances where, for example, President Truman threatened to draft striking steel workers into the army and force them back into the factories—advocate forced labor. Everyone surely has the right to quit. But that's not the issue. The issue is whether the employer has the right to hire replacement workers and continue in production.

Unions are now flexing their muscle politically as well, to pass legislation in Congress to prohibit employers from hiring permanent replacement workers, that is, from telling the strikers, in effect: "OK, you quit, so long!" Right now, employers are already severely restricted in this right: they cannot hire permanent replacement workers, that is, fire the strikers, in any strikes over "unfair labor" practices. What Congress should do is extend the right to fire to these "unfair labor" cases as well.

In addition to their habitual use of violence, the entire theory of labor unions is deeply flawed. Their view is that the worker somehow "owns" his job, and that therefore it should be illegal for an employer to bid permanent farewell to striking workers. The "ownership of jobs" is of course a clear violation of the property right of the employer to fire or not hire anyone he wants. No one has a "right to a job" in the future; one only has the right to be paid for work contracted and already performed. No one should have the "right" to have his hand in the pocket of his employer forever; that is not a "right" but a systematic theft of other people's property.

Even when the union does not commit violence directly, it should be clear that the much revered picket line, sanctified in song and story, is nothing but a thuggish attempt to intimidate workers or customers from crossing the line. The idea that picketing is simply a method of "free expression" is ludicrous: if you want to inform a town that there's a strike, you can have just one picket, or still less invasively, take out ads in the local media. But even if there is only one picket, the question then arises: on whose property does one have the right to picket, or to convey information? Right now, the courts are confused or inconsistent on the question: do strikers have the right to picket on the property of the targeted employer? This is clearly an invasion of the property right of the employer, who is forced to accept a trespasser whose express purpose is to denounce him and injure his business.

What of the question: does the union have the right to picket on the sidewalk in front of a plant or of a struck firm? So far, that right has been accepted readily by the courts. But the sidewalk is usually the responsibility of the owner of the building abutting it, who must maintain it, keep it unclogged, etc. In a sense, then, the building owner also "owns" the sidewalk, and therefore the general ban on picketing on private property should also apply here.

The union problem in the United States boils down to two conditions in crying need of reform. One is the systematic violence used by striking unions. That can be remedied, on the local level, by instructing the cops to defend private property, including that of employers; and, on the federal level by repealing the infamous Norris-LaGuardia Act of 1932, which prohibits the federal courts from issuing injunctions against the use of violence in labor disputes.

Before 1932, these injunctions were highly effective in blocking union violence. The act was passed on the basis of much-esteemed but phony research by Felix Frankfurter, who falsely claimed that the injunctions had been issued not against violence but against strikes *per se*. (For a masterful and definitive refutation of Frankfurter, which unfortunately came a half-century too late, see Sylvester Petro, "Unions and the Southern Courts—The Conspiracy and Tort Foundations of Labor Injunction," *The North Carolina Law Review* [March 1982]: 544–629.)

The second vital step is to repeal the sainted "Wagner Act" (National Labor Relations Act) of 1935, which still remains, despite modifications, the fundamental law of labor unions in the United States, and in those states that have patterned themselves after federal law. The Wagner Act is misleadingly referred to in economics texts as the bill that "guarantees labor the right to bargain collectively." Bunk. Labor unions have always had that right. What the Wagner Act did was to force employers to bargain collectively "in good faith" with any union which the federal National Labor Relations Board decides has been chosen in an NLRB election by a majority of the "bargaining unit"—a unit which is defined arbitrarily by the NLRB.

Workers in the unit who voted for another union, or for no union at all, are forced by the law to be "represented" by that union. To establish this compulsory collective bargaining, employers are prevented from firing union organizers, are forced to supply unions with organizing space, and are forbidden to "discriminate" against union organizers.

In other words, we have been suffering from compulsory collective bargaining since 1935. Unions will never meet on a "fair playing field" and we will never have a free economy until the Wagner and Norris-LaGuardia Acts are scrapped as a crucial part of the statism that began to grip this country in the New Deal, and has never been removed. ▶

38
THE LEGACY OF CESAR CHAVEZ

We live, increasingly, in a Jacobin Age. Memory, embodied in birthdays, anniversaries, and other commemorations, is vitally important to an individual, a family, or a nation. These ceremonies are critical for the self-identity and the renewed dedication to that identity, of a person or of a people. It was insight into this truth that led the Jacobins, during the French Revolution, to sweep away all the old religious festivals, birthdays, and even calendar of the French people, and to substitute new and artificial names, days, and months for commemoration.

First published in July 1993.

This Jacobinical process has been going on in the United States, albeit more gradually, in recent years. Festivals important for American self-identity and dedication have been purged or denigrated: e.g., Washington's Birthday has been denatured into an amorphous "President's Day" designed merely to insure one more holiday weekend. And in stark contrast to the great World Columbian Exposition in Chicago for the quadricentennial of the discovery of America, at its quincentenary in the fall of 1992, the discovery was universally reviled as a vicious genocidal act by a "dead white European male." Every week, it seems, the media come up with little-known substitute people or events whose anniversaries, or whose deaths, we are required to honor.

The latest *ersatz* hero is Cesar Estrada Chavez, who died last April at the age of 66. For days, TV and the press were filled with the lionization of Chavez and his supposed achievements. President Clinton asserted that "the labor movement and all Americans have lost a great leader," and he called Chavez "an authentic hero to millions of people throughout the world." And we were reminded of Bobby Kennedy's claim, in 1968, that Chavez "is one of the heroic figures of our time."

What had Chavez done to earn all these extravagant kudos? He had, for the first time, supposedly successfully organized low-paid and therefore "exploited" migrant farm workers, in California and other southwestern states, and thereby improved their lot. By living an austere lifestyle, and accepting only a small salary as founder and head of the United Farm Workers, he struck many gullible young left-liberals as a "saint." His admirers didn't realize that love of money is not the only emotion that motivates people; there is also the love of power.

Indeed, the Chavez movement was an "in" cause for New Left idealists in the late 1960s and early 1970s. Trained by the self-styled "professional radical" Saul Alinsky, Chavez successfully cultivated a quasi-political, quasi-religious aura for his union movement: including hymns, marches, fasts, and flags. He popularized such Spanish words as *"La Causa"* for his cause and "*Huelga!*" for "strike," and made it veritable radical chic to boycott grapes in support of his five-year strike against the California grape growers. The Chavez farm worker encampments attracted almost as many short-term priests, nuns, and young liberal idealists as the sugar cane-cutting Venceremos Brigade in Cuba.

In 1970, the boycott finally forced the grape growers to sign with UFW: five years later, Chavez reached his peak of seeming success when his newly-elected ally, Governor Jerry Brown, pushed through the Agricultural Labor Relations Act, for the first time, compelling collective bargaining in agriculture.

Indeed, the new California act came perilously close to imposing a closed shop: its "good standing clause" permitted union leaders to deny work to any worker who challenged decisions of union leaders.

Yet, despite the hosannahs of the nation's liberals, and the coercion supplied by the state of California, Cesar Chavez's entire life turned out to be a floperoo. Whereas he dreamed of his UFW organizing all of the nation's migrant farm workers, his union fell like a stone from a membership of 70,000 in the mid-1970s to only 5,000 today. In the UFW heartland, the Salinas Valley of California, the number of union contracts among vegetable growers has plummeted from 35 to only one at the present time. Only half of the meager union revenues now come from dues, the other half being supplied by nostalgic liberals. The UFW has had it.

What went wrong? Some of Chavez's critics point to his love of personal power, which led to his purging a succession of organizers, and to kicking all savvy non-Hispanic officials out of his union.

But the real problem is "the economy, stupid." In the long run, economics triumphs over symbolism, hoopla, and radical chic. Unions are only successful in a market economy where the union can control the supply of labor: that is, when workers are few in number, and highly skilled, so that they are not easily replaceable. Migrant farm workers, on the contrary, and almost by definition, are in abundant, ever-increasing, ever-moving, and therefore "uncontrollable" supply. And with their low skills and abundant numbers, they can be easily replaced.

The low wage of migrant farm workers is not a sign that they are "exploited" (whatever that term may mean), but precisely that they are low-skilled and easily replaceable. And anyone who is inclined to weep about their "exploitation" should ask himself why in the world these workers emigrate seasonally from Mexico to the United States to take these jobs. The answer is that it's all relative: what are "low wages" and miserable living conditions for Americans, are high wages and palatial conditions for Mexicans—or, rather, for those unskilled Mexicans who choose to make the trek each season.

In fact, it's a darned good thing for these migrant workers that their beloved union turned out to be a failure. For "success" of the union, imposed by the boycott and the coercion of the California legislature, would only have raised wage rates or improved conditions at the expense of massive unemployment of these workers, and forcing them to remain, in far more miserable conditions, in Mexico. Fortunately, not even that coercion could violate economic realities.

As the pseudonymous free-market economist "Angus Black" admonished liberals at the time of the grape boycott: if you *really* want to improve the lot of grape workers, don't boycott grapes; on the contrary, eat as many grapes as you can stand, and tell your friends to do the same. This will raise the consumer demand for grapes, and increase both the employment and the wages of grape workers.

But this lesson, of course, never sunk in. It was and still is easier for liberals to enjoy a pseudo-religious "sense of belonging" to a movement, and to "feel good about themselves" by getting a vicarious thrill of sanctification by not eating grapes, than actually to learn about economic realities and what will really help the supposed objects of their concern.

The real legacy of Cesar Chavez is negative: forget the charisma and the hype and learn some economics. ▶

39
PRIVATIZATION

Privatization is the "in" term, on local, state, and federal levels of government. Even functions that our civic textbooks tell us can only be performed by government, such as prisons, are being accomplished successfully, and far more efficiently, by private enterprise. For once, a fashionable concept contains a great deal of sense.

Privatization is a great and important good in itself. Another name for it is "desocialization." Privatization is the reversal of the deadly socialist process that had been proceeding unchecked for almost a century. It has the great virtue of taking resources from the coercive sector, the sector of politicians and bureaucrats—in short, the non-producers—and turning them over to the voluntary sector of creators and producers. The more resources remain in the private, productive sector, the less a dead weight of parasitism will burden the producers and cripple the standard of living of consumers.

In a narrower sense, the private sector will always be more efficient than the governmental because income in the private sector is only a function of efficient service to the consumers. The more efficient that service, the higher the income and profits. In the government sector, in contrast, income is unrelated to efficiency or service to the consumer. Income is extracted coercively from the taxpayers (or, by inflation, from the pockets of consumers). In the government sector, the consumer is not someone to be served and courted; he or she is an unwelcome "waster" of scarce resources owned or controlled by the bureaucracy.

Anything and everything is fair game for privatization. Socialists used to argue that all they wish to do is to convert the entire economy to function like one huge Post Office. No

---

First published in March 1986.

socialist would dare argue that today, so much of a disgrace is the monopolized governmental Postal Service. One standard argument is that the government "should only do what private firms or citizens cannot do." But *what* can't they do? Every good or service now supplied by government has, at one time or another, been successfully supplied by private enterprise. Another argument is that some activities are "too large" to be performed well by private enterprise. But the capital market is enormous, and has successfully financed far more expensive undertakings than most governmental activities. Besides the government has no capital of its own; everything it has, it has taxed away from private producers.

Privatization is becoming politically popular now as a means of financing the huge federal deficit. It is certainly true that a deficit may be reduced not only by cutting expenditures and raising taxes, but also by selling assets to the private sector. Those economists who have tried to justify deficits by pointing to the growth of government assets backing those deficits can now be requested to put up or shut up: in other words, to start selling those assets as a way of bringing the deficits down.

Fine. There is a huge amount of assets that have been hoarded, for decades, by the federal government. Most of the land of the Western states has been locked up by the federal government and held permanently out of use. In effect, the federal government has acted like a giant monopolist: permanently keeping out of use an enormous amount of valuable and productive assets: land, water, minerals, and forests. By locking up assets, the federal government has been reducing the productivity and the standard of living of every one of us. It has also been acting as a giant land and natural resource cartelist—artificially keeping up the prices of those resources by withholding their supply. Productivity would rise, and prices would fall, and the real income of all of us would greatly increase, if government assets were privatized and thereby allowed to enter the productive system.

Reduce the deficit by selling assets? Sure, let's go full steam. But let's not insist on too high a price for these assets. Sell, sell, at whatever prices the assets will bring. If the revenue is not enough to end the deficit, sell yet again.

A few years ago, at an international gathering of free-market economists, Sir Keith Joseph, Minister of Industry and alleged free-market advocate in the Thatcher government, was asked why the government, despite lip-service to privatization, had taken no steps to privatize the steel industry, which had been nationalized by the Labor government. Sir Keith explained that the steel industry was losing money in government hands, and "therefore" could not command a price if put up for sale. At which point, one prominent free-market American economist leaped to his feet, and shouted, waving a dollar bill in the air, "I hereby bid one dollar for the British steel industry!"

Indeed. There is no such thing as no price. Even a bankrupt industry would sell, readily, for its plant and equipment to be used by productive private firms.

And so even a low price should not stop the federal government in its quest to balance the budget by privatization. Those dollars will mount up. Just give freedom and private enterprise a chance. ▶

40

WHAT TO DO UNTIL PRIVATIZATION COMES

Free-market advocates are clear about what should be done about government services and operations: they should be privatized. While there is considerable confusion about how the process should be accomplished, the goal is crystal-clear. But apart from trying to speed up privatization, and also forcing that

---

First published in September 1991.

process indirectly by slashing the budgets of government agencies, what is supposed to be done in the meantime? Here, free-marketeers have scarcely begun to think about the problem, and much of that thinking is impossibly muddled.

In the first place, it is important to divide government operations into two parts: (a) where government is trying, albeit in a highly inefficient and botched manner, to provide private consumers and producers with goods and services; and (b) where government is being directly coercive against private citizens, and therefore being counter-productive. Both sets of operations are financed by the coercive taxing power, but at least Group A is providing desired services, whereas Group B is directly pernicious.

On the activities in Group B, what we want is not privatization but abolition. Do we really want regulatory commissions and the enforcement of blue laws privatized? Do we want the activities of the taxmen conducted by a really efficient private corporation? Certainly not. Short of abolition, and working always toward reducing their budgets as much as we can, we want these outfits to be as inefficient as possible. It would be best for the public weal if all that the bureaucrats infesting the Federal Reserve, the SEC, etc. ever did in their working lives was to play tiddlywinks and watch color TV.

But what of the activities in Group A: carrying the mail, building and maintaining roads, running public libraries, operating police and fire departments, and managing public schools, etc.? What is to be done with them? In the 1950s, John Kenneth Galbraith, in his first widely-known work, *The Affluent Society*, noted private affluence living cheek-by-jowl with public squalor in the United States. He concluded that there was something very wrong with private capitalism, and that the public sector should be drastically expanded at the expense of the private sector. After four decades of such expansion, public squalor is infinitely worse, as all of us know, while private affluence is crumbling around the edges. Clearly, Galbraith's diagnosis and solution were 180-degrees wrong: the problem is the public sector itself, and the solution is to privatize it (abolishing the counterproductive parts).

But what should be done in the meantime?

There are two possible theories. One, which is now predominant in our courts and among left-liberalism, and has been adopted by some libertarians, is that so long as any activity is public, the squalor must be maximized. For some murky reason, a public operation must be run as a slum and not in any way like a business, minimizing service to consumers on behalf of the unsupported "right" of "equal access" of everyone to those facilities. Among liberals and socialists, laissez-faire capitalism is routinely denounced as the "law of the jungle." But this "equal-access" view deliberately brings the rule of the jungle into every area of government activity, thereby destroying the very purpose of the activity itself.

For example: the government, owner of the public schools, does not have the regular right of any private school owner to kick out incorrigible students, to keep order in the class, or to teach what parents want to be taught. The government, in contrast to any private street or neighborhood owner, has no right to prevent bums from living on and soiling the street and harassing and threatening innocent citizens; instead, the bums have the right to free "speech" and a much broader term, free "expression," which they of course would not have in a truly private street, mall, or shopping center.

Similarly, in a recent case in New Jersey, the court ruled that public libraries did not have the right to expel bums who were living in the library, were clearly not using the library for scholarly purposes, and were driving innocent citizens away by their stench and their lewd behavior.

And finally, the City University of New York, once a fine institution with high academic standards, has been reduced to a hollow shell by the policy of "open admissions," by which, in effect, every moron living in New York City is entitled to a college education.

That the ACLU and left-liberalism eagerly promote this policy is understandable: their objective is to make the entire society the sort of squalid jungle they have already insured in the public sector, as well as in any area of the private sector they can find to be touched with a public purpose. But why do some libertarians support these "rights" with equal fervor?

There seem to be only two ways to explain the embrace of this ideology by libertarians. Either they embrace the jungle with the same fervor as left-liberals, which makes them simply another variant of leftist; or they believe in the old maxim of the worse the better, to try to deliberately make government activities as horrible as possible so as to shock people into rapid privatization. If the latter is the reason, I can only say that the strategy is both deeply immoral and not likely to achieve success.

It is deeply immoral for obvious reasons, and no arcane ethical theory is required to see it; the American public has been suffering from statism long enough, without libertarians heaping more logs onto the flames. And it is probably destined to fail, because such consequences are too vague and remote to count upon, and further because the public, as they catch on, will realize that the libertarians all along and in practice have been part of the problem and not part of the solution.

Hence, libertarians who might be sound in the remote reaches of high theory, are so devoid of common sense and out of touch with the concerns of real people (who, for example, walk the streets, use the public libraries, and send their kids to public schools) that they unfortunately wind up discrediting both themselves (which is no great loss) and libertarian theory itself.

What then is the second, and far preferable, theory of how to run government operations, within the goals for cutting the budget and ultimate privatization? Simply, to run it for the designed purpose (as a school, a thoroughfare, a library, etc.) as efficiently and in as businesslike a manner as possible. These operations will never do as well as when they are finally privatized; but in the meantime, that vast majority of us who live in the real world will have our lives made more tolerable and satisfying. ▶

41
POPULATION "CONTROL"

Most people exhibit a healthy lack of interest in the United Nations and its endless round of activities and conferences, considering them as boring busywork to sustain increasing hordes of tax-exempt bureaucrats, consultants, and pundits.

All that is true. But there is danger in underestimating the malice of UN activities. For underlying all the tedious nonsense is a continuing and permanent drive for international government despotism to be exercised by faceless and arrogant bureaucrats accountable to no one. The Fabian collectivist drive for power by these people remains unrelenting.

The latest exhibit, of course, is the recent Conference on Population, to be followed next year by an equally ominously entitled "Conference on Women." The television propaganda by the UN for this year's conference anticipates next year's as well, best encapsulated in one of the most idiotically true statements made by anyone in decades: "Raising the standard of living for women will raise the standard of living for everyone." Substitute "men" for "women" in this sentence, and the absurd banality of this statement becomes evident.

The underlying major problem and fallacy with the Population Conference has been lost in the fury over the abortion question. In the process, few people question the underlying premise of the conference: the widely held proposition that the major cause of poverty throughout the world, and at the very least in the undeveloped countries, is an excess of population.

First published in November 1994.

The solution, then, is the euphemistically named "population control," which in essence is the use of government power to encourage, or compel, restrictions on the growth, or on the numbers, of people in existence. Logically, of course, the anti-human-being fanatics (for what is "the population" but an array of humans?) should advocate the murder by government planners of large numbers of existing people, especially in the allegedly overpopulated developing world (or, to use older term, Third World) countries. But something seems to hold them back; perhaps the charge of "racism" that might ensue. Their concentration, then, is on restricting the number of future births.

In the palmy days of anti-population sentiment, cresting in the ZPG (Zero Population Growth) movement, the call was for an end to all population growth everywhere, including the U.S. Models based on simple extrapolation warned that by some fairly close date in the future, population growth would be such that there would be no room to stand upon the earth.

Indeed, the peak of ZPG hysteria in the U.S. came in the early 1970s, only to be put to rout when the census of 1970 was published, demonstrating that the ZPGers had actually achieved their goal and that the rate of population growth was already turning downward.

Interestingly enough, it took only a moment for the same people to complain that lower rates of population growth mean an aging population, and who or what is going to support the increasing number of the aged? It was at that point that the joys of early and "dignified" death for the elderly began to make its appearance in the doctrines of left-liberalism.

The standard call of the ZPGers was for a compulsory limit of two babies per woman, after which there would be government-forced sterilization or abortion for the offending female. (The Chinese communists, as is their wont, went the ZPGers one better by putting into force in the 1970s a compulsory limit of *one* baby per woman per lifetime.)

A grotesque example of a "free-market . . . expert" on efficiency slightly moderating totalitarianism was the proposal of the anti-population fanatic and distinguished economist, the late Kenneth E. Boulding. Boulding proposed the typical "reform" of an economist. Instead of forcing every woman to be sterilized after having two babies, the government would issue to each woman (at birth? at puberty?) two babyrights. She could have two babies, relinquishing a ticket after each birth, *or*, if she wanted to have three or more kids, she could *buy* the babyrights on a "free" market from a woman who only wanted to have one, or none. Pretty neat, eh? Well, if we start from the original ZPG plan, and we introduced the Boulding plan, wouldn't everyone be better off, and the requirements of "Pareto superiority" therefore obtain?

While the population controllers seem to have given up for advanced countries, they are still big on population control for the Third World. It's true that if you look at these countries, you see a lot of people starving and in bad economic shape. But it is an elementary fallacy to attribute this correlation to numbers of the population as cause.

In fact, population generally *follows* movement in standards of living; it doesn't cause them. Population rises when the demand for labor, and living standards rise, and *vice versa*. A rising population is generally a sign of, and goes along with, prosperity and economic development. Hong Kong, for example, has one of the densest populations in the world, and yet its standard of living is far higher than the rest of Asia, including, for example, the thinly populated Sinkiang province of China.

England, Holland, and Western Europe generally have a very dense population, and yet enjoy a high living standard. Africa, on the other hand, most people fail to realize, is very thinly populated. And no wonder, since its level of capital investment is so low it will not support the existence of many people. Critics point to Rwanda and Burundi as being densely populated, but the point is they are the exceptions in Africa. The city of Rome at the height of its empire, had a very large population; but during its collapse, its population greatly declined. The population decline was not a good thing for Rome. On the contrary, it was a sign of Rome's decay.

The world, even the Third World, does not suffer from too many people, or from excessive population growth. (Indeed, the *rate* of world population growth, although not yet its absolute numbers, is *already* declining.) The Third World suffers from a lack of economic development due to its lack of rights of private property, its government-imposed production controls, and its acceptance of government foreign aid that squeezes out private investment. The result is too little productive savings, investment, entrepreneurship, and market opportunity. What they desperately need is not more UN controls, whether of population or of anything else, but for international and domestic government to let them alone. Population will adjust on its own. But, of course, economic freedom is the one thing that neither the UN nor any other bureaucratic outfit will bring them. ◗

42
THE ECONOMICS OF GUN CONTROL

There is a continuing dispute about whether President Clinton is an Old "tax-and-spend" (read: socialistic) Democrat, or a New "centrist" Democrat. What a centrist New Democrat is supposed to be is vague, but the two examples of the New Democrat noted so far seem indistinguishable from the Old.

The first proposal was Clinton's collectivist "national service" program, in which the taxpayers provide college educations for selected youth. In return, the youth volunteer for governmental or community boondoggle-jobs, which are somehow held up as morally superior to productive paying jobs in the private sector which actually benefit consumers.

First published in March 1994.

The latest, and supposedly major piece of evidence for Mr. Clinton's "newness" is his emphasis on battling crime. But his crime control seems to consist in warring against every other entity except the real problem: criminals. Instead, there are drives to outlaw or severely restrict *symbolic* violence (toy guns, "violent" computer games, television cartoons, and other programs), and weapons which can be used either by criminals or innocent people in self-defense.

So far, guns are the favorite target of the new prohibitionist tendency. May we next expect an assault on knives, rocks, clubs, and sticks?

The latest gun control proposals from the Clinton administration provide an instructive, if unwitting, lesson in the economics of government intervention. Until this year, if you wanted to become a federally licensed gun dealer, you only needed to pay $10 a year. But the "Brady Bill" raised the federal license fee to *$66* a year—a more than 500 percent increase at one blow. Even this is not enough for Secretary of the Treasury Lloyd Bentsen, who proposes to raise fees by no less than another tenfold, to $600 a year.

One fascinating aspect of this drastic rise in license fees is that Bentsen actually proclaims and welcomes its effect as a device to cartelize the retail gun industry. Thus, Bentsen, in the *non sequitur* of the year, complains that there are 284,000 gun dealers in the country, "31 times more gun dealers than there are McDonald's restaurants."

So what? What is the basis for this asinine comparison? Why not a comparison with the total number of *all* restaurants? Or all retail stores? More to the point, who is to decide what the optimum number of gun dealers, McDonald's, shoe stores, all other retail outlets, etc. is supposed to be? In a free-market economy, the consumers make such decisions. Who is Bentsen or any other government planner to tell us how many of any kind of business establishments there should be? And on what possible basis are they making these selections?

Bentsen goes on to proclaim that the reason for so many gun dealers is that the license is cheap. No doubt. If we charged a $10 million a year license fee for each and every retail establishment, we might be able to deprive American consumers of all retail outlets of any kind.

Bentsen's proposal cheerily estimates that the enormous rise to $600 a year would eliminate 70–80 percent of existing gun dealers, who would be discouraged from renewing their licenses. The National Association of Federal Licensed Firearms Dealers reports that gun dealers are split on the increased license fee: large dealers, who could live with the increase, favor it precisely because their smaller competitors would be driven out of existence. Small dealers, who would be the ones driven out, are of course opposed to the scheme.

Indeed, the Bentsen plan explicitly terms the larger dealers, who sell from retail shops, "true" or "legitimate" gun dealers; whereas the smaller dealers, who sell from their homes or cars, are somehow illegitimate and are supposed to be driven out of business.

In addition to the fee increase, the Treasury wants to expand its pilot program in New York City, which it deems more successful. Here, City police and thuggish officers from the Treasury Department's notorious Bureau of Alcohol, Tobacco, and Firearms "pay a visit" to anyone applying for federal gun permits, explain the laws, and ask in detail what kind of sales operations they have in mind. These intimidating "visits" resulted in the withdrawal or denial of 90 percent of the applications, in contrast to the usual 90 percent approval rate.

There are several instructive lessons from this scheme and from the arguments in its favor.

First, a license "fee" is a euphemism for a tax, pure and simple.

Second, increased taxes discourage supply and drive firms out of business. The unspoken corollary, of course, is that the lower supply will raise prices and discourage consumer purchases.

Third, increased business taxes are not necessarily opposed by the taxed businesses, as is generally assumed. On the contrary, larger firms, especially those outcompeted by smaller competitors with lower overhead costs, will benefit from higher fixed costs imposed on the entire industry, since the smaller firms will not be able to pay these costs and will be driven out of business.

Fourth, here we have an example of a major force behind increases in taxation and government regulation: the use of such intervention, especially by larger firms, to cartelize the industry. They want to cut supply, and the number of suppliers, and thereby raise prices and profits.

In the gun control struggle, this measure is backed by a coalition of liberal anti-gun ideologues and big gun dealers—a perfect example of the major reason for continuing expansion of the welfare state: alliance between liberal ideologues and sectors of big business.

The most preposterous argument for the fee increase was offered by Bentsen and particularly by Senator Bill Bradley (D-NJ), who has been unaccountably hailed by some Beltway think-tanks as a champion of the free market. They said the raise is needed to cover the expenses of government licensing, which cost $28 million last year, while taking in only $3.5 million in fees. There is, of course, a far better way to save money for the taxpayers, the sudden subjects of Bentsen-Bradley solicitude: abolish gun-dealer licensing altogether. ▶

43
VOUCHERS: WHAT WENT WRONG?

California's Prop. 174 was the most ambitious school voucher plan to date. It was carefully planned well in advance, led by a veteran campaign manager, boosted by a nationwide propaganda effort of conservatives and libertarians,

First published in January 1994.

and tried out in a state where it is widely recognized that the public school system has failed abysmally. And yet, on the November 2 ballot, Prop. 174 was clobbered by the voters, losing in every county, and going down to defeat by 70–30 percent.

What went wrong? Proponents blame an overwhelming money advantage for the opposition, fueled by the teachers' unions. But public school teacher opposition was inevitable and discounted in advance. Besides, the property-tax-cutting Prop. 13 of 1978 in California was outspent by far more than the voucher scheme by the entire Establishment: big business as well as unions, and yet it swept the boards by more than 2-to-1. On the contrary, the lack of money in this case only reflected the lack of support at the polls.

The school voucher advocates, like the feminist forces who tried to push through the ERA, met their defeat with bluster, and vowed to keep trying forever. But the feminists, despite their protestations, dropped their proposal like a hot potato once they realized that it was a loser. Perhaps the school voucher forces will likewise face reality and rethink their entire plan—and one hopes they will not bypass the voters and try to impose their scheme through executive or judicial fiat. For the big problem was the voucher scheme itself.

The voucher forces began with the recognition that something was very wrong with the public school system. One problem with public schools inheres in every government operation: that being fueled by coercion rather than by the free market, the system will be grossly inefficient. But while inefficiency on a free market will fail the profit-and-loss test and force cutbacks, governmental inefficiency will only lead to accelerated waste. The tax system and lobbying by vested interests causes the system to grow like Topsy, or rather like a cancer on the civil society.

Another grave problem with public schools, in contrast to other government functions, such as water or transportation, is that schools perform the vital function of educating the young. Governmental schooling is bound to be biased in favor of statism and of inculcating obedience to the state apparatus and trendy political causes.

The conservatives and libertarians who conceived the voucher scheme began by noting these grave flaws of the public school system. But in their eagerness for a quick fix, they overlooked several equally important problems.

For there are two other deep flaws with the public school system: one, it constitutes a welfare scheme, by which taxpayers are forced to subsidize and educate other people's children, particularly the children of the poor. Second, an inherent ideal of the system is coercive egalitarian "democracy," whereby middle-class kids are forced to rub shoulders with children of the poor, many of whom are ineducable and some even criminal.

Third, as a corollary, while all public schools are unneccessary and replaceable, some are in significantly worse shape than others. In particular, many public schools in the suburbs are homogeneous enough and able enough in their student body, and sufficiently under local parental control, to function well enough to satisfy parents in the district.

As John J. Miller, a voucher advocate, wrote in the *Wall Street Journal*: "Most suburbanites—the folks who make up the GOP's rank-and-file—are happy with their kids' school systems. Their children already earn good grades . . . and gain admission into reputable colleges and universities. Moreover, suburban affluence grants a measure of freedom in choosing where to live and thus provides at least some control over school selection. . . . The last thing these satisfied parents want is an education revolution."

It behooves any revolutionaries, educational or other, to consider all problems and consequences before they start tearing up the social pea patch. The voucher revolutionaries, instead of curing problems caused by public schooling, would make matters immeasurably worse.

Vouchers would greatly extend the welfare system so that middle-class taxpayers would pay for private as well as public schooling for the poor. People without children, or parents who homeschool, would have to pay taxes for both public and private school. On the crucial principle that control always follows subsidy, the voucher scheme would extend government domination from the public schools to the as-yet more or less independent private schools.

Especially in regard to the suburbs, the voucher scheme would wreck the fairly worthwhile existing suburban schools in order to subject them to a new form of egalitarian forced busing, in which inner-city kids would be foisted upon the suburban schools. A most unwelcome "education revolution."

Moreover, by fatuously focussing on parental "choice," the voucher revolutionaries forget that expanding the "choices" of poor parents by giving them more taxpayer money also *restricts* the "choices" of the suburban parents and private-school parents from having the sort of education that *they* want for their kids. The focus should not be on abstract "choice," but on money earned. The more money you or your family earns, the more "choices" you necessarily have on how to spend that money.

Furthermore, there is no need for "vouchers" for particular goods or services: for education vouchers, food stamps, housing vouchers, television vouchers, or what have you. By far the best "voucher," and the only voucher needed, is the dollar bill that you earn honestly, and don't grab from others, even if they are merely taxpayers.

How in the world did conservatives and libertarians allow themselves to fall into this trap, where in the name of "political realism" they not only abandoned their principles of liberty and private property, but also found themselves expending effort and resources on a hopelessly losing cause? By taking their eye off the ball, off the central necessity for the rights of private property. Instead they ran after such seemingly "realistic" goals as helping the poor and pushing egalitarianism. Vouchers lost big because people wanted to protect their communities against state depredations. The voucher advocates got precisely what they deserved.

If the voucher fans are not irredeemably wedded to the welfare state and egalitarianism, how can they pursue a course that would be "positive" and realistic, and yet also cleave to their own professed principles of liberty and property rights? They could: (1) repeal regulations on private schools; (2) cut swollen public school budgets; (3) insure strictly local control of public schools by the parents and taxpayers of the respective neighborhoods; and (4) cut taxes so people can opt out of public schools.

Let each locality make its own decisions on its schools and let the state and federal government get out completely. But this also means that the voucher policy wonks—most of whom reside in D.C., New York, and Los Angeles—should get out as well, and devote their considerable energies to fixing up the admittedly horrible public schools in their own urban backyards. ▶

44

THE WHISKEY REBELLION: A MODEL FOR OUR TIME?

In recent years, Americans have been subjected to a concerted assault upon their national symbols, holidays, and anniversaries. Washington's Birthday has been forgotten, and Christopher Columbus has been denigrated as an evil Euro-White male, while new and obscure anniversary celebrations have been foisted upon us. New heroes have been manufactured to represent "oppressed groups" and paraded before us for our titillation.

There is nothing wrong, however, with the process of uncovering important and buried facts about our past. In particular,

---

First published in September 1994.

there is one widespread group of the oppressed that are still and increasingly denigrated and scorned: the hapless American taxpayer.

This year is the bicentenary of an important American event: the rising up of American taxpayers to refuse payment of a hated tax: in this case, an excise tax on whiskey. The Whiskey Rebellion has long been known to historians, but recent studies have shown that its true nature and importance have been distorted by friend and foe alike.

The Official View of the Whiskey Rebellion is that four counties of western Pennsylvania refused to pay an excise tax on whiskey that had been levied by proposal of the Secretary of Treasury Alexander Hamilton in the spring of 1791, as part of his excise tax proposal for federal assumption of the public debts of the several states.

Western Pennsylvanians failed to pay the tax, this view says, until protests, demonstrations, and some roughing up of tax collectors in western Pennsylvania caused President Washington to call up a 13,000-man army in the summer and fall of 1794 to suppress the insurrection. A localized but dramatic challenge to federal tax-levying authority had been met and defeated. The forces of federal law and order were safe.

This Official View turns out to be dead wrong. In the first place, we must realize the depth of hatred of Americans for what was called "internal taxation" (in contrast to an "external tax" such as a tariff). Internal taxes meant that the hated tax man would be in your face and on your property, searching, examining your records and your life, and looting and destroying.

The most hated tax imposed by the British had been the Stamp Tax of 1765, on all internal documents and transactions; if the British had kept this detested tax, the American Revolution would have occurred a decade earlier, and enjoyed far greater support than it eventually received.

Americans, furthermore, had inherited hatred of the excise tax from the British opposition; for two centuries, excise taxes in Britain, in particular the hated tax on cider, had provoked riots and demonstrations upholding the slogan, "liberty, property, and no excise!" To the average American, the federal government's assumption of the power to impose excise taxes did not look very different from the levies of the British crown.

The main distortion of the Official View of the Whiskey Rebellion was its alleged confinement to four counties of western Pennsylvania. From recent research, we now know that *no one* paid the tax on whiskey throughout the American "backcountry"; that is, the frontier areas of Maryland, Virginia, North and South Carolina, Georgia, and the entire state of Kentucky.

President Washington and Secretary Hamilton chose to make a fuss about Western Pennsylvania precisely because in that region there was cadre of wealthy officials who were willing to collect taxes. Such a cadre did not even exist in the other areas of the American frontier; there was no fuss or violence against tax collectors in Kentucky and the rest of the backcountry because there was no one willing to be a tax collector.

The whiskey tax was particularly hated in the back-country because whiskey production and distilling were widespread; whiskey was not only a home product for most farmers, it was often used as a money, as a medium of exchange for transactions. Furthermore, in keeping with Hamilton's program, the tax bore more heavily on the smaller distilleries. As a result, many large distilleries supported the tax as a means of crippling their smaller and more numerous competitors.

Western Pennsylvania, then, was only the tip of the iceberg. The point is that, in all the other back-country areas, the whiskey tax *was never paid*. Opposition to the federal excise tax program was one of the causes of the emerging Democrat-Republican Party, and of the Jeffersonian "Revolution" of 1800. Indeed, one of the accomplishments of the first Jefferson term as president was to repeal the entire Federalist excise tax program. In Kentucky, whiskey tax delinquents only paid up when it was clear that the tax itself was going to be repealed.

Rather than the whiskey tax rebellion being localized and swiftly put down, the true story turns out to be very different. The entire American back-country was gripped by a non-violent, civil disobedient refusal to pay the hated tax on whiskey. No local juries could be found to convict tax delinquents. The Whiskey Rebellion was actually widespread and successful, for it eventually forced the federal government to repeal the excise tax.

Except during the War of 1812, the federal government never again dared to impose an internal excise tax, until the North transformed the American Constitution by centralizing the nation during the War Between the States. One of the evil fruits of this war was the permanent federal "sin" tax on liquor and tobacco, to say nothing of the federal income tax, an abomination and a tyranny even more oppressive than an excise.

Why didn't previous historians know about this widespread non-violent rebellion? Because both sides engaged in an "open conspiracy" to cover up the facts. Obviously, the rebels didn't want to call a lot of attention to their being in a state of illegality.

Washington, Hamilton, and the Cabinet covered up the extent of the revolution because they didn't want to advertise the extent of their failure. They knew very well that if they tried to enforce, or send an army into, the rest of the back-country, they would have failed. Kentucky and perhaps the other areas would have seceded from the Union then and there. Both contemporary sides were happy to cover up the truth, and historians fell for the deception.

The Whiskey Rebellion, then, considered properly, was a victory for liberty and property rather than for federal taxation. Perhaps this lesson will inspire a later generation of American taxpayers who are so harried and downtrodden as to make the whiskey or stamp taxes of old seem like Paradise.

Note: Those interested in the Whiskey Rebellion should consult Thomas P. Slaughter, *The Whiskey Rebellion* (New York: Oxford University Press, 1986); and Steven R. Boyd, ed., *The*

Whiskey Rebellion (Westport, CT: Greenwood Press, 1985). Professor Slaughter notes that some of the opponents of the Hamilton excise in Congress charged that the tax would "let loose a swarm of harpies who, under the denominations of revenue offices, will range through the country, prying into every man's house and affairs, and like Macedonia phalanx bear down all before them." Soon, the opposition predicted, "the time will come when a shirt will not be washed without an excise." ▶

45
EISNERIZING MANASSAS

Many conservatives and free-marketeers believe that an inherent conflict exists between profits, free-markets, and "soulless capitalism," and money-making on the one hand, as against traditional values, devotion to older culture, and historical landmarks on the other. On the one hand, we have bumptious bourgeoisie devoted only to money; on the other, we have people who want to conserve a sense of the past.

The latest ideological and political clash between capitalist growth and development, and old-fogy preservation, is the bitter conflict over the Manassas battlefield, sacred ground to all who hold in memory the terrible War Between the States. The Disney Corporation wants to build a 3,000 acre theme park just five miles from the Manassas battlefield.

Disney, backed by the Virginia authorities and "conservative" Republican Governor George Allen, hails the new theme park as helping develop Virginia and "creating jobs," and also bringing the lessons of History to the millions of tourists. Virginia aristocrats, historians gathered together to preserve the American heritage, environmentalists, and paleoconservatives like Patrick Buchanan are ranged against the Disney theme park.

First published in August 1994.

Doesn't this show that right-wing social democrats and left-libertarians are right, and that paleoconservatives like Buchanan are only sand in the wheels of Economic Progress, that conservatism and free-market economics are incompatible?

The answer is No. There *are* soulless free-market economists who only consider monetary profit, but Austrian School free-marketeers are definitely not among them. Economic "efficiency" and "economic growth" are not goods in themselves, nor do they exist for their own sake. The relevant questions always are: "efficiency" in pursuit of what, or whose values? "Growth" for what?

There are two important points to be made about the Disney plan for Manassas. In the first place, whatever it is, it is in no sense free-market capitalism or free-market economic development.

Disney is scarcely content to purchase the land and invest in the theme park. On the contrary, Disney is calling for the state of Virginia to fork over $163 million in taxpayer money for roads and other "infrastructure" for the Disney park. Hence, this proposal constitutes not free-market growth, but state-subsidized growth.

The question then is: why should the taxpayers of Virginia subsidize the Disney Corporation to the tune of over $160 million? What we are seeing here is not free-market growth but subsidized, state-directed growth: the opposite of free markets.

The second problem is the content of the park that Virginia taxpayers are expected to subsidize. When Walt Disney was alive, the Disney output was overwhelmingly and deliberately charming and wholesome, if oriented almost exclusively toward kiddies. Since the death of Disney, however, and its acquisition by the buccaneer Michael Eisner, Disney content has been vulgarized, shlockized, and gotten less and less wholesome.

Moreover, since Manassas is an historical site and the Disney park will teach history, it is important to ask what the taxpayers of Virginia will be letting themselves in for. The type of history they will subsidize, alas, is calculated to send a shudder down the spine of all patriotic Virginians. This history will no longer be in the old Disney tradition; bland, but pro-American in the best sense. It is going to be debased history, multicultural history, Politically Correct history.

This sad truth is evident from the identity of the historian who has been chosen by Disney Corp. to be its major consultant on the history to be taught at the Manassas theme park. He is none other than the notorious Eric Foner, distinguished Marxist-Leninist historian at Columbia University, and the country's most famous Marxist historian of the Civil War and Reconstruction.

Foner, as might be gathered, is fanatically anti-South and a vicious smearer of the Southern cause. It was Foner who committed the unforgivable deed of writing the smear of the late great Mel Bradford as a "racist" and fascist for daring to be critical of the centralizing despotism of Abraham Lincoln.

Eric Foner is a member of the notorious Foner family of Marxist scholars and activists in New York City; one Foner was the head of the Communist-dominated Fur Workers Union; another the head of the Communist-dominated Drug and Hospital Workers Union; and two were Marxist-Leninist historians, one, Philip S. Foner, the author of a volume of a party-line history of American labor.

Eisnerizing and Fonerizing Manassas has nothing to do, on any level, with free-market ideology or free-market economic development. This impudent statist-project designed to denigrate the South should be stopped: in the name of conservatism and of genuine free-markets.

Once again, as in the case of the phony "free traders" pushing for Nafta and Gatt, it is important to look closely at what lies underneath the fair label of "free markets." Often, it's something else entirely. ▶

Enterprise Under Attack

46
STOCKS, BONDS, AND RULE BY FOOLS

The economic acumen of Establishment politicians, economists, and the financial press, never very high at best, has
plunged to new lows in recent years. The state of confusion,
self-contradiction, and general feather-brainedness has never
been so rampant. Almost any event can now be ascribed to any
cause, or to the contradiction of the very cause assigned the previous week.

If the Fed raises short-term interest rates, the same analyst
can say at one point that this is sure to raise long-term rates very
soon, while stating at another point that it is bound to lower
long-term rates: each contradictory pronouncement being
made with the same air of certitude and absolute authority. It is
a wonder that the public doesn't dismiss the entire guild of
economists and financial experts (let alone the politicians) as a
bunch of fools and charlatans.

In the past year and a half, the usual geyser of pseudo-eco-
nomic humbug has accelerated into virtual gibberish by the fervent desire of the largely Clintonian Establishment to put a
happy face on every possible morsel of economic news. Is
unemployment up? But that's good, you see, because it means
that inflation will be less of a menace, which means that interest rates will fall, which means that unemployment will soon be

---

First published in June 1994.

falling. And besides, we don't call layoffs "unemployment" any more, we call it "downsizing," and that means the economy will get more productive, soon decreasing unemployment.

In pre-Clinton economics, moreover, it was always considered—by all schools of economic thought—BAD to increase taxes during a recession. But *Clinton's* huge tax increase during a recession was an economic masterstroke, you see, because this will lower deficits, which in turn will lower interest rates, which in turn will bring us *out* of the recession.

What, you say that interest rates have gone up, despite the Clintonian budget staking much of its forecasts on the assurance that interest rates will go *down*? But *that's* okay; because, you see, higher interest rates will check inflation, bringing interest rates *down*, so we were right all along! And so down means up, up means down, and round and round she goes, and where she stops nobody knows.

Any sane assessment of the current economic situation is made still more problematic by the National Bureau of Economic Research's self-proclaimed "scientific" methodology of dating business cycles, which has been treated as Holy Writ by the economics profession for the past half-century. In this schema, there is exclusive concentration on finding the allegedly precise monthly date of the peak or trough of the business cycle, to the neglect of what is actually happening between these dates. Once a "trough" was officially proclaimed for some month in 1992, for example, every period since has to be an era of "recovery" by definition, even though the supposed recovery may be only one centimeter less feeble than the previous "recession." In any common sense view, however, the fact that we might be slightly better off now than at the depth of the recession scarcely makes the current period a "recovery."

Let us now try to dispel two of the most common—and most egregious—economic fallacies of our current epoch. First is the Low Interest Rate Fetish. It all reminds me of the Cargo Cult that took root in areas of the South Pacific during World War II. The primitive natives there saw big iron birds come down from the sky and emit U.S. soldiers replete with food, clothing, radios, and other goodies.

After the war, the U.S. Army left the area, and the old flow of abundant goodies disappeared. Whereupon the natives, using high-tech methods of empirical correlation, concluded that if these giant birds could be induced to return, the eagerly-sought goodies would come back with them. The natives then constructed *papier-mache* replicas of birds that would flap their wings and try to "attract" the large iron birds back to their villages.

In the same way, the British, the French and other countries saw, in the seventeenth century, that the Dutch were by far the most prosperous country in Europe. In casting around for the alleged cause of Dutch prosperity, the English concluded that the reason must be the lower interest rates that the Dutch enjoyed. Yet, many more plausible causal theories for Dutch prosperity could have been offered: fewer controls, freer markets, and lower taxes.

Low interest rates were merely a symptom of that prosperity, not the cause. But many English theorists, enchanted to have found the alleged causal chain called for creating prosperity by forcing down the rate of interest by government action: either by pushing down the interest rate below the "natural" or free market rate, determined by the rate of time preference. But bringing down the interest rate by government coercion lowers it below the true, "time preference" rate, thereby causing vast dislocations and distortions on the market.

The other point that should be made is the total amnesia of the financial press. In the old days, before World War II, one hallmark of a "recession" was the fact that prices were falling, as well as production and employment. And yet, in every recession since World War II, prices, especially consumer goods prices, have been *rising*.

In short, in the permanent post-World War II inflation attendant on the shift from a gold standard to fiat paper money, we have suffered through several "inflationary recessions," where we get hit by both inflation and recession at the same time, suffering the worst of both worlds. And yet, while consumer prices, or the "cost of living," has not fallen for a half-century, the overriding fact of inflationary recession has been poured down the Orwellian "memory hole," and everyone duly heaves a sigh of relief when inflation accelerates because "at least we won't have a recession," or when unemployment increases that "at least there is no threat of inflation." And in the meanwhile inflation has become permanent.

And yet everyone still acts as if the Keynesian hokum of the "inflation-unemployment tradeoff" (the so-called "Phillips curve") is a valid and self-evident insight. When will people realize that this "tradeoff" is about as correct as the forecast that the Soviet Union and the United States would have the same gross national product and standard of living by 1984. If we look, for example, at the benighted countries that suffer from the ravages of hyper-inflation (Russia, Brazil, Poland) they, at the same, time suffer from loss of production and unemployment; while, on the other hand, countries with almost zero inflation, such as Switzerland, also enjoy close to zero unemployment.

Finally, to sum up our current macroeconomic situation: During the 1980s, the Federal Reserve embarked on a decade of inflationary bank credit expansion, an expansion fueled by credit inflation of the Savings & Loans. The fact that prices only rose moderately was just as irrelevant as a similar situation during the inflationary boom of the 1920s. At the end of the 1980s, as at the end of the 1920s, the American—and the world—economy paid a heavy price in a lengthy recession that burst the "bubble" of the inflationary boom, that liquidated unsound investments, lowered industrial commodity prices, and, in particular, ravaged the real estate market that had been the major focus of the boom in the United States.

To try to get out of this recession, the Fed inflated bank reserves and pushed down short-term interest rates still further: with resulting bank credit expanding not so much the real industrial economy, which stayed pretty much depressed, but generating instead an artificial boom in the stock and bond markets. The stock and bond price boom of the last year or two has clearly been so out of line with current earnings that one of two things had to happen: either a spectacular recovery in the real world of industry to warrant the higher stock prices; or a collapse of the swollen financial markets.

For those of us skeptical about any magical economic recovery in the near future, and critical, too, of the feasibility of any permanent lowering by government manipulation of the rate of interest below the time-preference rate, a sharp stock and bond price decline was, and continues to be, in the cards. ▸

47
THE SALOMON BROTHERS SCANDAL

Financial scandals are juicy, dramatic, and fun, especially when they bring down such arrogant and aggressive social lions as Salomon Brothers' head, John Gutfreund and his crew. And even more so when they elevate, as the rugged Nebraskan in the white hat riding in to Wall Street to try to save the day, Mr. Integrity, billionaire Warren Buffett (coincidentally, the son of my old friend, the staunch libertarian and pro-gold Congressman, the late Howard Buffett). But when we have stopped exhilarating in Mr. Gutfreund's grievous fall, we might ponder the matter a bit more deeply.

In the first place, what did Salomon Brothers do that merits all the firings and the stripping of epaulets from the shoulders of the top Salomon executives? That they finagled a bit to get around rules on maximum share of government bond issues, doesn't seem to merit all this hysteria. Why should Salomon have cleaved solemnly to rules that make no sense whatever?

First published in November 1991.

But Salomon might have cornered the market temporarily on some new Treasury issues? So what? Why shouldn't they make some money at the expense of competitors?

The only thing clearly beyond the pale done by Salomon Brothers was to sign its customers' names to bond orders without their knowledge or consent. That, surely, was fraud and merits censure; but, again, it needs to be pointed out that such chicanery would not even have been considered were it not to evade the silly maximum purchase regulations imposed by the Treasury.

If much too much is being made of Salomon's bit of hanky-panky, does this mean that nothing is wrong on the government bond market? Quite the contrary. This fuss was made possible by a much more deeply-rooted scandal which no one has denounced: the fact that the U.S. Treasury has, for decades, conferred special privilege upon a handful of government bond dealers, whom it has picked out of the pack and designated as "primary dealers." Then, instead of selling its new bond issues at auction in the open market, the Treasury sells the great bulk of them to these primary dealers, who in turn resell them to the rest of the market.

In the meanwhile, there is cozy and continuing conferring by the Treasury with these privileged big bond-dealers, who are grouped together in an influential lobbying cartel called the Public Securities Association (once named the Primary Dealers Association).

The Treasury, of course, claims that it is more efficient to deal with these designated primary dealers, and it can thus finance its bond issues more cheaply. But surely the cozy closed partnership and the conflicts of interest it conjures up, more than makes up for the alleged benefit by bathing the entire proceedings in what looks very much like cartel privilege. The small group of large dealers benefits at the expense of their smaller competitors.

Moreover, the problem in the government bond market is even deeper. Once a small and relatively insignificant part of the capital market, the Treasury bond market now looms massively, casting its blight on all credit and capital. The total U.S. public debt now amounts to $3.61 trillion, of which no less than $117 billion of securities changes hands every day. But a flourishing government bond market means a market starved for private capital and credit; it means that increasingly, private savings are being siphoned away from productive investments and into the rathole of wasteful and counter-productive government expenditures.

It is doubtful, therefore, whether we really want a smoothly running and efficient government bond market. On the contrary, a government bond market in difficulty is a market where less of our savings is poured down a rathole, and more is channeled into productive investment that will raise our living standards.

We need, in fact, to do some long, hard thinking about the blight of government debt on our capital markets. Wouldn't it be better if such debt were to disappear altogether? One beneficial reform would be to return to the route of Britain in the nineteenth century, where much government debt was due not in six months, or five years, or 20 years, but was permanent debt, or "consols," that never came due at all.

The permanent consol paid perpetual interest, and was never contracted to pay its principal. If the British government wanted to reduce the public debt, it could use its fiscal surplus to buy back and cancel some of the consols. Replacing our current debt with consols would mean that the government would not have to keep coming back to the bond market, redeem principal, and refloat the debt; the crowding out of private credit and investment would be far smaller. Of course, the government would then have to pay higher interest since the principal would never be redeemed; but that would be a small price to pay for lifting so much of the debt burden from the capital markets.

Alternatively, and more radically, we could even ponder the old drastic Jeffersonian solution: simply repudiating the debt, and writing it off the books. Undoubtedly, repudiation would be a severe blow to American bondholders; on the other hand, think of the burden that would be lifted from U.S. taxpayers! Think of the spur to savings and productive investment! It might be replied, however, that, upon such a stark declaration of bad faith and bankruptcy, no one would lend money to the Treasury for a long time thereafter. But wouldn't this be a blessing? Surely a world where people refuse, for one reason or another, to trust or invest in the operations of government, would be a world happily inoculated against the temptations of statism.

Congress, in its wisdom, is trying to decide whether the Salomon Brothers scandal merits more severe regulation of the bond market. It should look first, however, to removing government privilege, from that market, such as the primary dealers' cartel and the vast scope of the government bond market. As in other parts of the economy, and as in the Communist countries seeking freedom, the best course for government, far from coining new plans and regulations, would be to get itself out of the way, as quickly as possible. Once again, the best way for government to benefit the economy is to disappear. ▶

48
NINE MYTHS ABOUT THE CRASH

Ever since Black, or Meltdown, Monday October 19, 1987, the public has been deluged with irrelevant and contradictory explanations and advice from politicians, economists, financiers, and assorted pundits. Let's try to sort out and rebut some of the nonsense about the nature, causes, and remedies for the crash.

First published in January 1988.

Myth 1: *It was not a crash, but a "correction."*

Rubbish. The market was in a virtual crash state since it started turning down sharply from its all-time peak at the end of August. Meltdown Monday simply put the seal on a contraction process that had gone on since early September.

Myth 2: *The crash occurred because stock prices had been "overvalued," and now the overvaluation has been cured.*

This adds a philosophical fallacy to Myth 1. To say that stock prices fell because they had been overvalued is equivalent to the age-old fallacy of "explaining" why opium puts people to sleep by saying that it "has dormitive power." A definition has been magically transmuted into a "cause." By definition, if stock prices fall, this means that they had been previously overvalued. So what? This "explanation" tells you nothing about why they were overvalued or whether or not they are "over" or "under" valued now, or what in the world is going to happen next.

Myth 3: *The crash came about because of computer trading, which in association with stock index futures, has made the stock market more volatile. Therefore either computer trading or stock index futures or both, should be restricted/outlawed.*

This is a variant of the scapegoat term "computer error" employed to get "people errors" off the hook. It is also a variant of the old Luddite fallacy of blaming modern technology for human error and taking a crowbar to wreck the new machines. People trade, and people program computers. Empirically, moreover, the "tape" was hours behind the action on Black Monday, and so computers played a minimal role. Stock index futures are an excellent new way for investors to hedge against stock price changes, and should be welcomed instead of fastened on—by its competitors in the old-line exchanges—to be tagged as the fall guy for the crash. Blaming futures or computer trading is like shooting the messenger—the markets that brings bad financial news. The acme of this reaction was the threat—and sometimes the reality—of forcibly shutting down the exchanges in a pitiful and futile attempt to hold back the news by destroying it. The Hong Kong exchange closed down for a week to try to stem the crash and, when it reopened, found that the ensuing crash was far worse as a result.

Myth 4: *A major cause of the crash was the big trade deficit in the U.S.*

Nonsense. There is nothing wrong with a trade deficit. In fact, there is no payment deficit at all. If U.S. imports are greater than exports, they must be paid for somehow, and the way they are paid is that foreigners invest in dollars, so that there is a capital inflow into the U.S. In that way, a big trade deficit results in a zero payment deficit.

Foreigners had been investing heavily in dollars—in Treasury deficits, in real estate, factories, etc.—for several years, and that's a good thing, since it enables Americans to enjoy a higher-valued dollar (and consequently cheaper imports) than would otherwise be the case.

But, say the advocates of Myth 4, the terrible thing is that the U.S. has, in recent years, become a debtor instead of a creditor nation. So what's wrong with that? The United States was in the same way a debtor nation from the beginning of the republic until World War I, and this was accompanied by the largest rate of economic and industrial growth and of rising living standards, in the history of mankind.

Myth 5: *The budget deficit is a major cause of the crash, and we must work hard to reduce that deficit, either by cutting government spending or by raising taxes or both.*

The budget deficit is most unfortunate, and causes economic problems, but the stock market crash was not one of them. Just because something is bad policy doesn't mean that all economic ills are caused by it. Basically, the budget deficit is as irrelevant to the crash, as the even larger deficit was irrelevant to the pre-September 1987 stock market boom. Raising taxes is now the favorite crash remedy of both liberal and conservative

Keynesians. Here, one of the few good points in the original, or "classical," Keynesian view has been curiously forgotten. How in the world can one cure a crash (or the coming recession), by raising taxes?

Raising taxes will clearly level a damaging blow to an economy already reeling from the crash. Increasing taxes to cure a crash was one of the major policies of the unlamented program of Herbert Hoover. Are we longing for a replay? The idea that a tax increase would "reassure" the market is straight out of Cloud Cuckoo-land.

Myth 6: *The budget should be cut, but not by much, because much lower government spending would precipitate a recession.*

Unfortunately, the way things are, we don't have to worry about a big cut in government spending. Such a cut would be marvelous, not only for its own sake, but because a slash in the budget would reduce the unproductive boondoggles of government spending, and therefore tip the social proportion of saving to consumption toward more saving and investment.

More saving and investment in relation to consumption is an Austrian remedy for easing a recession, and reducing the amount of corrective liquidation that the recession has to perform, in order to correct the malinvestments of the boom caused by the inflationary expansion of bank credit.

Myth 7: *What we need to offset the crash and stave off a recession is lots of monetary inflation (called by the euphemistic term "liquidity") and lower interest rates. Fed chairman Alan Greenspan did exactly the right thing by pumping in reserves right after the crash, and announcing that the Fed would assure plenty of liquidity for banks and for the entire market and the whole economy. (A position taken by every single variant of the conventional economic wisdom, from Keynesians to "free marketeers.")*

In this way, Greenspan and the federal government have proposed to cure the disease—the crash and future recession—by pouring into the economy more of the very virus (inflationary credit expansion) that caused the disease in the first place. Only in Cloud Cuckoo-land, to repeat, is the cure for inflation, more inflation. To put it simply: the reason for the crash was the credit boom generated by the double-digit monetary expansion engineered by the Fed in the last several years. For a few years, as always happens in Phase I of an inflation, prices went up less than the monetary inflation. This, the typical euphoric phase of inflation, was the "Reagan miracle" of cheap and abundant money, accompanied by moderate price increases.

By 1986, the main factors that had offset the monetary inflation and kept prices relatively low (the unusually high dollar and the OPEC collapse) had worked their way through the price system and disappeared. The next inevitable step was the return and acceleration of price inflation; inflation rose from about 1 percent in 1986 to about 5 percent in 1987.

As a result, with the market sensitive to and expecting eventual reacceleration of inflation, interest rates began to rise sharply in 1987. Once interest rates rose (which had little or nothing to do with the budget deficit), a stock market crash was inevitable. The previous stock market boom had been built on the shaky foundation of the low interest rates from 1982 on.

Myth 8: *The crash was precipitated by the Fed's unwise tight money policy from April 1987 onward, after which the money supply was flat until the crash.*

There is a point here, but a totally distorted one. A flat money supply for six months probably made a coming recession inevitable, and added to the stock market crash. But that tight money was a good thing nevertheless. No other school of economic thought but the Austrian understands that once an inflationary bank credit boom has been launched, a corrective recession is inevitable, and that the sooner it comes, the better.

The sooner a recession comes, the fewer the unsound investments that the recession has to liquidate, and the sooner the recession will be over. The important point about a recession is for the government not to interfere, not to inflate, not to regulate, and to allow the recession to work its curative way as quickly as possible. Interfering with the recession, either by inflating or regulating, can only prolong the recession and make it worse, as in the 1930s. And yet the pundits, the economists of all schools, the politicians of both parties, rush heedless into the agreed-upon policies of: Inflate and Regulate.

Myth 9: *Before the crash, the main danger was inflation, and the Fed was right to tighten credit. But since the crash, we have to shift gears, because recession is the major enemy, and therefore the Fed has to inflate, at least until price inflation accelerates rapidly.*

This entire analysis, permeating the media and the Establishment, assumes that the great fact and the great lesson of the 1970s, and of the last two big recessions, never happened: i.e., inflationary recession. The 1970s have gone down the Orwellian memory hole, and the Establishment is back, once again, spouting the Keynesian Phillips Curve, perhaps the greatest single and most absurd error in modern economics.

The Phillips Curve assumes that the choice is always either more recession and unemployment, or more inflation. In reality, the Phillips Curve, if one wishes to speak in those terms, is in reverse: the choice is either more inflation and bigger recession, or none of either. The looming danger is another inflationary recession, and the Greenspan reaction indicates that it will be a whopper. ▶

49
MICHAEL R. MILKEN VS. THE POWER ELITE

Quick: what do the following world-famous men have in common: John Kenneth Galbraith, Donald J. Trump, and David Rockefeller? What values could possibly be shared by the

First published in June 1989.

socialist economist who got rich by writing best-selling volumes denouncing affluence; the billionaire wheeler-dealer; and the fabulous head of the financially and politically powerful Rockefeller World Empire?

Would you believe: hatred of making money and of "capitalist greed?" Yes, at least when it comes to making money by one particular man, the Wall Street bond specialist Michael R. Milken. In an article in which the August *New York Times* was moved to drop its cherished veil of objectivity and shout in its headline, "Wages Even Wall St. Can't Stomach" (April 3, 1989), these three gentlemen each weighed in against the $550 million earned by Mr. Milken in 1987. Galbraith, of course, was Galbraith, denouncing the "process of financial aberration" under modern American capitalism.

More interesting were billionaires Trump and Rockefeller. Speaking from his own lofty financial perch, Donald Trump unctuously declared of Milken's salary, "you can be happy on a lot less money," going on to express his "amazement" that his former employers, the Wall Street firm of Drexel Burnham Lambert "would allow someone to benefit that greatly." Well, it should be easy enough to clear up Mr. Trump's alleged befuddlement. We would use economic jargon and say that the payment was justified by Mr. Milken's "marginal value product" to the firm, or simply say that Milken was clearly worth it, otherwise Drexel Burnham would not have happily continued the arrangement from 1975 until this year.

In fact, Mr. Milken was worth it because he has been an extraordinarily creative financial innovator. During the 1960s, the existing corporate power elite, often running their corporations inefficiently—an elite virtually headed by David Rockefeller—saw their positions threatened by takeover bids, in which outside financial interests bid for stockholder support against their own inept managerial elites.

The exiting corporate elites turned—as usual—for aid and bailout to the federal government, which obligingly passed the Williams Act (named for the New Jersey Senator who was later sent to jail in the Abscam affair) in 1967. Before the Williams Act, takeover bids could occur quickly and silently, with little hassle. The 1967 Act, however, gravely crippled takeover bids by decreeing that if a financial group amassed more than 5 percent of the stock of a corporation, it would have to stop, publicly announce its intent to arrange a takeover bid, and then wait for a certain time period before it could proceed on its plans. What Milken did was to resurrect and make flourish the takeover bid concept through the issue of high-yield bonds (the "leveraged buy-out").

The new takeover process enraged the Rockefeller-type corporate elite, and enriched both Mr. Milken and his employers, who had the sound business sense to hire Milken on commission, and to keep the commission going despite the wrath of the Establishment. In the process Drexel Burnham grew from a small, third-tier investment firm to one of the giants of Wall Street.

The Establishment was bitter for many reasons. The big banks who were tied in with the existing, inefficient corporate elites, found that the upstart takeover groups could make an end run around the banks by floating high-yield bonds on the open market. The competition also proved inconvenient for firms who issue and trade in blue-chip, but low-yield, bonds; these firms soon persuaded their allies in the Establishment media to sneeringly refer to their high-yield competition as "junk" bonds.

People like Michael Milken perform a vitally important economic function for the economy and for consumers, in addition to profiting themselves. One would think that economists and writers allegedly in favor of the free market would readily grasp this fact. In this case, such entrepreneurs aid the process of shifting the ownership and control of capital from inefficient to more efficient and productive hands—a process which is great for everyone, except, of course, for the inefficient Old Guard elites whose proclaimed devotion to the free markets does not stop them from using the coercion of the federal government to try to resist or crush their efficient competitors.

We should also examine the evident hypocrisy of left-liberals like Galbraith, who, ever since the 1932 book by Adolf Berle and Gardiner Means, *The Modern Corporation and Private Property*, have been weeping crocodile tears over the plight of the poor stockholders, who have been deprived of control of their corporation by a powerful managerial elite, responsible neither to consumers nor stockholders. These liberals have long maintained that if only this stockholder-controlled capitalism could be restored, they would no longer favor socialism or stringent government control of business and the economy.

The Berle-Means thesis was always absurdly overwrought, but to the extent it was correct, one would think that left-liberals would have welcomed takeover bids, leveraged buyouts, and Michael Milken with cheers and huzzahs. For here, at last, was an easy way for stockholders to take the control of their corporations into their own hands, and kick out inefficient or corrupt management that reduced their profits. Did liberals in fact welcome the new financial system ushered in by Milken and others? As we all know, quite the contrary; they furiously denounced these upstarts as exemplars of terrible "capitalist greed."

David Rockefeller's quotation about Milken is remarkably revealing: "Such an extraordinary income inevitably raises questions as to whether there isn't something unbalanced in the way our financial system is working." How does Rockefeller have the brass to denounce high incomes? Ludwig von Mises solved the question years ago by pointing out that men of great inherited wealth, men who get their income from capital or capital gains, have favored the progressive income tax, because they don't want new competitors rising up who make their money on personal wage or salary incomes. People like Rockefeller or Trump are not appalled, quite obviously, at high incomes *per se*; what appalls them is making money the old-fashioned way, i.e., by high personal wages or salaries. In other words, through labor income.

And yes, Mr. Rockefeller, this whole Milken affair, in fact, the entire reign of terror that the Department of Justice and the Securities and Exchange Commission have been conducting for the last several years in Wall Street, raises a lot of questions about the workings of our political as well as our financial system. It raises grave questions about the imbalance of political power enjoyed by our existing financial and corporate elites, power that can persuade the coercive arm of the federal government to repress, cripple, and even jail people whose only "crime" is to make money by facilitating the transfer of capital from less to more efficient hands. When creative and productive businessmen are harassed and jailed while rapists, muggers, and murderers go free, there is something very wrong indeed. ▶

50
PANIC ON WALL STREET

There is a veritable Reign of Terror rampant in the United States—and everyone's cheering. "They should lock those guys up and throw away the key. Nothing is bad enough for them," says the man-in-the-street.

Distinguished men are literally being dragged from their plush offices in manacles. Indictments are being handed down *en masse*, and punishments, including jail terms, are severe. The most notorious of these men (a) was forced to wire up and inform on his colleagues; (b) was fined $100 million; (c) was barred from his occupation for life; and (d) faces a possibility of five years in prison. The press, almost to a man, deplored the excessive lightness of this treatment.

First published in June 1987.

Who are these vicious criminals? Mass murderers? Rapists? Soviet spies? Terrorists bombing restaurants or kidnaping innocent people? No, far worse than these, apparently. These dangerous, sinister men have committed the high crime of "insider trading." As one knowledgeable lawyer explained to the *New York Times*: "Put yourself in the role of a young investment banker who sees one of your mentors led away by Federal marshals. It will have a very powerful effect on you and perhaps make you realize that insider trading is just as serious as armed robbery as far as the government is concerned."

This attorney's statement is grotesque enough, but it actually understates the case. Armed robbers are usually coddled by our judicial system. Columnists and social workers worry about their deprived backgrounds as youths, the friction between their parents, their lack of supervised playgrounds as children, and all the rest. And they are let off with a few months' probation to rob or mug again. But no one worries about the broken homes that may have spawned investment bankers and inside traders, and no social workers are there to hold their hands. They receive the full might of the law, and are sent straight to jail without stopping at "Go."

A major difference between the "crime" of insider trading and the other crimes is that insider trading is a "crime" with no victims. What is this dread inside trading? Very simply, it is using superior knowledge to make profits on stock (or other) markets. A terrible thing? But this, after all, is what entrepreneurship and the free-enterprise system is all about.

We live in a world of risk and uncertainty, and in that world, the more able and knowledgeable entrepreneurs make profits, while ignorant entrepreneurs suffer losses and eventually get out of business altogether.

This is what happens, not only in the financial markets, but in business in general. The assumption of risk by businessmen, seeking profits and hoping to avoid losses, is a voluntary assumption by businessmen themselves. Not only is this process the essence of the free market, but the market, by rewarding able and farsighted men and "punishing" the ignorant and short-sighted, places capital resources into the hands of the most knowledgeable and efficient, and thereby improves the workings of the entire economic system.

And yet there are no victims of inside trading as there are in robbery or murder. Suppose that A holds 1,000 shares of XYZ Co. stock, and wants to sell those shares. B has "inside knowledge" that XYZ will soon merge with Arbus Corp., with expected increase in value per share. B steps in and buys the 1,000 shares for $50 apiece; B, let us say, is right, the merger is soon announced, and the XYZ shares rise to $75 apiece. B sells and makes $25 per share, or $25,000 profit. B has profited from his inside knowledge. But has A been victimized? Certainly not, because if there had been no inside knowledge at all, A would *still* have sold his shares for $50.

The only difference is that someone else, say C, would have bought the shares, and made the $25,000 profit. The difference, of course, is that B would have made the profits as a knowledgeable investor, whereas C would have been simply lucky. But isn't it better for the economy to have capital resources owned by the knowledgeable and far-sighted rather than merely by the lucky? And, further, the point is that A hasn't been deprived of a dime by B's inside knowledge.

There is, in short, *nothing wrong and everything right with inside trading*. If anything, inside traders should be hailed as heroes of the free market instead of being apprehended in chains.

But, you say, it is "unfair" for some men to know more than others, and actually to *profit* by that knowledge. But what kind of a world-view dubs it "unfair" for some men to know more than others? It is the world-view of the egalitarian, who believes that any kind of superiority of one person over another—in ability, or knowledge, or income, or wealth—is somehow "unfair." But men are not ants or bees or robots; each individual is unique and different from others, and ability, talent, and wealth will therefore differ. That is the glory of the human race, to be admired and protected rather than destroyed, for in such destruction will perish human freedom and civilization itself.

There is another critical aspect to the current Reign of Terror over Wall Street. Freedom of speech, and the right of privacy, particularly cherished possessions of man, have disappeared. Wall Streeters are literally afraid to talk to one another, because muttering over a martini that "Hey, Jim, it looks like XYZ will merge," or even, "Arbus is coming out soon with a hot new product," might well mean indictment, heavy fines, and jail terms. And where are the intrepid guardians of the First Amendment in all this?

But of course, it is literally impossible to stamp out insider trading, or Wall Streeters talking to another, just as even the Soviet Union, with all its awesome powers of enforcement, has been unable to stamp out dissent or "black (free) market" currency trading. But what the outlawry of insider trading (or of "currency smuggling," the latest investment banker offense to be indicted) does is to give the federal government a hunting license to go after any person or firm who may be out of power in the financial-political struggles among our power elites. (Just as outlawing food would give a hunting license to get after people out of power who are caught eating.) It is surely no accident that the indictments have been centered in groups of investment bankers who are now out of power.

Specifically, the realities are that, since last November, firms such as Drexel Burnham Lambert; Kidder Peabody; and Goldman Sachs; have been under savage assault by the federal government. It is no accident that these are precisely the firms who have been financing takeover bids, which have benefited stockholders at the expense of inefficient, old-line corporate managerial elites. The federal crackdown on these and allied firms is the old-line corporate way of striking back. And looking on, the American public, blinded by envy of the intelligent and the wealthy, and by destructive egalitarian notions of "fairness," cheer to the rafters. ▶

51
GOVERNMENT-BUSINESS "PARTNERSHIPS"

The "partnership of government and business" is a new term for an old, old condition. We often fail to realize that the point of much of Big Government is precisely to set up such "partnerships," for the benefit of both government and business, or rather, of certain business firms and groups that happen to be in political favor.

We all know, for example, that "mercantilism," the economic system of Western Europe from the sixteenth through the eighteenth centuries, was a system of Big Government, of high taxes, large bureaucracy, and massive controls of trade and industry. But what we tend to ignore is that the point of many of these controls was to tax and restrict consumers and most merchants and manufacturers in order to grant monopolies, cartels, and subsidies to favored groups.

The king of England, for example, might confer upon John Jones a monopoly of the production of sale of all playing cards, or of salt, in the kingdom. This would mean that anyone else trying to produce cards or salt in competition with Jones would be an outlaw, that is, in effect, would be shot in order to preserve Jones's monopoly.

Jones either received this grant of monopoly because he was a particular favorite or, say, a cousin, of the king, or because he paid for a certain number of years for the monopoly grant by giving the king what was in effect the discounted sum of expected future returns from that privilege. Kings in that early modern period, as in the case of all governments in any and all times, were chronically short of money, and the sale of monopoly privilege was a favorite form of raising funds.

A common form of sale of privilege, especially hated by the public, was "tax farming." Here, the king would, in effect,

First published in September 1990.

"privatize" the collection of taxes by selling, "farming out," the right to collect taxes in the kingdom for a given number of years. Think about it: how would *we* like it if, for example, the federal government abandoned the IRS, and sold, or farmed out, the right to collect income taxes for a certain number of years to, say, IBM or General Dynamics? Do we *want* taxes to be collected with the efficiency of private enterprise?

Considering that IBM or General Dynamics would have paid handsomely in advance for the privilege, these firms would have the economic incentive to be ruthless in collecting taxes. Can you imagine how much we would hate these corporations? We then have an idea of how much the general public hated the tax farmers, who did not even enjoy the mystique of sovereignty or kingship in the minds of the masses.

In our enthusiasms for privatization, by the way, we should stop and think whether we would *want* certain government functions to be privatized, and conducted efficiently. Would it really have been better, for example, if the Nazis had farmed out Auschwitz or Belsen to Krupp or I.G. Farben?

The United States began as a far freer country than any in Europe; for we began in rebellion against the controls, monopoly privileges, and taxes of mercantilist Britain. Unfortunately, we started catching up to Europe during the Civil War. During that terrible fratricidal conflict, the Lincoln administration, seeing that the Democratic party in Congress was decimated by the secession of the Southern states, seized the opportunity to push the program of statism and Big Government that the Republican Party, and its predecessor, the Whigs, had long cherished.

For we must realize that the Democratic party, throughout the nineteenth century, was the party of laissez-faire, the party of separation of the government, and especially the federal government, from the economy and from virtually everything else. The Whig-Republican party was the party of the "American System," of the partnership of government and business.

Under cover of the Civil War, then, the Lincoln administration pushed through the following radical economic changes: a high protective tariff on imports; high federal excise taxes on liquor and tobacco (which they regarded as "sin taxes"); massive subsidies to newly established transcontinental railroads, in money per mile of construction and in enormous grants of land—all this fueled by a system of naked corruption; federal income tax; the abolition of the gold standard and the issue of irredeemable fiat money ("greenbacks") to pay for the war effort; and a quasi-nationalization of the previous relatively free banking system, in the form of the National Banking System established in acts of 1863 and 1864.

In this way, the system of minimal government, free trade, no excise taxes, a gold standard, and more or less free banking of the 1840s and 1850s was replaced by its opposite. And these changes were largely permanent. The tariffs and excise taxes remained; the orgy of subsidies to uneconomic and overbuilt transcontinental railroads was ended only with their collapse in the Panic of 1873, but the effects lingered on in the secular decline of the railroads during the twentieth century. It took a Supreme Court decision to declare the income tax unconstitutional (later reversed by the 16th Amendment); it took fourteen years after the end of the war to return to the gold standard.

And we were never able to shed the National Banking System, in which a few "national banks" chartered by the federal government were the only banks permitted to issue notes. All the private, state-chartered banks, had to keep deposits with the national banks permitting them to pyramid inflationary credit on top of those national banks. The national banks kept their reserves in government bonds, which they *inflated* on top of.

The chief architect of this system was Jay Cooke, long-time financial patron of the corrupt career of Republican Ohio politician Salmon P. Chase. When Chase became Secretary of the Treasury under Lincoln, he promptly appointed his patron Cooke monopoly underwriter of all government bonds issued during the war. Cooke, who became a multimillionaire investment banker from this monopoly grant and became dubbed "the Tycoon," added greatly to his boodle by lobbying for the

National Banking Act, which provided a built-in market for his bonds, since the national banks could inflate credit by multiple amounts on top of the bonds.

The National Banking Act, by design, was a halfway house to central banking, and by the time of the Progressive Era after the turn of the twentieth century, the failings of the system enabled the Establishment to push through the Federal Reserve System as part of the general system of neomercantilism, cartelization, and partnership of government and industry, imposed in that period. The Progressive Era, from 1900 through World War I, reimposed the income tax, federal, state, and local government regulations and cartels, central banking, and finally a totally collectivist "partnership" economy during the war. The stage was set for the statist system we know all too well.

The Bush administration carried on the old Republican tradition: still raising taxes, inflating, pushing a system of fiat paper money, expanding controls over and through the Federal Reserve System, and maneuvering to extend inflationary and regulatory controls still further over international currencies and goods.

The northeastern Republican Establishment is still cartelizing, controlling, regulating, handing out contracts to business favorites, and bailing out beloved crooks and losers. It is still playing the old "partnership" game—and still, of course, at our expense. ▶

52
AIRPORT CONGESTION:
A CASE OF MARKET FAILURE?

The press touted it as yet another chapter in the unending success story of "government-business cooperation." The

---

First published in January 1985.

traditional tale is that a glaring problem arises, caused by the unchecked and selfish actions of capitalist greed. And that then a wise and far-sighted government agency, seeing deeply and having only the public interest at heart, steps in and corrects the failure, its sage regulations gently but firmly bending private actions to the common good.

The latest chapter began in the summer of 1984, when it came to light that the public was suffering under a 73 percent increase in the number of delayed flights compared to the previous year. To the Federal Aviation Agency (FAA) and other agencies of government, the villain of the piece was clear. Its own imposed quotas on the number of flights at the nation's airports had been lifted at the beginning of the year, and, in response to this deregulation, the short-sighted airlines, each pursuing its own profits, over-scheduled their flights in the highly remunerative peak hours of the day. The congestion and delays occurred at these hours, largely at the biggest and most used airports. The FAA soon made it clear that it was prepared to impose detailed, minute-by-minute maximum limits on take-offs and landings at each airport, and threatened to do so if the airlines themselves did not come up with an acceptable plan. Under this bludgeoning, the airlines came up with a "voluntary" plan that was duly approved at the end of October, a plan that imposed maximum quotas of flights at the peak hours. Government-business cooperation had supposedly triumphed once more.

The real saga, however, is considerably less cheering. From the beginning of the airline industry until 1978, the Civil Aeronautics Board (CAB) imposed a coerced cartelization on the industry, parcelling out routes to favored airlines, and severely limiting competition, and keeping fares far above the free-market price. Largely due to the efforts of CAB chairman and economist Alfred E. Kahn, the Airline Deregulation Act was passed in 1978, deregulating routes, flights, and prices, and abolishing the CAB at the end of 1984.

What has really happened is that the FAA, previously limited to safety regulation and the nationalization of air traffic control services, has since then moved in to take up the torch of cartelization lost by the CAB. When President Reagan fired the air-traffic controllers during the PATCO strike in 1981, a little-heralded consequence was that the FAA stepped in to impose coerced maximum flights at the various airports, all in the name of rationing scarce air-traffic control services. An end of the PATCO crisis led the FAA to remove the controls in early 1984, but now here they are more than back again as a result of the congestion.

Furthermore, the quotas are now in force at the six top air-ports. Leading the parade in calling for the controls was East-ern Airlines, whose services using Kennedy and LaGuardia air-ports have, in recent years, been outcompeted by scrappy new People's Express, whose operations have vaulted Newark Air-port from a virtual ghost airport to one of the top six (along with LaGuardia, Kennedy, Denver, Atlanta, and O'Hare at Chicago). In imposing the "voluntary" quotas, it does not seem accidental that the peak hour flights at Newark Airport were drastically reduced (from 100 to 68), while the LaGuardia and Kennedy peak hour flights were actually increased.

But, in any case, was the peak hour congestion a case of mar-ket failure? Whenever economists see a shortage, they are trained to look immediately for the maximum price control below the free-market price. And sure enough, this is what has happened. We must realize that all commercial airports in this country are government-owned and operated—all by local gov-ernments except Dulles and National which are owned by the federal government. And governments are not interested, as is private enterprise, in rational pricing, that is, in a pricing that achieves the greatest profits. Other political considerations invariably take over. And so every airport charges fees for its "slots" (landing and takeoff spots on its runways) far below the market-clearing price that would be achieved under private ownership. Hence congestion occurs at valuable peak hours, with private corporate jets taking up space from which they would obviously be out-competed by the large commercial airliners.

The only genuine solution to airport congestion is to allow market-clearing pricing, with far higher slot fees at peak than at non-peak hours. And this would accomplish the task while encouraging rather than crippling competition by the compulsory rationing of underpriced slots imposed by the FAA. But such rational pricing will only be achieved when airports are privatized—taken out of the inefficient and political control of government.

There is also another important area to be privatized. Air-traffic control services are a compulsory monopoly of the federal government, under the aegis of the FAA. Even though the FAA promised to be back to pre-strike air-traffic control capacity by 1983, it still employs 19 percent fewer air-traffic controllers than before the strike, all trying to handle 6 percent greater traffic.

Once again, the genuine solution is to privatize air-traffic control. There is no real reason why pilots, aircraft companies, and all other aspects of the airline industry can be private, but that somehow air control must always remain a nationalized service. Upon the privatization of air control, it will be possible to send the FAA to join the CAB in the forgotten scrap heap of history. ▶

53
THE SPECTER OF AIRLINE RE-REGULATION

Empiricism without theory is a shaky reed on which to build a case for freedom. If a regulated airline system did not "work," and a deregulated system seemed for a time to work well, what happens when the winds of data happen to blow the other way? In recent months, crowding, delays, a few dramatic

---

First published in November 1987.

accidents, and a spate of bankruptcies and mergers among the airlines have given heart to the statists and vested interests who were never reconciled to deregulation. And so the hue and cry for re-regulation of airlines has spread like wildfire.

Airline deregulation began during the Carter regime and was completed under Reagan, so much so that the governing Civil Aeronautics Board (CAB) was not simply cut back, or restricted, but actually and flatly abolished. The CAB, from its inception, had cartelized the airline industry by fixing rates far above the free-market level and rationed supply by gravely restricting entry into the field and by allocating choice routes to one or two favored companies. A few airlines were privileged by government, fares were raised artificially, and competitors either were prevented from entering the industry or literally put out of business by the CAB's refusal to allow them to continue in operation.

One fascinating aspect of deregulation was the failure of experts to predict the actual operations of the free market. No transportation economist predicted the swift rise of the hub-and-spoke system. But the general workings of the market conformed to the insights of free-market economics: competition intensified, fares declined, the number of customers increased, and a variety of almost bewildering discounts and deals pervaded the airline market. Almost weekly, new airlines entered the field, old and inefficient lines went bankrupt, and mergers occurred as the airline market moved swiftly toward efficient service of consumer needs after decades of stultifying government cartelization

So why, then, the wave of agitation for re-regulation? (Setting aside the desire of former or would-be cartelists to rejoin the world of special privilege.) In the first place, many people forgot that while competition is marvelous for consumers and for efficiency, it provides no rose garden for the bureaucratic and the inefficient. After decades of cartelization, it was inevitable that inefficient airlines, or those who could not adapt successfully to the winds of competition, would have to go under, and a good thing, too.

The shakeout and the mergers have also revived an ancient fallacy carefully cultivated by would-be cartelists. There is already a mounting hysteria that the number of airlines is now declining, and that we are therefore "returning" to the "monopoly" or quasi-monopoly days of the CAB. Is not a new CAB needed to "enforce competition"? But this ignores the crucial difference between monopoly or large-scale firms created and bolstered by government privilege, as against such firms that have earned their position and are able to maintain it under free competition. The government-maintained firms are necessarily inefficient and a burden on progress; freely-competitive "monopoly" firms exist by virtue of being more efficient, providing better service at lower rates, than their existing or potential competitors. Even if the absurd fantasy transpired that only one U.S., presumably not worldwide airline, emerged from free competition, it would still be vital to avoid any governmental interference with such a free-market firm.

Note, in short, what the pro-cartelists are saying: they are saying that it is vital for the government to impose a coercive, inefficient monopoly *now* to avoid the shadowy possibility of an efficient, freely-competitive monopoly at some future date. Looked at this way, we can see that the call for re-regulation and cartelization makes no sense whatever except from the viewpoint of the cartelists.

Quite the contrary; it is now important to extend deregulation to the European sphere and end the international cartel of IATA, which has crippled intra-European travel and kept airline fares outrageously high.

What of the other unwelcome consequences of deregulation: crowded planes, delays, accidents? In the first place, as is typical, competition has led to lower fares and therefore brought airline travel into the mass market far more than before. So this means that those of us who used to fly on planes half or quarter-filled with business travelers now have to face flights on totally filled planes stocked with students, ethnics carrying all their possessions in paper bags, and squalling babies. But if deregulation has ended the gracious days of yore by making air travel more affordable, those of us who wish to restore that epoch will simply have to pay for the gracious amenities by traveling first class or chartering our own planes.

Delays, accidents, and near-accidents are another story completely. They are only "caused" by deregulation in the sense that air travel has been stimulated by free competition. The increased activity has run up against bottlenecks caused not by freedom but by government, and these unfortunate remnants of government have been causing and intensifying the problems.

There are two major difficulties. One is the fact that there are no privately-owned and operated commercial airports in this country; all such airports are owned by municipal governments (except the worst run, Dulles and National, owned and run by the federal government). Government runs airports in the same way it runs everything else—badly. Specifically, there is no incentive for government to price its services rationally. In consequence, government airports price their major service, landing on and taking off of runways, way below the market price.

The result is overcrowding, shortages of runway space at prime time, and a rationing policy by the airports to provide a first-come first-served policy which virtually insures circling and aggravating delays. A privately owned airport would price runways rationally in order to maximize its income by raising prices, especially at peak hours, and allowing airlines to purchase guaranteed time slots and push the far less revenue-productive private planes out of the runways in prime time. But government airports have failed to do so, and continue subsidizing runway prices, in deference to the politically powerful lobby of private plane owners.

The second big obstacle to the smooth use of the airways is the fact that the important service of air-traffic control has been nationalized by the federal government in its FAA (Federal

Aviation Administration). As usual, government provision of a labor service is far less efficient and sensitive to consumer needs than private firms would be. President Reagan's feat in de-unionizing the air-traffic controllers early in his administration has made people overlook the far more important fact that this vital service has remained in government hands, and poses, therefore, a growing threat to the safety of every air traveller.

As in every other case of government control and regulation, therefore, the cure for freedom is still more freedom. Halfway measures of deregulation are never enough. We must have the insight and the courage to go the whole way: in the airline case, to privatize commercial airports and the occupation of air traffic control. ▶

54
COMPETITION AT WORK: XEROX AT 25

L ittle over 25 years ago a revolutionary event occurred in the world of business and in American society generally. It was a revolution accomplished without bloodshed and without anyone being executed. The Xerox 914, the world's first fully-automated plain-paper copier, was exhibited to the press in New York City.

Before then copiers existed, but they were clumsy and complex, they took a long time, and the final product was a fuzzy mess imprinted on special, unattractive pink paper. The advent of Xerox ushered in the photocopying age, and was successful to such an extent that within a decade the word "xerox" was in danger of slipping out of trademark and becoming a generic term in the public domain.

Many people, and even some economists, believe that large, highly capitalized firms can always outcompete small ones.

First published in February 1985.

Nothing could be further from the truth. In the pre-Xerox age, the photography industry was dominated, at least in the United States, by one giant, Eastman Kodak. And yet it was not Kodak or any other giant business or massive research facility that invented or even developed the Xerox process. It was invented, instead, by one man, Chester Carlson, a New York City patent attorney, who did the initial experiments in the kitchen of his apartment home in 1938. Carlson then looked around for a firm that would develop a commercial product from his invention. He first thought of Eastman Kodak, but Kodak told him it would never work, that it was too complex, would be too costly to develop, and, most remarkably of all, would have only a small potential market! The same answer was given to Carlson by 21 other large firms such as IBM. They were the "experts"; how could they all be wrong?

Finally, one small firm in Rochester took a gamble on the Xerox project. Haloid Co., a photographic paper manufacturer with annual sales of less than $7 million, bought the rights to the process from Carlson in 1947, and spent $20 million and 12 years before the mighty Xerox 914 came on the market in the fateful fall of 1959. Horace Becket, who was chief engineer on the Xerox 914, explains that "technically, it did not look like a winner. . . . That which we did, a big company could not have afforded to do. We really shot the dice, because it didn't make any difference." Small business can outcompete, and outinnovate, the giants.

Haloid Co., then Haloid Xerox Co., and finally Xerox, became one of the great business and stock-market success stories of the 1960s. By the early 1970s, it had captured almost all of the new, huge photocopier market, and its 1983 revenues totaled $8.5 billion. But by the mid 1970s, Xerox, too, was getting big, bureaucratic, and sluggish, and Japan invaded the photocopy market with the successful Savin copier. As competition by new originally small firms accelerated, Xerox's share of the market fell to 75 percent in 1975, 47 percent in 1980, and less than 40 percent in 1982. As one investment analyst commented, "They had an aging product line. They were caught off guard."

In the world of business, no firm, even the giants, can stand still for long. In trouble, Xerox fought back with its new and improved 10 Series of "Marathon" copiers, and in 1983 the company increased its share of the photocopy market for the first time since 1970; and its record considerably improved in 1984.

So, Happy Birthday Xerox! The Xerox success story is a monument to what a brilliant and determined lone inventor can accomplish. It is a living testimony of how a small firm can innovate and outcompete giant firms, and of how a small firm, become a giant, can rethink and retool in order to keep up with a host of new competitors. But above all, the Xerox story is a tribute to what free competition and free enterprise can accomplish, in short, what people can do if they are allowed to think and work and invest and employ their energies in freedom. Human progress and human freedom go hand in hand. ▶

55
THE WAR ON THE CAR

One of the fascinating features of the current political scene is its bitter, and nearly unprecedented, polarization. On the one hand, there has been welling up in recent months a palpable, intense, and very extensive *popular* grass-roots movement of deep-seated loathing for President Clinton the man, for his ideology and for his politics, for all those associated with Clinton, and for the Leviathan government in Washington.

This movement is remarkably broad-based, stretching from rural citizens to customarily moderate intellectuals and professors. The movement is reflected in all indicators, from personal conversations to grass-roots activity, to public opinion polls.

First published in December 1994.

The bizarre new element is that usually, in response to such an intense popular movement, the other side, in this case, the Clinton administration, would pull in its horns and tack to the wind. Instead, they are barreling ahead, heedlessly, and thereby helping to create, more and more, a virtual social crisis and what the Marxists would call a "revolutionary situation."

Response of the Clinton administration has been to try to suppress, literally, the freedom of speech of its opponents. Two prominent recent examples: the Clinton bill to expand the definition of lobbying (which would mean coerced registration and other onerous regulations) to include virtually all grass-roots political activity. Fortunately, this "lobbying reform" bill was killed by "obstructionists" in the Senate after passing the House.

Second, was the federal Housing and Urban Development's systematic legal action to crack down on the freedom of political speech and assembly of those opposing public housing developments for the "homeless" in their neighborhoods. It turns out that this elemental political activity of free men and women was "discriminatory," and therefore "illegal," and HUD legal harassment of these citizens was only pulled back under the glare of severe public criticism. And even then, HUD never admitted that it was wrong.

The latest Clintonian march toward totalitarianism has not yet been unleashed. It seems that the White House has established an advisory panel known as the "White House Car Talks" committee, slated to submit its recommendations for action in September. The need for "car talks" is supposed to be the menace of the automobile as polluter.

The fact that the demonized chemical element, lead, has already been eliminated from gasoline, or that federal mandates have repeatedly made auto engines more "fuel efficient" at the expense of car safety, cuts no ice with these people. It is impossible to appease an aggressive movement bent on full-scale collectivism: gains or concessions simply encourage them and whet their appetite for escalating their demands. And so to the car talkers, automobile pollution remains as severe a menace as ever.

The Car Talks panel consists of the usual suspects: Clintonian officials, environmentalists, sympathetic economists, and a few stooges from the automobile industry. Some of the innovative ideas under discussion, in addition to higher taxes on "gasguzzling" cars and trucks (query: does any car ever sip daintily instead of "guzzle?"):

- establishing a higher minimum age for drivers' licenses;
- forcing drivers over a maximum age to give up their licenses;
- placing maximum limits on how many cars any family will be allowed to own;
- enforcing alternative driving days for car commuters.

In short, the coercive rationing of automobiles, by forcing some groups to stop driving altogether, and by forcing others to stop using the cars they are still graciously allowed to possess.

If that isn't totalitarianism, what exactly would qualify? If the American public is enraged about "gun-grabbers," and they indeed are, wait until they realize that Leviathan is coming to grab their cars!

Now, of course, the White House aide who discussed these ideas with the press admitted that some of the "wilder ideas" will get killed in committee. Is that all we can rely on to preserve our liberty?

Meanwhile, as usual, the only public criticism of these ruminations has come from the Left, griping that the Car Talkers are not acting fast enough. Dan Becker, of the Sierra Club, complains that "each second this yammering goes on in the White house," hundreds of gallons of pollution are being sent into the air. Who knows? Maybe Dr. David Kessler, apparently the permanent head of the Food and Drug Administration, can issue a finding that the fuel emissions are "toxic," and the administration can then ban all cars overnight.

We should realize that the war against the car did not begin with the discovery of pollution. Hatred of the private automobile has been endemic among left-liberals for decades. It first surfaced in the disproportionate hysteria over what seemed to be a minor esthetic complaint: tailfins on Cadillacs in the 1950s. The amount of ink and energy expended on attacking the horrors of tailfins was prodigious.

But it soon emerged that the left-liberal complaint against automobiles had little to do either with tailfins or pollution. What they hate, with a purple passion, is the private car as a deeply individualistic, comfortable, and even luxurious mode of transportation.

In contrast to the railroad, the automobile liberated Americans from the collectivist tyranny of mass transit: of being forced to rub elbows with a "cross-section of democracy" on bus or train, of being dominated by fixed timetables and fixed terminals. Instead, the private automobile made each individual "King of the Road"; he could ride wherever and whenever he wanted, with no compulsion to clear it with his neighbors or his "community."

And furthermore, the driver and car-owner could perform all these miracles in comfort and luxury, in an ambiance far more pleasurable than in jostling his fellow "democrats" for hours at a time.

And so the systemic war on private automobiles began and moved into high gear. If they couldn't get our cars straight away, they could, in the name of "fuel efficiency . . . pollution," the joys of physical exercise, or even esthetics, persuade and coerce us into using cars that were costlier, smaller, lighter, and therefore less safe, and less luxurious and even less comfortable.

If they grudgingly and temporarily allowed us to keep our cars, they could punish us by making the ride more difficult. But now, the Clintonians, in a multi-faceted drive toward collectivism from health to gun-grabbing to assaults on free speech, and on the rights of smokers have demonstrated that they never give up.

Unlike previous administrations, they are tireless, implacable, and overlook nothing. Yesterday, the slogan: "If you let them come for our cigarettes or for our guns, next they will come for our cars," would have seemed like absurd hyperbole. Now, that prospect is becoming all too much a sober portrayal of political reality. ▶

Fiscal Mysteries Revealed

56
ARE WE UNDERTAXED?

Every day that passes brings further evidence, in the marvelous phrase of Bill Kauffman in *Chronicles*, of "the enormous gulf between those who live in America and those who run it." We who live in America are firmly convinced that we are taxed far too much, that government spending and taxation are eating out our substance to support a growing parasitic army of crooks and moochers, and that the accelerating burden of government has caused our economy to stagnate over the last two decades.

The ruling elites who run America, including the sophisticated technocratic economists who lend a patina of "science" to their rule, see the American problem, of course, in a very different way. This economist elite, whose task it is to apologize for Leviathan rule, and to take highly-placed jobs directing that elite rule is, if nothing else, cool and calm about their own counter-theme: "the trouble with America is that it is *under-taxed.*"

To the cries of understandable outrage that greet this claim, the elite is sophisticated and "scientific." It is typical of us cloddish types to be narrow and "selfish," greedily trying to keep some of our own money from the depredations of the taxman. For they, the elite, are wise and all-seeing; in contrast to us

---

First published in April 1992.

narrow and selfish resisters, they have only the common good, the general welfare, and the public weal at heart. To point out that their version of the common good coincides suspiciously with the narrow and selfish interests of the selfsame technocratic economic elite, is to lay ourselves open to one of the worst cuss phrases in our contemporary lexicon: "conspiracy theorist of history."

Leading the most recent parade of "many" (if not all) economists calling for long-range tax increases are Nobel Laureate Robert M. Solow of MIT, Benjamin Friedman of Harvard, and Charles L. Schultze, chairman of the Council of Economic Advisers under Carter. ("Economists See Long-Run Need to Raise Taxes," *New York Times*, Jan. 27, 1992.) One familiar ploy used by the nation's serried ranks of economists is to point to other countries in Europe and elsewhere, whose percentage of national product absorbed in taxes is greater than in the U.S. Well, bully. On that reasoning, why not point to the glorious economic successes of the Soviet Union, whose government output absorbed and constituted *all* of the nation's resources?

On a closer look, the Solow, *et al.* claim is a replay of the old Galbraith thesis, publicized in his best-selling, *The Affluent Society* (1958), which looked around at America and saw the private sector prosperous and thriving, while the public sector, or the "socialized" sector, lay in squalor and disarray. Assuming that the prosperity and efficiency of a sector depends only upon the resources spent, Galbraith concluded that "too much" was being spent on the private sector, and "too little" on public. Hence, Galbraith called for a massive transfer of resources from the private to the public sector.

And after 24 years of following such a transfer program, of taxing the private sector ever more to feed the swollen public sector, what has been the result? What has been the consequence of following Galbraithian doctrine? Patently: aggravated squalor of the public sector, accompanied by a noticeable fraying of the edges in the private sector. The answer of Solow, Galbraith and others is that we still haven't done enough: that the government must tax and spend ever more. If we keep doing so, we can look forward to the economic situation of the Soviet Union in 1991 as the end result.

The crucial fallacy at the root of this nonsense is the idea that government spending really *is* saving and investing, indeed a superior form of saving and investing to the private sector. Solow and company agree with free-market economists that a rise in the standard of living can only come about via increased saving and investment, but their *idea* of such saving is collectivist and can only be effected through government spending.

Thus, in the *New York Times* paraphrase, Professor Solow has the nerve to conclude that "if Americans are seeking to insure that their children live better than they do, they must learn to consume less, meaning live less well, and to save and invest more." Unfortunately, due to higher taxes, they are *already* living less well, but this sacrifice will scarcely help their future state or their children's. Solow's conception is very much like Stalin's, in which the State sweats the consumers, taxes them and keeps down their living standards, all for the sake of a future pie-in-the-sky that never comes true.

In contrast, in a free-market economy of private savings and investment, no one is forced to sacrifice, for those who are able and eager to save and invest do so, and the others can consume to their hearts' content.

The crucial fallacy, then, of this economic elite, is to designate virtually every bit of government spending with the honorific label "investment." But on the contrary, government spending is not "investment" at all; it is simply money spent for the edification or the power of the unproductive ruling elite in the government. All government spending, far from deserving the term "investment," is in reality consumption spending by politicians and bureaucrats. Any increase in the government budget is therefore a push toward more consumption and less saving and investment; and the reverse is true for any cut in the budget.

There is nothing noble, or public-interest-oriented, or "unselfish" about the call of Solow and other Establishment economists for more government and higher taxes. Quite the contrary.

And what of the original Galbraithian claim about private prosperity and public squalor, a gap that is even more glaring now than it was in the 1950s? The observation is true enough, but the conclusion is wrongheaded. If the public sector is the big problem, may not the answer lie in the contrasting nature of the two sectors? May not the answer be to get rid of, or at the very least to shrink drastically, the failed public sector?

In short, privatize the public sector, and the noteworthy squalor would rapidly disappear. And if anyone should prove skeptical, let's try it for a while. Let's privatize the government for, say, ten years, and see what happens; we can even call it a "Great Social Experiment," performed in the best interests of "value-free science." Any takers? ▶

57
THE RETURN OF THE TAX CREDIT

Modern liberalism works in a simple but effective manner: liberals Find Problems. This is not a difficult task, considering that the world abounds with problems waiting to be discovered. At the heart of these problems is the fact that we do not live in the Garden of Eden: that there is a scarcity of resources available for us to achieve all of our desired goals.

Thus: there is the Problem of X number (to be discovered by sociological research) of people over 65 with hangnails; and the Problem that there are over 200 million Americans who cannot afford the BMW of their dreams. Having Found the Problem,

---

First published in July 1988.

the liberal researcher examines it and worries about it until it becomes a full-fledged Crisis.

A typical procedure: the liberal finds two or three cases of people with beri-beri. On television, we are treated to graphic portrayals of suffering beri-beri victims, and we are flooded with direct-mail appeals to help conquer the dread beri-beri outbreak. After ten years, and billions of federal tax dollars poured into beri-beri research, beri-beri treatment centers, beri-beri maintenance doses, and whatever, a survey of the results of the great struggle demonstrates the potentially disquieting fact that there is more beri-beri around than ever before. The idea that federal funding for beri-beri has been a waste of time and money and perhaps even counterproductive is quickly dismissed. Instead, the liberal draws the lesson that beri-beri is even more of a menace than he had thought, and that there must be a prompt across-the-board tripling of federal funding. And, moreover, he points out that we *now* enjoy the advantage in the struggle of having in place 200,000 highly trained beri-beri professionals, ready to devote the rest of their lives, on suitably lavish federal grants, to the great Cause.

Since voicing the idea that perhaps it is not the government's place to go around Solving Social Problems had subjected them to the withering charge of "insensitivity" and "lack of compassion," some conservatives latched onto a shrewd end-run strategy. "Yes, yes," they agreed, "we too are convinced of the urgency of your Social Crisis, and we thank you for calling it to our attention. But we believe that the way to solve the problem is *not* through increased government spending and higher taxes, but by allowing private persons and groups to spend money solving the problem, to be financed by tax credits."

In short, the social crisis would be solved by allowing people to keep more of their own money, provided they spend it on: aiding hangnail research, BMWs, or combatting beri-beri. While the fundamental philosophical problem was sidestepped, at least people were allowed to spend their money themselves, and taxes would fall instead of increase. It is true that people were still not being allowed to keep their money, *period*, but at least the tax credit was a welcome step away from government and toward private action and operation.

In 1986, however, everything changed. Conservatives joined liberals in scorning the tax credit as a "subsidy" (as if allowing people to spend their own money is the same thing as giving them some of other people's money!) and in rejecting the tax credit approach as a "loophole," a breach in the noble ideal of a monolithic uniformity of taxation. Instead of trying to get people's taxes as low as possible, reducing taxes where they could, conservatives now adopted the ideal of a monolithic, "fair," imposition of an equal pain on everyone in society.

The Tax Reform Act of 1986 was supposed to bring sweet simplicity to our tax forms, and to bring about fairness without changing total revenue. But when Americans finally got through wending their way through the thickets of their tax forms, they found everything so complex that even the IRS couldn't understand what was going on and most of them found that their tax payments had gone up. And there were no tax credits to bring them solace.

But there is hope. The Liberal Crisis of 1988, displacing the Homeless of the previous year and the Hungry of the year before, is the fact that upper-middle class, two-wage-earner families, the very backbone of the liberal constituency, can't afford the child care services to which they would like to become accustomed. Hence, the call, heeded on all sides, for many billions of federal taxpayer dollars, by which relatively low-income, single-wage-earner families would be forced to subsidize wealthier families with working mothers. Truly the Welfare State in action!

In despair, and not prepared to say either (a) that this problem is none of the government's business, or (b) that child care would be both cheaper and more abundant if government regulations requiring minimum cubic feet of space, licensed RNs on the premises, etc. were abolished, the conservatives, in their desperation, came up with our old, forgotten taxpayers' friend:

the tax credit. That credit would apply, not only toward professional child care, but also for mothers choosing to tend their children at home.

Let us hope that the tax credit will return in full force. And then we can revive the lost tactic, not of "closing the loopholes," but of ever-widening them, opening them so widely for all indeed, that everyone will be able to drive a Mack truck through them, until that wondrous day when the entire federal revenue system will be one gigantic loophole. ❯

58
DEDUCTIBILITY AND SUBSIDY

One of the most controversial aspects (because it involves scores of billions of dollars) of the Reagan administration's tax "reform" plan is its proposal to eliminate the deductibility of state and local taxes from the federal income tax. The argument rests on the view that, under deductibility, the citizens of the low-tax states are "subsidizing" the high-tax states. Since subsidies are presumed to be unfortunate and non-neutral to the market, deductibility is supposed to be eliminated in a quest for neutrality and an approximation to the workings of the free market. The opponents make the obvious reply that since taxation is supposed to be on net income, eliminating deductibility would mean that people are being taxed twice on the same income; once by the federal, and again by the state or local authorities.

But, in the meanwhile, the subsidy argument has not faced enough discussion. For the proponents of the reform have engaged in tricky semantics on the word "subsidy." Subsidy has always meant that one set of people has been taxed and the funds transferred to another group: that Peter has been taxed to

First published in November 1985.

pay Paul. But if the tax-oppressed citizens of New York are taxed less because of deductibility, in what way are they "subsidized"? All that has happened is that New Yorkers are suffering less expropriation of their hard-earned property than they would otherwise. But they are only being "subsidized" in precisely the same sense as when a robber, assaulting someone on the highway, graciously allows his victim to keep bus fare home. How can allowing you to keep more of your own money be called a "subsidy?"

Only on one assumption. For the hidden assumption of those who want to eliminate deductibility (not only of state and local taxes but of many other expenditures and "loopholes"), is that the government is really the just owner of all of our income and property, and that allowing us to keep any of it, or any more of it than before, constitutes an illegitimate "subsidy." Or, more specifically, that the federal government must collect a certain amount of taxes from its subjects, that this amount is somehow written in stone, and that any person or group paying less than some arbitrarily allotted figure means that someone else will have to pick up his tab. Only then does the idea that a tax cut is equivalent to a subsidy make any sense at all. But this is a curious argument indeed. There is no warrant for the notion that payment of some grand allotted total is so vital that it must override any devotion to the rights of person and property, to the idea that people are entitled to keep the property they have earned.

The recent emphasis on tax allocation, on concentrating on "fair shares" or alleged "subsidies," has been a clever and largely successful device to divert people's attention from the real problem: that taxes are burdensome and oppressive for everyone. The agitation for tax "reform" has managed to deflect people's attention from the need to lower everyone's taxes to a great crusade to try to make sure that the other guy pays his "fair share" and is not being "subsidized." In that way, the long suffering citizens are encouraged to fight among themselves, to try to get someone else's taxes increased, instead of maintaining taxpayer solidarity and keeping their eyes on lowering taxes, period, wherever and however they can. Such a grand taxpayers' coalition can only be maintained if there is a tacit agreement that, regardless of whose taxes are cut and by how much, no person or group will have to suffer an increase of taxes, and this means all coerced payments to government, whether they be called taxes, fees, revenues, contributions, or "closing of loopholes." ▶

59
THAT GASOLINE TAX

The big bad gasoline tax, one of the favorite programs of left-liberalism, is back in the limelight. After having denounced the scheme during the campaign as a tax on the middle class, then President-elect Clinton professed surprise that so many luminaries at the interregnum "economic summit" championed the idea.

Of course, he should not have been surprised at all, since Clinton's much-vaunted love of "diversity" clearly does not extend to the intellectual realm. At the Little Rock economic summit, the economists and businessmen ran the full gamut from left-liberal to left-liberal (my own invitation, as they say, got lost in the mail). The only questions seem to be: how high should the gas tax increase go—the "moderate" 50 cents a gallon suggested by Tsongas (the mainstream) or the more rigorous $1 or more a gallon suggested by Rivlin (the administration)—and how many months or years are we to be allowed for the tax to be phased in?

The official arguments for the gas tax are general (helping to cut the deficit) as well as specific to this particular tax. On the glories of the gas tax *per se*, one common argument is that the tax would force the consumer to "conserve" more gasoline by

---

First published in March 1993.

purchasing less. That it will, but why is it such a good idea to force people to buy less gas?

If the federal government slapped a $500 tax on the sale of chess sets, it would surely "conserve" them by forcing people to purchase a lot less. But why is this dictatorial coercion, this forcing a lower standard of living upon American consumers, supposed to be a good thing in a free society?

One favorite answer of the pro-gas-taxers is that consumers will be led, by the tax, to conserve scarce fuel. But conservation of resources is one of the major functions of the *free price* system. The market economy is continually being forced to choose: how much of product X or product Y, of resource X or Y, should be produced now, and how much should be "conserved" to be produced in the future? Not just of oil and gas, but of everything else: copper, iron, timber, etc.

In every area, this "conservation," this decision on how to allocate production over time, takes place smoothly and harmoniously on the free market. The price of every resource and product is set on the market by the interaction of demand (ultimately consumer demand) and the relative scarcities of supply. If the supply of X, now and in the expected near future, falls, then the current price of X will rise. In this way, an expected future decline in supply is met right now with a rise in price, which will induce buyers to purchase less, and producers to mine or manufacture more of the product in response to the higher price. You don't need a tax to accomplish the task of allocation and conversation.

In fact, a tax is a most clumsy way of meeting the problem. In the first place, since government knows very little and the market knows a lot, the government will not hit the proper target; indeed, since government's coercion comes on top of market action, a tax is bound to "overconserve," to reduce the production of a good below the optimum. And second, unlike a price rise accruing to producers, a tax provides no incentive for supply to increase or productivity to improve.

And why is gasoline supposed to need non-market conservation measures? On the contrary, over the past decade, the *real* price of gasoline (corrected for inflation) has fallen by 40 percent; in short an increasing abundance of oil and gas relative to demand has demonstrated that there is no need to worry about conservation of oil.

Another argument for a gas tax is that it will force consumers to use gas in a more "fuel-efficient" way. But the entire worry about "fuel efficiency" is absurd and ill-conceived. Why should automobiles only be efficient in using *fuel?* There are many aspects of "efficiency," including efficiency per man hour, efficiency in use of tires, and efficiency in the car taking you where you want to go. The market coordinates all these efficiencies in the most optimal way for the consumer.

Why the fuel fetish? Moreover, federal rules mandating ever-greater miles-per-gallon have already greatly increased the cost of cars and crippled auto safety by forcing upon us ever-lighter-weight automobiles.

Another argument claims that a higher gas tax would "reduce our dependence on foreign oil." But in the first place, the tax would discourage the use and production of domestic oil as well as foreign; and second, haven't we demonstrated, with the Gulf War, the willingness to use the direst coercion against even the sniff of a possible threat to our foreign oil supplies? And besides, what's wrong with free trade and the international division of labor?

Probably the dopiest, though one of the common, arguments is that other countries have a much higher gas tax: the United States now has a gas tax that is "only" 37 percent of the retail price, whereas in Western Europe the gas tax averages over 70 percent.

Maybe we can find lots of countries with a higher TB rate. Are we supposed to rush to emulate them too? This is an absurd twist on a typical kid's argument to his parents: "Jimmy's parents let him stay up till 11" or, a few years later, "Jimmy's parents bought him a bigger car." I understand what the *kids* are getting out of these other-directed arguments. But what do *we* get out of pointing to other countries that are even more socialistic than our own?

Even the media recognize a couple of problems with the gas tax. First, that it penalizes rural people and Westerners, where distances are great and cars are driven far more than in Eastern or urban areas. A feeble response is that the proceeds of the tax will be used to "invest" in America's highways, thereby aiding the drivers. But if it goes into highways, how will it help reduce the deficit?

The second recognized difficulty is that the gas tax which injures the broad middle class, is "regressive" and is therefore "unfair." This was Clinton's reason for rejecting a higher gas tax in the first place. But presumably, this argument can be countered by giving some other tax or spending goody to the middle class (a process which again defies the deficit argument).

The general argument for the gas tax is, of course, that it will cut the deficit; official estimates claim that a 50 cent a gallon tax rise will cut the deficit by $50 billion. It is strange that liberals only worry about the deficit when they can use it as an excuse to raise taxes.

How come there is no similar enthusiasm for the only deficit reduction scheme that works: *cutting government expenditures?* When have tax increases ever worked to cut deficits? The huge tax increases under Reagan? Under Bush? This is apart from the problem that these estimates are only shots in the dark, since no one knows by how much people will reduce their purchases from any given increase.

Cutting through the raft of specious arguments, we must ask: why the persisting yen for a gas increase among left-liberals? In the first place, of course, it is the essence of the liberal creed that they have never met a tax, or for that matter a government expenditure, they haven't liked. Both taxes and expenditures take away from producers money they have earned, and shift resources from private citizens to the maw of government.

In short, taxes and expenditures both fulfill the Fabian liberal objective of moving the country ever closer to full-scale socialism. This accounts for the general itch for taxation, but why the long-time special fondness for the gas tax?

Because, of all the features of modern American life, liberals have special hatred for the automobile. For the first time in history, the automobile permits each individual to travel about cheaply and comfortably on his own. In contrast to mass transport, which liberals find satisfyingly collective, egalitarian, and rigidly fixed to time and place schedules, the automobile is gloriously individualistic.

Above all, liberals detest cars which are plush, luxuriant "gas guzzlers," cars that embody and glorify the values and the lifestyle of the bourgeoisie, the productive middle-class whom liberal intellectuals, in their deep resentment of non-intellectuals so yearn to cripple and bring down. ▶

60
BABBITRY AND TAXES: A PROFILE IN COURAGE?

There is no question that the media darling of the early 1988 presidential election season was former governor Bruce Babbitt of Arizona. As time neared for the Iowa caucuses, pundits for virtually every organ of the Establishment media weighed in with *serioso* think-pieces about the glory and the wonder, the intelligence and especially the high courage of a great man who suffered the misfortune of looking like Ichabod Crane on television.

Gloomily, the pundits figured that the Iowa masses would lack the perception and the wisdom of being able to look beyond the TV surface and see the statesman lurking underneath. Fortunately perhaps for America, the pundits proved

---

First published in April 1988.

correct, and the number of voters for Bruce Babbitt barely exceeded the number of his ardent fans in the national media.

Of what does the great courage of Bruce Babbitt, as trumpeted by the media, consist? The answer is his intrepid valor in coming out, frankly and squarely, for higher taxes to slash the federal deficit. The similar gallantry of Mondale in 1984 is then recalled. Set aside the palpable fact that Mondale had a lot more to lose, in contrast to Bruce Babbitt, who began close to zero percent popularity in any case. The interesting question to ask is: what kind of "courage" is this?

It used to be thought that heroism and "courage" meant being willing to go out into the lists, candidly and unafraid, to battle the mighty and despotic powers-that-be. Can we really call it "courage" when a Mondale or a Babbitt frankly calls upon the eager state apparatus to *increase* still further its already outrageous and parasitic plunder of the hard-earned money of honest and productive American citizens? Whooping it up for higher taxes is the moral equivalent of some Ugandan theoretician of a few years ago publicly urging Idi Amin to pile on his looting and his despotism still further, or of a Mafia *consigliere* advising the *capo* to add an extra ten percent to the "protection fee" imposed on neighborhood stores. We can think of many names for this sort of activity, but "courage" is surely not one of them.

It might be objected that, after all, a politician who urges higher taxes is not only imposing suffering on *other* people; he himself as a taxpayer will also have to bear the same deprivations as other citizens. Isn't there, then, a kind of nobility, even if misguided, in his plea for "belt-tightening" common sacrifice?

To meet this question, we must realize a vital truth that has long remained discreetly veiled to the tax-burdened citizenry. And that is: contrary to carefully instilled myth, politicians and bureaucrats *pay no taxes*. Take, for example, a politician who receives a salary of, say, $80,000; assume he duly files his income tax return, and pays $20,000. We must realize that he does not in reality pay $20,000 in taxes; instead, he is simply a *net tax-receiver* of $60,000. The notion that he pays taxes is simply an accounting fiction, designed to bamboozle the citizenry into believing that he and the rest of us are on the same moral and financial footing before the law. He pays nothing; he simply is extracting $60,000 *per annum* from our pockets. The only virtue of United Nations' employees is that they are frankly and openly exempt from all taxes levied by any nation-state—which simply makes their position the same as other national bureaucrats, except uncamouflaged and unadorned.

The same principle, too, applies to sales or property or any other tax. Bureaucrats and politicians do not pay them; they are simply subtracted from the net transfer to themselves from the body of taxpayers.

Unfortunately in current American politics, we are trapped between purveyors of false choices: the "courageous" who call for higher taxes, and the supply-siders who say that there's nothing really wrong with deficits, and that we should learn to relax and enjoy them. It seems to be forgotten that there is another tried and true, and perhaps far more "courageous," way of slashing the deficits: *cutting government spending.*

It would seem embarrassingly trivial to mention it, except somehow this alternative has gotten lost down the Orwellian memory hole. "But *where* would you cut?" asks the cunning critic, hoping to get us all bogged down in the numbing minutiae of whether $50,000 should be cut from a grant to some New Jersey *avant-garde* theater group.

The proper answer is: anywhere and everywhere; only wholesale flailing away with a meat axe could possibly do justice to the task. An immediate 50 percent across-the-board slash in literally everything; abolishing every other government agency at random; a line-by-line reduction of the budget to some previous president's—the further back in time the better; all these will do nicely for openers. The important thing is to adopt the spirit, the mind-set; and a balanced budget will be the least of the wondrous results to follow. ▶

61
FLAT TAX OR FLAT TAXPAYER?

Hosannas poured in from all parts of the academic spectrum—left, right, and center—hailing the Treasury's 1986 draft plan as an approach to the ideal of the "flat tax." (Since the plan calls for three classes of income tax rates, it has been called a "flat tax with bumps.")

This near-unanimity should not be surprising, because a flat tax appeals to the sort of academic who, regardless of ideology, likes to push people around like pawns on a chessboard. The great nineteenth-century Swiss historian Jacob Burckhardt called such intellectual social engineers "terrible simplifiers." The label applies beautifully to the legion of flat-taxers because one of their prime arguments is that they would replace our bewildering mosaic of tax laws by one of limpid simplicity, one that "you could make out on a postcard."

Unfortunately, this proposed simplicity is more childlike and naive than a great burst of clarifying intelligence. For our Terrible Simplifiers fail to stop and ask themselves *why* the tax laws are so complicated. No one likes complexity for its own sake. There is a good reason for the current complexity: it is the result of a myriad of individuals, groups, and businesses trying their darndest to get out from under the crippling income tax.

And, in contrast to the flat-tax academic who sneers at all *other* groups than his own as slaves of sinister special interests, there is *nothing wrong* with this often messy process. For these are people who, quite simply and even admirably, are trying to keep some of their hard-earned money from being snatched up in the maw of the tax-collector.

And these people have already found out what our flat-tax academics seem not to have cottoned to: there are things in this

---

First published in June 1995.

life worse than complexity, and one of them is paying more taxes. Complexity is good if it allows you to keep more of your own money.

In the name of sacred simplicity, in fact, our flat-taxers are cheerfully willing to impose enormous losses on a very large number of individuals and businesses, in the following ways:

RAISE the tax on capital gains to treat it like income, thereby crippling saving and investment, particularly in new and growing firms. One of the things that has kept the English economy from going totally down the tubes is that England, despite its cripplingly high income taxation, has no tax at all on capital gains.

ELIMINATE accelerated depreciation, thereby destroying an excellent 1981 tax reform that allowed businesses to depreciate rapidly and reinvest. This change will particularly hurt heavily capitalized "smokestack" industries, already in economic trouble.

ELIMINATE OR RESTRICT income-tax deductions for mortgage payments, *plus* treat homeowners as having a taxable income from "imputed" rent, i.e., from the rent they would otherwise have paid if they had been tenants instead of homeowners. This double blow to homeowners is so politically explosive that it will probably not go through—but such is the full intention of the flat-taxers. Unfortunately, those who are taxed on "imputed" income will not be able to pay their taxes in "imputed" form. *They* will have to pay Uncle Sam in money.

ELIMINATE oil depletion allowances, a neat way to send the oil industry into a depression. Flat-tax academics persist in regarding depreciation payments and depletion allowances as "subsidies" to capitalists and oil or mining companies. They are not subsidies, however, they are ways of permitting these firms to keep more of their own money, something which at least pro-free enterprise academics are *supposed* to believe in. Furthermore, only income is supposed to be taxed, and not accumulated wealth; taxing "income" which is merely the loss of capital value (either by depreciation or depletion) is really a tax on capital or wealth.

ELIMINATE tax deductions for uninsured medical payments or losses due to accident or fire. Does one get a glimmer of why economists are sometimes called "heartless"?

Note that, unlike some welfare economists, I am in no sense a slave to the ideal of "Pareto-optimality" (the notion that no government action must impose a loss on anyone). I am willing to advocate radical measures that impose losses on some people, but only to achieve a substantial increase in freedom. But severe losses merely for the sake of symmetry?!

We are left with the final Argument From Simplicity: that the flat tax will enable all of us to dispense with tax lawyers and accountants. A powerful lure, perhaps, but fallacious and untrue on many levels. In the first place, those taxpayers who want simplicity can achieve it now: they can fill out the simplified tax forms. Two-thirds of American taxpayers do so now.

The rest of us who struggle with complex forms are doing so for a good reason: to pay less taxes. Second, those of us who have our own businesses, including the business of writing and lecturing, will enjoy no reduction in the complexity of our tasks; we will still be struggling at great length to see what our net business gain (or loss) might be. None of this will change under the reign of the Simplifiers.

And finally, there is, once again, a good reason for our paying money to tax lawyers and accountants. Spending money on them is no more a social waste that our purchase of locks, safes, or fences. *If there were no crime*, expenditure on such safety measures would be a waste, but there is crime. Similarly, we pay money to the lawyers and accountants because, like fences or locks, they are our defense, our shield and buckler, against the tax man.

Many years ago, my friend and mentor Frank Chodorov, during the midst of the McCarthy era, wrote that "the way to get rid of Communists in government jobs is to get rid of the jobs." Similarly, the way to get rid of tax lawyers and accountants is to abolish the income tax. That would be Sweet Simplicity indeed! ▸

62
MRS. THATCHER'S POLL TAX

R iots in the streets; protest against a hated government; cops arresting protesters. A familiar story these days. But suddenly we find that the protests are directed, not against a hated Communist tyranny in Eastern Europe, but against Mrs. Thatcher's regime in Britain, a supposed paragon of liberty and the free market. What's going on here? Are anti-government demonstrators heroic freedom-fighters in Eastern Europe, but only crazed anarchists and alienated punks in the West?

The anti-government riots in London at the end of March were, it must be noted, *anti-tax* riots, and surely a movement in opposition to taxation can't be all bad. But wasn't the protest movement at bottom an envy-ridden call for soaking the rich, and hostility to the new Thatcher tax a protest against its abstention from egalitarian leveling?

Not really. There is no question that the new Thatcher "community charge" was a bold and fascinating experiment. Local government councils, in many cases havens of the left-wing Labour Party, have been engaging in runaway spending in recent years. As in the case of American local governments, basic local revenue in great Britain has been derived from the property tax ("rates" in Britain) which are levied proportionately on the value of property.

Whereas in the United States, conservative economists tend to hail proportionate taxation (especially on incomes) as ideal and "neutral" to the market, the Thatcherites have apparently understood the fallacy of this position. On the market, people do *not* pay for goods and services in proportion to their incomes. David Rockefeller does *not* have to pay $1,000 for a loaf of bread for which the rest of us pay $1.50. On the contrary,

---

First published in June 1990.

on the market there is a strong tendency for a good to be priced the same throughout the market; one good, one price. It would be far more neutral to the market, indeed, for everyone to pay, not the same tax in proportion to his income, but the same tax as everyone else, period. Everyone's tax should therefore be equal. Furthermore, since democracy is based on the concept of one man or woman, one vote, it would seem no more than fitting to have a principle of one man, one tax. Equal voting, equal taxation.

The concept of an equal tax per head is called the "poll tax," and Mrs. Thatcher decided to bring the local councils to heel by legislating the abolition of the local rates, and their replacement by an equal poll tax per adult, calling it by the euphemism, "community charge." At least on the local level, then, soaking the rich has been replaced by an equal tax.

But there are several deep flaws in the new tax. In the first place, it is still not neutral to the market, since—a crucial difference—market prices are paid voluntarily by the consumer purchasing the good or service, whereas the tax (or "charge") is levied coercively on each person, even if the value of the "service" of government to that person is far less than the charge, or is even negative.

Not only that: but a poll tax is a charge levied on a person's very existence, and the person must often be hunted down at great expense to be forced to pay the tax. Charging a man for his very existence seems to imply that the government owns all of its subjects, body and soul.

The second deep flaw is bound up with the problem of coercion. It is certainly heroic of Mrs. Thatcher to want to scrap the property tax in behalf of an equal tax. But she seems to have missed the major point of the equal tax, one that gives it its unique charm. For the truly great thing about an equal tax is that in order to make it payable, it has to be drastically reduced from the levels before the equality is imposed.

Assume, for example, that our present federal tax was suddenly shifted to become an equal tax for each person. This would mean that the average person, and particularly the low-income person, would suddenly find himself paying enormously more per year in taxes—about $5,000. So that the great charm of equal taxation is that it would necessarily force the government to lower drastically its levels of taxing and spending. Thus, if the U.S. government instituted, say, a universal and equal tax of $10 per year, confining it to the magnificent sum of $2 billion annually, we would all live quite well with the new tax, and no egalitarian would bother about protesting its failure to soak the rich.

But instead of drastically lowering the amount of local taxation, Mrs. Thatcher imposed no such limits, and left the total expenditure and tax levels, as before, to the local councils. These local councils, Conservative as well as Labour, proceeded to raise their tax levels substantially, so that the average British citizen is being forced to pay approximately one-third more in local taxes. No wonder there are riots in the streets! The only puzzle is that the riots aren't more severe.

In short, the great thing about equal taxation is using it as a club to force an enormous lowering of taxes. To increase tax levels after they become equal is absurd: an open invitation for tax evasion and revolution. In Scotland, where the equal tax had already gone into effect, there are no penalties for non-payment and an estimated one-third of citizens have refused to pay. In England, where payment is enforced, the situation is rougher. In either case, it is no wonder that popularity of the Thatcher regime has fallen to an all-time low. The Thatcher people are now talking about placing caps on local tax rates, but capping is scarcely enough: drastic reductions are a political and economic necessity, if the poll tax is to be retained.

Unfortunately, the local tax case is characteristic of the Thatcher regime. Thatcherism is all too similar to Reaganism: free-market rhetoric masking statist content. While Thatcher has engaged in some privatization, the percentage of government spending and taxation to GNP has increased over the course of her regime, and monetary inflation has now led to price inflation. Basic discontent, then, has risen, and the increase in local tax levels has come as the vital last straw. It seems to me that a minimum criterion for a regime receiving the accolade of "pro-free-market" would require it to cut total spending, cut overall tax rates, and revenues, and put a *stop* to its own inflationary creation of money. Even by this surely modest yardstick, no British or American administration in decades has come close to qualifying. ▶

63
EXIT THE IRON LADY

Mrs. Thatcher's departure from British rule befitted her entire reign: blustering in rhetoric ("the Iron Lady will never quit") accompanied by very little concrete action (as the Iron Lady quickly departed).

Her rhetoric did bring free-market ideas back to respectability in Britain for the first time in a half-century, and it is certainly gratifying to see the estimable people at the Institute of Economic Affairs in London become Britain's most reputable think-tank. It is also largely to the credit of the Thatcher Era that the Labour Party has moved rightward, and largely abandoned its loony left-wing views, and that the British have decisively abandoned their post-Depression psychosis about unemployment rates ever being higher than 1 percent.

The Thatcher accomplishments, however, are a very different story, and very much of a mixed-bag. On the positive side, there was a considerable amount of denationalization and privatization, including the sale of public housing units to the tenants, thereby converting former Labour voters to staunchly Conservative property owners. Another of her successes was breaking the massive power of the British trade unions.

First published in February 1991.

Unfortunately, the pluses of the Thatcher economic record are more than offset by the stark fact that the State ends the Thatcher era more of a parasitic burden on the British economy and society than it was when she took office. For example, she never dared touch the sacred cow of socialized medicine, the National Health Service. For that and many other reasons, British government spending and revenues are more generous than ever.

Furthermore, despite Mrs. Thatcher's lip-service to monetarism, her early successes against inflation have been reversed, and monetary expansion, inflation, government deficits, and accompanying unemployment are higher than ever. Mrs. Thatcher left office, after eleven years, in the midst of a disgraceful inflationary recession: with inflation at 11 percent, and unemployment at 9 percent. In short, Mrs. Thatcher's macroeconomic record was abysmal.

To top it off, her decisive blunder was the replacement of local property taxes by an equal tax per person (a "poll tax"). In England, in contrast to the United States, the central government has control over the local governments, many of which are ruled by wild-spending left Labourites. The equal tax was designed to curb the free-spending local governments.

Instead, what should have been predictable happened. The local governments generally increased their spending and taxes, the higher equal tax biting fiercely upon the poor and middle-class, and then effectively placed the blame for the higher taxes upon the Thatcher regime. Moreover, in all this maneuvering, the Thatcherites forgot that the great point about an equal tax is precisely that taxes have to be drastically lowered so that the poorest can pay them; to raise equal tax rates above the old property tax, or to allow them to be raised, is a species of economic and political insanity, and Mrs. Thatcher reaped the proper punishment for egregious error.

Why then didn't the Thatcher government, upon installing the equal tax for local governments, directly decree drastically lower tax rates for each locale? Then the British masses would have welcomed instead of combatted the poll tax. The Thatcherite answer is that the central government would have had to assume funding of such local government activities as education, which would have raised either central taxes or the central government deficit.

But that only pushed the analysis one step further: why wasn't the Thatcher government prepared to slash such spending, which is almost as bloated as in the U.S.? Clearly the answer is either that the Thatcherites did not truly believe their own rhetoric or that they didn't have the guts to raise the issue. In either case, Mrs. Thatcher deserved her eventual fate.

In one area of the macro-economy we must regret the exit of Mrs. Thatcher: hers was the only voice raising a cry against the creation of the European Central Bank, issuing a new European currency unit. Unfortunately, and especially since the firing of her monetarist economic adviser, Sir Alan Walters, Mrs. Thatcher failed to make a convincing case for her opposition to this coming new order, putting it solely in cranky, hectoring terms of British national glory as against subordination to "Europe." She therefore came off as a narrow anti-European obstructionist as against a seemingly enlightened and benefi-cent "united Europe."

The problem in almost all analyses of the new European Community is the usual conflation of State and society. Socially and economically, to the extent that the new Europe will be a vast free-trade and free-capital investment area, this new order will be all to the good: expanding the division of labor, the pro-ductivity, and the living standards of all the participating nations. Unfortunately, the essence of the new Europe will not be its free-trade area, but a giant new State bureaucracy, head-quartered in Strasbourg and Brussels, controlling, regulating, and "equalizing" tax rates everywhere by coercing the raising of taxes in low-tax countries.

And the worst aspect of this united Europe is precisely the area that Mrs. Thatcher zeroed in on: money and banking. While the monetarists are dead wrong in preferring a Europe (or a world) of nationally fragmented fiat monies to an international gold money, they are right in warning of the dangers of the new scheme. For the problem is that the new currency will of course not be gold, a market-produced money, but a fiat paper issued in new currency units. So that the result of this neo-Keynesian scheme will be inflationary fiat money, the issue of which is controlled by the regional Central Bank, i.e., by the new regional government.

This collaboration will then make it much easier for the Central Banks of the U.S., Britain, and Japan, to collaborate with the new European Central Bank, and thereby to move rapidly toward the old Keynesian dream: a World Central Bank issuing a new world paper currency unit. And then, we would be truly off to the races, with the world's Money and macro-economy totally at the mercy of a worldwide inflation, centrally controlled by self-proclaimed all-wise Keynesian masters. It is unfortunate that Mrs. Thatcher would not articulate her opposition to the new monetary Europe in such terms. ▶

64
THE BUDGET CRISIS

In politics fall, not spring, is the silly season. How many times have we seen the farce: the crisis deadline in October, the budget "summit" between the Executive and Congress, and the piteous wails of liberals and centrists that those wonderful, hard-working, dedicated "federal workers" may be "furloughed," which unfortunately does not mean that they are thrown on the beach to find their way in the productive private sector. The dread furlough means that for a few days or so, the oppressed taxpaying public gets to keep a bit more of its own money, while the federal workers get a rare chance to apply

---

First published in December 1990.

their dedication without mulcting the taxpayers: an opportunity that these bureaucrats invariably seem to pass up.

Has it occurred to many citizens that, for the few blessed days of federal shutdown, the world does not come to an end? That the stars remain in their courses, and everyone goes about their daily life as before?

I would like to offer a modest proposal, giving us a chance to see precisely how vital to our survival and prosperity is the Leviathan federal government, and how much we are truly willing to pay for its care and feeding. Let us try a great social experiment: for one year, one exhilarating jubilee year, we furlough, without pay, the Internal Revenue Service and the rest of the revenue-gathering functions of the Department of Treasury.

That is, for one year, suspend all federal taxes and float no public debt, either newly incurred or even for payment of existing interest or principal. And then let us see how much the American public is willing to kick into, purely voluntarily, the public till.

We make these voluntary contributions strictly anonymous, so that there will be no incentive for individuals and institutions to collect brownie-points from the feds for current voluntary giving. We allow no carryover of funds or surplus, so that any federal spending for the year—including the piteous importuning of Americans for funds takes place strictly out of next year's revenue.

It will then be fascinating to see how much the American public is truly willing to pay, how much it thinks the federal government is really worth, how much it is really convinced by all the slick cons: by the spectre of roads falling apart, cancer cures aborted, by invocations of the "common good," the "public interest," the "national security," to say nothing of the favorite economists' ploys of "public goods" and "externalities."

It would be even more instructive to allow the various anonymous contributors to check off what specific services or agencies they wish to earmark for expenditure of their funds. It would be still more fun to see vicious and truthful competitive advertising between bureaus: "No, no, don't contribute to those lazy louts in the Department of Transportation (or whatever), give to us." For once, government propaganda might even prove to be instructive and enjoyable.

The precedent has already been set: if it is proper and legitimate for President Bush and his administration to beg Japan, Germany, and other nations for funds for our military adventures in the Persian Gulf, why shouldn't they be forced, at least for one glorious year, to beg for funds from the American people, instead of wielding their usual bludgeon?

The 1990 furlough crisis highlights some suggestive but neglected aspects of common thinking about the budget. In the first place, all parties are talking about "fair sharing of the pain," of the "necessity to inflict pain," etc. How come that government, and only government, is regularly associated with a systematic infliction of pain?

In contemplating the activities of Sony or Proctor and Gamble or countless other private firms, do we ask ourselves how much pain they propose to inflict upon us in the coming year? Why is it that government, and only government, is regularly coupled with pain: like ham-and-eggs, or . . . death-and-taxes? Perhaps we should begin to ask ourselves why government and pain are Gemini twins, and whether we really need an institution that consists of a massive engine for the imposition and administration of pain and suffering. Is there no better way to run our affairs?

Another curious note: it is now the accepted orthodoxy of our liberal—and centrist—Establishment that taxes must be raised, regardless of where we are in the business cycle. So strong is this article of faith that the fact that we are already in a recession (and intelligent observers do not have to wait for the National Bureau of Economic Research to tell us that retroactively) seems to make no dent whatever in the thirst for higher taxes.

And yet there is no school of economic thought—be it New Classical, Keynesian, monetarist, or Austrian that advocates raising taxes in a recession. Indeed, both Keynesians and Austrians would advocate cutting taxes in a recession, albeit for different reasons.

So whence this fanatical devotion to higher taxes? The liberal-centrists profess its source to be deep worry about the federal deficit. But since these very same people, not too long ago, scoffed at worry about the deficit as impossibly Neanderthal and reactionary, and since right now these same people brusquely dismiss any call for lower government spending as *ipso facto* absurd, one suspects a not very cleverly hidden agenda at work.

Namely: a love for higher taxes and for higher government spending for their own sake, or, rather, for the sake of expanding statism and collectivism as contrasted with the private sector.

There is one way we can put our hypothesis to the test: shouldn't these newfound worriers about the deficit delight in our modest proposal one year with no deficit at all, one year with no infliction of pain whatever? Wanna bet? ▶

65

THE BALANCED-BUDGET AMENDMENT HOAX

It is a hallmark of the triumph of image over substance in modern society that an administration which has submitted to Congress budgets with the biggest deficits in American history should propose as a cure-all a constitutional amendment mandating a balanced budget. Apart from the high irony of such a proposal from such a source, the amendment-mongers don't

---

First published in October 1987.

seem to realize that the same pressures of the democratic process that have led to permanent and growing deficits will also be at work on the courts that have acquired the exclusive power to interpret the Constitution. The federal courts are appointed by the executive and confirmed by the legislature, and are therefore part and parcel of the government structure.

Apart from these general strictures on rewriting the Constitution as a panacea for our ills, the various proposed balanced-budget amendments suffer from many deep flaws in themselves. The major defect is that they only require a balance of the future *estimated* budget, and not of the actual budget at the end of a given fiscal year. As we all should know by this time, economists and politicians are expert at submitting glittering projected future budgets that have only the foggiest relation to the actual reality of the future year. It will be duck soup for Congress to estimate a future balance; not so easy, however, to actually balance it. At the very least, any amendment should require the actual balancing of the budget at the end of each particular year.

Second, balancing the budget by increasing taxes is like curing influenza by shooting the patient; the cure is worse than the disease. Dimly recognizing this fact, most of the amendment proposals include a clause to limit federal taxation. But unfortunately, they do so by imposing a limit on revenues as a percentage of the national income or gross national product. It is absurd to include such a concept as "national income" in the fundamental law of the land; there is no such real entity, but only a statistical artifact, and an artifact that can and does wobble according to the political breeze. It is all too easy to include or exclude an enormous amount from this concept.

A third flaw highlights again the problem of treating "the budget" as a constitutional entity. As a means of making the deficit look less bleak, there has been an increasing tendency for the government to spend money on "off-budget" items that simply don't get included in official expenses, and therefore don't get added to the deficit. Any balanced-budget amendment would provide a field day for this kind of mass trickery on the American public.

We must here note a disturbing current tendency for "born again" prodeficit economists in conservative ranks to propose that "capital" items be excluded from the federal budget altogether. This theory is based on an analogy with private firms and their "capital" versus "operating" budgets. One would think that allegedly free-market economists would not have the effrontery to apply this to government. Get this adopted, and the government could happily throw away money on any boondoggle, no matter how absurd, so long as they could call it an "investment in the future." Here is a loophole in the balanced-budget amendment that would make any politician's day!

A fourth problem is that the various proposals make it all too easy for Congress to override the amendment. Suppose Congress or the president violate the amendment. What then? Would the Supreme Court have the power to call the federal marshals and lock up the whole crew? To ask that question is to answer it. (Of course, by making the budget balance *prospective* instead of real, this problem would not even arise, since it would be almost impossible to violate the amendment at all.)

But isn't half a loaf better than none? Isn't it better to have an imperfect amendment than none at all? Half a loaf is indeed better than none, but *even worse* than no loaf is an elaborate camouflage system that fools the public into thinking that a loaf exists where there is really none at all. Or, to mix our metaphors, that the naked Emperor is really wearing clothes.

We now see the role of the balanced budget amendment in the minds of many if not most of its supporters. The purpose is not actually to balance the budget, for that would involve massive spending cuts that the Establishment, "conservative" or liberal, is not willing to contemplate.

The purpose is to continue deficits while deluding the public into thinking that the budget is, or will soon be, balanced. In that way, the public's slipping confidence in the dollar will be shored up. Thus, the balanced-budget amendment turns out to be the fiscal counterpart of the supply-siders' notorious proposal for a phony gold standard. In that scheme, the public would not be able to redeem its dollars in gold coin, the Fed would continue to manipulate and inflate, but all the while this inflationist policy would now be cloaked in the confidence-building mantle of gold.

In both plans, we would be dazzled by the shadow, the rhetoric of sound policy, while the same old program of cheap money and huge deficits would proceed unchecked. In both cases, the dominant ideology seems to be that of P.T. Barnum: "There's a sucker born every minute." ▶

Economic Ups and Downs

66

THE NATIONAL BUREAU AND BUSINESS CYCLES

Not only is there confusion about whether or not a recession is imminent, but some economists think that we're already *in* one (1988). Thus, Richard W. Rahn, chief economist for the U.S. Chamber of Commerce, recently declared: "The economic slowdown is not coming: it's here, and soon it will be gone." Not knowing whether or not we're in a recession is not as silly as it sounds. It takes a while for data to come in, and then to figure out if a decline is a mere glitch or if it constitutes a new trend. But the natural confusion is compounded by the thrall in which virtually all economists, statisticians, and financial writers have been held by the National Bureau of Economic Research.

Everyone waits for the National Bureau to speak; when the oracle finally makes its pronouncement, it is accepted without question. Thus, in 1966, the economy slowed down and receded to such an extent that I, for one, concluded that we were in a recession. But no, GNP had not declined quite long enough to meet the Bureau's definition of a recession, and that, unfortunately, was that. And since we were not in what the Bureau called a "recession," we by definition continued to be in a "boom." The reason is that, by the Bureau's peculiar and arbitrary standards and methods, the economy *cannot* be just sort of

---

First published in June 1988.

lolling along, in neither a boom nor a recession. It *has* to be in one or the other.

To say that the Bureau is fallible should go without saying; but instead, its pronouncements are taken as divine writ. Why is that? Precisely because the Bureau was cleverly designed, and so proclaimed, to be an allegedly value-free, purely "scientific" institution.

The Bureau is a private institution, supported by a large group of associations and institutions, business and union groups, banks, foundations, and scholarly associations, which confer upon it an almost painful respectability. Its numerous books and monographs are very long on statistics, short on text or interpretation. Its proclaimed methodology is Baconian: that is, it trumpets the claim that it *has no* theories, that it collects myriads of facts and statistics, and that its cautiously worded conclusions arise solely, Phoenix-like, out of the data themselves. Hence, its conclusions are accepted as unquestioned holy "scientific" writ.

And yet, despite its proclamations, the National Bureau's procedures themselves necessarily manipulate the data to arrive at conclusions. And these procedures are *not* free of theory, indeed they rest on faulty and questionable theoretical assumptions. Hence, the conclusions, far from being strictly "scientific," are skewed and misshaped to the extent that they are determined by the procedures themselves.

Specifically, the Bureau selects "reference cycles," of the general economy, and then examines "specific cycles" of particular prices, production, etc. and compares these with the reference cycles. Unfortunately, all depends on the Bureau's dating theory, that is, it picks out only the trough and peak months, first for the general cycles, and then for each specific cycle. But suppose, as in many cases, the curve is flat, or there are several peaks or troughs close to each other.

In these cases, the Bureau arbitrarily takes the last month of the plateau, or the multi-peak or trough period, and calls *that* the peak or trough month. There is no earthly economic reason for this; why not take the whole period as a peak or trough period, or average the data, or whatever? Instead, the Bureau takes *only* the last month and calls that the peak or trough, and then compounds that error by arbitrarily squeezing the distance between the designated "peak month" and "trough month" into three equal parts, and assuming that everything in between peak and trough is a straight line of expansion or contraction, boom or bust.

In other words, in the real world, any given time series, say copper prices, or housing starts in California, might have dawdled near the trough, gone quickly upward, and stayed at a plateau or multi-peak for many months. But on the Procrustean rack of National Bureau doctrine, the activity is squeezed into a single, one-month trough; a straight line expansion, divided into three parts by time; reaching a single-month peak; and then going down in a similar linear, jagged-line contraction. In short, National Bureau methods inevitably force the economy to look falsely like a series of jagged, saw-toothed, straight lines upward and downward. The triumphant conclusion that "life is a series of sawtooth lines" is imposed by the way the Bureau massages the data in the first place.

That massaging is bad enough. But then the Bureau compounds the error by averaging all the specific cycles, its leads and lags, etc. as far as the data will go back, say from the 1860s to the 1980s. It is from that averaging that the Bureau has developed its indices of "leading . . . coincident," and "lagging" indicators, the first of which are supposed to (but not very successfully) forecast the future.

The problem with this averaging of cycle data over the decades is that it assumes a "homogeneous population," that is, it assumes that all these cycles, say for copper prices or housing starts in California, are the same thing, and operate in the same context over all these decades. But that is a whopping assumption; history means change, and it is absurd to assume that the underlying population of all this data remains constant and unchanging, and therefore can be averaged meaningfully.

When the National Bureau set forth this methodology in Arthur F. Burns and Wesley C. Mitchell, *Measuring Business Cycles* (National Bureau of Economic Research, 1946), it was correctly criticized by a distinguished econometrician for being "Measurement without Theory" in the *Journal of Political Economy*, but still it quickly swept the board to achieve oracular status.

Particularly irritating were the claims of the Bureau that those of us who held definite business cycle theories were partial and arbitrary, whereas the Bureau spoke only from the facts of hard, empirical reality. Yet the Bureau has had far less respect for empirical reality than have allegedly "anti-empirical" Austrians. Austrians realize that empirical reality is unique, particularly raw statistical data. Let that data be massaged, averaged, seasonals taken out, etc. and then the data necessarily falsify reality. Their Baconian methodology has not saved the Bureau from this trap; it has only succeeded in blinding them to the ways that they have been manipulating data arbitrarily. ▶

67
INFLATIONARY RECESSION, ONCE MORE

I am by no means a complete "contrarian," but I have one contrarian index to offer as a sound "leading indicator" of recession: every time Establishment economists and financial writers trumpet the existence of a brave new world of permanent boom with no more recessions, I know that a big recession is just around the corner.

It never fails. During the late 1920s the Establishment, led by proto-Friedmanite economist Irving Fisher, proclaimed a "New Era," an era of permanent boom with no more depressions—all

---

First published in January 1991.

because of the wise fine-tuning of that wonderful new institution, the Federal Reserve System. And then came 1929.

During the 1960s we were assured by the Keynesian Establishment that business cycles were a relic of the bygone Bad Old Days of laissez-faire: that wise fine-tuning by Keynesian officials would insure a world of continuous full employment without inflation. So sure of themselves were Establishment economists that "Business Cycle" courses in graduate school were abolished.

Why linger in the antiquities of a pre-modern world? Instead, they were replaced by courses in "Macroeconomics" and "Economic Growth." And then bingo! came not only the deep recessions, but the seemingly impossible phenomenon of inflationary recessions: recessions and price inflation at the same time, first in 1973–75, and then the two-humped recession of 1980–82, the biggest and steepest recession since the Great Depression. (In the old days, such major recessions would have routinely been called "depressions," but therapy-by-semantics has taken over, and the word "depression" has been effectively outlawed as too . . . depressing.)

And now, in the middle and late 1980s, the Reaganite Establishment began to assure us that, once again, a new economic era had arrived, that the miracle of the Reagan tax cuts (actually non-existent) had, along with a more global and technologically sophisticated technology, assured us that there would never be any more recessions, except perhaps some painless rolling readjustments in specific industries or regions.

It was time for another Big One, and sure enough, here we are. Not only has the Establishment forgotten about recessions, but in particular they totally forgot that postwar recessions have been inflationary. Combining the worst of both worlds, unemployment, bankruptcies, and declines of activity have been accompanied by steep increases in the cost of living. A half-century of Keynesian fine-tuning (from which we still suffer, despite the Reaganaut label) has not cured inflation or recessions; it has only accomplished the feat of bringing us both at the same time.

Everyone is afraid to use his judgment on whether we are in a recession; it has become the custom of everyone to await breathlessly the pronouncement of the National Bureau of Economic Research (NBER), a much revered private institution which has established a Dating Committee of a handful of experts, who sift the data to figure out when, if ever, a recession has begun. The problem is that it takes many months into a recession for the NBER to make up its mind: by the time it pronounces that we're in a recession, it is almost over. Thus, the steep recession that started in November 1973 was only pronounced a recession a year later; but six months after that, by March 1975, we were on the way to recovery. Most recessions are over in a year or year and a half. Of course, maybe that's the point: for the Establishment to lull us all to sleep until the recession is over.

The reason why it takes the NBER such a long time to make up its mind, is because it feels that it has to get the precise month of the onset of the recession absolutely right; and the reason it suffers from this precise month fetish (which, in all reason and common sense, doesn't make a heck of a lot of difference) is because the entire deeply flawed NBER approach to business cycles depends on getting the "reference month" down precisely, and then basing all of its averages, and leads and lags, on that particular month. To date the recession one or two months either way would mess up all the calculations based on the NBER paradigm. And that, of course, comes first, way before trying to figure out what is going on and getting the knowledge to the public as quickly as possible.

Looking at the housing market, unemployment, debt liquidation, and many other factors in 1988, I am willing to state flatly that we are in another inflationary recession. What does this mean? It is heartwarming to see some economists welcoming the recession as having an important cleansing effect on malinvestment and unsound debt, paving the way for more rapid and more sustainable economic growth. Thus, Victor Zarnowitz of the University of Chicago states that "it may be healthier for the economy to endure an occasional recession . . . than to grow sluggishly for a prolonged period," and David A. Poole, economist of Van Eck Management Corp., warns that there shouldn't be a recovery too soon, presumably stimulated by government, for then "the recessionary cleansing process will not have had time to work." Welcome to Austrian Economics!

But how is the current Establishment (the Bush administration center plus Democratic left-liberalism) proposing to deal with this recession? Remarkably, by violating every tenet of every school of thought known to economics: by steeply raising taxes! Every school: Austrian, Keynesian, monetarist, or classical, would react in horror to such a plan, which obviously worsens a recession by lowering saving and investment, and productive (as opposed to parasitic and wasteful government) consumption. Raising taxes does nothing to help the inflation, and does a lot to make the recession more severe; and it aggravates the deadweight burden of government on the economy.

But wouldn't raising taxes cure the budget deficit? No, it would only give government an excuse (as if they needed one!) to increase the burden of government spending still further. The one thing worse than a deficit, furthermore, is higher taxes; increasing taxes will only bring us more of both.

Can't the government do anything to alleviate our current inflationary recession? Yes, it can, and quickly. (Never say that Austrians can't come up with positive, even short-run, suggestions for government policy.)

First, to stop the inflationary part of current crisis, the Federal Reserve can stop, permanently, all further purchase of any assets, or lowering of reserve ratios. This will stop all future inflationary credit expansion. Second, it can cut all taxes drastically: sales, excise, capital gains, medicare, social security, and income (for upper, middle, and lower incomes). Third, it can cut government spending, everywhere, even more drastically:

thus cutting the deficit as well as all its other benefits. And that's for openers. You think Newt Gingrich is tough? ▶

68
DEFLATION, FREE OR COMPULSORY

Few occurrences have been more dreaded and reviled in the history of economic thought than deflation. Even as perceptive a hard-money theorist as Ricardo was unduly leery of deflation, and a positive phobia about falling prices has been central to both Keynesian and monetarist thought.

Both the inflationary spending and credit prescriptions of Irving Fisher and the early Chicago School, and the famed Friedmanite "rule" of fixed rates of money growth, stemmed from a fervid desire to keep prices from falling, at least in the long run.

It is precisely because free markets and the pure gold standard lead inevitably to falling prices that monetarists and Keynesians alike call for fiat money. Yet, curiously, while free or voluntary deflation has been invariably treated with horror, there is general acclaim for the draconian, or compulsory, deflationary measures adopted recently—especially in Brazil and the Soviet Union—in attempts to reverse severe inflation.

But first, some clarity is needed in our age of semantic obfuscation in monetary matters. "Deflation" is usually defined as generally falling prices, yet it can also be defined as a decline in the money supply which, of course, will also tend to lower prices. It is particularly important to distinguish between changes in prices or the money supply that arise from voluntary changes in people's values or actions on the free market; as against deliberate changes in the money supply imposed by governmental coercion.

First published in April 1991.

Price deflation on the free market has been a particular victim of deflation-phobia, blamed for depression, contraction in business activity, and unemployment. There are three possible causes for such deflation. In the first place, increased productivity and supply of goods will tend to lower prices on the free market. And this indeed is the general record of the Industrial Revolution in the West since the mid-eighteenth century.

But rather than a problem to be dreaded and combatted, falling prices through increased production is a wonderful long-run tendency of untrammelled capitalism. The trend of the Industrial Revolution in the West was falling prices, which spread an increased standard of living to every person; falling costs, which maintained general profitability of business; and stable monetary wage rates—which reflected steadily increasing real wages in terms of purchasing power.

This is a process to be hailed and welcomed rather than to be stamped out. Unfortunately, the inflationary fiat money world since World War II has made us forget this home truth, and inured us to a dangerously inflationary economic horizon.

A second cause of price deflation in a free economy is in response to a general desire to "hoard" money which causes people's stock of cash balances to have higher real value in terms of purchasing power. Even economists who accept the legitimacy of the first type of deflation react with horror to the second, and call for government to print money rapidly to prevent it.

But what's wrong with people desiring higher real cash balances, and why should this desire of consumers on the free market be thwarted while others are satisfied? The market, with its perceptive entrepreneurs and free price system, is precisely geared to allow rapid adjustments to any changes in consumer valuations.

Any "unemployment" of resources results from a failure of people to adjust to the new conditions, by insisting on excessively high real prices or wage rates. Such failures will be quickly corrected if the market is allowed freedom to adapt—

that is, if government and unions do not intervene to delay and cripple the adjustment process.

A third form of market-driven price deflation stems from a contraction of bank credit during recessions or bank runs. Even economists who accept the first and second types of deflation balk at this one, indicting the process as being monetary and external to the market.

But they overlook a key point: that contraction of bank credit is always a healthy reaction to previous inflationary bank credit intervention in the market. Contractionary calls upon the banks to redeem their swollen liabilities in cash is precisely the way in which the market and consumers can reassert control over the banking system and force it to become sound and non-inflationary. A market-driven credit contraction speeds up the recovery process and helps to wash out unsound loans and unsound banks.

Ironically enough, the only deflation that is unhelpful and destructive generally receives favorable press: compulsory monetary contraction by the government. Thus, when "free market" advocate Collor de Mello became president of Brazil in March 1990, he immediately and without warning blocked access to most bank accounts, preventing their owners from redeeming or using them, thereby suddenly deflating the money supply by 80 percent.

This act was generally praised as a heroic measure reflecting "strong" leadership, but what it did was to deliver the Brazilian economy the second blow of a horrible one-two punch. After governmental expansion of money and credit had driven prices into severe hyperinflation, the government now imposed further ruin by preventing people from using their own money. Thus, the Brazilian government imposed a double destruction of property rights, the second one in the name of the free market and "of combatting inflation."

In truth, price inflation is not a disease to be combatted by government; it is only necessary for the government to cease inflating the money supply. That, of course, all governments are reluctant to do, including Collor de Mello's. Not only did his sudden blow bring about a deep recession, but the price inflation rate, which had fallen sharply to 8 percent per month by May 1990, started creeping up again.

Finally, in the month of December, the Brazilian government quickly expanded the money supply by 58 percent, driving price inflation up to 20 percent per month. By the end of January, the only response the "free market" government could think of was to impose a futile and disastrous price and wage freeze.

In the Soviet Union, President Gorbachev, perhaps imitating the Brazilian failure, similarly decided to combat the "ruble overhang" by suddenly withdrawing large-ruble notes from circulation and rendering most of them worthless. This severe and sudden 33 percent monetary deflation was accompanied by a promise to stamp out the "black market," i.e., the market, which had until then been the only Soviet institution working and keeping the Soviet people from mass starvation.

But the black marketeers had long since gotten out of rubles and into dollars and gold, so that Gorby's meat axe fell largely on the average Soviet citizen, who had managed to work hard and save from his meager earnings. The only slightly redeeming feature of this act is that at least it was not done in the name of privatization and the free market; instead, it was part and parcel of Gorbachev's recent shift back to statism and central control.

What Gorbachev should have done was not worry about the rubles in the hands of the public, but pay attention to the swarm of new rubles he keeps adding to the Soviet economy. The prognosis is even gloomier for the Soviet future if we consider the response of a leading allegedly free-market reformer, Nicholas Petrakov, until recently Gorbachev's personal economic adviser. Asserting that Gorbachev's brutal action was "sensible," Petrakov plaintively added that "if, in the future, we go on just printing more money everything will just go back to square one." And why should anyone think this will not happen? ▶

69
BUSH AND THE RECESSION

Unfortunately, John Maynard Keynes, the disastrous and discredited spokesman and inspiration for the macroeconomics of virtually the entire world since the 1930s (and that includes the Western World, the Third World, the Gorbachev era, as well as the Nazi economic system), still lives. President Bush's reaction to this grim recession has been Keynesian through and through not surprising, since his economic advisers are Keynesian to the core.

Since Keynesians are perpetual trumpeters for inflationary credit expansion, they of course do not talk about the basic cause of every recession; previous excesses of inflationary bank credit, stimulated and controlled by the central bank—in the U.S., the Federal Reserve system. To Keynesians, recessions come about via a sudden collapse in spending—by consumers and by investors. This collapse, according to Keynesians, comes about because of a decline in what Keynes called "animal spirits": people become worried, depressed, apprehensive about the future, so they invest, borrow, and spend less.

The Keynesian remedy to this "market failure" brought about by private citizens being irrational worry-warts, is provided by good old government, the benevolent Mr. Fixit. When guided by wise and coolheaded Keynesian economists, government is able, as a judicious seacaptain at the helm, to compensate for the foolish whims of the public and to steer the economy on a proper and rational course.

First published in February 1992.

There are, then, two anti-recession weapons available to government in the Keynesian schema. One is to spend a lot more money, particularly by incurring large-scale deficits. The problem with this weapon, as we all know far too well, is that government deficits are now permanently and increasingly stratospheric, in good times as well as bad. Current estimates for the federal deficit, which almost always prove too low, are approaching the annual rate of $500 billion (especially if we eliminate the phony accounting "surplus" of $50 billion in the Social Security account).

If increasing the deficit further is no longer a convincing tool of government, the only thing left is to try to stimulate *private* spending. And the principal way to do *that* is for the government to soft-soap the public, to treat the public as if it were a whiny kid, that is: to stimulate its confidence that things are really fine and getting better so that the public will open its purses and wallets and borrow and spend more.

In other words, to lie to the public "for its own good." Except that many of us are convinced that it's really lying for the good of the *politicians*, so that the deluded public will continue to have confidence in them. Hence all the disgraceful gyrations of the Bush administration: the year-long claim that we weren't in a recession, then the idea that we had been in it but were now out, then the soft-soap about a "weak recovery," then the non-sense about "double-dip" recession, and all the rest. Only when an aroused public hit him in the face did the President acknowledge that there's a real problem, and that maybe something should be done about it.

But what to do, within the Keynesian framework? First, the Fed drove down interest rates, expecting that now people would borrow and spend. But no one feels like lending and borrowing in recessions, and so nothing much happened, except that short-term Treasury securities got cheaper to buy—not very useful for the private economy. But, darn it, credit card rates stayed high, so Bush got the idea of talking down credit card rates, stimulating more consumers to borrow.

The resulting fiasco is well-known. Senator Al D'Amato (R-NY), ever the eager beaver, figured that forcing rates down is more effective than talking them down, and so Congress only just missed passing this disaster by a vigorous protest of the banks and a mini-crash in the stock market bringing it to its senses. Outgoing chief-of-staff John Sununu, as ever attentive to the actions of "this President," tried to justify Bush's jawboning as correct, asserting that Congress's error was to try coercion.

But Bush's idea of talking credit card rates down was only slightly less idiotic than forcing them down. The point is that prices on the market, including interest rates, are not set arbitrarily, or according to the good or bad will of the sellers or lenders. Prices are set according to the market forces of supply and demand.

Credit card rates did not stay high because bankers decided to put the screws to this particular group of borrowers. The basic reason for credit card rates staying high is because the public—in its capacity as borrowers, *not* in its capacity as economic pundits—doesn't care that much about these rates. Consumers are not credit-card rate sensitive.

Why? Because basically there are two kinds of credit-card users. One is the sober, responsible types who pay off their credit cards each month, and for whom interest charges are simply not important. The other group is the more live-it-up types such as myself, who tend to borrow up to the limit on their cards. But for them, interest rates are not that important either: because in order to take advantage of low-rate cards (and there are such around the country), they would have to pay off existing cards first—a slow process at best.

There was another gaping fallacy in the Bush-D'Amato attitude, which the bankers quickly set them straight about. Interest rates are not the only part of the credit-card package. There is also the *quality* of the credit: the ease of getting the card, the requirements for getting it and keeping it, as well as the annual fee, etc. As the banks pointed out, at a 14 instead of a 19 percent rate, far fewer people are going to be granted credit cards. Pathetically, the only positive thing that President Bush can think of to speed the recovery is to spend money *faster*, that is: to step up government spending, and hence the deficit, early in the year, presumably to be offset later by a fall in its rate of spending.

What about tax cuts? Here the Bush administration is trapped in the current Keynesian view that, the deficits already being too high, every tax cut must be balanced by a tax increase somewhere else: i.e., be "revenue neutral." Hence, the administration feels limited to the correct but picayune call for a cut in the capital gains tax, since this presumably will be made up by a supply-side increase to keep total revenue constant.

What is needed is the courage to bust out of this entire fallacious and debilitating Keynesian paradigm. Massive tax cuts, especially in the income tax are needed (a) to reduce the parasitic and antiproductive burden of government on the taxpayer, and (b) to encourage the public to spend and especially to save more, because only through increased private savings will there come greater productive investment.

Moreover, the increased saving will speed recovery by validating some of the shaky and savings-starved investments of the previous boom. First of all, massive tax cuts may force the government to reduce its own swollen spending, and thereby reduce the burden of government on the system. And second, if this means that total government revenue is lower, *so much the better*. The burden of tax-rates is twofold: rates that are high and cripple savings and investment activity; and revenues that are high and siphon off money from the productive private sector into wasteful government boondoggles. The trouble with the supply-siders is that they ignore the second burden, and hence fall into the Keynesian-Bush "revenue-neutral" trap.

And finally, if the Bush administration is so worried about the deficit, it should do its part by proposing drastic cuts in government spending, and justify it to the public by showing that government spending is not helpful to a prosperous economy but precisely the opposite. Then, if Congress rejects this proposition, and keeps increasing spending, the Administration could put the onus for prolonging the recession squarely upon Congress. But of course it can't do so, because that would mean a fundamental break with the Keynesian doctrine that has formed the paradigm for the world's macroeconomics for the past half-century.

We will never break out of our economic stagnation or our boom-bust cycles and achieve permanent prosperity until we have repudiated Keynes as thoroughly and as intensely as the peoples of Eastern Europe and the Soviet Union have repudiated Marx and Lenin. The real way to achieve freedom and prosperity is to hurl all three of these icons of the twentieth century into the dustbin of history. ▶

70
LESSONS OF THE RECESSION

It's official! Long after everyone in America knew that we were in a severe recession, the private but semi-official and incredibly venerated National Bureau of Economic Research has finally made its long-awaited pronouncement: we've been in a recession ever since last summer. Well! Here is an instructive example of the reason why the economics profession, once revered as a seer and scientific guide to wealth prosperity, has been sinking rapidly in the esteem of the American public. It couldn't have happened to a more deserving group. The current recession, indeed, has already brought us several valuable lessons:

Lesson # 1: You don't need an economist. . . . One of the favorite slogans of the 1960s New Left was: "You don't need a weatherman to tell you how the wind is blowing." Similarly, it

---

First published in July 1991.

is all too clear that you don't need an economist to tell you whether you've been in a recession. So how is it that the macro-mavens not only can't forecast what will happen next, they can't even tell us where we are, and can barely tell us where we've been? To give them their due, I am pretty sure that Professors Hall, Zarnowitz, and the other distinguished solons of the famed Dating Committee of the National Bureau have known we've been in a recession for quite a while, maybe even since the knowledge percolated to the general public.

The problem is that the Bureau is trapped in its own methodology, the very methodology of Baconian empiricism, meticulous data-gathering and pseudo-science that has brought it inordinate prestige from the economics profession.

For the Bureau's entire approach to business cycles for the past five decades has depended on dating the precise month of each cyclical turning point, peak and trough. It was therefore not enough to say, last fall, that "we entered a recession this summer." That would have been enough for common-sense, or for Austrians, but even one month off the precise date would have done irreparable damage to the plethora of statistical manipulations—the averages, reference points, leads, lags, and indicators—that constitute the analytic machinery, and hence the "science," of the National Bureau. If you want to know whether we're in a recession, the last people to approach is the organized economics profession.

Of course, the general public might be good at spotting where we are at, but they are considerably poorer at causal analysis, or at figuring out how to get out of economic trouble. But then again, the economics profession is not so great at that either.

Lesson #2: There ain't no such thing as a "new era." Every time there is a long boom, by the final years of that boom, the press, the economics profession, and financial writers are rife with the pronouncement that recessions are a thing of the past, and that deep structural changes in the economy, or in knowledge among economists, have brought about a "new era." The bad old days of recessions are over. We heard that first in the 1920s, and the culmination of that first new era was 1929; we heard it again in the 1960s, which led to the first major inflationary recession of the early 1970s; and we heard it most recently in the later 1980s. In fact, the best leading indicator of imminent deep recession is not the indices of the National Bureau; it is the burgeoning of the idea that recessions are a thing of the past.

More precisely, recessions will be around to plague us so long as there are bouts of inflationary credit expansion which bring them into being.

Lesson #3: You don't need an inventory boom to have a recession. For months into the current recession, numerous pundits proclaimed that we couldn't be in a recession because business had not piled up excessive inventories. Sorry. It made no difference, since malinvestments brought about by inflationary bank credit don't necessarily have to take place in inventory form. As often happens in economic theory, a contingent symptom was mislabeled as an essential cause.

Unlike the above, other lessons of the current recession are not nearly as obvious. One is:

Lesson #4: Debt is not the crucial problem. Heavy private debt was a conspicuous feature of the boom of the 1980s, with much of the publicity focused on the floating of high-yield ("junk") bonds for buyouts and takeovers. Debt *per se*, however, is not a grave economic problem.

When I purchase a corporate bond I am channeling savings into investment much the same way as when I purchase stock equity. Neither way is particularly unsound. If a firm or corporation floats too much debt as compared to equity, that is a miscalculation of its existing owners or managers, and not a problem for the economy at large. The worst that can happen is that, if indebtedness is too great, the creditors will take over from existing management and install a more efficient set of managers. Creditors, as well as stockholders, in short, are entrepreneurs.

The problem, therefore, is not debt but credit, and not all credit but bank credit financed by inflationary expansion of bank money rather than by the genuine savings of either shareholders or creditors. The problem in other words, is not debt but loans generated by fractional-reserve banking.

Lesson #5: Don't worry about the Fed "pushing on a string." Hard money adherents are a tiny fraction in the economics profession; but there are a large number of them in the investment newsletter business. For decades, these writers have been split into two warring camps: the "inflationists" versus the "deflationists." These terms are used not in the sense of advocating policy, but in predicting future events.

"Inflationists," of whom the present writer is one, have been maintaining that the Fed, having been freed of all restraints of the gold standard and committed to not allowing the supposed horrors of deflation, will pump enough money into the banking system to prevent money and price deflation from ever taking place.

"Deflationists," on the other hand, claim that because of excessive credit and debt, the Fed has reached the point where it cannot control the money supply, where Fed additions to bank reserves cannot lead to banks expanding credit and the money supply. In common financial parlance, the Fed would be "pushing on a string." Therefore, say the deflationists, we are in for an imminent, massive, and inevitable deflation of debt, money, and prices.

One would think that three decades of making such predictions that have never come true would faze the deflationists somewhat, but no, at the first sign of trouble, especially of a recession, the deflationists are invariably back, predicting imminent deflationary doom. For the last part of 1990, the money supply was flat, and the deflationists were sure that their day had come at last. Credit had been so excessive, they claimed, that businesses could no longer be induced to borrow, no matter how low the interest rate is pushed.

What deflationists always overlook is that, even in the unlikely event that banks could not stimulate further loans, they can always use their reserves to purchase securities, and thereby push money out into the economy. The key is whether or not the banks pile up excess reserves, failing to expand credit up to the limit allowed by legal reserves. The crucial point is that never have the banks done so, in 1990 or at any other time, apart from the single exception of the 1930s. (The difference was that not only were we in a severe depression in the 1930s, but that interest rates had been driven down to near zero, so that the banks were virtually losing nothing by not expanding credit up to their maximum limit.) The conclusion must be that the Fed pushes with a stick, not a string.

Early this year, moreover, the money supply began to spurt upward once again, putting an end, at least for the time being, to deflationist warnings and speculations.

Lesson #6: The banks might collapse. Oddly enough there is a possible deflation scenario, but not one in which the deflationists have ever expressed interest. There has been, in the last few years, a vital, and necessarily permanent, sea-change in American opinion. It is permanent because it entails a loss of American innocence. The American public, ever since 1933, had bought, hook, line and sinker, the propaganda of all Establishment economists, from Keynesians to Friedmanites, that the banking system is safe, SAFE, because of federal deposit insurance.

The collapse and destruction of the savings and loan banks, despite their "deposit insurance" by the federal government, has ended the insurance myth forevermore, and called into question the soundness of the last refuge of deposit insurance, the FDIC. It is now widely known that the FDIC simply doesn't have the money to insure all those deposits, and that in fact it is heading rapidly toward bankruptcy.

Conventional wisdom now holds that the FDIC will be shored up by taxpayer bailout, and that it will be saved. But no matter: the knowledge that the commercial banks might fail has been tucked away by every American for future reference. Even if the public can be babied along, and the FDIC patched up for this recession, they can always remember this fact at some future crisis, and then the whole fractional-reserve house of cards will come tumbling down in a giant, cleansing bank run. To offset such a run, no taxpayer bailout would suffice.

But wouldn't that be deflationary? Almost, but not quite. Because the banks could still be saved by a massive, hyper-inflationary printing of money by the Fed, and who would bet against such emergency rescue?

Lesson #7: There is no "Kondratieff cycle," no way, no how. There is among many people, even including some of the better hard-money investment newsletter writers, an inexplicable devotion to the idea of an inevitable 54-year "Kondratieff cycle" of expansion and contraction. It is universally agreed that the last Kondratieff trough was in 1940. Since 51 years have elapsed since that trough, and we are still waiting for the peak, it should be starkly clear that such a cycle does not exist.

Most Kondratieffists confidently predicted that the peak would occur in 1974, precisely 54 years after the previous peak, generally accepted as being in 1920. Their joy at the 1974 recession, however, turned sour at the quick recovery. Then they tried to salvage the theory by analogy to the alleged "plateau" of the 1920s, so that the visible peak, or contraction, would occur nine or ten years after the peak, as *1929* succeeded 1920.

The Kondratieffists there fell back on 1984 as the preferred date of the beginning of the deep contraction. Nothing happened, of course; and, now, seven years later, we are in the last gasp of the Kondratieff doctrine. If the current recession does not, as we have maintained, turn into a deep deflationary spiral, and the recession ends, there will simply be no time left for any plausible cycle of anything approaching 54 years. The Kondratieffist practitioners will, of course, never give up, any more than other seers and crystal-ball gazers; but presumably, their market will at last be over. ▶

71
THE RECESSION EXPLAINED

"**I** told you so!" may not be considered polite among Recession friends or acquaintances, but in ideological clashes it is important to remind one and all of your successes, since neither the indifferent nor your enemies are likely to do the job for you.

In the case of Austrian business cycle theory, shouldering this task is particularly important. For not only have our ideological and methodological enemies been all too quick to bury Austrian theory as either (a) hopelessly Neanderthal and reactionary, and/or (b) obsolete in today's world, but also many of our erstwhile friends and adherents have been joining the chorus, maintaining that Austrian theory might have been applicable in the 1930s, or, more radically, only in the 19th century, but that it definitely has no application in the modern economy.

Well, to paraphrase the great philosopher Etienne Gilson on natural law, Austrian cycle theory always survives to bury its enemies. In contrast to conventional wisdom, from Keynesian to monetarist to eclectic, Austrian theory has recently triumphed over its host of detractors in the following ways:

1. The perpetual boom of the '80s. As the 1980s went on, the Conventional Wisdom (CW) trumpeted that recessions were a thing of the dead and unlamented past. Here was a new era, of perpetual prosperity. Wise governmental fiscal and monetary policies, combined with structural changes such as the age of the computer and global capital markets, have made sure that

---

First published in January 1992.

we never have a recession again, that 1981-82 was the Last Recession.

I have long asserted that the best "leading indicator" of a recession is when the CW has started proclaiming the end of the business cycle and perpetual prosperity. Sure enough, here we are, and, as Austrians point out, the bigger and the longer the boom, the greater and deeper will tend to be the recession necessary to wash out the distortions and malinvestment of the inflationary boom, brought on by bank credit expansion.

2. The end of inflation. During the great boom of the '80s, the CW also proclaimed that inflation was a thing of the past. It was over, licked. Again: wise government monetary and fiscal policies, coupled with structural economic changes, and "efficient markets," insured that inflation was finished. And yet, inflation, which never really disappeared, is back in full force, and is even stronger now, in the depths of recession, than it was during most of the boom—a sure sign that not only is inflation still with us, but that it is going to pose a severe and accelerating problem as soon as recovery occurs.

3. (A corollary of one and two.) They forgot about inflationary recession. Inflation has persisted in every post-World War II recession since 1973–74, and indeed really began in the 1957–58 recession, after a couple of years of recovery. Yet everyone—and that means everyone including all wings of Establishment economics, and financial writers and forecasters—forgets all about the new reality of inflationary recession (also called "stagflation"), and writes and talks as if the choice in the coming months is always between inflation or recession.

There is a long-running dispute among Austrian economists on whether market participants can or do learn from experience. Whatever the answer is (and I believe it is "yes"), it becomes increasingly clear that the body of economists and the financial press seem to be incapable of this simple learning experience. Look fellas: every recession is going to be inflationary from now on.

Presumably, the reason for this failure to learn is because it violates the basic theoretical prejudices of both Keynesian and monetarist economists: that either we are experiencing an inflationary boom or we are in a recession, never both. And indeed, no one can truly learn about these matters without a correct theory. But it just so happens that Austrian theory alone predicts and explains why all recessions, precisely in the modern world, will be inflationary. The reason: the scrapping of the gold standard and the shift to fiat money in the 1930s meant that there is no longer any restraint on the government or the Federal Reserve from creating as much money as it wishes—and it always wishes. This act does not eliminate business cycles; in fact, it makes them worse, by adding inflation and rising costs of living on top of recessions, falling asset values, bankruptcies, and unemployment.

4. The average person knows when we're in a recession long before economists do. Establishment economists, mired in their methodology of statistical correlation based on precise dating of cycle peaks and troughs, take a very long time to decide the precise month of the peak—in the current recession, July 1990. It took almost a year after that point before economists deigned to tell us what we already all knew: that we were in a big recession.

5. The average person knows we're in a recession long after the economists have proclaimed "recovery." Here we have a failing among economists far less excusable than methodological error. For hardly were we told, at long last, that we were in a recession, when the Establishment hastened to tell us that recovery was already under way. In a spectacular mistake, Establishment economists, professionally and politically bedded, as any Administration is, to Pollyanna optimism, hastened to assure us that the recession was over by the beginning of the third quarter of 1991.

When it came to forecasting recovery, professional economic caution was shamefully thrown to the winds. Ever since the middle of 1991, the political and economic establishment has been desperately searching for signs of "recovery." "Well, it's there but it's feeble"; "recoveries always begin weakly"; and on and on. Finally, by November, as most indices were clearly getting worse, economists, reluctant to admit their glaring error of the summer, started muttering about a possible "double-dip recession," about the danger of "slipping back into recession," etc. Look, let's face reality, and let the revered Dating Committee of the National Bureau of Economic Research, the semi-official but universally exclaimed gurus of business cycle dating, go hang.

6. Once a recession has taken hold, the government cannot inflate out of it; government can only delay recovery, not hasten it. This is a vital truth of Austrian economics that has been absorbed by virtually no one. Once a recession is underway, Keynesian-monetarist type stimulation: cheap money, accelerating the money supply, etc., can only make things worse. But look at what has happened to such alleged anti-inflation "hawks" as Alan Greenspan and the Cleveland Fed: as soon as the recession took hold, and even though inflation is now worse than it has been in years, they have all thrown over their alleged anti-inflation principles and have been cutting interest rates like mad, trying rashly and vainly to hype the sick horse with another shot of inflationary stimulus.

7. Tax cuts are good in a recession, or any other time. Students of human folly can only stand in wonder at the Keynesian, one of whose traditional proposals was for tax cuts during recession, suddenly adopting a conservative, monetarist stance. During this recession, Keynesians declare that "yes, well, tax cuts are good in theory (?) but they won't help us out of recession, because of inevitable lag in the results of fiscal policy." The complaint is that the cuts will only take effect after a recovery (they hope) has already begun. Well, so what?

Tax cuts are good at any time, especially for the long run. Apart from the business cycle, the American economy has been suffering from stagnation for the past twenty years; since 1973, the American standard of living has been level and even slightly declining. This is a highly worrisome feature of the modern

American economy. One way to remedy this problem is tax cuts, the deeper the better. Keynesian tax cuts were only designed to stimulate consumer spending in recession; Austrian tax cuts are a means of partially loosening the fetters by which the government has been chaining and binding down the private and productive sector of the economy, a crippling effect that has gotten steadily worse in recent years.

But what about the deficit? The deficit is indeed monstrous and out of control, but the one way it should not and cannot be combatted is by raising taxes or keeping them high. Lower taxes would mean that government spending would have to be cut, and government spending cuts are the only sound way to cure deficits. Indeed, Austrian theory is unique in advocating government spending cuts even in a recession as a way to shift social spending from excessive consumption to much needed saving-and-investment. For, contrary to Keynesian myth, government spending is not "investment" at all (a cruel joke), but is wasteful "consumption" spending. The "consumers," in this case, are the politicians and government officials who leech off the productive private sector. ▶

The Fiat Money Plague

72

TAKING MONEY BACK

Money is a crucial command post of any economy, and therefore of any society. Society rests upon a network of voluntary exchanges, also known as the "free-market economy"; these exchanges imply a division of labor in society, in which producers of eggs, nails, horses, lumber, and immaterial services such as teaching, medical care, and concerts, exchange their goods for the goods of others. At each step of the way, every participant in exchange benefits immeasurably, for if everyone were forced to be self-sufficient, those few who managed to survive would be reduced to a pitiful standard of living.

Direct exchange of goods and services, also known as "barter," is hopelessly unproductive beyond the most primitive level, and indeed every "primitive" tribe soon found its way to the discovery of the tremendous benefits of arriving, on the market, at one particularly marketable commodity, one in general demand, to use as a "medium" of "indirect exchange." If a particular commodity is in widespread use as a medium in a society, then that general medium of exchange is called "money."

The money-commodity becomes one term in every single one of the innumerable exchanges in the market economy. I sell my services as a teacher for money; I use that money to buy

First published in *The Freeman*, September and October 1995.

groceries, typewriters, or travel accommodations; and these producers in turn use the money to pay their workers, to buy equipment and inventory, and pay rent for their buildings. Hence the ever-present temptation for one or more groups to seize control of the vital money-supply function.

Many useful goods have been chosen as moneys in human societies. Salt in Africa, sugar in the Caribbean, fish in colonial New England, tobacco in the colonial Chesapeake Bay region, cowrie shells, iron hoes, and many other commodities have been used as moneys. Not only do these moneys serve as media of exchange; they enable individuals and business firms to engage in the "calculation" necessary to any advanced economy. Moneys are traded and reckoned in terms of a currency unit, almost always units of weight. Tobacco, for example, was reckoned in pound weights. Prices of other goods and services could be figured in terms of pounds of tobacco; a certain horse might be worth 80 pounds on the market. A business firm could then calculate its profit or loss for the previous month; it could figure that its income for the past month was 1,000 pounds and its expenditures 800 pounds, netting it a 200 pound profit.

GOLD OR GOVERNMENT PAPER

Throughout history, two commodities have been able to outcompete all other goods and be chosen on the market as money; two precious metals, gold and silver (with copper coming in when one of the other precious metals was not available). Gold and silver abounded in what we can call "moneyable" qualities, qualities that rendered them superior to all other commodities. They are in rare enough supply that their value will be stable, and of high value per unit weight; hence pieces of gold or silver will be easily portable, and usable in day-to-day transactions; they are rare enough too, so that there is little likelihood of sudden discoveries or increases in supply. They are durable so that they can last virtually forever, and so they provide a sage "store of value" for the future. And gold and silver are divisible, so that they can be divided into small pieces without losing their value; unlike diamonds, for example, they are homogeneous, so that one ounce of gold will be of equal value to any other.

The universal and ancient use of gold and silver as moneys was pointed out by the first great monetary theorist, the eminent fourteenth-century French scholastic Jean Buridan, and then in all discussions of money down to money and banking textbooks until the Western governments abolished the gold standard in the early 1930s. Franklin D. Roosevelt joined in this deed by taking the United States off gold in 1933.

There is no aspect of the free-market economy that has suffered more scorn and contempt from "modern" economists, whether frankly statist Keynesians or allegedly "free market" Chicagoites, than has gold. Gold, not long ago hailed as the basic staple and groundwork of any sound monetary system, is now regularly denounced as a "fetish" or, as in the case of Keynes, as a "barbarous relic." Well, gold is indeed a "relic" of barbarism in one sense; no "barbarian" worth his salt would ever have accepted the phony paper and bank credit that we modern sophisticates have been bamboozled into using as money.

But "gold bugs" are not fetishists; we don't fit the standard image of misers running their fingers through their hoard of gold coins while cackling in sinister fashion. The great thing about gold is that it, and only it, is money supplied by the free market, by the people at work. For the stark choice before us always is: gold (or silver), or government. Gold is market money, a commodity which must be supplied by being dug out of the ground and then processed; but government, on the contrary, supplies virtually costless paper money or bank checks out of thin air.

We know, in the first place, that all government operation is wasteful, inefficient, and serves the bureaucrat rather than the consumer. Would we prefer to have shoes produced by competitive private firms on the free market, or by a giant monopoly of the federal government? The function of supplying money could be handled no better by government. But the situation in money is far worse than for shoes or any other commodity. If the government produces shoes, at least they might be worn, even though they might be high-priced, fit badly, and not satisfy consumer wants.

Money is different from all other commodities: other things being equal, more shoes, or more discoveries of oil or copper benefit society, since they help alleviate natural scarcity. But once a commodity is established as a money on the market, no more money at all is needed. Since the only use of money is for exchange and reckoning, more dollars or pounds or marks in circulation cannot confer a social benefit: they will simply dilute the exchange value of every existing dollar or pound or mark. So it is a great boon that gold or silver are scarce and are costly to increase in supply.

But if government manages to establish paper tickets or bank credit as money, as equivalent to gold grams or ounces, then the government, as dominant money-supplier, becomes free to create money costlessly and at will. As a result, this "inflation" of the money supply destroys the value of the dollar or pound, drives up prices, cripples economic calculation, and hobbles and seriously damages the workings of the market economy.

The natural tendency of government, once in charge of money, is to inflate and to destroy the value of the currency. To understand this truth, we must examine the nature of government and of the creation of money. Throughout history, governments have been chronically short of revenue. The reason should be clear: unlike you and I, governments do not produce useful goods and services which they can sell on the market; governments, rather than producing and selling services, live parasitically off the market and off society. Unlike every other person and institution in society, government obtains its revenue from coercion, from taxation. In older and saner times, indeed, the King was able to obtain sufficient revenue from the products of his own private lands and forests, as well as through highway tolls. For the State to achieve regularized, peacetime taxation was a struggle of centuries. And even after taxation was established, the kings realized that they could not easily impose new taxes or higher rates on old levies; if they did so, revolution was very apt to break out.

CONTROLLING THE MONEY SUPPLY

If taxation is permanently short of the style of expenditures desired by the State, how can it make up the difference? By getting control of the money supply, or, to put it bluntly, by counterfeiting. On the market economy, we can only obtain good money by selling a good or service in exchange for gold, or by receiving a gift; the only other way to get money is to engage in the costly process of digging gold out of the ground. The counterfeiter, on the other hand, is a thief who attempts to profit by forgery, e.g., by painting a piece of brass to look like a gold coin. If his counterfeit is detected immediately, he does no real harm, but to the extent his counterfeit goes undetected, the counterfeiter is able to steal not only from the producers whose goods he buys. For the counterfeiter, by introducing fake money into the economy, is able to steal from everyone by robbing every person of the value of his currency. By diluting the value of each ounce or dollar of genuine money, the counterfeiter's theft is more sinister and more truly subversive than that of the highwayman; for he robs everyone in society, and the robbery is stealthy and hidden, so that the cause-and-effect relation is camouflaged.

Recently, we saw the scare headline: "Iranian Government Tries to Destroy U.S. Economy by Counterfeiting $100 Bills." Whether the ayatollahs had such grandiose goals in mind is dubious; counterfeiters don't need a grand rationale for grabbing resources by printing money. But all counterfeiting is indeed subversive and destructive, as well as inflationary.

But in that case, what are we to say when the government seizes control of the money supply, abolishes gold as money, and establishes its own printed tickets as the only money? In other words, what are we to say when the government becomes the legalized, monopoly counterfeiter?

Not only has the counterfeit been detected, but the Grand Counterfeiter, in the United States the Federal Reserve System, instead of being reviled as a massive thief and destroyer, is hailed and celebrated as the wise manipulator and governor of our "macroeconomy," the agency on which we rely for keeping us out of recessions and inflations, and which we count on to determine interest rates, capital prices, and employment. Instead of being habitually pelted with tomatoes and rotten eggs, the Chairman of the Federal Reserve Board, whoever he may be, whether the imposing Paul Volcker or the owlish Alan Greenspan, is universally hailed as Mr. Indispensable to the economic and financial system.

Indeed, the best way to penetrate the mysteries of the modern monetary and banking system is to realize that the government and its central bank act precisely as would a Grand Counterfeiter, with very similar social and economic effects. Many years ago, the *New Yorker* magazine, in the days when its cartoons were still funny, published a cartoon of a group of counterfeiters looking eagerly at their printing press as the first $10 bill came rolling off the press. "Boy," said one of the team, "retail spending in the neighborhood is sure in for a shot in the arm."

And it was. As the counterfeiters print new money, spending goes up on whatever the counterfeiters wish to purchase: personal retail goods for themselves, as well as loans and other "general welfare" purposes in the case of the government. But the resulting "prosperity" is phony; all that happens is that more money bids away existing resources, so that prices rise. Furthermore, the counterfeiters and the early recipients of the new money bid away resources from the poor suckers who are down at the end of the line to receive the new money, or who never even receive it at all. New money injected into the economy has an inevitable ripple effect; early receivers of the new money spend more and bid up prices, while later receivers or those on fixed incomes find the prices of the goods they must buy unaccountably rising, while their own incomes lag behind or remain the same. Monetary inflation, in other words, not only raises prices and destroys the value of the currency unit; it also acts as a giant system of expropriation of the late receivers by the counterfeiters themselves and by the other early receivers. Monetary expansion is a massive scheme of hidden redistribution.

When the government is the counterfeiter, the counterfeiting process not only can be "detected"; it proclaims itself openly as monetary statesmanship for the public weal. Monetary expansion then becomes a giant scheme of hidden taxation, the tax falling on fixed income groups, on those groups remote from government spending and subsidy, and on thrifty savers who are naive enough and trusting enough to hold on to their money, to have faith in the value of the currency.

Spending and going into debt are encouraged; thrift and hard work discouraged and penalized. Not only that: the groups that benefit are the special interest groups who are politically close to the government and can exert pressure to have the new money spent on them so that their incomes can rise faster than the price inflation. Government contractors, politically connected businesses, unions, and other pressure groups will benefit at the expense of the unaware and unorganized public.

৯৹   ৯৹   ৯৹   ৯৹   ৯৹

We have already described one part of the contemporary flight from sound, free market money to statized and inflated money: the abolition of the gold standard by Franklin Roosevelt in 1933, and the substitution of fiat paper tickets by the Federal Reserve as our "monetary standard." Another crucial part of this process was the federal cartelization of the nation's banks through the creation of the Federal Reserve System in 1913.

Banking is a particularly arcane part of the economic system; one of the problems is that the word "bank" covers many different activities, with very different implications. During the

Renaissance era, the Medicis in Italy and the Fuggers in Germany, were "bankers"; their banking, however, was not only private but also began at least as a legitimate, non-inflationary, and highly productive activity. Essentially, these were "merchant-bankers," who started as prominent merchants. In the course of their trade, the merchants began to extend credit to their customers, and in the case of these great banking families, the credit or "banking" part of their operations eventually overshadowed their mercantile activities. These firms lent money out of their own profits and savings, and earned interest from the loans. Hence, they were channels for the productive investment of their own savings.

To the extent that banks lend their own savings, or mobilize the savings of others, their activities are productive and unexceptionable. Even in our current commercial banking system, if I buy a $10,000 CD ("certificate of deposit") redeemable in six months, earning a certain fixed interest return, I am taking my savings and lending it to a bank, which in turn lends it out at a higher interest rate, the differential being the bank's earnings for the function of channeling savings into the hands of credit-worthy or productive borrowers. There is no problem with this process.

The same is even true of the great "investment banking" houses, which developed as industrial capitalism flowered in the nineteenth century. Investment bankers would take their own capital, or capital invested or loaned by others, to underwrite corporations gathering capital by selling securities to stockholders and creditors. The problem with the investment bankers is that one of their major fields of investment was the underwriting of government bonds, which plunged them hip-deep into politics, giving them a powerful incentive for pressuring and manipulating governments, so that taxes would be levied to pay off their and their clients' government bonds. Hence, the powerful and baleful political influence of investment bankers in the nineteenth and twentieth centuries: in particular, the Rothschilds in Western Europe, and Jay Cooke and the House of Morgan in the United States.

By the late nineteenth century, the Morgans took the lead in trying to pressure the U.S. government to cartelize industries they were interested in—first railroads and then manufacturing: to protect these industries from the winds of free competition, and to use the power of government to enable these industries to restrict production and raise prices.

In particular, the investment bankers acted as a ginger group to work for the cartelization of commercial banks. To some extent, commercial bankers lend out their own capital and money acquired by CDs. But most commercial banking is "deposit banking" based on a gigantic scam: the idea, which most depositors believe, that their money is down at the bank, ready to be redeemed in cash at any time. If Jim has a checking account of $1,000 at a local bank, Jim knows that this is a "demand deposit," that is, that the bank pledges to pay him $1,000 in cash, on demand, anytime he wishes to "get his money out." Naturally, the Jims of this world are convinced that their money is safely there, in the bank, for them to take out at any time. Hence, they think of their checking account as equivalent to a warehouse receipt. If they put a chair in a warehouse before going on a trip, they expect to get the chair back whenever they present the receipt. Unfortunately, while banks depend on the warehouse analogy, the depositors are systematically deluded. Their money ain't there.

An honest warehouse makes sure that the goods entrusted to its care are there, in its storeroom or vault. But banks operate very differently, at least since the days of such deposit banks as the Banks of Amsterdam and Hamburg in the seventeenth century, which indeed acted as warehouses and backed all of their receipts fully by the assets deposited, e.g., gold and silver. This honest deposit or "giro" banking is called "100 percent reserve" banking. Ever since, banks have habitually created warehouse receipts (originally bank notes and now deposits) out of thin air. Essentially, they are counterfeiters of fake warehouse-receipts to cash or standard money, which circulate as if they were genuine, fully-backed notes or checking accounts. Banks make money by literally creating money out of thin air, nowadays exclusively deposits rather than bank notes. This sort of swindling or counterfeiting is dignified by the term "fractional-reserve banking," which means that bank deposits are backed by only a small fraction of the cash they promise to have at hand and redeem. (Right now, in the United States, this minimum fraction is fixed by the Federal Reserve System at 10 percent.)

FRACTIONAL-RESERVE BANKING

Let's see how the fractional reserve process works, in the absence of a central bank. I set up a Rothbard Bank, and invest $1,000 of cash (whether gold or government paper does not matter here). Then I "lend out" $10,000 to someone, either for consumer spending or to invest in his business. How can I "lend out" far more than I have? Ahh, that's the magic of the "fraction" in the fractional reserve. I simply open up a checking account of $10,000 which I am happy to lend to Mr. Jones. Why does Jones borrow from me? Well, for one thing, I can charge a lower rate of interest than savers would. I don't have to save up the money myself, but simply can counterfeit it out of thin air. (In the nineteenth century, I would have been able to issue bank notes, but the Federal Reserve now monopolizes note issues.) Since demand deposits at the Rothbard Bank function as equivalent to cash, the nation's money supply has just, by magic, increased by $10,000. The inflationary, counterfeiting process is under way.

The nineteenth-century English economist Thomas Tooke correctly stated that "free trade in banking is tantamount to free trade in swindling." But under freedom, and without government support, there are some severe hitches in this counterfeiting process, or in what has been termed "free banking." First: why should anyone trust me? Why should anyone accept the checking deposits of the Rothbard Bank? But second, even if I were trusted, and I were able to con my way into the trust of the gullible, there is another severe problem, caused by the fact that the banking system is competitive, with free entry into the field. After all, the Rothbard Bank is limited in its clientele. After

Jones borrows checking deposits from me, he is going to spend it. Why else pay money for a loan? Sooner or later, the money he spends, whether for a vacation, or for expanding his business, will be spent on the goods or services of clients of some other bank, say the Rockwell Bank. The Rockwell Bank is not particularly interested in holding checking accounts on my bank; it wants reserves so that it can pyramid its own counterfeiting on top of cash reserves. And so if, to make the case simple, the Rockwell Bank gets a $10,000 check on the Rothbard Bank, it is going to demand cash so that it can do some inflationary counterfeit-pyramiding of its own. But, I, of course, can't pay the $10,000, so I'm finished. Bankrupt. Found out. By rights, I should be in jail as an embezzler, but at least my phony checking deposits and I are out of the game, and out of the money supply.

Hence, under free competition, and without government support and enforcement, there will only be limited scope for fractional-reserve counterfeiting. Banks could form cartels to prop each other up, but generally cartels on the market don't work well without government enforcement, without the government cracking down on competitors who insist on busting the cartel, in this case, forcing competing banks to pay up.

CENTRAL BANKING

Hence the drive by the bankers themselves to get the government to cartelize their industry by means of a central bank. Central Banking began with the Bank of England in the 1690s, spread to the rest of the Western world in the eighteenth and nineteenth centuries, and finally was imposed upon the United States by banking cartelists via the Federal Reserve System of 1913. Particularly enthusiastic about the Central Bank were the investment bankers, such as the Morgans, who pioneered the cartel idea, and who by this time had expanded into commercial banking.

In modern central banking, the Central Bank is granted the monopoly of the issue of bank notes (originally written or printed warehouse receipts as opposed to the intangible receipts of bank deposits), which are now identical to the government's paper money and therefore the monetary "standard" in the country. People want to use physical cash as well as bank deposits. If, therefore, I wish to redeem $1,000 in cash from my checking bank, the bank has to go to the Federal Reserve, and draw down its own checking account with the Fed, "buying" $1,000 of Federal Reserve Notes (the cash in the United States today) from the Fed. The Fed, in other words, acts as a bankers' bank. Banks keep checking deposits at the Fed and these deposits constitute their reserves, on which they can and do pyramid ten times the amount in checkbook money.

Here's how the counterfeiting process works in today's world. Let's say that the Federal Reserve, as usual, decides that it wants to expand (i.e., inflate) the money supply. The Federal Reserve decides to go into the market (called the "open market") and purchase an asset. It doesn't really matter what asset it buys; the important point is that it writes out a check. The Fed could, if it wanted to, buy any asset it wished, including corporate stocks, buildings, or foreign currency. In practice, it almost always buys U.S. government securities.

Let's assume that the Fed buys $10,000,000 of U.S. Treasury bills from some "approved" government bond dealer (a small group), say Shearson, Lehman on Wall Street. The Fed writes out a check for $10,000,000, which it gives to Shearson, Lehman in exchange for $10,000,000 in U.S. securities. Where does the Fed get the $10,000,000 to pay Shearson, Lehman? It creates the money out of thin air. Shearson, Lehman can do only one thing with the check: deposit it in its checking account at a commercial bank, say Chase Manhattan. The "money supply" of the country has already increased by $10,000,000; no one else's checking account has decreased at all. There has been a net increase of $10,000,000.

But this is only the beginning of the inflationary, counterfeiting process. For Chase Manhattan is delighted to get a check on the Fed, and rushes down to deposit it in its own checking account at the Fed, which now increases by $10,000,000. But this checking account constitutes the "reserves" of the banks, which have now increased across the nation by $10,000,000. But this means that Chase Manhattan can create deposits based on these reserves, and that, as checks and reserves seep out to other banks (much as the Rothbard Bank deposits did), each one can add its inflationary mite, until the banking system as a whole has increased its demand deposits by $100,000,000, ten times the original purchase of assets by the Fed. The banking system is allowed to keep reserves amounting to 10 percent of its deposits, which means that the "money multiplier"—the amount of deposits the banks can expand on top of reserves—is 10. A purchase of assets of $10 million by the Fed has generated very quickly a tenfold, $100,000,000 increase in the money supply of the banking system as a whole.

Interestingly, all economists agree on the mechanics of this process even though they of course disagree sharply on the moral or economic evaluation of that process. But unfortunately, the general public, not inducted into the mysteries of banking, still persists in thinking that their money remains "in the bank."

Thus, the Federal Reserve and other central banking systems act as giant government creators and enforcers of a banking cartel; the Fed bails out banks in trouble, and it centralizes and coordinates the banking system so that all the banks, whether the Chase Manhattan, or the Rothbard or Rockwell banks, can inflate together. Under free banking, one bank expanding beyond its fellows was in danger of imminent bankruptcy. Now, under the Fed, all banks can expand together and proportionately.

"DEPOSIT INSURANCE"

But even with the backing of the Fed, fractional-reserve banking proved shaky, and so the New Deal, in 1933, added the lie of "bank deposit insurance," using the benign word "insurance" to mask an arrant hoax. When the savings and loan system went down the tubes in the late 1980s, the "deposit insurance" of the federal FSLIC [Federal Savings and Loan Insurance Corporation] was unmasked as sheer fraud. The "insurance" was simply the smoke-and-mirrors term for the unbacked name of the federal government. The poor taxpayers finally bailed out the S & Ls, but now we are left with the formerly sainted FDIC [Federal Deposit Insurance Corporation], for commercial banks, which is now increasingly seen to be shaky, since the FDIC itself has less than one percent of the huge number of deposits it "insures."

The very idea of "deposit insurance" is a swindle; how does one insure an institution (fractional-reserve banking) that is inherently insolvent, and which will fall apart whenever the public finally understands the swindle? Suppose that, tomorrow, the American public suddenly became aware of the banking swindle, and went to the banks tomorrow morning, and, in unison, demanded cash. What would happen? The banks would be instantly insolvent, since they could only muster 10 percent of the cash they owe their befuddled customers. Neither would the enormous tax increase needed to bail everyone out be at all palatable. No: the only thing the Fed could do, and this would be in their power, would be to print enough money to pay off all the bank depositors. Unfortunately, in the present state of the banking system, the result would be an immediate plunge into the horrors of hyperinflation.

Let us suppose that total insured bank deposits are $1,600 billion. Technically, in the case of a run on the banks, the Fed could exercise emergency powers and print $1,600 billion in cash to give to the FDIC to pay off the bank depositors. The problem is that, emboldened at this massive bailout, the depositors would promptly redeposit the new $1,600 billion into the banks, increasing the total bank reserves by $1,600 billion, thus permitting an immediate expansion of the money supply by the banks by tenfold, increasing the total stock of bank money by

$16 trillion. Runaway inflation and total destruction of the currency would quickly follow.

❧ ❧ ❧ ❧ ❧

To save our economy from destruction and from the eventual holocaust of run away inflation, we the people must take the money-supply function back from the government. Money is far too important to be left in the hands of bankers and of Establishment economists and financiers. To accomplish this goal, money must be returned to the market economy, with all monetary functions performed within the structure of the rights of private property and of the free-market economy.

It might be thought that the mix of government and money is too far gone, too pervasive in the economic system, too inextricably bound up in the economy, to be eliminated without economic destruction. Conservatives are accustomed to denouncing the "terrible simplifiers" who wreck everything by imposing simplistic and unworkable schemes. Our major problem, however, is precisely the opposite: mystification by the ruling elite of technocrats and intellectuals, who, whenever some public spokesman arises to call for large-scale tax cuts or deregulation, intone sarcastically about the dimwit masses who "seek simple solutions for complex problems." Well, in most cases, the solutions are indeed clear-cut and simple, but are deliberately obfuscated by people whom we might call "terrible complicators." In truth, taking back our money would be relatively simple and straightforward, much less difficult than the daunting task of denationalizing and decommunizing the Communist countries of Eastern Europe and the former Soviet Union.

Our goal may be summed up simply as the privatization of our monetary system, the separation of government from money and banking. The central means to accomplish this task is also straightforward: the abolition, the liquidation of the Federal Reserve System—the abolition of central banking. How could the Federal Reserve System possibly be abolished? Elementary: simply repeal its federal charter, the Federal Reserve

Act of 1913. Moreover, Federal Reserve obligations (its notes and deposits) were originally redeemable in gold on demand. Since Franklin Roosevelt's monstrous actions in 1933, "dollars" issued by the Federal Reserve, and deposits by the Fed and its member banks, have no longer been redeemable in gold. Bank deposits are redeemable in Federal Reserve Notes, while Federal Reserve Notes are redeemable in nothing, or alternatively in other Federal Reserve Notes. Yet, these Notes are our money, our monetary "standard," and all creditors are obliged to accept payment in these fiat notes, no matter how depreciated they might be.

In addition to cancelling the redemption of dollars into gold, Roosevelt in 1933 committed another criminal act: literally confiscating all gold and bullion held by Americans, exchanging them for arbitrarily valued "dollars." It is curious that, even though the Fed and the government Establishment continually proclaim the obsolescence and worthlessness of gold as a monetary metal, the Fed (as well as all other central banks) clings to its gold for dear life. Our confiscated gold is still owned by the Federal Reserve, which keeps it on deposit with the Treasury at Fort Knox and other gold depositaries. Indeed, from 1933 until the 1970s, it continued to be illegal for any Americans to own monetary gold of any kind, whether coin or bullion or even in safe deposit boxes at home or abroad. All these measures, supposedly drafted for the Depression emergency, have continued as part of the great heritage of the New Deal ever since. For four decades, any gold flowing into private American hands had to be deposited in the banks, which in turn had to deposit it at the Fed. Gold for "legitimate" non-monetary purposes, such as dental fillings, industrial drills, or jewelry, was carefully rationed for such purposes by the Treasury Department.

Fortunately, due to the heroic efforts of Congressman Ron Paul it is now legal for Americans to own gold, whether coin or bullion. But the ill-gotten gold confiscated and sequestered by the Fed remains in Federal Reserve hands. How to get the gold out from the Fed? How privatize the Fed's stock of gold?

PRIVATIZING FEDERAL GOLD

The answer is revealed by the fact that the Fed, which had promised to redeem its liabilities in gold, has been in default of that promise since Roosevelt's repudiation of the gold standard in 1933. The Federal Reserve System, being in default, should be liquidated, and the way to liquidate it is the way any insolvent business firm is liquidated: its assets are parceled out, pro rata, to its creditors. The Federal Reserve's gold assets are listed, as of October 30, 1991, at $11.1 billion. The Federal Reserve's liabilities as of that date consist of $295.5 billion in Federal Reserve Notes in circulation, and $24.4 billion in deposits owed to member banks of the Federal Reserve System, for a total of $319.9 billion. Of the assets of the Fed, other than gold, the bulk are securities of the U.S. government, which amounted to $262.5 billion. These should be written off posthaste, since they are worse than an accounting fiction: the taxpayers are forced to pay interest and principle on debt which the Federal Government owes to its own creature, the Federal Reserve. The largest remaining asset is Treasury Currency, $21.0 billion, which should also be written off, plus $10 billion in SDRs, which are mere paper creatures of international central banks, and which should be abolished as well. We are left (apart from various buildings and fixtures and other assets owned by the Fed, and amounting to some $35 billion) with $11.1 billion of assets needed to pay off liabilities totalling $319.9 billion.

Fortunately, the situation is not as dire as it seems, for the $11.1 billion of Fed gold is a purely phony evaluation; indeed it is one of the most bizarre aspects of our fraudulent monetary system. The Fed's gold stock consists of 262.9 million ounces of gold; the dollar valuation of $11.1 billion is the result of the government's artificially evaluating its own stock of gold at $42.22 an ounce. Since the market price of gold is now about $350 an ounce, this already presents a glaring anomaly in the system.

DEFINITIONS AND DEBASEMENT

Where did the $42.22 come from?

The essence of a gold standard is that the monetary unit (the "dollar," "franc," "mark," etc.) is defined as a certain weight of gold. Under the gold standard, the dollar or franc is not a thing-in-itself, a mere name or the name of a paper ticket issued by the State or a central bank; it is the name of a unit of weight of gold. It is every bit as much a unit of weight as the more general "ounce," "grain," or "gram." For a century before 1933, the "dollar" was defined as being equal to 23.22 grains of gold; since there are 480 grains to the ounce, this meant that the dollar was also defined as .048 gold ounce. Put another way, the gold ounce was defined as equal to $20.67.

In addition to taking us off the gold standard domestically, Franklin Roosevelt's New Deal "debased" the dollar by redefining it, or "lightening its weight," as equal to 13.714 grains of gold, which also defined the gold ounce as equal to $35. The dollar was still redeemable in gold to foreign central banks and governments at the lighter $35 weight; so that the United States stayed on a hybrid form of international gold standard until August 1971, when President Nixon completed the job of scuttling the gold standard altogether. Since 1971, the United States has been on a totally fiat paper standard; not coincidentally, it has suffered an unprecedented degree of peace-time inflation since that date. Since 1971, the dollar has no longer been tied to gold at a fixed weight, and so it has become a commodity separate from gold, free to fluctuate on world markets.

When the dollar and gold were set loose from each other, we saw the closest thing to a laboratory experiment we can get in human affairs. All Establishment economists—from Keynesians to Chicagoite monetarists—insisted that gold had long lost its value as a money, that gold had only reached its exalted value of $35 an ounce because its value was "fixed" at that amount by the government. The dollar allegedly conferred value upon gold rather than the other way round, and if gold and the dollar were ever cut loose, we would see the price of gold sink rapidly to its estimated non-monetary value (for jewelry, dental fillings, etc.) of approximately $6 an ounce. In contrast to this unanimous Establishment prediction, the followers of Ludwig von Mises and other "gold bugs" insisted that gold was undervalued at 35 debased dollars, and claimed that the price of gold would rise far higher, perhaps as high as $70.

Suffice it to say that the gold price never fell below $35, and in fact vaulted upward, at one point reaching $850 an ounce, in recent years settling at somewhere around $350 an ounce. And yet since 1973, the Treasury and Fed have persistently evaluated their gold stock, not at the old and obsolete $35, to be sure, but only slightly higher, at $42.22 an ounce. In other words, if the U.S. government only made the simple adjustment that accounting requires of everyone—evaluating one's assets at their market price—the value of the Fed's gold stock would immediately rise from $11.1 to $92.0 billion.

From 1933 to 1971, the once very large but later dwindling number of economists championing a return to the gold standard mainly urged a return to $35 an ounce. Mises and his followers advocated a higher gold "price," inasmuch as the $35 rate no longer applied to Americans. But the majority did have a point: that any measure or definition, once adopted, should be adhered to from then on. But since 1971, with the death of the once-sacred $35 an ounce, all bets are off. While definitions once adopted should be maintained permanently, there is nothing sacred about any initial definition, which should be selected at its most useful point. If we wish to restore the gold standard, we are free to select whatever definition of the dollar is most useful; there are no longer any obligations to the obsolete definitions of $20.67 or $35 an ounce.

ABOLISHING THE FED

In particular, if we wish to liquidate the Federal Reserve System, we can select a new definition of the "dollar" sufficient to pay off all Federal Reserve liabilities at 100 cents to the dollar. In the case of our example above, we can now redefine "the dollar" as equivalent to 0.394 grains of gold, or as 1 ounce of gold equalling $1,217. With such redefinition, the entire Federal Reserve stock of gold could be minted by the Treasury into gold coins that would replace the Federal Reserve Notes in circulation, and also constitute gold coin reserves of $24.4 billion at the various commercial banks. The Federal Reserve System would be abolished, gold coins would now be in circulation replacing Federal Reserve Notes, gold would be the circulating medium, and gold dollars the unit of account and reckoning, at the new rate of $1,217 per ounce. Two great desiderata—the return of the gold standard, and the abolition of the Federal Reserve—would both be accomplished at one stroke.

A corollary step, of course, would be the abolition of the already bankrupt Federal Deposit Insurance Corporation. The very concept of "deposit insurance" is fraudulent; how can you "insure" an entire industry that is inherently insolvent? It would be like insuring the Titanic after it hit the iceberg. Some free-market economists advocate "privatizing" deposit insurance by encouraging private firms, or the banks themselves, to "insure" each others' deposits. But that would return us to the unsavory days of Florentine bank cartels, in which every bank tried to shore up each other's liabilities. It won't work; let us not forget that the first S & Ls to collapse in the 1980s were those in Ohio and in Maryland, which enjoyed the dubious benefits of "private" deposit insurance.

This issue points up an important error often made by libertarians and free-market economists who believe that all government activities should be privatized; or as a corollary, hold that any actions, so long as they are private, are legitimate. But, on the contrary, activities such as fraud, embezzlement, or counterfeiting should not be "privatized"; they should be abolished.

This would leave the commercial banks still in a state of fractional reserve, and, in the past, I have advocated going straight to 100 percent, non-fraudulent banking by raising the gold price enough to constitute 100 percent of bank demand liabilities. After that, of course, 100 percent banking would be legally required. At current estimates, establishing 100 percent to all commercial bank demand deposit accounts would require going back to gold at $2,000 an ounce; to include all checkable deposits would require establishing gold at $3,350 an ounce, and to establish 100 percent banking for all checking and savings deposits (which are treated by everyone as redeemable on demand) would require a gold standard at $7,500 an ounce.

But there are problems with such a solution. A minor problem is that the higher the newly established gold value over the current market price, the greater the consequent increase in gold production. This increase would cause an admittedly modest and one-shot price inflation. A more important problem is the moral one: do banks deserve what amounts to a free gift, in which the Fed, before liquidating, would bring every bank's gold assets high enough to be 100 percent of its liabilities? Clearly, the banks scarcely deserve such benign treatment, even in the name of smoothing the transition to sound money; bankers should consider themselves lucky they are not tried for embezzlement. Furthermore, it would be difficult to enforce and police 100 percent banking on an administrative basis. It would be easier, and more libertarian, to go through the courts. Before the Civil War, the notes of unsound fractional reserve banks in the United States, if geographically far from home base, were bought up at a discount by professional "money brokers," who would then travel to the banks' home base and demand massive redemption of these notes in gold.

The same could be done today, and more efficiently, using advanced electronic technology, as professional money brokers try to make profits by detecting unsound banks and bringing them to heel. A particular favorite of mine is the concept of ideological Anti-Bank Vigilante Leagues, who would keep tabs on banks, spot the errant ones, and go on television to proclaim that banks are unsound, and urge note and deposit holders to call upon them for redemption without delay. If the Vigilante Leagues could whip up hysteria and consequent bank runs, in which noteholders and depositors scramble to get their money out before the bank goes under, then so much the better: for then, the people themselves, and not simply the government, would ride herd on fractional reserve banks. The important point, it must be emphasized, is that at the very first sign of a bank's failing to redeem its notes or deposits on demand, the police and courts must put them out of business. Instant justice, period, with no mercy and no bailouts.

Under such a regime, it should not take long for the banks to go under, or else to contract their notes and deposits until they are down to 100 percent banking. Such monetary deflation, while leading to various adjustments, would be clearly one-shot, and would obviously have to stop permanently when the total of bank liabilities contracted down to 100 percent of gold assets. One crucial difference between inflation and deflation, is that inflation can escalate up to an infinity of money supply and prices, whereas the money supply can only deflate as far as the total amount of standard money, under the gold standard the supply of gold money. Gold constitutes an absolute floor against further deflation.

If this proposal seems harsh on the banks, we have to realize that the banking system is headed for a mighty crash in any case. As a result of the S &L collapse, the terribly shaky nature of our banking system is at last being realized. People are openly talking of the FDIC being insolvent, and of the entire banking structure crashing to the ground. And if the people ever get to realize this in their bones, they will precipitate a mighty "bank run" by trying to get their money out of the banks and into their own pockets. And the banks would then come tumbling down, because the people's money isn't there. The only thing that could save the banks in such a mighty bank run is if the Federal Reserve prints the $1.6 trillion in cash and gives it to the banks—igniting an immediate and devastating runaway inflation and destruction of the dollar.

Liberals are fond of blaming our economic crisis on the "greed of the 1980s." And yet "greed" was no more intense in the 1980s than it was in the 1970s or previous decades or than it will be in the future. What happened in the 1980s was a virulent episode of government deficits and of Federal Reserve-inspired credit expansion by the banks. As the Fed purchased assets and pumped in reserves to the banking system, the banks happily multiplied bank credit and created new money on top of those reserves.

There has been a lot of focus on poor quality bank loans: on loans to bankrupt Third World countries or to bloated and, in retrospect, unsound real estate schemes and shopping malls in the middle of nowhere. But poor quality loans and investments are always the consequence of central bank and bank-credit expansion. The all-too-familiar cycle of boom and bust, euphoria and crash, prosperity and depression, did not begin in the 1980s. Nor is it a creature of civilization or the market economy. The boom-bust cycle began in the eighteenth century with the beginnings of central banking, and has spread and intensified ever since, as central banking spread and took control of the economic systems of the Western world. Only the abolition of the Federal Reserve System and a return to the gold standard can put an end to cyclical booms and busts, and finally eliminate chronic and accelerating inflation.

Inflation, credit expansion, business cycles, heavy government debt, and high taxes are not, as Establishment historians claim, inevitable attributes of capitalism or of "modernization." On the contrary, these are profoundly anti-capitalist and parasitic excrescences grafted onto the system by the interventionist State, which rewards its banker and insider clients with hidden special privileges at the expense of everyone else.

Crucial to free enterprise and capitalism is a system of firm rights of private property, with everyone secure in the property that he earns. Also crucial to capitalism is an ethic that encourages and rewards savings, thrift, hard work, and productive enterprise, and that discourages profligacy and cracks down sternly on any invasion of property rights. And yet, as we have seen, cheap money and credit expansion gnaw away at those rights and at those virtues. Inflation overturns and transvalues values by rewarding the spendthrift and the inside fixer and by making a mockery of the older "Victorian" virtues.

Restoring the Old Republic

The restoration of American liberty and of the Old Republic is a multi-faceted task. It requires excising the cancer of the Leviathan State from our midst. It requires removing Washington, D.C., as the power center of the country. It requires restoring the ethics and virtues of the nineteenth century, the taking back of our culture from nihilism and victimology, and restoring that culture to health and sanity. In the long run, politics, culture, and the economy are indivisible. The restoration of the Old Republic requires an economic system built solidly on the inviolable rights of private property, on the right of every person to keep what he earns, and to exchange the products of his labor. To accomplish that task, we must once again have money that is produced on the market, that is gold rather than paper, with the monetary unit a weight of gold rather than the name of a paper ticket issued *ad lib* by the government. We must have investment determined by voluntary savings on the market, and not by counterfeit money and credit issued by a knavish and State-privileged banking system. In short, we must abolish central banking, and force the banks to meet their obligations as promptly as anyone else. Money and banking have been made to appear as mysterious and arcane processes that must be guided and operated by a technocratic elite. They are nothing of the sort. In money, even more than the rest of our affairs, we have been tricked by a malignant Wizard of Oz. In money, as in other areas of our lives, restoring common sense and the Old Republic go hand in hand. ▶

73
THE WORLD CURRENCY CRISIS

The world is in permanent monetary crisis, but once in a while, the crisis flares up acutely, and we noisily shift gears from one flawed monetary system to another. We go back and forth from fixed paper rates to fluctuating rates, to some inchoate and aborted blend of the two. Each new system, each basic change, is hailed extravagantly by economists, bankers, the financial press, politicians, and central banks, as the final and permanent solution to our persistent monetary woes.

Then, after some years, the inevitable breakdown occurs, and the Establishment trots out another bauble, another wondrous monetary nostrum for us to admire. Right now, we are on the edge of another shift.

To stop this shell game, we must first understand it. First, we must realize that there are three coherent systems of international money, of which only one is sound and non-inflationary. The sound money is the genuine gold standard; "genuine" in the sense that each currency is defined as a certain unit of weight of gold, and is redeemable at that weight.

Exchange rates between currencies were "fixed" in the sense that each was defined as a given weight of gold; for example, since the dollar was defined as one-twentieth of a gold ounce and the pound sterling as .24 of a gold ounce, the exchange rate between the two was naturally fixed at their proportionate gold weight, i.e., £ 1 = $4.87.

The other two systems are the Keynesian ideal, where all currencies are fixed in terms of an international paper unit, and fluctuating independent fiat-paper moneys. Keynes wanted to call his new world paper unit the *bancor* while U.S. Treasury official (and secret Communist) Harry Dexter White wanted to

---

First published in February 1986.

name it the *unita*. *Bancor* or *unita*, these new paper tickets would ideally be issued by a World Reserve Bank and would form the reserves of the various central banks. Then, the World Reserve Bank could inflate the *bancor* at will, and the *bancor* would provide reserves upon which the Fed, the Bank of England, etc. could pyramid a multiple expansion of their respective national fiat currencies.

The whole world would then be able to inflate together, and therefore not suffer the inconvenience of inflationary countries losing either gold or income to sound-money countries. All the countries could inflate in a centrally-coordinated fashion, and we could suffer manipulation and inflation by a world government-banking elite without check or hindrance. At the end of the road would be a horrendous worldwide hyper-inflation, with no way of escaping into sounder or less inflated currencies.

Fortunately, national rivalries have prevented the Keynesians from achieving their goal, and so they had to settle for "second best," the Bretton Woods system that the U.S. and Britain foisted on the world in 1944, and which lasted until its collapse in 1971. Instead of the *bancor*, the dollar served as the international reserve upon which other currencies could pyramid their money and credit. The dollar, in turn, was tied to gold in a mockery of a genuine gold standard, at the pre-war par of $35 per ounce. In the first place, dollars were not redeemable in gold coins, as they had been before, but only in large and heavy gold bars, which were worth many thousands of dollars. And second, only foreign governments and central banks could redeem their dollars in gold even on this limited basis.

For two decades, the system seemed to work well, as the U.S. issued more and more dollars, and they were then used by foreign central banks as a base for their own inflation. In short, for years the U.S. was able to "export inflation" to foreign countries without suffering the ravages itself. Eventually, however, the ever-more inflated dollar became depreciated on the gold market, and the lure of high priced gold they could obtain from the U.S. at the bargain $35 per ounce led European central banks to cash in dollars for gold. The house of cards collapsed when President Nixon, in an ignominious declaration of bankruptcy, slammed shut the gold window and went off the last remnants of the gold standard in August 1971.

With Bretton Woods gone, the Western powers now tried a system that was not only unstable but also incoherent: fixing exchange rates without gold or even any international paper money with which to make payments. The Western powers signed the ill-fated Smithsonian Agreement on December 18, 1971, which was hailed by President Nixon as "the greatest monetary agreement in the history of the world." But if currencies are purely fiat, with no international money, they become goods in themselves, and fixed exchange rates are then bound to violate the market rates set by supply and demand.

At that time the inflated dollar was heavily overvalued in regard to Western European and Japanese currencies. At the overvalued dollar rate, there were repeated scrambles to buy European and Japanese moneys at bargain rates, and to get rid of dollars. Repeated "shortages" of the harder moneys resulted from this maximum price control of their exchange rates. Finally, panic selling of the dollar broke the Smithsonian system apart in March 1973. With the collapse of Bretton Woods and the far more rapid disintegration of the "greatest monetary agreement" in world history, both the phony gold standard and the fixed paper exchange rate systems were widely and correctly seen to be inherent failures. The world now embarked, almost by accident on a new era: a world of fluctuating fiat paper moneys. Friedmanite monetarism was to have its day in the sun.

The Friedmanite monetarists had come into their own, replacing the Keynesians as the favorites of the financial press and of the international monetary establishment. Governments and central banks began to hail the soundness and permanence of fluctuating exchange rates as fervently as they had once trumpeted the eternal virtues of Bretton Woods. The monetarists proclaimed the ideal international monetary system to be freely fluctuating exchange rates between different moneys, with no government intervention to try to stabilize or even moderate the fluctuations. In that way, exchange rates would reflect, from day to day, the fluctuations of supply and demand, just as prices do on the free market.

Of course, the world *had* suffered mightily from fluctuating fiat money in the not too distant past: the 1930s, when every country had gone off gold (a phony gold standard preserved for foreign central banks by the United States). The problem is that each nation-state kept fixing its exchange rates, and the result was currency blocs, aggressive devaluations attempting to expand exports and restrict imports, and economic warfare cul-minating in World War II. So the monetarists were insistent that the fluctuations must be absolutely free of all government intervention.

But, in the fist place, the Friedmanite plan is *politically* so naive as to be almost impossible to put into practice. For what the monetarists do, in effect, is to make each currency fiat paper issued by the national government. They give total power over money to that government and its central bank, and then they issue stern admonitions to the wielders of absolute power: "Remember, use your power wisely, *don't* under any circum-stances interfere with exchange rates." But inevitably, govern-ments will find many reasons to interfere: to force exchange rates up or down, or stabilize them, and there is nothing to stop them from exercising their natural instincts to control and intervene.

And so what we have had since 1973 is an incoherent blend of "fixed" and fluctuating, unhampered and hampered, foreign currency markets. Even Beryl W. Sprinkel, a dedicated mone-tarist who served as Undersecretary of Treasury for Monetary Policy in the first Reagan administration, was forced to back-track on his early achievement of persuading the administration to decontrol exchange rates. Even he was compelled to inter-vene in "emergency" situations, and now the second Reagan administration moved insistently in the direction of refixing exchange rates.

The problem with freely fluctuating rates is not only political. One virtue of fixed rates, especially under gold, but even to some extent under paper, is that they keep a check on national inflation by central banks. The virtue of fluctuating rates—that they prevent sudden monetary crises due to arbitrarily valued currencies—is a mixed blessing, because at least those crises provided a much-needed restraint on domestic inflation. Freely fluctuating rates mean that the only damper on domestic inflation is that the currency might depreciate. Yet countries often *want* their money to depreciate, as we have seen in the recent agitation to soften the dollar and thereby subsidize exports and restrict imports—a back-door protectionism. The current refixers have one sound point: that worldwide inflation only became rampant in the mid and late 1970s, after the last fixed-rate discipline was removed.

The refixers are on the march. During November 1985, a major, well-publicized international monetary conference took place in Washington, organized by U.S. Representative Jack Kemp and Senator Bill Bradley, and including representatives from the Fed, foreign central banks, and Wall Street banks. This liberal-conservative spectrum agreed on the basic objective: refixing exchange rates. But refixing is no solution; it will only bring back the arbitrary valuations, and the breakdowns of Bretton Woods and the Smithsonian. Probably what we will get eventually is a worldwide application of the current "snake," in which Western European currencies are tied together so that they can fluctuate but only within a fixed zone. This pointless and inchoate blend of fixed and fluctuating currencies can only bring us the problems of both systems.

When will we realize that only a genuine gold standard can bring us the *virtues* of both systems and a great deal more: free markets, absence of inflation, and exchange rates that are fixed not arbitrarily by government but as units of weights of a precious market commodity, gold? ▸

74

NEW INTERNATIONAL MONETARY SCHEME

Ever since the Western world abandoned the gold coin standard in 1914, the international monetary system has been rocketing from one bad system to another, from the frying pan to the fire and back again, fleeing the problems of one alternative only to find itself deeply unhappy in the other. Basically, only two alternative systems have been considered: (1) fiat money standards, each national fiat currency being governed by its own central bank, with relative values fluctuating in accordance with supply and demand; and, (2) some sort of fixed exchange rate system, governed by international coordination of economic policies.

Our current System 1 came about willy-nilly in 1973, out of the collapse of Bretton Woods System 2 that had been imposed on the world by the United States and Britain in 1944. System 1, the monetarist or Friedmanite ideal, at best breaks up the world monetary system into national fiat enclaves, adds great uncertainties and distortions to the monetary system, and removes the check of external discipline from the inflationary propensities of every central bank. At worst, System 1 offers irresistible temptations to every government to intervene heavily in exchange rates, precipitating the world into currency blocs, protectionist blocs, and "beggar-my-neighbor" policies of competing currency devaluations such as the economic warfare of the 1930s that helped generate World War II.

The problem is that shifting to System 2 is truly a leap from the frying pan into the fire. The national fiat blocs of the 1930s emerged out of the System 2 pound sterling standard in which other countries pyramided an inflation of their currencies on top of inflating pounds sterling, while Britain retained a nominal but

First published in September 1987.

phony gold standard. The 1930s system was itself replaced by Bretton Woods, a world dollar standard, in which other countries were able to inflate their own currencies on top of inflating dollars, while the United States maintained a nominal but phony gold standard at $35 per gold ounce.

Now the problems of the Friedmanite System 1 are inducing plans for some sort of return to a fixed exchange rate system. Unfortunately, System 2 is even worse than System 1, for any successful coordination permits a concerted worldwide inflation, a far worse problem than particular national inflations. Exchange rates among fiat moneys have to fluctuate, since fixed exchange rates inevitably create Gresham's Law situations, in which undervalued currencies disappear from circulation. In the Bretton Woods system, American inflation permitted worldwide inflation, until gold became so undervalued at $35 an ounce that demands to redeem dollars in gold became irresistible, and the system collapsed.

If System 1 is the Friedmanite ideal, then the Keynesian one is the most pernicious variant of System 2. For what Keynesians have long sought, notably in the Bernstein and Triffin Plans of old, and in the abortive attempt to make SDRs (special drawing rights) a new currency unit, is a World Reserve Bank issuing a new world paper-money unit, replacing gold altogether. Keynes called his suggested new unit the "bancor," and Harry Dexter White of the U.S. Treasury called his the "unita."

Whatever the new unit may be called, such a system would be an unmitigated disaster, for it would allow the bankers and politicians running the World Reserve Bank to issue paper "bancors" without limit, thereby engineering a coordinated worldwide inflation. No longer would countries have to lose gold to each other, and they could fix their exchange rates without worrying about Gresham's Law. The upshot would be an eventual worldwide runaway inflation, with horrendous consequences for the entire world.

Fortunately, a lack of market confidence, and inability to coordinate dozens of governments, have so far spared us this

Keynesian ideal. But now, a cloud no bigger than a man's hand, an ominous trial balloon toward a World Reserve Bank had been floated. In a meeting in Hamburg, West Germany, 200 leading world bankers in an International Monetary Conference, urged the elimination of the current volatile exchange rate system, and a move towards fixed exchange rates.

The theme of the Conference was set by its chairman, Willard C. Butcher, chairman and chief executive of Rockefeller's Chase Manhattan Bank. Butcher attacked the current system, and warned that it could not correct itself, and that a search for a better world currency system "must be intensified" (*New York Times*, June 23, 1987).

It was not long before Toyo Gyoten, Japan's vice-minister of finance for international affairs, spelled out some of the concrete implications of this accelerated search. Gyoten proposed a huge multinational financial institution, possessing "at least several hundred billion dollars," that would be empowered to intervene in world financial markets to reduce volatility.

And what is this if not the beginnings of a World Reserve Bank? Are Keynesian dreams at least beginning to come true? ▶

75
"ATTACKING" THE FRANC

An all-too-familiar melodrama was played out in full on the stage of the world media. It was the same phony story, with the same Heroes and Villains.

The French franc, a supposed noble currency, was "under attack." Previously in September, it was the British pound, and before that the Swedish krona. The "attack" is as fierce and mysterious as a shark attack in the coastal waters. The Hero is

---

First published in November 1993.

the Prime Minister or Finance Minister of the country, who tries desperately to "defend the value" of the currency.

Prime Minister Eduard Balladur of France, pledged himself to defend the "strong franc" (the *franc fort*) or go under (that is resign) in the attempt. The "defense" was waged, not with guns and planes, but with hard-currency reserves spent by the Bank of France, as well as many billions of dollars expended in the same cause by the German central bank, the Bundesbank. In many cases, international institutions and the Federal Reserve lend a hand in trying to support the value of the "threatened" currency.

If national and international statesmen and governments are the Heroes, the Villains are speculators whose "attack" consists simply of selling the currency, the franc or pound, in exchange for currencies they consider "harder" and sounder, in this case the German mark, in other cases the U.S. dollar.

The upshot is always the same. After weeks of hysteria and denunciation, the speculators win, even after repeated pledges by the prime minister or finance minister that such devaluations would never ever occur. The krona, the pound, or the franc is, one way or another, devalued. Its old official value is no more. The government loses a lot of money, but the promised resignations never take place. Prime Minister Balladur is still there, having saved face by widening the "permitted bands" of movement of the franc.

And, as usual, after the hysteria passes, and the franc or pound or krona is finally lowered in value, everyone begins to realize, as if in a wonder of new insight, that the economy is really in better or at least more promising shape now than it was before the "attack" succeeded in its wicked work.

Why the repeated subjection of currencies to attack? And why do the villains always win? And why do things always seem *better* after the "defeat" than before?

It's really fairly simple. A currency's value is determined like any commodity: the greater the supply, the lower the value;

the greater the demand, the higher the value. Before the twentieth century, national currencies were not independent commodities but definitions of weight of either gold or silver (sometimes, unfortunately, both). In the twentieth century, and especially since the last vestige of the gold standard was eliminated in 1971, each currency has been an independent commodity. The supply of francs or dollars consist in whatever francs or dollars are in existence. The "demand" to hold these currencies depends largely on people's expectations of what will happen to price, or to the value of the currency.

The more a government inflates its currency, then, the lower will be the "value" of that currency in two ways: its purchasing power in terms of goods and services, and its value in other currencies. Inflationary currencies, therefore, will tend to suffer from rising prices domestically and from falling exchange rates in terms of other, less inflated currencies. A severely inflated currency will lead to a "flight" from that currency, since people expect greater inflation, and a flight into harder currencies.

The best and least inflated form of money is a worldwide gold currency. But absent gold redeemability, and given our existing fiat national currencies, by far the best course is to allow exchange rates to float freely in the foreign exchange markets, where they at least clear the market and insure no shortage or oversupply of currencies. At least, the values reflect supply and demand.

Governments like to pretend that the value of their currency is greater than it really is. If France really wants a "franc fort," the central bank should stop increasing the supply of francs on the market. Instead, governments habitually want to enjoy the goodies of inflation (higher prices, high government spending, subsidies, and cheap loans to friends and allies of the government), without suffering any loss of prestige. As a result, governments habitually set a value of their currency higher than the free-market rate.

Fixing the exchange rate amounts to an artificial overvaluation (minimum price floor) of their own currency, and an artificial undervaluation (maximum price ceilings) of such harder currencies as dollars and marks. The result is a "surplus" of francs or krona and a "shortage" of the harder currencies.

To maintain this artificially high rate, the government and its allies have to pour in (waste) many billions of dollars in what is equivalent to price supports, which eventually must run down as the government runs out of money and patience. And since the overvalued currency under attack has only one way to go—down—speculators can move in for a handsome and sure profit.

Blaming speculators for these crises is as absurd as blaming "black marketeers" for higher prices under price controls. The true villains are the supposed "heroes," those government officials trying, like King Canute, to command the tides, and to maintain artificial and unsound valuations.

The alleged Heroes are even more villainous these days than usual. Since 1979, the European governments have been trying to maintain a fixed exchange rate system among themselves; in the last few years, they have been trying to close the allowed bands of fluctuation—2.25 percent plus or minus the official rate—in preparation for a single European Currency Unit (ECU) that was supposed to begin at the end of 1993 and would be issued by a single European central bank.

A single European currency and central bank was sold to the world public as a giant "free trade unit," but it actually was a giant step toward centralized government in Brussels. It was a step toward the old Keynesian dream of a world paper unit by a World Reserve Bank administered by a world government.

Fortunately, with the resistance to Maastricht, and then with the pullout of Britain from the European Currency System and the face-saving new system of very wide exchange rate bands, the ECU and the Keynesian dream lie all but dead. The world market has once against triumphed over Keynesian statism, even though the power seemed to be in the Establishment's hands.

In the French case, there was another villain condemned by all. The German Bundesbank, worried about German inflation as a result of the mammoth subsidies to East Germany, has not been as inflationary as France would have liked. One way for France or Britain to be able to enjoy the goodies of inflation without the embarrassment of a falling currency is to try to *muscle* harder currencies to inflate, dragging them down to the level of the weaker currencies.

Fortunately, the Germans, even though they inflated a bit and wasted billions supporting the franc, did not inflate nearly as much as the French or British would have liked. Yet for pursuing a relatively sound monetary course, the Germans were condemned as "selfish," for they had not sacrificed their all for "Europe"—that is, for Keynesian inflationists and centralizing collectivists.

It is all too easy to despair as we look around and see the world's governments and opinion organs in the hands of power-seeking collectivists. But there is mighty force in our favor. Free markets, not only the long run but often in the short run, will triumph over government power. The market proved mightier than communism and the gulag. Even in the much despised form of shadowy speculators, it has once again triumphed over unworkable and malevolent plans of statesmen and international Keynesians. ▶

76
BACK TO FIXED EXCHANGE RATES

Hold on to your hats: the world has now embarked on yet another "new economic order"—which means another disaster in the making. Ever since the abandonment of the "classical" gold-coin standard in World War I (by the United States in 1933), world authorities have been searching for a way

First published in December 1987.

to replace the peaceful world rule of gold by the coordinated, coercive rule of the world's governments.

They have searched for a way to replace the sound money of gold by an internationally coordinated inflation which would provide cheap money, abundant increases in the money supply, increasing government expenditures, and prices that do not rise too wildly or too far out of control, and with no embarrassing monetary crises or excessive declines in any one country's currency. In short, governments have tried to square the circle, or, to have their pleasant inflationary cake without "eating" it by suffering decidedly unpleasant consequences.

The first new economic order of the twentieth century was the New Era dominated by Great Britain, in which the world's countries were induced to ground their currencies on a phony gold standard, actually based on the British pound sterling, which was in turn loosely based on the dollar and gold. When this recipe for internationally coordinated inflation collapsed and helped create the Great Depression of the 1930s, a new and very similar international order was constructed at Bretton Woods in 1944. In *this* case, another phony gold standard was created, this time with all currencies based on the U.S. dollar, in turn supposedly redeemable, *not* in gold coin to the public, but in gold bullion to foreign central banks and governments at $35 an ounce.

In the late 1920s, governments of the various nations could inflate their currencies by pyramiding on top of an inflating pound; similarly in the Bretton Woods system, the U.S. exported its own inflation by encouraging other countries to inflate on top of their expanding accumulation of dollar reserves. As world currencies, and especially the dollar, kept inflating, it became evident that gold was undervalued and dollars overvalued at the old $35 par, so that Western European countries, reluctant to continue inflationary policies, began to demand gold for their accumulated dollars (in short, Gresham's Law, that money overvalued by the government will drive undervalued money out of circulation, came into effect). Since the U.S. was not able to redeem its gold obligations, President Nixon went off the Bretton Woods standard, which had come to its inevitable demise, in 1971.

Since that date, or rather since 1933, the world has had a fluctuating fiat standard, that is, exchange rates of currencies have fluctuated in accordance with supply and demand on the market. There are grave problems with fluctuating exchange rates, largely because of the abandonment of one world money (i.e., gold) and the shift to international barter. Because there is no world money, every nation is free to inflate its own currency at will—and hence to suffer a decline in its exchange rates. And because there is no longer a world money, unpredictably fluctuating uncertain exchange rates create a double uncertainty on top of the usual price system—creating, in effect, multiprice systems in the world.

The inflation and volatility under the fluctuating exchange rate regime has caused politicians and economists to try to resurrect a system of fixed exchange rates—but this time, without even the element of the gold standard that marked the Bretton Woods era. But without a world gold money, this means that nations are fixing exchange rates arbitrarily, without reference to supply and demand, and on the alleged superior wisdom of economists and politicians as to what exchange rates should be.

Politicians are pressured by conflicting import and export interests, and economists have made the grave error of mistaking a long-run tendency (of exchange rates on a fluctuating market to rest at the proportion of purchasing-powers of the various currencies) for a criterion by which economists can correct the market. This attempt to place economists above the market overlooks the fact that the market properly sets exchange rates on the basis, not only of purchasing power proportions, but also expectations of the future, differences in interest rates, differences in tax policy, fears of future inflation or confiscation, etc. Once again, the market proves wiser than economists.

This new coordinated attempt to fix exchange rates is a hysterical reaction against the high dollar. The Group of Seven nations (the U.S., Britain, France, Italy, West Germany, Japan, and Canada) helped drive down the value of the dollar, and then, in their wisdom, in February 1987, decided that the dollar was now somehow at a perfect rate, and coordinated their efforts to keep the dollar from falling further.

In reality, the dollar was high until early 1986 because foreigners had been unusually willing to invest in dollars—purchasing government bonds as well as other assets. While this happy situation continued, they were willing to finance Americans in buying cheap imports. After early 1987, this unusual willingness disappeared, and the dollar began to fall in order to equilibrate the U.S. balance of payments. Artificially propping up the dollar in 1987 has led the other countries of the Group of Seven to purchase billions of dollars with their own currencies—a shortsighted effort which cannot last forever, especially because West Germany and Japan have fortunately not been willing to inflate their own currencies and lower their interest rates further, to divert capital from themselves toward the U.S.

Instead of realizing that this coordination game is headed toward inevitable crisis and collapse, Secretary of Treasury James Baker, the creator of the new system, proposes to press ahead to a more formal New Order. In his September speech to the IMF and World Bank, Secretary Baker proposed a formal, coordinated regime of fixed exchange rates, in which—as a sop to public sentiment for gold—gold is to have an extremely shadowy, almost absurd, role. In the course of fine tuning the world economy, the central banks and treasuries of the world, in addition to looking at various "indicators" on their control panels-price levels, interest rates, GNP, unemployment rates, etc.—will also be consulting a new commodity price index of their own making which, by *secret* formula, would also include gold.

Such a ludicrous substitute for genuine gold money will certainly fool no one, and is an almost laughable example of the love of central bankers and treasury officials for secrecy and mystification for its own sake, so as to bewilder and bamboozle the public. I do not often agree with J.K. Galbraith, but he is certainly on the mark when he calls this new secret index a "marvelous exercise in fantasy and obfuscation."

Politically, the secret index embodies a ruling alliance within the Reagan administration between such conservative Keynesians as Secretary Baker and such supply-siders as Professor Robert Mundell and Congressman Jack Kemp (who have both hailed the scheme as a glorious step in the right direction). The supply-siders have long desired the restoration of a Bretton Woods-type system that would allow coordinated cheap money and inflation worldwide, *coupled* with a phony gold standard as camouflage, so as to build unjustified confidence in the new scheme among the pro-gold public.

The conservative Keynesians have long desired a new Bretton Woods, based eventually on a new world paper unit issued by a World Central Bank. Hence the new alliance. The alliance was made politically possible by the disappearance from the Reagan administration of the Friedmanite monetarists, such as former Undersecretary of Treasury for Monetary Policy Beryl W. Sprinkel and Jerry Jordan, spokesmen for fluctuating exchange rates. With monetarism discredited by the repeated failures of their monetary predictions over the last several years, the route was cleared for a new international, fixed-rates system.

Unfortunately, the only thing worse than fluctuating exchange rates is fixed exchange rates based on fiat money and international coordination. Before rates were allowed to fluctuate, and after the end of Bretton Woods, the U.S. government tried such an order, in the international Smithsonian Agreement of December 1971. President Nixon hailed this agreement as "the greatest monetary agreement in the history of the world." This exercise in international coordination lasted no more than a year and a half, foundering on monetary crises brought about by Gresham's Law from overvaluation of the dollar.

How long will it take this new, New Order, along with its puerile secret index, to collapse as well? ▶

77

THE CROSS OF FIXED EXCHANGE RATES

Governments, especially including the U.S. government, seem to be congenitally incapable of keeping their mitts off any part of the economy. Government, aided and abetted by its host of apologists among intellectuals and policy wonks, likes to regard itself as a *deus ex machina* (a "god out of the machine") that surveys its subjects with Olympian benevolence and omniscience, and then repeatedly descends to earth to fix up the numerous "market failures" that mere people, in their ignorance, persist in committing.

The fact that history is a black record of continual gross failure by this "god," and that economic theory explains why it must be so, makes no impression on official political discourse.

Every Nation-State, for example, is continually tempted to intervene to fix its exchange rates, the rates of its fiat paper money in terms of the scores of other moneys issued by all the other governments in the world.

Governments don't know, and don't want to know, that the only successful fixing of exchange rates occurred, not coincidentally, in the era of the gold standard. In that era, money was a market commodity, produced on the market rather than manufactured *ad lib* by a government or a central bank. Fixed exchange rates worked because these national money units—the dollar, the pound, the lira, the mark, etc.—were not independent things or entities. Rather each was defined as a certain weight of gold.

Like all definitions such as the yard, the ton, etc., the point of the definition was that, once set, it was fixed forever. Thus,

---

First published in July 1994.

for example, if, as was roughly the case in the nineteenth century, "the dollar" was defined as 1/20 of a gold ounce, "the pound" as 1/4 of a gold ounce, and "the French franc" as 1/100 of a gold ounce, the "exchange rates" were simply proportional gold weights of the various currency units, so that the pound would automatically be worth $5, the franc would automatically be worth 20 cents, etc.

The United States dropped the gold standard in 1933, with the last international vestiges discarded in 1971. After the whole world followed, each national currency became a separate and independent entity, or good, from all the others. Therefore a "market" developed immediately among them, as a market will always develop among different tradable goods.

If these exchange markets are left alone by governments, then exchange rates will fluctuate freely. They will fluctuate in accordance with the supplies and demands for each currency in terms of the others, and the day-to-day rates will reflect supply and demand conditions and, as in the case of all other goods, "clear the market" so as to equate supply and demand, and therefore assure that there will be no shortages or unsold surpluses of any of the moneys.

Fluctuating fiat moneys, as the world has discovered once again, since 1971, are unsatisfactory. They cripple the advantages of international money and virtually return the world to barter. They fail to provide the check against inflation by governments and central banks once supplied by the stern necessity of redeeming their monetary issues in gold.

What the world has failed to grasp is that there is one thing much worse than fluctuating fiat moneys: and that is fiat money where governments try to fix the exchange rates. For, as in the case of any price control, governments will invariably fix their rates either above or below the free market rate. Whichever route they take, government fixing will create undesirable consequences, will cause unnecessary monetary crises, and, in the long run, cannot be sustained and will end up in ignominious failure.

One crucial point is that government fixing of exchange rates will inevitably set "Gresham's Law" to work: that is, the money artificially undervalued by the government (set at a price too low by the government) will tend to disappear from the market ("a shortage"), while money overvalued by government (price set too high) will tend to pour into circulation and constitute a "surplus."

The Clinton administration, which seems to have a homing instinct for economic fallacy, has been as bumbling and inconsistent in monetary policy as in all other areas. Thus, until recently, the administration, absurdly worried about a seemingly grave (but actually non-existent) balance of payments "deficit," has tried to push down the exchange rate of the dollar in order to stimulate exports and restrict imports.

There is no way, however, that government can ever find and set some sort of "ideal" exchange rate. A cheaper dollar encourages exports all right, but the administration eventually came to realize that there is an inevitable down side: namely, that import prices of course are higher, which removes competition that will keep domestic prices down.

Instead of learning the lesson that there is no ideal exchange rate apart from determination by the free market, the Clinton administration, as is its wont, reversed itself abruptly, and orchestrated a multi-billion campaign by the Fed and other major central banks to prop up the sinking dollar, as against the German mark and the Japanese yen. The dollar rate rose slightly, and the media congratulated Clinton for propping up the dollar.

Overlooked in the hosannahs are several intractable problems. First, billions of taxpayers money, here and abroad, are being devoted to distorting market exchange rates. Second, since the exchange rate is being coercively propped up, such "successes" cannot be repeated for long. How long before the Fed runs out of marks and yen with which to keep up the dollar? How long before Germany, Japan, and other countries tire of inflating their currencies in order to keep the dollar artificially high?

If the Clinton administration persists, even in the face of these consequences, in trying to hold the dollar artificially high, it will have to meet the developing mark and yen "shortages" by imposing exchange controls and mark-and-yen-rationing on American citizens.

In the meantime, one of the first bitter fruits of Nafta has already appeared. Like all other modern "free trade" agreements, Nafta serves as a back-channel to international currency regulation and fixed exchange rates. One of the unheralded aspects of Nafta was joint government action in propping up each others' exchange rates. In practice, this means artificial overvaluation of the Mexican peso, which has been dropping sharply on the market, in response to Mexican inflation and political instability.

Thus, Nafta originally set up a "temporary" $6 billion credit pool to aid mutual overvaluation of exchange rates. With the peso slipping badly, falling 6 percent against the dollar since January, the Nafta governments, in late April, made the credit pool permanent, and raised it to $8.8 billion. Moreover, the three Nafta countries created a new North American Financial Group, consisting of the respective finance ministers and central bank chairman, to "oversee economic and financial issues affecting the North American partners."

Robert D. Hormats, vice-chairman of Goldman Sachs International, hailed the new arrangement as "a logical progression from trade and investment cooperation between the three countries to greater monetary and fiscal cooperation." Well, that's *one* way to look at it. Another way is to point out that this is one more step of the U.S. government toward arrangements that will distort exchange rates, create monetary crises and currency shortages, and waste taxpayers' money and economic resources.

Worst of all, the U.S. is marching inexorably toward economic regulation and planning by regional, and even world, governmental bureaucracies, out of control and accountable to no one, to none of the subject peoples anywhere on the globe. ▶

78
THE KEYNESIAN DREAM

For a half-century, the Keynesians have harbored a Dream. They have long dreamed of a world without gold, a world rid of any restrictions upon their desire to spend and spend, inflate and inflate, elect and elect. They have achieved a world where governments and Central Banks are free to inflate without suffering the limits and restrictions of the gold standard. But they still chafe at the fact that, although national governments are free to inflate and print money, they yet find themselves limited by depreciation of their currency. If Italy, for example, issues a great many lira, the lira will depreciate in terms of other currencies, and Italians will find the prices of their imports and of foreign resources skyrocketing.

What the Keynesians have dreamed of, then, is a world with one fiat currency, the issues of that paper currency being generated and controlled by one World Central Bank. What you *call* the new currency unit doesn't really matter: Keynes called his proposed unit at the Bretton Woods Conference of 1944, the "bancor"; Harry Dexter White, the U.S. Treasury negotiator at that time, called his proposed money the "unita"; and the London *Economist* has dubbed its suggested new world money the "phoenix." Fiat money by any name smells as sour.

Even though the United States and its Keynesian advisers dominated the international monetary scene at the end of World War II, they could not impose the full Keynesian goal; the jealousies and conflicts of national sovereignty were too intense. So the Keynesians reluctantly had to settle for the jerry-built dollar-gold international standard at Bretton Woods, with exchange rates flexibly fixed, and with no World Central Bank at its head.

As determined men with a goal, the Keynesians did not fail from not trying. They launched the Special Drawing Right

First published in July 1989.

(SDR) as an attempt to replace gold as an international reserve money, but SDRs proved to be a failure. Prominent Keynesians such as Edward M. Bernstein of the International Monetary Fund and Robert Triffin of Yale, launched well-known Plans bearing their names, but these too were not adopted.

Ever since the Bretton Woods system, hailed for nearly three decades as stable and eternal, collapsed in 1971, the Keynesians have had to suffer the indignity of floating exchange rates. Ever since the accession of Keynesian James R. Baker as Secretary of Treasury in 1985, the United States has abandoned its brief commitment to a monetarist hands-off the foreign exchange market policy, and has tried to engineer a phase transformation of the international monetary system. First, fixed exchange rates would be obtained by coordinated action of the large Central Banks. This has largely been achieved, at first covertly and then openly; the leading Central Banks picked a target point or zone, for, say, the dollar, and then by buying and selling dollars, manipulated exchange rates to stay within that zone. Their main difficulty has been figuring out what target to pick, since, indeed, they have no wisdom in rate-fixing beyond that of the market. Indeed, the concept of a just exchange-rate for the dollar is just as inane as the notion of the "just price" for a particular good.

A tempting opportunity for mischief has been offered the Keynesians by the coming of the European Community in 1992. The Keynesians, led by now Secretary of State James Baker, have been pushing for a new currency unit for this United Europe, to be issued by a European-wide Central Bank. This would not only mean an international economic government for Europe, it would also mean that it would become relatively easy for the post-1992 European Central Bank to become coordinated with the Central Banks of the United States and Japan, and to segue without too much trouble to the long-cherished goal of the World Central Bank and world currency unit.

Inflationist European countries, such as Italy and France, are eager for the coordinated European-wide inflation that a regional Central Bank would bring about. Hard-money countries such as West Germany, however, are highly critical of inflationary schemes. You would expect Germany, therefore, to resist these Europeanist demands; so why don't they? The problem is that, ever since World War II, the United States has had enormous political leverage upon West Germany and the United States and its Keynesian foreign secretary Baker have been pushing hard for European monetary unity. Only Great Britain, happily, has been throwing a monkey-wrench into these Keynesian proceedings. Hard-money oriented, and wary of infringements on its sovereignty—and also influenced by Monetarist adviser Sir Alan Wakers—Britain might just succeed in blocking the European Central Bank indefinitely.

At best, the Keynesian Dream is a long shot. It is always possible that, not only British opposition, but also the ordinary and numerous frictions between sovereign nations will insure that the Dream will never be achieved. It would be heartening, however, if principled opposition to the Dream could also be mounted. For what the Keynesians want is no less than an internationally coordinated and controlled worldwide, paper-money inflation, a fine-tuned inflation that would proceed unchecked upon its merry way until, whoops!, it landed the entire world smack into the middle of the untold horrors of global runaway hyperinflation. ▸

79
MONEY INFLATION AND PRICE INFLATION

The Reagan administration seemed to have achieved the culmination of its "economic miracle" of the last several years: while the money supply had skyrocketed upward in double digits, the consumer price index remained virtually flat. Money cheap and abundant, stock and bond markets boomed, and yet

---

First published in September 1986.

prices remaining stable: what could be better than that? Had the President, by inducing Americans to feel good and stand tall, really managed to repeal economic law? Had soft soap been able to erase the need for "root-canal" economics?

In the first place, we have heard that song before. During every boom period, statesmen, economists, and financial writers manage to find reasons for proclaiming that now, this time, we are living in a new age where old-fashioned economic law has been nullified and cast into the dust bin of history. The 1920s is a particularly instructive decade, because then we had expanding money and credit, and a stock and bond market boom, while prices remained constant. As a result, all the experts as well as the politicians announced that we were living in a brand "new era," in which new tools available to government had eliminated inflations and depressions.

What were these marvelous new tools? As Bernard M. Baruch explained in an optimistic interview in the spring of 1929, they were (a) expanded cooperation between government and business; and (b) the Federal Reserve Act, "which gave us coordinated control of our financial resources and . . . a unified banking system." And, as a result, the country was brimming with "self-confidence." But, also as a result of these tools, there came 1929 and the Great Depression. Unfortunately both of these mechanisms are with us today in aggravated form. And great self confidence, which persisted in the market and among the public into 1931, didn't help one whit when the fundamental realities took over.

But the problem is not simply history. There are very good reasons why monetary inflation cannot bring endless prosperity. In the first place, even if there were no price inflation, monetary inflation is a bad proposition. For monetary inflation is counterfeiting, plain and simple. As in counterfeiting, the creation of new money simply diverts resources from producers, who have gotten their money honestly, to the early recipients of the new money—to the counterfeiters, and to those on whom they spend their money.

Counterfeiting is a method of taxation and redistribution—from producers to counterfeiters and to those early in the chain when counterfeiters spend their money and the money gets respent. Even if prices do not increase, this does not alleviate the coercive shift in income and wealth that takes place. As a matter of fact, some economists have interpreted price inflation as a desperate method by which the public, suffering from monetary inflation, tries to recoup its command of economic resources by raising prices at least as fast, if not faster, than the government prints new money.

Second, if new money is created via bank loans to business, as much of it is, the money inevitably distorts the pattern of productive investments. The fundamental insight of the "Austrian," or Misesian, theory of the business cycle is that monetary inflation via loans to business causes overinvestment in capital goods, especially in such areas as construction, long-term investments, machine tools, and industrial commodities. On the other hand, there is a relative underinvestment in consumer goods industries. And since stock prices and real-estate prices are titles to capital goods, there tends as well to be an excessive boom in the stock and real-estate markets. It is not necessary for consumer prices to go up, and therefore to register as price inflation. And this is precisely what happened in the 1920s, fooling economists and financiers unfamiliar with Austrian analysis, and lulling them into the belief that no great crash or recession would be possible. The rest is history. So, the fact that prices have remained stable recently does not mean that we will not reap the whirlwind of recession and crash.

But why didn't prices rise in the 1920s? Because the enormous increase in productivity and the supply of goods offset the increase of money. This offset did not, however, prevent a crash from developing, even though it did avert price inflation. Our good fortune, unfortunately, is not due to increased productivity.

Productivity growth has been minimal since the 1970s, and real income and the standard of living have barely increased since that time.

The offsets to price inflation in the 1980s have been very different. At first, during the Reagan administration, a severe depression developed in 1981 and continued into 1983, of course dragging down the price inflation rate. Recovery was slow at first, and in the later years, three special factors held down price inflation. An enormous balance of trade deficit of $150 billion was eagerly enhanced by foreign investors in American dollars, which kept the dollar unprecedentedly high, and therefore import prices low, despite the huge deficit.

Second, and unusually, a flood of cash dollars stayed overseas, in hyperinflating countries of Asia and Latin America, to serve as underground money in place of the increasingly worthless domestic currency. And third, the well-known collapse of the OPEC cartel at last brought down oil and petroleum product prices to free-market levels. But all of these offsets were obviously one-shot, and rapidly came to an end. In fact, the dollar declined in value, compared to foreign currencies, by about 30 percent in the year following the "recovery."

We are left with the fourth offset to price inflation, the increased willingness by the public to hold money rather than spend it, as the public has become convinced that the Reagan administration has discovered the secrets to an economic miracle in which prices will never rise again. But the public has not been deeply convinced of this, because real interest rates (interest rates in money minus the inflation rate) are at the highest level in our history. And interest rates are strongly affected by people's expectations of future price inflation; the higher the expectation, the higher the interest rate.

We may therefore expect a resumption of price inflation before long, and, as the public begins to wake up to the humbug nature of the "economic miracle," we may expect that inflation to accelerate. ▶

80
BANK CRISIS!

There has been a veritable revolution in the attitude of the nation's economists, as well as the public, toward our banking system. Ever since 1933, it was a stern dogma—a virtual article of faith—among economic textbook authors, financial writers, and all Establishment economists from Keynesians to Friedmanites, that our commercial banking system was super-safe. Because of the wise Establishment of the Federal Deposit Insurance Corporation in 1933, that dread scourge—the bank run—was a thing of the reactionary past. Depositors are now safe because the FDIC "insures," that is, guarantees, all bank deposits. Those of us who kept warning that the banking system was inherently unsound and even insolvent were considered nuts and crackpots, not in tune with the new dispensation.

But since the collapse of the S & Ls, a catastrophe destined to cost the taxpayers between a half-trillion and a trillion-and-a-half dollars, this Pollyanna attitude has changed. It is true that by liquidating the Federal Savings and Loan Insurance Corporation into the FDIC, the Establishment has fallen back on the FDIC, its last line of defense, but the old assurance is gone. All the pundits and moguls are clearly whistling past the graveyard.

In 1985, however, the bank-run—supposedly consigned to bad memories and old movies on television—was back in force—replete with all the old phenomena: night-long lines waiting for the bank to open, mendacious assurances by the bank's directors that the bank was safe and everyone should go home, insistence by the public on getting their money out of the bank, and subsequent rapid collapse. As in 1932–33, the governors of the respective states closed down the banks to prevent them from having to pay their sworn debts.

First published in March 1991.

The bank runs began with S & Ls in Ohio and then Maryland that were insured by private insurers. Runs returned again this January among Rhode Island credit unions that were "insured" by private firms. And a few days later, the Bank of New England, after announcing severe losses that rendered it insolvent, experienced massive bank runs up to billions of dollars, during which period Chairman Lawrence K. Fish rushed around to different branches falsely assuring customers that their money was safe. Finally, to save the bank the FDIC took it over and is in the highly expensive process of bailing it out.

A fascinating phenomenon appeared in these modern as well as the older bank runs: when one "unsound" bank was subjected to a fatal run, this had a domino effect on all the other banks in the area, so that they were brought low and annihilated by bank runs. As a befuddled Paul Samuelson, Mr. Establishment Economics, admitted to the *Wall Street Journal* after this recent bout, "I didn't think I'd live to see again the day when there are actually bank runs. And when good banks have runs on them because some unlucky and bad banks fail . . . we're back in a time warp."

A time warp indeed: just as the fall of Communism in Eastern Europe has put us back to 1945 or even 1914, banks are once again at risk.

What is the reason for this crisis? We all know that the real estate collapse is bringing down the value of bank assets. But there is no "run" on real estate. Values simply fall, which is hardly the same thing as everyone failing and going insolvent. Even if bank loans are faulty and asset values come down, there is no need on that ground for all banks in a region to fail.

Put more pointedly, why does this domino process affect only banks, and not real estate, publishing, oil, or any other industry that may get into trouble? Why are what Samuelson and other economists call "good" banks so all-fired vulnerable, and then in what sense are they really "good"?

The answer is that the "bad" banks are vulnerable to the familiar charges: they made reckless loans, or they overinvested in Brazilian bonds, or their managers were crooks. In any case, their poor loans put their assets into shaky shape or made them actually insolvent. The "good" banks committed none of these sins; their loans were sensible. And yet, they too, can fall to a run almost as readily as the bad banks. Clearly, the "good" banks are in reality only slightly less unsound than the bad ones.

There therefore must be something about all banks—commercial, savings, S & L, and credit union—which make them inherently unsound. And that something is very simple although almost never mentioned: fractional-reserve banking. All these forms of banks issue deposits that are contractually redeemable at par upon the demand of the depositor. Only if all the deposits were backed 100 percent by cash at all times (or, what is the equivalent nowadays, by a demand deposit of the bank at the Fed which is redeemable in cash on demand) can the banks fulfill these contractual obligations.

Instead of this sound, non-inflationary policy of 100 percent reserves, all of these banks are both allowed and encouraged by government policy to keep reserves that are only a fraction of their deposits, ranging from 10 percent for commercial banks to only a couple of percent for the other banking forms. This means that commercial banks inflate the money supply tenfold over their reserves a policy that results in our system of permanent inflation, periodic boom-bust cycles, and bank runs when the public begins to realize the inherent insolvency of the entire banking system.

That is why, unlike any other industry, the continued existence of the banking system rests so heavily on "public confidence," and why the Establishment feels it has to issue statements that it would have to admit privately were bald lies. It is also why economists and financial writers from all parts of the ideological spectrum rushed to say that the FDIC "had to" bail out all the depositors of the Bank of New England, not just those who were "insured" up to $100,000 per deposit account. The FDIC had to perform this bailout, everyone said, because "otherwise the financial system would collapse." That is, everyone would find out that the entire fractional-reserve system is held together by lies and smoke and mirrors; that is, by an Establishment con.

Once the public found out that their money *is not* in the banks, and that the FDIC has no money either, the banking system would quickly collapse. Indeed, even financial writers are worried since the FDIC has less than 0.7 percent of deposits they "insure," estimated soon be down to only 0.2 percent of deposits. Amusingly enough, the "safe" level is held to be 1.5 percent! The banking system, in short, is a house of cards, the FDIC as well as the banks themselves.

Many free-market advocates wonder: why is it that I am a champion of free markets, privatization, and deregulation everywhere else, but not in the banking system? The answer should now be clear: Banking is not a legitimate industry, providing legitimate service, so long as it continues to be a system of fractional-reserve banking: that is, the fraudulent making of contracts that it is impossible to honor.

Private deposit insurance—the proposal of the "free-banking" advocates—is patently absurd. Private deposit insurance agencies are the first to collapse, since everyone *knows* they haven't got the money. Besides, the "free bankers" don't answer the question why, if banking is as legitimate as every other industry, it *needs* this sort of "insurance"? What other industry tries to insure itself?

The only reason the FDIC is still standing while the FSLIC and private insurance companies have collapsed, is because the people believe that, even though it technically doesn't have the money, if push came to shove, the Federal Reserve would simply *print* the cash and *give it* to the FDIC. The FDIC in turn would give it to the banks, not even burdening the taxpayer as the government has done in the recent bailouts. After all, isn't the FDIC backed by "full faith and credit" of the federal government, whatever that may mean?

Yes, the FDIC *could*, in the last analysis, print all the cash and give it to the banks, under cover of some emergency decree or statute. But . . . there's a hitch. If it does so, this means that all the trillion or so dollars of bank deposits would be turned into cash. The problem, however, is that if the cash is redeposited in the banks, their reserves would increase by that hypothetical trillion, and the banks could then multiply new money immediately by 10–20 trillion, depending upon their reserve requirements. And that, of course, would be unbelievably inflationary, and would hurl us immediately into 1923 German-style hyperinflation. And that is why no one in the Establishment wants to discuss this ultimate failsafe solution. It is also why it would be far better to suffer a one-shot deflationary contraction of the fraudulent fractional-reserve banking system, and go back to a sound system of 100 percent reserves. ▶

81
ANATOMY OF THE BANK RUN

It was a scene familiar to any nostalgia buff: all-night lines waiting for the banks (first in Ohio, then in Maryland) to open; pompous but mendacious assurances by the bankers that all is well and that the people should go home; a stubborn insistence by depositors to get their money out; and the consequent closing of the banks by government, while at the same time the banks were permitted to stay in existence and collect the debts due them by their borrowers.

In other words, instead of government protecting private property and enforcing voluntary contracts, it deliberately violated the property of the depositors by barring them from retrieving their own money from the banks.

All this was, of course, a replay of the early 1930s: the last era of massive runs on banks. On the surface the weakness was the fact that the failed banks were insured by private or state deposit insurance agencies, whereas the banks that easily withstood the

First published in September 1985.

storm were insured by the federal government (FDIC for commercial banks; FSLIC for savings and loan banks).

But why? What is the magic elixir possessed by the federal government that neither private firms nor states can muster? The defenders of the private insurance agencies noted that they were technically in better financial shape than FSLIC or FDIC, since they had greater reserves per deposit dollar insured. How is it that private firms, so far superior to government in all other operations, should be so defective in this one area? Is there something unique about money that requires federal control? The answer to this puzzle lies in the anguished statements of the savings and loan banks in Ohio and in Maryland, after the first of their number went under because of spectacularly unsound loans. "What a pity," they in effect complained, "that the failure of this one unsound bank should drag the sound banks down with them!"

But in what sense is a bank "sound" when one whisper of doom, one faltering of public confidence, should quickly bring the bank down? In what other industry does a mere rumor or hint of doubt swiftly bring down a mighty and seemingly solid firm? What is there about banking that public confidence should play such a decisive and overwhelmingly important role?

The answer lies in the nature of our banking system, in the fact that both commercial banks and thrift banks (mutual-savings and savings-and-loan) have been systematically engaging in fractional-reserve banking: that is, they have far less cash on hand than there are demand claims to cash outstanding. For commercial banks, the reserve fraction is now about 10 percent; for the thrifts it is far less.

This means that the depositor who thinks he has $10,000 in a bank is misled; in a proportionate sense, there is only, say, $1,000 or less there. And yet, both the checking depositor and the savings depositor think that they can withdraw their money at any time on demand. Obviously, such a system, which is considered fraud when practiced by other businesses, rests on a confidence trick: that is, it can only work so long as the bulk of depositors do not catch on to the scare and try to get their money out. The confidence is essential, and also misguided. That is why once the public catches on, and bank runs begin, they are irresistible and cannot be stopped.

We now see why private enterprise works so badly in the deposit insurance business. For private enterprise only works in a business that is legitimate and useful, where needs are being fulfilled. It is impossible to "insure" a firm, even less so an industry, that is inherently insolvent. Fractional reserve banks, being inherently insolvent, are uninsurable.

What, then, is the magic potion of the federal government? Why does everyone trust the FDIC and FSLIC even though their reserve ratios are lower than private agencies, and though they too have only a very small fraction of total insured deposits in cash to stem any bank run? The answer is really quite simple: because everyone realizes, and realizes correctly, that only the federal government—and not the states or private firms—can print legal tender dollars. Everyone knows that, in case of a bank run, the U.S. Treasury would simply order the Fed to print enough cash to bail out any depositors who want it. The Fed has the unlimited power to print dollars, and it is this unlimited power to inflate that stands behind the current fractional-reserve banking system.

Yes, the FDIC and FSLIC "work," but only because the unlimited monopoly power to print money can "work" to bail out any firm or person on earth. For it was precisely bank runs, as severe as they were that, before 1933, kept the banking system under check, and prevented any substantial amount of inflation.

But now bank runs—at least for the overwhelming majority of banks under federal deposit insurance—are over, and we have been paying and will continue to pay the horrendous price of saving the banks: chronic and unlimited inflation.

Putting an end to inflation requires not only the abolition of the Fed but also the abolition of the FDIC and FSLIC. At long last, banks would be treated like any firm in any other industry.

In short, if they can't meet their contractual obligations they will be required to go under and liquidate. It would be instructive to see how many banks would survive if the massive governmental props were finally taken away. ▶

82
Q & A ON THE S & L MESS

Q. When is a tax not a tax?

A. When it's a "fee." It was only a question of time before we would discover what form of creative semantics President Bush would use to wiggle out of his "read my lips" pledge (bolstered by the Richard Darman "walks like a duck" corollary) never ever to raise taxes. Unfortunately, it took only a couple of weeks to discover the answer. No, it wasn't "revenue enhancement" or "equity" or "closing of loopholes" this time; it was the good old chestnut, the "fee."

When Secretary of the Treasury Brady came up with the ill-fated "fee" proposal for all bank depositors to bail out the failed, insolvent S & L industry, President Bush likened it to the user fee the federal government charges for people to enter Yellowstone Park. But the federal government—unfortunately—*owns* Yellowstone and, as its owner, may arguably charge a fee for its use without it being labeled a "tax" (although even here problems can be raised since the government does not have the same philosophical or economic status as would a private owner). But on what basis can someone's use of his own money to deposit in an allegedly private savings and loan bank be called a "fee"? To *whom*, and for what?

No, in the heartwarming firestorm of protest that arose, from the general public, and from all politicians and political observers, it was clear that to everyone except the Bush

---

First published in April 1989.

administration, the proposed levy on savers looked, talked, and waddled very much like a tax-duck.

Q. When is insurance not insurance?

A. When you are trying to "insure" an industry that is already bankrupt. Sometimes, the tax that is supposedly not a tax is called, not a "fee" but an "insurance premium." When the barrage of public protest virtually sank the "fee" on savers, the Bush administration began to backpedal and to shift its proposal to a levy on other banks that are not yet officially insolvent, this new tax on banks to be termed a higher "insurance premium."

But there are far more problems here than creative semantics. The very concept of "insurance" is fallacious. To "insure" a fractional-reserve banking system, whether it be the deposits of commercial banks, or of savings and loan banks, is absurd and impossible. It is very much like "insuring" the Titanic *after it hit the iceberg*.

Insurance is only an appropriate term and a feasible concept when there are certain near-measurable risks that can be pooled over large numbers of cases: fire, accident, disease, etc. But an entrepreneurial firm or industry cannot be "insured," since the entrepreneur is undertaking the sort of risks that precisely cannot be measured or pooled, and hence cannot be insured against.

All the more is this true for an industry that is inherently and philosophically bankrupt anyway: fractional-reserve banking. Fractional-reserve S & L banking is pyramided dangerously on top of the fractional-reserve commercial banking system. The S & Ls use their deposits in commercial banks as their own reserves. Fractional reserve banks are philosophically bankrupt because they are engaged in a gigantic con-game: pretending that your deposits are there to be redeemed at any time you wish, while actually lending them out to earn interest.

It is because fractional reserves are a giant con that these banks rely almost totally on public "confidence," and that is why

President Bush rushed to assure S & L depositors that their money is safe and that they should not be worried.

The entire industry rests on gulling the public, and making them think that their money is safe and that everything is OK; fractional-reserve banking is the only industry in the country that can and will collapse as soon as that "confidence" falls apart. Once the public realizes that the whole industry is a scam, the jig is up, and it goes crashing down; in short, the whole operation is done with mirrors, and falls apart once the public finds out the score.

The whole point of "insurance," then, is not to insure, but to swindle the public into placing its confidence where it does not belong. A few years ago, private deposit insurance fell apart in Ohio and Maryland because one or two big banks failed, and the public started to take their money out (which was not there) because their confidence was shaken. And now that one-third of the S & L industry is officially bankrupt—and yet allowed to continue operations—and the Federal Savings and Loan Insurance Corporation (FSLIC) is officially bankrupt as well, the tottering banking system is left with the Federal Deposit Insurance Corporation (FDIC). The FDIC, which "insures" commercial banks, is still officially solvent. It is only in better shape than its sister FSLIC, however, because everyone perceives that behind the FDIC stands the unlimited power of the Federal Reserve to print money.

Q. Why did deregulation fail in the case of the S & Ls? Doesn't this violate the rule that free enterprise always works better than regulation?

A. The S & L industry is no free-market industry. It was virtually created, cartelized, and subsidized by the federal government. Formerly the small "building and loan" industry in the 1920s, the thrifts were totally transformed into the government-created and cartelized S & L industry by legislation of the early New Deal. The industry was organized under Federal Home Loan Banks and governed by a Federal Home Loan Board, which cartelized the industry, poured in reserves, and inflated the nation's money supply by generating subsidized cheap credit and mortgages to the nation's housing and real-estate industry.

FSLIC was the Federal Home Board's form of "insurance" subsidy to the industry. Furthermore, the S & Ls persuaded the Federal Reserve to cartelize the industry still further by imposing low maximum interest rates that they would have to pay their gulled and hapless depositors. Since the average person, from the 1930s through the 1970s, had few other outlets for their savings than the S & Ls, their savings were coercively channeled into low-interest deposits, guaranteeing the S & Ls a hefty profit as they loaned out the money for higher-interest mortgages. In this way, the exploited depositors were left out in the cold to see their assets decimated by continuing inflation.

The dam burst in the late 1970s, however, with the invention of the money-market mutual fund, which allowed the fleeced S & L depositors to take out their money in droves and put it into the funds paying market interest rates. The thrifts began to go bankrupt, and they were forced to clamor for elimination of the cartelized low rates to depositors, otherwise they would have gone under from money-market fund competition. But then, in order to compete with the high-yield funds, the S & Ls had to get out of low-yield mortgages, and go into swinging, speculative, and high-risk assets.

The federal government obliged by "deregulating" the assets and loans of the S & Ls. But, of course, this was phony deregulation, since the FSLIC continued to guarantee the S & Ls' liabilities: their deposits. An industry that finds its assets unregulated while its liabilities are guaranteed by the federal government may be, in the short-run, at least, in a happy position; but it can in no sense be called an example of a free-enterprise industry. As a result of nearly a decade of wild speculative loans, official S & L bankruptcy has now piled up, to the tune of at least $100 billion.

Q. How will the federal government get the funds to bail out the S & Ls and FSLIC, and, down the road, the FDIC?

A. There are three ways the federal government can bail out the S & Ls: increasing taxes, borrowing, or printing money and handing it over. It has already floated the lead balloon of raising "fees" on the depositing public, which is not only an outrageous tax on the public to bail out their own exploiters, but is also a massive tax on savings, which will decrease our relatively low amount of savings still further. On borrowing, it faces the much ballyhooed Gramm-Rudman obstacle, so the government is borrowing to bail out the S & Ls by floating special bonds that would not count in the federal budget. An example of creative accounting: if you want to balance a budget, spend money and don't count it in the budget!

Q. So why doesn't the Fed simply print the money and give it to the S & Ls?

A. It could easily do so, and the perception of the Fed's unlimited power to print provides the crucial support for the entire system. But there is a grave problem. Suppose that the ultimate bailout were $200 billion. After much hullaballoo and crisis management, the Fed simply printed $200 billion and handed it over to the S & L depositors, in the course of liquidating the thrifts. This in itself would not be inflationary, since the $200 billion of increased currency would only replace $200 billion in disappeared S & L deposits. But the big catch is the next step.

If the public then takes this cash, and redeposits it in the commercial banking system, as they probably would, the banks would then enjoy an increase of $200 billion in reserves, which would then generate an immediate and enormously inflationary increase of about $2 trillion in the money supply. Therein lies the rub.

Q. What's the solution to the S & L mess?

A. What the government *should* do, if it had the guts, is to "fess up" that the S & Ls are broke, that its own "insurance" fund is broke, and therefore, that since the government has no money which it does not take from the taxpayer, that the S & Ls should be allowed to go under and the mass of their depositors to lose their non-existent funds.

In a genuine free-market economy, no one may exploit anyone else in order to acquire an ironclad guarantee against loss.

The depositors must be allowed to go under along with the S & Ls. The momentary pain will be more than offset by the salutary lessons these depositors will have learned: don't trust the government, and don't trust fractional-reserve banking. One hopes that the depositors in fractional-reserve commercial banks will profit from this example and get their money out posthaste. All the commentators prate that the government "has to" borrow or tax to raise funds to pay off the S & L depositors. There is no "has to" about it; we live in a world of free will and free choice.

Eventually, the only way to avoid similar messes is to scrap the current inflationist and cartelized system and move to a regime of truly sound money. That means a dollar defined as, and redeemable in, a specified weight of gold coin, and a banking system that keeps its cash or gold reserves 100 percent of its demand liabilities. ▸

83
INFLATION REDUX

Inflation is back. Or rather, since inflation never really left, inflation is back, with a vengeance. After being driven down by the severe recession of 1981–82 from over 13 percent in 1980 to 3 percent in 1983, and even falling to 1 percent in 1986, consumer prices in the last few years have begun to accelerate upward. Back up to 4–5 percent in the last two years, price inflation finally

---

First published in May 1989.

drove its way into public consciousness in January 1989, rising at an annual rate of 7.2 percent.

Austrians and other hard-money economists have been chided for the last several years: the money supply increased by about 13 percent in 1985 and 1986; why didn't inflation follow suit? The reason is that, unlike Chicago School monetarists, Austrians are not mechanists. Austrians do not believe in fixed leads and lags. After the money supply is increased, prices do not rise automatically; the resulting inflation depends on human choices and the public's decisions to hold or not to hold money. Such decisions depend on the insight and the expectations of individuals, and there is no way by which such perceptions and choices can be charted by economists in advance.

As people began to spend their money, and the special factors such as the collapse of OPEC and the more expensive dollar began to disappear or work through their effects in the economy, inflation has begun to accelerate in response.

The resumption and escalation of inflation in the last few years has inexorably drawn interest rates ever higher in response. The Federal Reserve, ever timorous and fearful about clamping down too tightly on money and precipitating a recession, allowed interest rates to rise only very gradually in reaction to inflation. In addition, Alan Greenspan has been talking a tough line on inflation so as to hold down inflationary expectations and thereby keep down interest yields on long-term bonds. But by insisting on gradualism, the Fed has only managed to prolong the agony for the market, and to make sure that interest rates, along with consumer prices, can only increase in the foreseeable future. Most of the nation's economists and financial experts are, as usual, caught short by the escalating inflation, and can make little sense out of the proceedings. One of the few perceptive responses was that of Donald Ratajczak of Georgia State University. Ratajczak scoffed: "The Fed always follows gradualism, and it never works. And you have to ask after a while, Don't they read their own history?"

Whatever the Fed does, it unerringly makes matters worse. First it pumps in a great deal of new money because, in the depth of recession, prices go up very little in response. Emboldened by this "economic miracle," it pumps more and more new money into the system. Then, when prices finally start accelerating, it tries to prolong the inevitable and thereby only succeeds in delaying market adjustments.

Apart from a few exceptions, moreover, the nation's economists prove to be duds in anticipating the new inflation. In fact, it was only recently that many economists began to opine that the economy had undergone some sort of mysterious "structural change," and that, as a result, inflation was no longer possible. No sooner do such views begin to take hold, than the economy moves to belie the grandiose new doctrine.

Ironically, despite the gyrations and interventions of the Fed and other government authorities, recession is inevitable once an inflationary boom has been set into motion, and will occur after the inflationary boom stops or slows down. As investment economist Giulio Martino states: "We've never had a soft landing, where the Fed brought inflation down without a recession."

We can see matters particularly clearly if we rely on M-A (for Austrian), rather than on the various Ms issued by the Fed which are statistical artifacts devoid of real meaning. After increasing rapidly for several years, the money supply remained flat from April to August 1987, long enough to help precipitate the great stock market crash of October. Then, M-A rose by about 2.5 percent per year, increasing from $1,905 billion in August 1987 to $1,948 billion in July 1988. Since July, however, this modest increase has been reversed, and the money supply remained level until the end of the year, then fell sharply to $1,897 billion by the end of January 1989. From the middle of 1988, then, until the end of January 1989, the total money supply, M-A, fell in absolute terms by no less than an annual rate of 5.2 percent. The last time M-A fell that sharply was in 1979–80, precipitating the last great recession.

This is not an argument for the Fed to expand money again in panic. Quite the contrary. Once an inflationary boom is launched, a recession is not only inevitable but is also the only way of correcting the distortions of the boom and returning the economy to health. The quicker a recession comes the better, and the more it is allowed to perform its corrective work, the sooner full recovery will arrive. ▶

84
INFLATION AND THE SPIN DOCTORS

We are all too familiar with the phenomenon of the "spin doctors," those political agents who rush to provide the media with the proper "spin" after each campaign poll, speech, or debate. What we sometimes fail to realize is that the Establishment has its spin doctors in the economic realm as well. For every piece of bad economic news, there is a scramble to provide a pleasantly soothing interpretation.

One perennial favorite is our permanent state of inflation. During the halcyon days of the 1950s and 1960s, the Fed and the other monetary authorities believed that inflation was out of control if it went above 2 percent a year. But such is the narcotizing effect of habit and desensitization that nowadays our standard 4 percent rate is held to be equivalent to inflation having disappeared. In fact, the implication is that we have no need to worry so long as inflation stays below the dread "double digit," reached for the first time in peacetime during the inflationary recessions of the early and late 1970s.

Well, in January 1990, the cost of living index at least reached well over double-digit proportions. During that month, the cost of living shot up by 1.1 percent, which amounts to more

---

First published in May 1990.

than 13 percent per year, reaching the disturbing inflationary peaks of the 1970s. Was there any grave concern? Did the Fed and the administration, at long last, reach for the panic button?

Certainly not, for the economic spin doctors were quick to leap to their tasks. You see, if you take out the fastest rising price categories—food and energy—things don't look so bad. Food went up by 1.8 percent in January—an annual rise of almost 22 percent; while energy prices went up by no less than 5.1 percent—an annual increase of over 61 percent. But that's OK, because the culprit was the record cold snap in December, which drove food and vegetable prices up by 10.2 percent the following month (an annual rise of over 122 percent), and pushed up heating oil prices by 26.3 percent (an annual increase of over 315 percent).

Take out those volatile (though important) categories of food and energy, then, and we get a far more satisfactory "core rate" (defined as consumer price movements minus food and energy) of "only" 0.6 percent for January, an annual rise of 7.5 percent. This, the Establishment admitted, is definitely cause for concern, but it is, after all, well under the baleful levels of double-digit.

But, we must remember, there are often cold snaps during the winter, and the allegedly random effects of the weather always seem to work more strongly in the inflationary than in the deflationary direction.

The concoction of the "core rate" is a plausible-seeming example of a racketeering general principle: if you want to make inflation go away, simply take out the price categories that are rising most rapidly. Lop off enough prices, and you can make it seem that there is no inflation at all, ever. Find some excuse for taking out all the rising categories, call whatever is left the "base rate," and presto-changeo! inflation is gone forever.

Thus, during the early years of the Reagan administration, housing prices were going up by an embarrassing degree, and so they were simply taken out of the index, on the excuse that consumers pay annual rents, actual or imputed, and at that point rents had not yet caught up to the increases in the prices of housing. During the infamous German hyperinflation of 1923, for another example, there were respected Establishment economists who maintained that there was no inflation in Germany at all, but rather deflation, since prices in terms of gold (which was no longer redeemable for marks) were going down!

Unfortunately, the poor benighted consumers are paying through the nose in higher prices for all the goods in the index (and even more for goods that never get on the index, such as brand-name products and books), even including houses, food, and energy. We consumers don't have the privilege of paying only for "core" goods; nor, unfortunately, do we enjoy the luxury of paying in gold.

Since even the core rate is getting disturbingly high, the Establishment economists are beginning to look around for explanations. One old candidate for blame has therefore resurfaced, with several economists pointing out that wage rates went up by a disquietingly high 5.0 percent last year; but since prices went up by the now traditional 4.5 percent, this hardly seems a major point of worry.

Wage rates have been lagging behind price increases for years. The real culprit for the accelerating inflation is the one candidate that the Establishment always tries its best to avoid fingering: the money supply created by the federal government itself.

After years of the government's creating new money and pouring it into the economy, the people are now spending that money, and hence driving prices upward. But the last group the federal government wants to blame is itself; besides, money creation is too pleasant for the creator and his beneficiaries to give up without a struggle. And only when the power to create money, that is, to counterfeit, is taken totally out of the hands of government will the curse of inflation truly disappear forever. ▶

85
ALAN GREENSPAN:
A MINORITY REPORT ON THE FED CHAIRMAN

The press is resounding with acclaim for the accession to Power of Alan Greenspan as chairman of the Fed; economists from right, left, and center weigh in with hosannas for Alan's greatness, acumen, and unparalleled insights into the "numbers." The only reservation seems to be that Alan might not enjoy the enormous power and reverence accorded to his predecessor, for he does not have the height of a basketball player, is not bald, and does not smoke imposing cigars.

The astute observer might feel that anyone accorded such unanimous applause from the Establishment couldn't be all good, and in this case he would be right on the mark. I knew Alan 30 years ago, and have followed his career with interest ever since.

I found particularly remarkable the recent statements in the press that Greenspan's economic consulting firm of Townsend-Greenspan might go under, because it turns out that what the firm *really* sells is not its econometric forecasting models, or its famous numbers, but Greenspan himself, and his gift for saying absolutely nothing at great length and in rococo syntax with no clearcut position of any kind.

As to his eminence as a forecaster, he ruefully admitted that a pension fund managing firm he founded a few years ago just folded for lack of ability to apply the forecasting where it counted: when investment funds were on the line.

Greenspan's real qualification is that he can be trusted never to rock the Establishment's boat. He has long positioned himself in the very middle of the economic spectrum. He is, like

_____

First published in August 1987.

most other long-time Republican economists, a conservative Keynesian, which in these days is almost indistinguishable from the liberal Keynesians in the Democratic camp. In fact, his views are virtually the same as Paul Volcker, also a conservative Keynesian. Which means that he wants moderate deficits and tax increases, and will loudly worry about inflation as he pours on increases in the money supply.

There is one thing, however, that makes Greenspan unique, and that sets him off from his Establishment buddies. And that is that he is a follower of Ayn Rand, and therefore "philosophically" believes in laissez-faire and even the gold standard. But as the *New York Times* and other important media hastened to assure us, Alan only believes in laissez-faire "on the high philosophical level." In practice, in the policies he advocates, he is a centrist like everyone else because he is a "pragmatist."

As an alleged "laissez-faire pragmatist," at no time in his prominent 20-year career in politics has he ever advocated anything that even remotely smacks of laissez-faire, or even any approach toward it. For Greenspan, laissez-faire is not a lodestar, a standard, and a guide by which to set one's course; instead, it is simply a curiosity kept in the closet, totally divorced from his concrete policy conclusions.

Thus, Greenspan is only in favor of the gold standard if all conditions are right: if the budget is balanced, trade is free, inflation is licked, everyone has the right philosophy, etc. In the same way, he might say he only favors free trade if all conditions are right: if the budget is balanced, unions are weak, we have a gold standard, the right philosophy, etc. In short, never are one's "high philosophical principles" applied to one's actions. It becomes almost piquant for the Establishment to have this man in its camp.

Over the years, Greenspan has, for example, supported President Ford's imbecilic Whip Inflation Now buttons when he was Chairman of the Council of Economic Advisers. Much worse is the fact that this "high philosophic" adherent of laissez-faire saved the racketeering Social Security program in 1982, just when the general public began to realize that the program was bankrupt and there was a good chance of finally slaughtering this great sacred cow of American politics. Greenspan stepped in as head of a "bipartisan" (i.e., conservative and liberal centrists) Social Security Commission, and "saved" the system from bankruptcy by slapping on higher Social Security taxes.

Alan is a long-time member of the famed Trilateral Commission, the Rockefeller-dominated pinnacle of the financial-political power elite in this country. And as he assumes his post as head of the Fed, he leaves his honored place on the board of directors of J.P. Morgan & Co. and Morgan Guaranty Trust. Yes, the Establishment has good reason to sleep soundly with Greenspan at our monetary helm. And as icing on the cake, they know that Greenspan's "philosophical" Randianism will undoubtedly fool many free-market advocates into thinking that a champion of their cause now perches high in the seats of power. ▶

86
THE MYSTERIOUS FED

Alan Greenspan has received his foreordained reappointment as chairman of the Fed, to the smug satisfaction and contentment of the entire financial Establishment. For them, Greenspan's still in his heaven, and all's right with the world. No one seems to wonder at the mysterious process by which each succeeding Fed chairman instantly becomes universally revered and indispensable to the soundness of the dollar, to the banking and financial system, and to the prosperity of the economy.

When it looked for a while that the great Paul Volcker might not be reappointed as Fed chairman, the financial press went into a paroxysm of agony: no, no, without the mighty Volcker

---

First published in October 1991.

at the helm, the dollar, the economy, nay even the world, would fall apart. And yet, when Volcker finally left the scene years later, the nation, the economy, and the world, somehow did not fall apart; in fact, ever since, none of those who once danced around Volcker for every nugget of wit and wisdom, seem to care any longer that Paul Volcker is still alive.

What was Volcker's mysterious power? Was it his towering, commanding presence? His pomposity and charisma? His strong cigars? It turns out that these forces really played no role, since Alan Greenspan, now allegedly the Indispensable Man, enjoys none of Volcker's qualities of personality and presence. Greenspan, a nerd with the charisma of a wet mackerel, drones on in an uninspired monotone. So what makes him indispensable now? He is supposed to be highly "knowledgeable," but of course there are hundreds of possible Fed chairmen who would know at least as much.

So if it is not qualities of personality or intellect, what makes all Fed chairmen so indispensable, so widely beloved? To paraphrase the famous answer of Sir Edmond Hilary, who was asked why he persisted in climbing Mt. Everest, it is because the Fed chairman is there. The very existence of the office makes its holder automatically wonderful, revered, deeply essential to the world economy, etc. Anyone in that office, up to and including Lassie, would receive precisely the same hagiographic treatment. And anyone out of office would be equally forgotten; if Greenspan should ever leave the Fed, he will be just as ignored as he was before.

It's too bad that people aren't more suspicious: that they don't ask what's wrong with an economy, or a dollar, that supposedly depends on the existence of one man. For the answer is that there's lots wrong. The health of Sony or Honda depends on the quality of their product, on the continuing satisfaction of their consumers. No one particularly cares about the personal qualities of the head of the company. In the case of the Fed, the acolytes of the alleged personal powers of the chairman are never specific about what exactly he does, except for maintaining the "confidence" of the public or the market, in the dollar or the banking system.

The air of majesty and mystery woven around the Fed chairman is deliberate, precisely because no one knows his function and no one consumes the Fed's "product." What would we think of a company where the president and his P.R. men were constantly urging the public: "Please, please. Have confidence in our product—our Sonys, Fords, etc." Wouldn't we think that there was something fishy about such an enterprise? On the market, confidence stems from tried and tested consumer satisfaction with the product. The proclaimed fact that our banking system relies so massively on our "confidence" demonstrates that such confidence is sadly misplaced.

Mystery, appeals to confidence, lauding the alleged qualities of the head: all this amounts to a con-game. Volcker, Greenspan, and their handlers are tricksters pulling a Wizard of Oz routine. The mystery, the tricks, are necessary, because the fractional-reserve banking system over which the Fed presides is bankrupt. Not just the S & Ls and the FDIC are bankrupt, but the entire banking system is insolvent. Why? Because the money that we are supposed to be able to call upon in our bank deposit accounts is simply not there. Or only about 10 percent of that money is there.

The mystery and the confidence trick of the Fed rests on its function: which is that of a banking cartel organized and enforced by the federal government in the form of the Fed. The Fed continually enters the "open market" to buy government securities. With what does the Fed pay for those bonds? With nothing, simply with checking accounts created out of thin air. Every time the Fed creates $1 million of checkbook money to buy government bonds, this $1 million quickly finds its way into the "reserves" of the banks, which then pyramid $10 million more of bank deposits, newly created out of thin air. And if someone sensibly wants cash instead of these open book deposits, why that's okay, because the Fed just prints the cash which immediately become standard "dollars" (Federal

Reserve notes) which pay for this system. But even these fiat paper tickets only back 10 percent of our bank deposits.

It is interesting that, of the rulers of the Fed, the only ones that seem to be worried about the inflationary nature of the system are those Fed regional bank presidents who hail from outside the major areas of bank cartels. The regional presidents are elected by the local bankers themselves, the nominal owners of the Fed. Thus, the Fed presidents from top cartel areas such as New York or Chicago, or the older financial elites from Philadelphia and Boston, tend to be pro-inflation "doves," whereas the relatively anti-inflation "hawks" within the Fed come from the periphery outside the major cartel centers: e.g., those from Minneapolis, Richmond, Cleveland, Dallas, or St. Louis. Surely, this constellation of forces is no coincidence.

Of course, anyone who thinks that these regional bank presidents are insufferable anti-inflation "hawks" ain't seen nothing yet. Wait till they meet some Misesians! ▶

87
FIRST STEP BACK TO GOLD

September 1986 was an historic month in the history of United States monetary policy. For it is the first month in over 50 years—thanks to the heroic leadership of Ron Paul during his four terms in Congress—that the United States Treasury minted a genuine gold coin.

Gold coins were the standard money in the United States until Franklin Roosevelt repudiated the gold standard and confiscated the gold coins Americans possessed in 1933. Not only were these gold coins confiscated, under cover of the depression emergency, but possession not only of gold coins but of all gold (with the exception of designated amounts grudgingly allowed

---

First published in November 1986.

to collectors, dentists, jewelers, and industrial users) was prohibited.

During the 1970s, Congress made possession of gold by Americans legal, and now the Treasury itself acknowledges at least some monetary use by minting its own gold coins. We have come a long way, in only a decade, from total outlawry to Treasury minting.

It is true that the political motives for the new coin were not all of the purest. One of them was a way of trying to attract the gold coin business from the South African krugerrands, which somehow acquired a taint of apartheid by their mere production in South Africa. But the important thing is that gold is at least partially back in monetary use, and also that the public has a chance to see, look at, and invest in gold coins.

One of the ways by which government was able to weaken the gold standard, even before 1933, was to discourage its broad circulation as coins, and to convince the public that all the gold should be safely tucked away in the banks, in the form of bullion, rather than in general use as money in the form of coins. Since Americans were not using coins directly as money by 1933, it was relatively easy for the government to confiscate their coins without raising very much of an opposition.

The new American Eagle coin is a very convenient one for possible widespread use in the future. It usefully weighs exactly one troy ounce, and the front of the coin bears the familiar Saint-Gaudens design for the goddess Liberty that had been used on American gold coins from 1907 until 1933.

But while the minting of the new American Eagle coin is an excellent first step on the road back to sound money, much more needs to be done. It is important not to rest on our laurels.

For one thing, even though gold coins are now legal, the U.S. government has never relinquished its possession of the confiscated coins, nor given them back to their rightful owners, the possessors of U.S. dollars. So it is vitally important to denationalize the U.S. gold stock by returning it to private hands.

Second, there is what can only be considered a grisly joke perpetrated on us by the U.S. Treasury. The one-ounce gold coin is designated, like the pre-1933 coins, as "legal tender," but only at $50. In other words, if you owe someone $500, you can legally pay your creditor in ten one-ounce coins. But of course you would only do so if you were an idiot, since on the market gold is now worth approximately $420 an ounce. At the designated rate, who would choose to pay their creditors in $4,200 of gold to discharge a $500 debt?

The phony, artificially low gold price, is of course designed by the U.S. Treasury so as to make sure that no one would use these gold coins as money, that is, to make payments and discharge debt. Suppose, for example, that the government designated the one-ounce coin at a bit higher than the market price, say at $500. Then, everyone would rush to exchange their dollars for gold coins, and gold would swiftly replace dollars in circulation.

All this is a pleasant fantasy, of course, but even this superior system would not solve the major problem: what to do about the Federal Reserve and the banking system.

To solve that problem, it would not be enough merely to find a way to get the gold out of the hands of the Treasury. For that gold is technically owned by the Federal Reserve Banks, although kept in trust for the Fed by the Treasury at Fort Knox and other depositories. Furthermore, the Federal Reserve has the absolute monopoly on the printing of dollars, and that monopoly would remain even if people began to trade in dollars for Treasury gold coins.

It is indeed important to denationalize gold—to get it out of Fort Knox and into the hands of the people. But it is just as, if not more, important to denationalize the dollar—that is, to tie the name "dollar" firmly and irretrievably to a fixed weight of gold. Every piece of gold at Fort Knox would be tied to the dollar, and then, and only then, the Federal Reserve System could be swiftly abolished, and the gold poured back into the hands of the public at the fixed dollar weights. To accomplish this task, those who wish to return the gold of the nation and the dollar from the government to the people will have to agree on the fixed weight.

It is best to pick the initial definition of the gold dollar at the most convenient rate. Certainly $50 an ounce of gold is not it. There are good arguments for the current market price, for higher than the current price, and for a price sufficiently high (or a dollar weight sufficiently low) so as to enable the Fed, upon liquidation, to pay off not only its own debts but also all bank demand deposits one-for-one in gold (which would require a gold price of approximately $1,600 per ounce). But within those parameters, it almost doesn't matter what price is chosen, so long as these reforms are effected as soon as possible, and the country returns to sound money. ▶

88
FIXED-RATE FICTIONS

Governments, especially including the U.S. government, seem to be congenitally incapable of keeping their mitts off any part of the economy. Government, aided and abetted by its host of apologists among intellectuals and policy wonks, likes to regard itself as a *deus ex machina* (a "god out of the machine") that surveys its subjects with Olympian benevolence and omniscience, and then repeatedly descends to earth to fix up the numerous "market failures" that mere people, in their ignorance, persist in committing.

The fact that history is a black record of continual gross failure by this "god," and that economic theory explains why it must be so, makes no impression on official political discourse.

Every nation-state, for example, is continually tempted to intervene to fix its exchange rates, the rates of its fiat paper

First published in July 1994.

money in terms of the scores of other moneys issued by all the other governments in the world.

Governments don't know, and don't want to know, that the only successful fixing of exchange rates occurred, not coincidentally, in the era of the gold standard. In that era, money was a market commodity, produced on the market rather than manufactured *ad lib* by a government or a central bank. Fixed exchange rates worked because these national money units—the dollar, the pound, the lira, the mark, etc.—were not independent entities. Rather each was defined—as a certain weight of gold.

Like all definitions such as the yard, the ton, etc., the point of the definition was that, once set, it was fixed. Thus, for example, if, as was roughly the case in the nineteenth century, "the dollar" was defined as 1/20 of a gold ounce, "the pound" as 1/4 of a gold ounce, and "the French franc" as 1/100 of a gold ounce, the "exchange rates" were simply proportional gold weights of the various currency units, so that the pound would automatically be worth $5, the franc would automatically be worth 20 cents, etc.

The United States dropped the gold standard in 1933, with the last international vestiges discarded in 1971. After the whole world followed, each national currency became a separate and independent entity from all the others. Therefore a "market" developed immediately among them, as a market will always develop among different tradable goods.

If these exchange markets are left alone by governments, then exchange rates will fluctuate freely. They will fluctuate in accordance with the supplies and demands for each currency in terms of the others, and the day-to-day rates will, as in the case of all other goods, "clear the market" so as to equate supply and demand, and therefore assure that there will be no shortages or unsold surpluses of any of the moneys.

Fluctuating fiat moneys, as the world has discovered, once again since 1971, are unsatisfactory. They cripple the advantages of international money and virtually return the world to barter. They fail to provide the check against inflation by governments and central banks once supplied by the stern necessity of redeeming their monetary issues in gold.

What the world has failed to grasp is that there is one thing much worse than fluctuating fiat moneys: and that is fiat money where governments try to fix the exchange rates. For, as in the case of any price control, governments will invariably fix their rates either above or below the free-market rate. Whichever route they take, government fixing will create undesirable consequences, will cause unnecessary monetary crises, and, in the long run, will end up in ignominious failure. One crucial point is that government fixing of exchange rates will inevitably set "Gresham's Law" to work: that is, the money artificially undervalued by the government (set at a price too low by the government) will tend to disappear from the market ("a shortage"), while money overvalued by government (price set too high) will tend to pour into circulation and constitute a "surplus."

The Clinton administration, which seems to have a homing instinct for economic fallacy, has been as bumbling and inconsistent in monetary policy as in all other areas. Thus, until recently, the administration, absurdly worried about a seemingly grave (but actually non-existent) balance of payments "deficit," has tried to push down the exchange rate of the dollar to stimulate exports and restrict imports.

There is no way, however that government can ever find and set some sort of "ideal" exchange rate. A cheaper dollar encourages exports all right, but the administration eventually came to realize that there is an inevitable downside: namely, that import prices are higher, which removes competition that will keep domestic prices down.

Instead of learning the lesson that there is no ideal exchange rate apart from determination by the free market, the Clinton administration, as is its wont, reversed itself abruptly, and orchestrated a multi-billion dollar campaign by the Fed and other major central banks to prop up the sinking dollar, as against the German mark and the Japanese yen. The dollar rate rose slightly, and the media congratulated Clinton for propping up the dollar.

Overlooked in the hosannahs are several intractable problems. First, billions in taxpayers' money, here and abroad, are being devoted to distorting market exchange rates. Second, since the exchange rate is being coercively propped up, such "successes" cannot be repeated for long. How long before the Fed runs out of marks and yen with which to keep up the dollar? How long before Germany, Japan, and other countries tire of inflating their currencies to keep the dollar artificially high?

If the Clinton administration persists, even in the face of these consequences, in trying to hold the dollar artificially high, it will have to meet the developing mark and yen "shortages" by imposing exchange controls and mark-and-yen-rationing on American citizens.

In the meantime, one of the first bitter fruits of Nafta has already appeared. Like all other modern "free-trade" agreements, Nafta serves as a backchannel to international currency regulation and fixed exchange rates. One of the unheralded aspects of Nafta was joint government action in propping up each others' exchange rates. In practice, this means artificial overvaluation of the Mexican peso, which has been dropping sharply on the market, in response to Mexican inflation and political instability.

Thus, Nafta originally set up a "temporary" $6 billion credit pool to aid mutual overvaluation of exchange rates. With the peso slipping badly, the Nafta governments made the credit pool permanent and raised it to $8.8 billion. Moreover, the three Nafta countries created a new North American Financial Group, consisting of the respective finance ministers and central bank chairmen, to "oversee economic and financial issues affecting the North American partners."

Robert D. Hormats, vice-chairman of Goldman Sachs International, hailed the new arrangement as "a logical progression from trade and investment cooperation between the three countries to greater monetary and fiscal cooperation." Well, that's one way to look at it. Another way is to point out that this is one more step by the U.S. government toward arrangements that will distort exchange rates, create monetary crises and shortages, and waste taxpayers' money and economic resources.

Worst of all, the U.S. is marching inexorably toward economic regulation and planning by regional, and even world, governmental bureaucracies, out of control and accountable to none of the subject peoples anywhere on the globe. ▸

Economics Beyond the Borders

89

PROTECTIONISM AND THE
DESTRUCTION OF PROSPERITY

Protectionism, often refuted and seemingly abandoned, has returned, and with a vengeance. The Japanese, who bounced back from grievous losses in World War II to astound the world by producing innovative, high-quality products at low prices, are serving as the convenient butt of protectionist propaganda.

Memories of wartime myths prove a heady brew, as protectionists warn about this new "Japanese imperialism," even "worse than Pearl Harbor." This "imperialism" turns out to consist of selling Americans wonderful TV sets, autos, microchips, etc., at prices more than competitive with American firms.

Is this "flood" of Japanese products really a menace, to be combatted by the U.S. government? Or is the new Japan a godsend to American consumers?

In taking our stand on this issue, we should recognize that all government action means coercion, so that calling upon the U.S. government to intervene means urging it to use force and violence to restrain peaceful trade. One trusts that the protectionists

---

First published as a monograph in 1986.

are not willing to pursue their logic of force to the ultimate in the form of another Hiroshima and Nagasaki.

KEEP YOUR EYE ON THE CONSUMER

As we unravel the tangled web of protectionist argument, we should keep our eye on two essential points: (1) protectionism means force in restraint of trade; and (2) the key is what happens to the consumer. Invariably, we will find that the protectionists are out to cripple, exploit, and impose severe losses not only on foreign consumers but especially on Americans. And since each and every one of us is a consumer, this means that protectionism is out to mulct all of us for the benefit of a specially privileged, subsidized few—and an inefficient few at that: people who cannot make it in a free and unhampered market.

Take, for example, the alleged Japanese menace. All trade is mutually beneficial to both parties—in this case Japanese producers and American consumers—otherwise they would not engage in the exchange. In trying to stop this trade, protectionists are trying to stop American consumers from enjoying high living standards by buying cheap and high-quality Japanese products. Instead, we are to be forced by government to return to the inefficient, higher-priced products we have already rejected. In short, inefficient producers are trying to deprive all of us of products we desire so that we will have to turn to inefficient firms. American consumers are to be plundered.

HOW TO LOOK AT TARIFFS AND QUOTAS

The best way to look at tariffs or import quotas or other protectionist restraints is to forget about political boundaries. Political boundaries of nations may be important for other reasons, but they have no economic meaning whatever. Suppose, for example, that each of the United States were a separate nation. Then we would hear a lot of protectionist bellyaching that we are now fortunately spared. Think of the howls by high-priced New York or Rhode Island textile manufacturers who would then be complaining about the "unfair," "cheap labor" competition from various low-type "foreigners" from Tennessee or North Carolina, or *vice versa*.

Fortunately, the absurdity of worrying about the balance of payments is made evident by focusing on interstate trade. For nobody worries about the balance of payments between New York and New Jersey, or, for that matter, between Manhattan and Brooklyn, because there are no customs officials recording such trade and such balances.

If we think about it, it is clear that a call by New York firms for a tariff against North Carolina is a pure ripoff of New York (as well as North Carolina) consumers, a naked grab for coerced special privilege by less efficient business firms. If the 50 states were separate nations, the protectionists would then be able to use the trappings of patriotism, and distrust of foreigners, to camouflage and get away with their looting the consumers of their own region.

Fortunately, inter-state tariffs are unconstitutional. But even with this clear barrier, and even without being able to wrap themselves in the cloak of nationalism, protectionists have been able to impose interstate tariffs in another guise. Part of the drive for continuing increases in the federal minimum-wage law is to impose a protectionist devise against lower-wage, lower-labor-cost competition from North Carolina and other southern states against their New England and New York competitors.

During the 1966 Congressional battle over a higher federal minimum wage, for example, the late Senator Jacob Javits (R-NY) freely admitted that one of his main reasons for supporting the bill was to cripple the southern competitors of New York textile firms. Since southern wages are generally lower than in the north, the business firms hardest hit by an increased minimum wage (and the workers struck by unemployment) will be located in the south.

Another way in which interstate trade restrictions have been imposed has been in the fashionable name of "safety." Government-organized state milk cartels in New York, for example, have prevented importation of milk from nearby New Jersey under the patently spurious grounds that the trip across the Hudson would render New Jersey milk "unsafe."

If tariffs and restraints on trade are good for a country, then why not indeed for a state or region? The principle is precisely the same. In America's first great depression, the Panic of 1819, Detroit was a tiny frontier town of only a few hundred people. Yet protectionist cries arose—fortunately not fulfilled—to prohibit all "imports" from outside of Detroit, and citizens were exhorted to buy only Detroit. If this nonsense had been put into effect, general starvation and death would have ended all other economic problems for Detroiters.

So why not restrict and even prohibit trade, i.e., "imports," into a city, or a neighborhood, or even on a block, or, to boil it down to its logical conclusion, to one family? Why shouldn't the Jones family issue a decree that from now on, no member of the family can buy any goods or services produced outside the family house? Starvation would quickly wipe out this ludicrous drive for self-sufficiency.

And yet we must realize that this absurdity is inherent in the logic of protectionism. Standard protectionism is just as preposterous, but the rhetoric of nationalism and national boundaries has been able to obscure this vital fact.

The upshot is that protectionism is not only nonsense, but dangerous nonsense, destructive of all economic prosperity. We are not, if we were ever, a world of self-sufficient farmers. The market economy is one vast latticework throughout the world, in which each individual, each region, each country, produces what he or it is best at, most relatively efficient in, and exchanges that product for the goods and services of others. Without the division of labor and the trade based upon that division, the entire world would starve. Coerced restraints on trade—such as protectionism—cripple, hobble, and destroy trade, the source of life and prosperity. Protectionism is simply a plea that consumers, as well as general prosperity, be hurt so as to confer permanent special privilege upon groups of less efficient producers, at the expense of more competent firms and of consumers. But it is a peculiarly destructive kind of bailout, because it permanently shackles trade under the cloak of patriotism.

THE NEGATIVE RAILROAD

Protectionism is also peculiarly destructive because it acts as a coerced and artificial increase in the cost of transportation between regions. One of the great features of the Industrial Revolution, one of the ways in which it brought prosperity to the starving masses, was by reducing drastically the cost of transportation. The development of railroads in the early nineteenth century, for example, meant that for the first time in the history of the human race, goods could be transported cheaply over land. Before that, water—rivers and oceans—was the only economically viable means of transport. By making land transport accessible and cheap, railroads allowed interregional land transportation to break up expensive inefficient local monopolies. The result was an enormous improvement in living standards for all consumers. And what the protectionists want to do is lay an axe to this wondrous principle of progress.

It is no wonder that Frédéric Bastiat, the great French laissez-faire economist of the mid-nineteenth century, called a tariff a "negative railroad." Protectionists are just as economically destructive as if they were physically chopping up railroads, or planes, or ships, and forcing us to revert to the costly transport of the past—mountain trails, rafts, or sailing ships.

"FAIR" TRADE

Let us now turn to some of the leading protectionist arguments. Take, for example, the standard complaint that while the protectionist "welcomes competition," this competition must be "fair." Whenever someone starts talking about "fair competition" or indeed, about "fairness" in general, it is time to keep a sharp eye on your wallet, for it is about to be picked. For the genuinely "fair" is simply the voluntary terms of exchange, mutually agreed upon by buyer and seller. As most of the medieval scholastics were able to figure out, there is no "just" (or "fair") price outside of the market price.

So what could be "unfair" about the free-market price? One common protectionist charge is that it is "unfair" for an American firm to compete with, say, a Taiwanese firm which needs to pay only one-half the wages of the American competitor. The U.S. government is called upon to step in and "equalize" the wage rates by imposing an equivalent tariff upon the Taiwanese. But does this mean that consumers can never patronize low-cost firms because it is "unfair" for them to have lower costs than inefficient competitors? This is the same argument that would be used by a New York firm trying to cripple its North Carolina competitor.

What the protectionists don't bother to explain is why U.S. wage rates are so much higher than Taiwan. They are not imposed by Providence. Wage rates are high in the U.S. because American employers have bid these rates up. Like all other prices on the market, wage rates are determined by supply and demand, and the increased demand by U.S. employers has bid wages up. What determines this demand? The "marginal productivity" of labor.

The demand for any factor of production, including labor, is constituted by the productivity of that factor, the amount of revenue that the worker, or the pound of cement or acre of land, is expected to bring to the brim. The more productive the factory, the greater the demand by employers, and the higher its price or wage rate. American labor is more costly than Taiwanese because it is far more productive. What makes it productive? To some extent, the comparative qualities of labor, skill, and education. But most of the difference is not due to the personal qualities of the laborers themselves, but to the fact that the American laborer, on the whole, is equipped with more and better capital equipment than his Taiwanese counterparts. The more and better the capital investment per worker, the greater the worker's productivity, and therefore the higher the wage rate.

In short, if the American wage rate is twice that of the Taiwanese, it is because the American laborer is more heavily capitalized, is equipped with more and better tools, and is therefore, on the average, twice as productive. In a sense, I suppose, it is not "fair" for the American worker to make more than the Taiwanese, not because of his personal qualities, but because savers and investors have supplied him with more tools. But a wage rate is determined not just by personal quality but also by relative scarcity, and in the United States the worker is far scarcer compared to capital than he is in Taiwan.

Putting it another way, the fact that American wage rates are on the average twice that of the Taiwanese, does not make the cost of labor in the U.S. twice that of Taiwan. Since U.S. labor is twice as productive, this means that the double wage rate in the U.S. is offset by the double productivity, so that the cost of labor per unit product in the U.S. and Taiwan tends, on the average, to be the same. One of the major protectionist fallacies is to confuse the price of labor (wage rates) with its cost, which also depends on its relative productivity.

Thus, the problem faced by American employers is not really with the "cheap labor" in Taiwan, because "expensive labor" in the U.S. is precisely the result of the bidding for scarce labor by U.S. employers. The problem faced by less efficient U.S. textile or auto firms is not so much cheap labor in Taiwan or Japan, but the fact that other U.S. industries are efficient enough to afford it, because they bid wages that high in the first place.

So, by imposing protective tariffs and quotas to save, bail out, and keep in place less efficient U.S. textile or auto or microchip firms, the protectionists are not only injuring the American consumer. They are also harming efficient U.S. firms and industries, which are prevented from employing resources now locked into incompetent firms, and who could otherwise be able to expand and sell their efficient products at home and abroad.

"Dumping"

Another contradictory line of protectionist assault on the free market asserts that the problem is not so much the low costs enjoyed by foreign firms, as the "unfairness" of selling their products "below costs" to American consumers, and thereby engaging in the pernicious and sinful practice of "dumping." By such dumping they are able to exert unfair advantage over American firms who presumably never engage in such practices and make sure that their prices are always high enough to cover costs. But if selling below costs is such a powerful weapon, why isn't it ever pursued by business firms within a country?

Our first response to this charge is, once again, to keep our eye on consumers in general and on American consumers in particular. Why should it be a matter of complaint when consumers so clearly benefit? Suppose, for example, that Sony is willing to injure American competitors by selling TV sets to Americans for a penny apiece. Shouldn't we rejoice at such an absurd policy of suffering severe losses by subsidizing us, the American consumers? And shouldn't our response be: "Come on, Sony, subsidize us some more!" As far as consumers are concerned, the more "dumping" that takes place, the better.

But what of the poor American TV firms, whose sales will suffer so long as Sony is willing to virtually give their sets away? Well, surely, the sensible policy for RCA, Zenith, etc. would be to hold back production and sales until Sony drives itself into bankruptcy. But suppose that the worst happens, and RCA, Zenith, etc. are themselves driven into bankruptcy by the Sony price war? Well, in that case, we the consumers will still be better off, since the plants of the bankrupt firms, which would still be in existence, would be picked up for a song at auction, and the American buyers at auction would be able to enter the TV business and outcompete Sony because they now enjoy far lower capital costs.

For decades, indeed, opponents of the free market have claimed that many businesses gained their powerful status on the market by what is called "predatory price-cutting," that is, by driving their smaller competitors into bankruptcy by selling their goods below cost, and then reaping the reward of their unfair methods by raising their prices and thereby charging "monopoly prices" to the consumers. The claim is that while consumers may gain in the short run by price wars, "dumping," and selling below costs, they lose in the long run from the alleged monopoly. But, as we have seen, economic theory shows that this would be a mug's game, losing money for the "dumping" firms, and never really achieving a monopoly price. And sure enough, historical investigation has not turned up a single case where predatory pricing, when tried, was successful, and there are actually very few cases where it has even been tried.

Another charge claims that Japanese or other foreign firms can afford to engage in dumping because their governments are willing to subsidize their losses. But again, we should still welcome such an absurd policy. If the Japanese government is really willing to waste scarce resources subsidizing American purchases of Sony's, so much the better! Their policy would be just as self-defeating as if the losses were private.

There is yet another problem with the charge of "dumping," even when it is made by economists or other alleged "experts" sitting on impartial tariff commissions and government bureaus. There is no way whatever that outside observers, be they economists, businessmen, or other experts, can decide what some other firm's "costs" may be. "Costs" are not objective entities that can be gauged or measured. Costs are subjective to the businessman himself, and they vary continually, depending on the businessman's time horizon or the stage of production or selling process he happens to be dealing with at any given time.

Suppose, for example, a fruit dealer has purchased a case of pears for $20, amounting to $1 a pound. He hopes and expects to sell those pears for $1.50 a pound. But something has happened to the pear market, and he finds it impossible to sell most of the pears at anything near that price. In fact, he finds that he must sell the pears at whatever price he can get before they become overripe. Suppose he finds that he can only sell his stock of pears at 70 cents a pound. The outside observer might say that the fruit dealer has, perhaps "unfairly," sold his pears "below costs," figuring that the dealer's costs were $1 a pound.

"INFANT" INDUSTRIES

Another protectionist fallacy held that the government should provide a temporary protective tariff to aid, or to bring into being, an "infant industry." Then, when the industry was well-established, the government would and should remove the tariff and toss the now "mature" industry into the competitive swim.

The theory is fallacious, and the policy has proved disastrous in practice. For there is no more need for government to protect a new, young, industry from foreign competition than there is to protect it from domestic competition.

In the last few decades, the "infant" plastics, television, and computer industries made out very well without such protection. Any government subsidizing of a new industry will funnel too many resources into that industry as compared to older firms, and will also inaugurate distortions that may persist and render the firm or industry permanently inefficient and vulnerable to competition. As a result, "infant-industry" tariffs have tended to become permanent, regardless of the "maturity" of the industry. The proponents were carried away by a misleading biological analogy to "infants" who need adult care. But a business firm is not a person, young or old.

OLDER INDUSTRIES

Indeed, in recent years, older industries that are notoriously inefficient have been using what might be called a "senile-industry" argument for protectionism. Steel, auto, and other outcompeted industries have been complaining that they "need a breathing space" to retool and become competitive with foreign rivals, and that this breather could be provided by several years of tariffs or import quotas. This argument is just as full of holes as the hoary infant-industry approach, except that it will be even more difficult to figure out when the "senile" industry will have become magically rejuvenated. In fact, the steel industry has been inefficient ever since its inception, and its chronological age seems to make no difference. The first protectionist movement in the U.S. was launched in 1820, headed by the Pennsylvania iron (later iron and steel) industry, artificially force-fed by the War of 1812 and already in grave danger from far more efficient foreign competitors.

THE NON-PROBLEM OF THE BALANCE OF PAYMENTS

A final set of arguments, or rather alarms, center on the mysteries of the balance of payments. Protectionists focus on the horrors of imports being greater than exports, implying that if market forces continued unchecked, Americans might wind up buying everything from abroad, while selling foreigners nothing, so that American consumers will have engorged themselves to the permanent ruin of American business firms. But if the exports really fell to somewhere near zero, where in the world would Americans still find the money to purchase foreign products? The balance of payments, as we said earlier, is a pseudo-problem created by the existence of customs statistics.

During the day of the gold standard, a deficit in the national balance of payments was a problem, but only because of the nature of the fractional-reserve banking system. If U.S. banks, spurred on by the Fed or previous forms of central banks, inflated money and credit, the American inflation would lead to higher prices in the U.S., and this would discourage exports and encourage imports. The resulting deficit had to be paid for in some way, and during the gold standard era this meant being paid for in gold, the international money. So as bank credit expanded, gold began to flow out of the country, which put the fractional reserve banks in even shakier shape. To meet the threat to their solvency posed by the gold outflow, the banks eventually were forced to contract credit, precipitating a recession and reversing the balance of payment deficits, thus bringing gold back into the country.

But now, in the fiat-money era, balance of payments deficits are truly meaningless. For gold is no longer a "balancing item." In effect, there is no deficit in the balance of payments. It is true that in the last few years, imports have been greater than exports by $150 billion or so per year. But no gold flowed out of the country. Neither did dollars "leak" out. The alleged "deficit" was paid for by foreigners investing the equivalent amount of money in American dollars: in real estate, capital goods, U.S. securities, and bank accounts.

In effect, in the last couple of years, foreigners have been investing enough of their own funds in dollars to keep the dollar high, enabling us to purchase cheap imports. Instead of worrying and complaining about this development, we should rejoice that foreign investors are willing to finance our cheap imports. The only problem is that this bonanza is already coming to an end, with the dollar becoming cheaper and exports more expensive.

We conclude that the sheaf of protectionist arguments, many plausible at first glance, are really a tissue of egregious fallacies. They betray a complete ignorance of the most basic economic analysis. Indeed, some of the arguments are almost embarrassing replicas of the most ridiculous claims of seventeenth-century mercantilism: for example, that it is somehow a calamitous problem that the U.S. has a balance of trade deficit, not overall, but merely with one specific country, e.g., Japan.

Must we even relearn the rebuttals of the more sophisticated mercantilists of the eighteenth century: namely, that balances with individual countries will cancel each other out, and therefore that we should only concern ourselves with the overall balance? (Let alone realize that the overall balance is no problem either.) But we need not reread the economic literature to realize that the impetus for protectionism comes not from preposterous theories, but from the quest for coerced special privilege and restraint of trade at the expense of efficient competitors and consumers. In the host of special interests using the political process to repress and loot the rest of us, the protectionists are among the most venerable. It is high time that we get them, once and for all, off our backs, and treat them with the righteous indignation they so richly deserve. ❯

90
"FREE TRADE" IN PERSPECTIVE

There is no time like a presidential election year for truth to become buried under an avalanche of mendacious propaganda. No sooner did Patrick J. Buchanan enter the presidential race when the Bush administration, aided by its battalion of apologists in the media, attacked Buchanan as a "protectionist" violating the Bushian devotion to "free trade."

Indeed, the esoterics of international trade have not played such a visible role in national elections for many decades, perhaps since the nineteenth century. The very idea of Bush administration dedication to free trade is patently laughable, its absurdity punctuated by the president's Asian trip in tandem with the highly-paid, grossly inefficient, professional Japan basher Lee Iacocca.

For years, in fact, the administration has been doing its best to keep Japan from selling us high-quality, moderately priced cars, while also trying to force the hapless Japanese to purchase overpriced American lemons that they don't want to buy. *This* is "free trade"—now rechristened by President Bush "free *and fair* trade"? Indeed, the entire emphasis on trade deficits between two countries is a nightmarish fallacy already discarded by the sophisticated mercantilists of the seventeenth century.

In addition to this patent duplicity, however, it is generally overlooked that there is far more to freedom of trade than not obstructing it via tariffs or import quotas. More importantly,

---

First published in March 1992.

genuine freedom of trade must be, in addition, unregulated and unsubsidized. In addition to slapping on tariffs and quotas, the Bush administration has greatly intensified the regulations on American business that prevent them from competing or producing efficiently, either at home or abroad. Not only that: these intensified regulations are always pointed to as the administration's proudest—if not only—achievements: including the quota-imposing Civil Rights Act, the Clean Air Act, and the Americans with Disabilities Act.

But let us shift our focus from the Bush administration to the neoconservative columnists who infest the media, and who claim to be dedicated enemies of protectionism and advocates of pure and unrestricted freedom of trade. Here are some of the policies about which these "free traders" habitually wax enthusiastic:

1. *Regional "free-trade" zones,* embodied in the U.S.-Canada treaty, and in whatever "fast-track" Mexican treaty the president may come up with. It is blithely assumed that anyone skeptical of such treaties is a blankety-blank protectionist. And yet, such regional blocs can be dangerous. An example is the European Economic Community, highly vaunted by "free traders" as a noble example of a vast regional free-trade area. And yet, the reality is just the opposite.

Externally, the EC can and does use its power to raise general tariffs with nations outside the bloc. But even internally, the result has increased trade restrictions and regulations inside the bloc. Thus, the EC has been building a burgeoning European super-government and bureaucracy in Brussels, that has often increased regulation throughout the area. One pernicious measure of the EC has been to require low-tax countries in Europe to raise their taxes so as to make sure that each country enjoys a "fair and level playing field" with the others. In the same way, minimum wage laws and other pernicious "social" measures have been imposed on relatively freer economies within the EC. Mrs. Thatcher's much-publicized opposition to Britain's entry into the EC was not simply paranoia or blind resistance to a noble "new Europe."

The same evils can befall the United States in any regional trade bloc, and giving the president a blank check to negotiate and virtually impose a treaty is hardly a favorable omen for the future.

The major point is that genuine free trade requires no negotiations, treaties, super-power creations, or presidential jetting abroad. All it requires is for the United States to cut tariffs and quotas, as well as taxes and regulations. Period. And yes, unilaterally. No other nations or governments need get into the act.

2. *Foreign aid.* The neoconservative and Bushian "free traders" are invariably staunch supporters of massive foreign aid programs for the United States. And yet, since genuine free trade requires unsubsidized trade, these massive programs for export subsidies constitute an enormous interference with free trade that is never acknowledged, let alone defended by these alleged opponents of protectionism.

The arguments for foreign aid keep changing over the years (from "reconstructing" Europe, to stopping Communism, to developing the Third World, to humanitarian relief of famine), but throughout the various twists and turns the essence of the process remains the same: a systematic racket by which money is seized from the American taxpayers, and handed over to the following groups: (1) the U.S. government bureaucracy, for its handling fee; (2) recipient foreign governments, whose wealth and power is strengthened *vis-à-vis* their own hapless subjects; and (3) last and foremost, the U.S. export firms and industries upon whom the foreign governments necessarily spend their purloined dollars.

Apart from the questionable morality of looting you and me and other American taxpayers in order to subsidize U.S. export firms and their bankers, we must see the enormous distortion of trade that this system entails.

3. *Cartelized World Paper Money.* A far greater danger to trade than a couple of tariffs is the seemingly inexorable drive of the entire Keynesian Establishment (from left-Keynesian Democrats to conservative-Keynesian Bushians to neoconservatives)

for world collaboration and cartelization of central banks, moving toward what will effectively be world economic government, with a world central bank issuing world fiat paper money.
This fulfillment of the long-time Keynesian dream will enable
worldwide inflation, engineered and controlled by a world central bank.

The European monetary unit would only be the first step in
such a scheme. Once again: the distortion of trade to be
imposed by worldwide control of money and banking is far
more dangerous than a tariff or two, and far less easy to get rid
of.

In gauging the extent of free trade or protectionism among
such presidential candidates as Pat Buchanan or President Bush
or the neoconservative hero-in-waiting, Jack Kemp, we should
consider that, unlike the other two, Buchanan favors the abolition of foreign aid. And while he has never pronounced on the
world fiat money scheme, it is certain that as a professed "economic nationalist," he would strongly oppose that as well.

We might also consider Buchanan's reply to George Will's
charge of protectionism on the Brinkley TV program: "What
you have to do, George, is take off the burdens of taxes, of regulations, from American business and industry, and then the
United States can start to compete." Who in the public arena is
closer to free trade than that? ▶

91
THE NAFTA MYTH

Americans—or at least the American Establishment—may
be the most gullible people on earth. When Gorbachev
tried to sell his timid reforms as "market socialism," only the
American Establishment cheered. The Soviet public immediately

---

First published in October 1993.

spotted the phoniness and would have none of it. When the Polish Stalinist Oskar Lange touted "market socialism" for Poland, only American economists shouted huzzahs. The Polish public knew the score all too well.

For some people, it seems, all you have to do to convince them of the free enterprise nature of something is to label it "market," and so we have the spawning of such grotesque creatures as "market socialists" or "market liberals." The word "freedom," of course, is also a grabber, and so another way to gain adherents in an age that exalts rhetoric over substance is simply to *call* yourself or your proposal "free market" or "free trade." Labels are often enough to nab the suckers.

And so, among champions of free trade, the *label* "North American Free Trade Agreement" (Nafta) is supposed to command unquestioning assent. "But how can you be against *free trade?*" It's very easy. The folks who have brought us Nafta and presume to call it "free trade" are the same people who call government spending "investment," taxes "contributions," and raising taxes "deficit reduction." Let us not forget that the Communists, too, used to call their system "freedom."

In the first place, genuine free trade doesn't require a treaty (or its deformed cousin, a "trade agreement"; Nafta is called a trade agreement so it can avoid the constitutional requirement of approval by two-thirds of the Senate). If the Establishment truly wants free trade, all it has to do is to repeal our numerous tariffs, import quotas, anti-"dumping" laws, and other American-imposed restrictions on trade. No foreign policy or foreign maneuvering is needed.

If authentic free trade ever looms on the policy horizon, there'll be one sure way to tell. The government/media/big-business complex will oppose it tooth and nail. We'll see a string of op-eds "warning" about the imminent return of the nineteenth century. Media pundits and academics will raise all the old canards against the free market, that it's exploitative and anarchic without government "coordination." The Establishment would react to instituting true free trade about as enthusiastically as it would to repealing the income tax.

In truth, the bipartisan Establishment's trumpeting of "free trade" since World War II fosters the opposite of genuine freedom of exchange. The Establishment's goals and tactics have been consistently those of free trade's traditional enemy, "mercantilism"—the system imposed by the nation-states of sixteenth to eighteenth century Europe. President Bush's infamous trip to Japan was only one instance: trade policy as a continuing system of maneuverings to try to force other countries to purchase more American exports.

Whereas genuine free traders look at free markets and trade, domestic or international, from the point of view of the consumer (that is, all of us), the mercantilist, of the sixteenth century or today, looks at trade from the point of view of the power elite, big business in league with the government. Genuine free traders consider exports a means of paying for imports, in the same way that goods in general are produced in order to be sold to consumers. But the mercantilists want to privilege the government business elite *at the expense* of all consumers, be they domestic or foreign.

In negotiations with Japan, for example, be they conducted by Reagan or Bush or Clinton, the point is to force Japan to buy more American products, for which the American government will graciously if reluctantly permit the Japanese to sell their products to American consumers. Imports are the price government pays to get other nations to accept our exports.

Another crucial feature of post-World War II Establishment trade policy in the name of "free trade" is to push heavy subsidies of exports. A favorite method of subsidy has been the much beloved system of foreign aid, which, under the cover of "reconstructing Europe . . . stopping Communism," or "spreading democracy," is a racket by which the American taxpayers are forced to subsidize American export firms and industries as well as foreign governments who go along with this system. Nafta represents a continuation of this system by enlisting the U.S. government and American taxpayers in this cause.

Yet Nafta is more than just a big business trade deal. It is part of a very long campaign to integrate and cartelize government in order to entrench the interventionist mixed economy. In Europe, the campaign culminated in the Maastricht Treaty, the attempt to impose a single currency and central bank on Europe and force its relatively free economies to rachet up their regulatory and welfare states.

In the United States, this has taken the form of transferring legislative and judicial authority away from the states and localities to the executive branch of the federal government. Nafta negotiations have pushed the envelope by centralizing government power continent-wide, thus further diminishing the ability of taxpayers to hinder the actions of their rulers.

Thus the siren-song of Nafta is the same seductive tune by which the socialistic Eurocrats have tried to get Europeans to surrender to the superstatism of the European Community: wouldn't it be wonderful to have North America be one vast and mighty "free trade unit" like Europe? The reality is very different: socialistic intervention and planning by supernational Nafta Commission or Brussels bureaucrats accountable to no one.

And just as Brussels has forced low-tax European countries to raise their taxes to the Euro-average or to expand their welfare state in the name of "fairness," a "level playing field," and "upward harmonization," so too Nafta Commissions are to be empowered to "upwardly harmonize," to ride roughshod over labor and other laws of American state governments.

President Clinton's trade representative Mickey Kantor has crowed that, under Nafta, "no country in the agreement can lower its environmental standards—ever." Under Nafta, we will not be able to roll back or repeal the environmental and labor provisions of the welfare state because the treaty will have locked us in—forever.

In the present world, as a rule of thumb, it is best to oppose *all* treaties, absent the great Bricker Amendment to the Constitution, which could have passed Congress in the 1950s but was shot down by the Eisenhower administration. Unfortunately, under the Constitution, every treaty is considered "the supreme law of the land," and the Bricker Amendment would have prevented any treaty from overriding any pre-existing Constitutional rights. But if we must be wary of *any* treaty, we must be particularly hostile to a treaty that builds supranational structures, as does Nafta.

The worst aspects of Nafta are the Clintonian side agreements, which have converted an unfortunate Bush treaty into a horror of international statism. We have the side agreements to thank for the supra-national Commissions and their coming "upward harmonization." The side agreements also push the foreign aid aspect of the Establishment's "free trade" hoax. They provide for the U.S. to pour an estimated $20 billion into Mexico for an "environmental cleanup" along the U.S.-Mexican border. In addition, the United States has informally agreed to pour billions into Mexican government coffers through the World Bank when and if Nafta is signed.

As with any policy that benefits the government and its connected interests, the Establishment has gone all out in its propaganda efforts on behalf of Nafta. Its allied intellectuals have even formed networks to champion the cause of government centralization. Even if Nafta were a worthy treaty, this outpouring of effort by the government and its friends would raise suspicions.

The public is rightly suspicious that this effort is related to the vast amount of money that the Mexican government and its allied special interests are spending on lobbying for Nafta. That money is, so to speak, the down payment on the $20 billion that the Mexicans hope to mulct from the American taxpayers once Nafta passes.

Nafta advocates say we must sacrifice to "save" Mexican President Carlos Salinas and his allegedly wonderful "free-market" policies. But surely Americans are justly tired of making eternal "sacrifices," of cutting their own throats, on behalf of cloudy foreign objectives which never seem to benefit them. If Nafta dies, Salinas and his party may fall. But what that means is that Mexico's vicious one-party rule by the PRI (Institutional Revolutionary Party) may at last come to an end after many corrupt decades. What's wrong with that? Why should such a fate cause our champions of "global democracy" to tremble?

We should look at the supposed nobility of Carlos Salinas in the same way we look at the other ersatz heroes served up to us by the Establishment. How many Americans know, for example, that under Annex 602.3 of the Nafta treaty, the "free-market" Salinas government "reserves to itself" all exploration and use, all investment and provision, all refining and processing, all trade, transportation and distribution, of oil and natural gas? All private investment in and operation of oil and gas in Mexico, in other words, is to be prohibited. *This* is the government Americans have to sacrifice to preserve?

Most English and German conservatives are fully aware of the dangers of the Brussels-Maastricht Eurocracy. They understand that when the people and institutions whose existence is devoted to promoting statism suddenly come out for freedom, something is amiss. American conservatives and free-marketers should also be aware of the equivalent dangers of Nafta. ▶

92
IS THERE LIFE AFTER NAFTA?

The great historian Charles A. Beard used to talk about the vital gulf between "appearance" and "reality" that pervades our politics and our political system. Rarely has that gulf been as striking and as revealing as in the bitter and intense struggle over Nafta. On the surface, Nafta dealt with a few puny tariffs

---

First published in February 1994.

covering a small fraction of American trade. So why the fuss and feathers? Why did the Clinton administration pull out all the stops, throwing caution to the winds by openly and shamelessly buying Congressional votes? And why the coming together of the entire Establishment: Democrats, Republicans, Big Business, Big Finance, Big Media, ex-Presidents and Secretaries of State, including the ubiquitous Henry Kissinger, and the last but surely not least, Big Economists and Nobel Laureates? What was going on here?

Perhaps the most shocking performance was that of America's self-styled free-market economists, periodicals, and think-tanks. Surely it would have been legitimate for them to say, in response to those of us who denounced Nafta from a free-trade perspective: "Your concerns are legitimate, but taken all in all, we think that Nafta cuts more in favor of free trade than against." Surely that would be the behavior one would expect from one free-market economist to a colleague who differed on the issue. But with only one or two exceptions, this was not the response of the Nafta forces.

From the time when Lew Rockwell first laid out the free-market case against Nafta in the *Los Angeles Times* (10/19/92), the reaction has been hysteria. Consider what happened when the excellent analysts of the Competitive Enterprise Institute, Jim Sheehan and Matt Hoffman, proved in meticulous detail that Nafta was a statist mockery of free trade. Instead of being persuaded, or considering their views soberly, other and larger free-market think-tanks inside the Beltway played vicious hardball, suitable for a political brawl rather than for a discussion of ideas. They put tremendous pressure on CEI, not only to suppress the Sheehan-Hoffman Report, but also to fire its authors. Fortunately, Fred Smith, head of CEI, firmly resisted these pressures.

So what was the frenzy all about, from Clinton and Kissinger down to Beltway think-tanks? It was indeed not about trade, certainly not about "free" trade. As the Clinton administration and their Republican auxiliaries stressed as the vote went down to the wire, the fight was about foreign policy, about the globalist policy that the United States has been pursuing since Woodrow Wilson, and certainly since World War II. It was about the Establishment-Keynesian dream of a New World Order. Nafta was a vital step down the road to that order.

Politically, such an order means a United States totally committed to a form of world government, in which U.S./UN "police" forces dominate the world, and impose institutions to our liking around the globe. Economically, it means a global system devoted not to free trade but to managed, cartelized trade and production, the economy to be governed by an oligarchic ruling coalition of Big Government, Big Business, and Big Intellectuals/Big Media. On the vital currency front the New World Order is slated to fulfill the Keynesian dream: of a World Reserve Bank issuing world paper money *ad lib*, to make sure that all countries can inflate and enjoy easy money together, with no country's currency inflating more than the others, and thereby suffering declines in exchange rates or outflow of a reserve currency. Internationally coordinated fiat money inflation is the Keynesian goal.

As for the shibboleths about "free trade," the "freedom" is strictly Orwellian. The Establishment's concept of "free" trade, since World War II, is exports subsidized by the taxpayers. The idea is to privilege American exports, either by foreign aid or by the international inflation which will pour more buying power into the hands of foreigners who will purchase American products. The U.S. business Establishment is willing to accept imports only as a bargaining chip to pressure foreigners into buying American exports.

Within American business, the war over Nafta was a war between exporters, and the bankers who finance them, as against business firms that suffer from import competition. It was a contest which the domestic oriented firms and their union supporters were doomed to lose, since their arguments, by denouncing competition and "loss of jobs," were clearly both special pleading and economically ignorant. As a result, the exporters and their financiers came across as wise statesmen, and their opponents appeared as both dumb and narrow-minded.

The truth is that the exporters were simply more sophisticated and better con artists; for one thing, they had in their camp the articulate economists and self-proclaimed champions of the free market. Well, the exporters and their bankers have, and have had for decades, the money and the power. And, unfortunately, in this world, if they have the money and the power, all too often the Big Intellectuals and Economists and Free-Market Champions will follow in their wake.

The good news, on the other hand, is that Nafta is only the beginning of the struggle. The New World Order is a Utopian project. Not only is it statist and cartelist and opposed to genuine free trade and free enterprise; it cuts against the interests and the freedom of the broad mass of the people. Furthermore, it also cuts against the rising and rampant nationalisms that have been reawakened throughout the world upon the collapse of Communism and the Soviet Empire. The broad public in the U.S. and in other nations, coupled with renascent nationalisms, could well be enough to put the boots to the New World Order. All that is needed are intellectuals and leaders courageous enough to tell the truth.

The truth can make us free; and the panic of the entire Establishment in the weeks before Nafta shows that *they* know what they will be up against once the public is on to their game. ▶

93
"FAIRNESS" AND THE STEEL STEAL

Whenever anyone talks about "fairness," the average American had better look to his wallet. When social

---

First published in February 1993.

pressure groups invoke "fairness," it means that American business must be saddled with quotas for mandatory hiring or promoting of myriad special interest groups, depending on who can get themselves organized and win the ear of the politicians.

When businessmen talk of "fair trade" or "fair competition," it means that they are pressuring the government to use coercion to cartelize their industry, to restrict production, raise prices, and allow the flourishing of inefficient and uncompetitive practices.

In business, the other guy, your competitor, if he is efficient and is successfully cutting into your business, is by definition engaging in "unfair competition" and "unfair trading practices." Such strictures, of course and again by definition, never seem to apply to the subsidies *you* may be receiving from government or to these very cartel policies that you are calling for.

Of all the industries in the United States, the one that has most consistently and successfully run whining for special privilege to the U.S. government has been iron and steel. Since 1969, the iron and steel industry, facing new competition from European firms that had recovered from World War II, lobbied for and received from the U.S. a system of steel import quotas, which severely restricted steel imports, drove up steel prices sharply, and caused repeated shortages for American steel-using manufacturers. Such steel import quotas, strong-armed and enforced by the U.S. government, were referred to in Orwellian fashion as "voluntary restraint agreements," though agreed to under substantial duress by the foreign governments.

These import quotas were always supposed to be temporary, to allow American steel companies to recover from whatever crises they claimed to have suffered, but the quotas of course kept being renewed. Finally, in the spring of 1992, they were allowed to lapse, but not because of an attack of free-trade fervor in the steel industry or in the "free trade" Bush administration. On the contrary, the steel industry decided that they had captured so much of the market share under cover of the quotas, that they were ready to shift the *form* of their protection from import quotas to higher tariffs, since the quotas were no longer keeping out very much foreign steel.

The Bush Commerce Department decided that a dozen countries, Mexico plus mainly European nations, were "unfairly" subsidizing their own steel industries, and that the tariffs against them must rise to offset this advantage. The fact that the U.S. steel companies are themselves heavily subsidized by the government (e.g., with special loans, development grants, and pension guarantees), did not of course enter into the equation. Tariffs on various forms of steel must now rise up to 90 percent. The result will be higher costs, restricted production, and higher prices imposed on a myriad of American steel-using industries, notably appliances, automobiles, and construction, which will harm the American consumer and hurt the competitiveness of American industry at home and abroad.

Moreover, the Commerce Department and the U.S. government's ultimate decision-maker, the International Trade Commission, will rule on still higher steel tariffs, to offset the alleged "dumping" of steel by 20 foreign countries, that is selling at prices below what the U.S. government designates to be "fair market value"—in plain English, a "value" set not by the *market* but high enough to make it easy for inefficient U.S. companies to compete.

This is not a new story for the steel industry, which has been a pernicious influence on American political life for nearly two centuries. During the War of 1812, the American iron industry, centered in Pennsylvania was able to take advantage of the cut-off of foreign trade during the war to expand and fill the place naturally taken by imports from England. After the war, however, the artificially swollen and inefficient Pennsylvania iron plants were unable to compete with imports from England. In response, the Pennsylvania iron industry established the first nationwide mass movement for a protective tariff, employing the Philadelphia newspaper publisher and printer Matthew Carey to head the agitation; Carey was particularly interested in a protective tariff against foreign printers. A bill for a protective tariff was introduced in Congress by Rep. Henry Baldwin of Pittsburgh, himself an ironmaster (an older term for iron manufacturer).

By the 1840s, the national Democratic Party was able to defeat the northern protectionists and establish freedom of trade. During the Civil War, however, the protectionist Republicans were able to use the virtual one-party Congress to drive through their entire national-statist economic program, including protective tariffs on iron and steel and other manufactures.

Heading the protectionist forces and the Radical Republicans was Pennsylvania Congressman Thaddeus Stevens, himself an ironmaster and interested in crushing the pro-free trade and anti-protectionist South. And every week at his Philadelphia salon, the venerable economist Henry C. Carey, son of Matthew and himself an ironmaster, instructed the Pennsylvania power elite at his "Carey Vespers," why they should favor fiat money and a depreciating greenback as well as a protective tariff on iron and steel. Carey showed the assembled Republican bigwigs, ironmasters, and propagandists, that expected future inflation is discounted far earlier in the foreign exchange market than in domestic sales, so that the dollar will weaken faster in foreign exchange markets under inflation than it will lose in purchasing power at home. So long as the inflation continues, then, the dollar depreciation will act like a second "tariff," encouraging exports as well as discouraging imports.

The arguments of the steel industry differed from one century to the next. In the nineteenth century, their favorite was the "infant industry argument": how can a new, young, weak, struggling "infant" industry as in the United States, possibly compete with the well-established mature, and strong iron industry in England without a few years, at least, of protection until the steel baby was strong enough to stand on its two feet?

Of course, "infancy" for protectionists never ends, and the "temporary" period of support stretched on forever. By the post-World War II era, in fact, the steel propagandists, switching their phony biological metaphors, were using what amounted to a "senescent industry argument": that the American steel industry was old and creaky, stuck with old equipment, and that they needed a "breathing space" of a few years to retool and rejuvenate.

One argument is as fallacious as the other. In reality, protection is a subsidy for the inefficient and tends to perpetuate and aggravate the inefficiency, be the industry young, mature, or "old." A protective tariff or quota provides a shelter for inefficiency and mismanagement to multiply, and for the excessive bidding up of costs and pandering to steel unions. The result is a perpetually uncompetitive industry. In fact, the American steel industry has always been laggard and sluggish in adopting technological innovation—be it the nineteenth-century Bessemer process, or the twentieth-century oxygenation process. Only exposure to competition can make a firm or an industry competitive.

As for "unfairly" low pricing or dumping, this is trumped-up nonsense by American firms who are being out-competed. But if a foreign country should be silly enough to engage in this practice, we should rush to take advantage of it rather than penalizing it. Suppose, for example, that Mexico, by some quirk, decides to "dump" steel by giving it away free, or charging a nominal penny a ton. Instead of barring these goodies, we should applaud as American buyers—in this case steel-using manufacturers—rush to buy these bargains so long as they might last. Until the inevitable day comes when Mexico goes bankrupt and reverses this nutty policy, the American buyers and the consumers will enjoy a bargain bonanza. "Dumping" can harm only the dumper; it always benefits the dumpee. ▶

94
THE CRUSADE AGAINST SOUTH AFRICA

For many years, America's campuses have been sunk in political apathy. The values of the 1950s are supposed to be back, including concentration on one's career and lack of interest in social or political causes.

But now, suddenly, it begins to seem like a replay of the late 1960s: demonstrations, placards, even sit-ins on campus. The issue is apartheid in South Africa, and the campaign hopes to bring down apartheid by pressuring colleges and universities to disinvest in South Africa. Coercion against South Africa is also being pursued on the legislative front, including drives to embargo that country as well as prohibit the importation of Krugerrands.

I yield to no one in my abhorrence of the apartheid system, but it must never be forgotten what the road to Hell is paved with. Good intentions are scarcely enough, and we must always be careful that in trying to do good, we don't do harm instead.

The object of the new crusade is presumably to help the oppressed blacks of South Africa. But what would be the impact of U.S. disinvestment?

The demand for black workers in South Africa would fall, and the result would be loss of jobs and lower wage rates for the oppressed people of that country. Not only that: presumably the U.S. firms are among the highest-paying employers in South Africa, so that the impact on black wages and working conditions would be particularly severe. In short: the group we are most trying to help by our well-meaning intervention will be precisely the one to lose the most. As on so many other occasions, doing good *for* becomes doing harm *to*.

First published in July 1985.

The same result would follow from the other legislative actions against South Africa. Prohibition of Krugerrands, for example, would injure, first and foremost, the black workers in the gold mining industry. And so on down the line.

I suppose that demonstrating and crusading against apartheid gives American liberals a fine glow of moral righteousness. But have they really pondered the consequences? Some American black leaders are beginning to do so. A spokesman for the National Urban League concedes that "We do not favor disinvestment. . . . We believe that the workers would be the ones that would be hurt." And Ted Adams, executive director of the National Association of Blacks Within Government, warns that disinvestment would "come down hard on black people," and could wind up "throwing the baby out with the bath water."

But other black leaders take a sterner view. A spokesman for Chicago Mayor Harold Washington admits "some concern that the most immediate effect of disinvestment may be felt by the laborers themselves," but then adds, on a curious note, "that's never an excuse not to take action." Michelle Kourouma, executive director of the National Conference of Black Mayors, explains the hard-line position: "How could it get any worse? We have nothing to lose and everything to gain: freedom."

The profound flaw is an equivocation on the word "we," a collective term covering a multitude of sins. Unfortunately, it is not Ms. Kourouma or Mr. Washington or any American liberal who stands to lose by disinvestment; it is only the blacks in South Africa.

It is all too easy for American liberals, secure in their well-paid jobs and their freedom in the United States, to say, in effect, to the blacks of South Africa: "We're going to make you sacrifice for your own benefit." It is doubtful whether the blacks in South Africa will respond with the same enthusiasm. Unfortunately, they have nothing to say in the matter; once again, their lives will be the pawns in other people's political games.

How can we in the United States help South African blacks? There is no way that we can end the apartheid system. But one thing we can do is the exact opposite of the counsel of our mis-led crusaders.

During the days of the national grape boycott, the economist Angus Black wrote that the only way for consumers to help the California grape workers was to buy as many grapes as they possibly could, thereby increasing the demand for grapes and raising the wage rate and employment of grape workers.

Similarly, all we can do is to encourage as much as possible American investment in South Africa and the importation of Krugerrands. In that way, wages and employment, in relatively well-paid jobs, will improve for the black laborers.

Free-market capitalism is a marvelous antidote for racism. In a free market, employers who refuse to hire productive black workers are hurting their own profits and the competitive position of their own company. It is only when the state steps in that the government can socialize the costs of racism and establish an apartheid system.

The growth of capitalism in South Africa will do far more to end apartheid than the futile and counterproductive grand-standing of American liberals. ▶

95
ARE DIAMONDS REALLY FOREVER?

The international diamond cartel, the most successful cartel in history, far more successful than the demonized OPEC, is at last falling on hard times. For more than a century, the powerful DeBeers Consolidated Mines, a South African corporation controlled by the Rothschild Bank in London, has managed to organize the cartel, restricting the supply of diamonds

First published in June 1986.

on the market and raising the price far above what would have been market levels.

It is not simply that DeBeers mines much of the world's diamonds; DeBeers has persuaded the world's diamond miners to market virtually all their diamonds through DeBeers's Central Selling Organization (CSO), which then grades, distributes, and sells all the rough diamonds to cutters and dealers further down on the road toward the consumer.

Even an unchallenged cartel, of course, does not totally control its price or its market; even it is at the mercy of consumer demand. One of the reasons that diamond prices and profits are slumping is the current world recession. World demand, and particularly consumer demand in the U.S. for diamonds, has fallen sharply, with consumers buying fewer diamonds and downgrading their purchases to cheaper gems, which of course particularly hits the market in the expensive stones.

But how could even this degree of cartel success occur in a free market? Economic theory and history both tell us that maintaining a cartel, for any length of time, is almost impossible on the free market, as the firms who restrict their supply are challenged by cartel members who secretly cut their prices in order to expand their share of the market as well as by new producers who enter the fray enticed by their higher profits attained by the cartelists. So, how could DeBeers maintain such a flourishing, century-long cartel on the free market?

The answer is simple: the market has not been really free. In particular, in South Africa, the major center of world diamond production, there has been no free enterprise in diamond mining. The government long ago nationalized all diamond mines, and anyone who finds a diamond mine on his property discovers that the mine immediately becomes government property. The South African government then licenses mine operators who lease the mines from the government and, it so happened, that lo and behold!, the only licensees turned out to be either DeBeers itself or other firms who were willing to play ball with the DeBeers cartel. In short: the international diamond cartel was only maintained and has only prospered because it was enforced by the South African government.

And enforced to the hilt: for there were severe sanctions against any independent miners and merchants who tried to produce "illegal" diamonds, even though they were mined on what used to be private property. The South African government has invested considerable resources in vessels that constantly patrol the coast, firing on and apprehending the supposedly pernicious diamond "smugglers."

Back in the pre-Gorbachev era, it was announced that Russia had discovered considerable diamond resources. For a while, there was fear among DeBeers and the cartelists that the Russians would break the international diamond cartel by selling in the open market abroad. Never fear, however. The Soviet government, as a professional monopolist itself, was happy to cut a deal with DeBeers and receive an allocation of their own quota of diamonds to sell to the CSO.

But now the CSO and DeBeers are in trouble. The problem is not only the recession; the very structure of the cartel is at stake, with the problem centering on the African country of Angola. Not that the communist government (or formerly communist, but now quasicommunist, government) refuses to cooperate with the cartel. It always has. The problem is three-fold. First, even though the Angolan civil war is over, the results have left the government powerless to control most of the country. Second, the end of the war has given independent wildcatters access to the Cuango River in northern Angola, a territory rich in diamonds. And third, the African drought has dried up the Cuango along with other rivers, leaving the rich alluvial diamond deposits in the beds and on the banks of the Cuango accessible to the eager prospectors.

With the diamond deposits available and free of war, and the central government unable to enforce the cartel, 50,000 prospectors have happily poured into the Cuango Valley of Angola. Furthermore, the prospectors are being protected by a private army of demobilized but armed Angolan soldiers. As one Johannesburg broker pointed out, "If you fly a patrol over the province you can get shot down by a missile. And it's a 100-mile river. You can't put a fence around it."

So far, DeBeers has been holding the line by buying up the "oversupply" caused by the influx of Angolan diamonds; this year, the cartel may be forced to buy no less than $500 million in "illegal" Angolan diamonds, twice as much as that country's official output. Consequently, DeBeers is taking heavy losses; as a result, Julian Ogilvie Thompson, the arrogant and aristocratic chairman of DeBeers, was forced to announce that the company was slashing its dividend, for only the second time since World War II. Immediately, DeBeers's shares plummeted by one-third, taking with it much of the Johannesburg Stock Exchange.

Overall, DeBeers's CSO had to purchase $4.8 billion of rough diamonds in 1992, while being able to sell only $3.5 billion. This huge pileup of inventory could break the cartel price; to stave off such a perceived disaster, DeBeers ordered cartel members to cut back 25 percent on the diamonds they had already contracted to market through the cartel. Such a large cutback sets the stage for individual firms to sneak supplies into the market and evade the cartel restrictions. No wonder that Sir Harry Oppenheimer, the octogenarian head of DeBeers, decided to "vacation" in Russia at the end of August, presumably to persuade the Russians to resist any temptation to engage in free-market competition in the diamond market. With luck, however, the forces of free competition—as well as the world's consumers of diamonds—may triumph. ▶

96
OIL PRICES AGAIN

Sometimes it seems that our entire apparatus of economic education: countless courses, students, professors, textbooks,

---

First published in October 1990.

backed up—in the case of oil pricing—by a decade of experience in the 1970s, is a gigantic waste of time. Certainly it seems that way when we ponder the near-universal reaction to the Kuwait crisis.

When Iraq invaded Kuwait on August 2, 1990, and the Bush administration quickly organized an oil embargo and military action to try to restore the hereditary emirate, gasoline prices, wholesale and retail, began going up immediately. In two days, gasoline price rises throughout the country ranged from four to 17 cents a gallon. Immediately, hysteria hit.

Wherever one turned—media pundits, the financial press, professional consumerists, politicians of all parties, the general public, even parts of the oil industry itself—the reaction was unanimous. The price increases were unacceptable, a "ripoff by Big Oil," they constituted evil "price gouging," and the cause was all too clear: "unconscionable greed."

Not content with "desecrating" pristine beaches and blue water by wantonly dumping oil upon them, Big Oil, in the words of Edwin Rothschild (all over TV as energy policy director of the Naderite Citizen Action), had launched a "preemptive strike: they are doing to American consumers what Saddam Hussein did to Kuwait." Federal, state, and local governments hastily began investigations of the "gouging." Senator Stevens (R-AK) ominously predicted "gas lines by Christmas," and Senator Lieberman (D-CT), leading the anti-oil hawks in the Senate, declared "there is absolutely no reason consumers should already be paying more for oil and gas . . . it must be stopped."

Under this bludgeoning, ARCO quickly announced a one-week freeze of gasoline prices, and there was general talk of "voluntary" freezes by other oil companies.

We are mired, once again, in a farrago of economic fallacies. Let us start with "greed." There is absolutely no evidence that Big Oil is any greedier than small oil, or that oil businesses are any greedier than any other firms. It is even less likely that oil businessmen, whether big or small, were suddenly seized by a monumental intensification of greed on August 2.

In fact, pricing on the market is not an act of will by sellers. Businessmen do not determine their selling prices on the basis of whether they feel greedy or "responsible" that morning. The entire apparatus of economic theory, built up over centuries, is devoted to demonstrating a great truth: that prices are set only by the demand of purchasers (how much of a good or service purchasers will buy at any given price), and by the supply or stock of the good.

Prices are set so as to "clear the market" by equating supply and demand; at the market price the supply of a good will exactly equal the amount of the good that people are willing to buy or hold. If the demand for the good increases, purchases will bid the price up; if the supply increases, the price will fall. Demanders consist of consumers, whose purchases are determined by the values they place on the goods, and various producers or businessmen, whose demands are determined by how much they expect consumers to pay for the final product. Current production, and therefore future supply, will be determined by how much businessmen expect that consumers will be paying in the future for the final product.

When Iraq invaded Kuwait, knowledgeable people in the oil market immediately and understandably forecast a future drop in the supply of oil. (In fact, as soon as Iraq began to mass troops on the Kuwait border a few weeks before the invasion, crude prices began to rise sharply, in expectation of a possible invasion.) Actions on the market, e.g., demands for the purchase or accumulation of oil, are not at all mechanistic: they are a function of what knowledgeable people on the market anticipate will happen.

Far from being disruptive or "unconscionable," this sort of speculative demand performs an important economic function. If people were mechanistic and did not anticipate the future, a cutoff of Middle Eastern oil would disrupt the economy by causing a sudden drop in supply and a huge jump in prices.

Speculative anticipation eases this volatility by raising prices more gradually; then, if supply is sharply cut off, speculators can unload their oil or gasoline stocks at a profit and lower prices from what they would have been. In short, speculators, by anticipating the future, help to smooth fluctuations and to allocate oil or any other commodity to its most-valued uses, over time.

The general public, media pundits, politicians, and even some businessmen, seem to have a mechanistic, cost-plus model of "just" pricing in their heads. It is all right, they concede, for each businessman to pay his costs of production and then add on some "reasonable" markup; but any price beyond that is morally condemned as excessive "greed." But cost of production has no direct influence on price; prices are only determined by supply and demand.

Assume, for example, that manna from heaven, an extremely valuable product, falls on some piece of land in New Jersey. The manna (extremely scarce and useful) will command a high price even though its "cost" to the landowner was zero (or is limited to the costs of advertising and marketing his find). There is no guaranteed profit margin on the free market. A businessman may find that he can only sell his product below his costs, and thereby suffer losses; or that he can sell above costs, and enjoy a profit. The better he forecasts, the more profit he makes. That, in fact, is what entrepreneurship and our profit-and-loss system is all about.

Ideas have consequences; and the danger is that we will repeat the calamities of the early and late 1970s. Then, too, suddenly higher prices (caused by current and anticipated supply cutoffs) were treated as moral failures on the part of oil men and combatted by maximum price controls imposed by government.

Imposing controls to stop a price increase is like trying to cure a fever by pushing down the mercury on a thermometer. They work on the symptoms instead of the causes. As a result, controls do not stop price increases; they create consumer shortages, misallocations, and drive the price increases underground into black markets. The consumers wind up far worse off than before. The consumer gas lines and shortages of both the early and late 1970s were caused by price controls; these gas lines (including the shooting of drivers who tried to muscle through the line) disappeared as if by magic as soon as gas prices were allowed to rise to clear the market and equate demand and supply.

If the politicians and pundits have their way, there may well be gas lines by Christmas; but the cause will be they themselves, and not small or Big Oil. ▶

97
WHY THE INTERVENTION IN ARABIA?

Amidst the near-universal hoopla for President Bush's massive intervention into the Arabian Peninsula, a few sober observers have pointed out the curious lack of clarity in Mr. Bush's strategic objective: is it to defend Saudi Arabia (and is that kingdom really under attack?); to kick Iraq out of Kuwait; to restore what Bush has oddly referred to as the "legitimate government" of Kuwait (made "legitimate" by what process?); to depose or murder Saddam Hussein (and to replace him with whom or what?); or to carpet-bomb Iraq back to the Stone Age?

There has been even less discussion, however, about a somewhat different even more puzzling question: why, exactly, are we suddenly hip-deep into Saudi Arabia? Why the hysteria? Why the most massive military buildup since Vietnam, and the placing of almost our entire army, air force, navy, marines, and a chunk of reserves in this one spot on the globe where there is not even a U.S. treaty obligation?

(1) Big guy, little guy. What is puzzling to some of us is crystal clear to General H. Norman Schwarzkopf, commander of U.S. forces in "Operation Desert Shield." Growing testy under

---

First published in November 1990.

media questioning, the general replied: "Don't you read the papers? You all know why we're here. A big guy beat up a little guy and we're here to stop it." The general was obviously using the Police Action metaphor. A big guy is beating up a little guy, and the cop on the corner intervenes to put a stop to the aggression.

Unfortunately, on further analysis, the Police Action metaphor raises far more questions than it answers. Aside from the obvious problem: why is the U.S. the self-appointed international cop? The cops, seeing the bad guy flee and lose himself in his neighborhood, do not surround that neighborhood with massive force and starve out the entire neighborhood looking for the bad guy. Still less do cops carpet-bomb the area hoping the bad guy is killed in the process. Cops operate on the crucial principle that innocent civilians do not get killed or targeted in the course of trying to apprehend the guilty.

Another crucial point: governments are not akin to individuals. If a big guy sets upon a little guy, the aggressor is invading his victim's right to his person and to his property. But governments cannot be assumed to be innocent individuals possessing just property rights in their territory. Government boundaries are not productive acquisitions, as is private property. They are almost always the result of previous aggressions and coercion by governments on both sides. We cannot assume that every existing state has the absolute right to "own" or control all the territory within its generally arbitrary borders.

Another problem with the alleged principle of the U.S. cop defending all borders, especially those of little states: what about the big U.S. government's own invasion of decidedly little Panama only a short time ago? Who gets to put the manacles on the U.S.? The usual retort was that the U.S. was "restoring" free elections in Panama. An odd way to justify intervention against Iraq, however, since Kuwait and Saudi Arabia are each absolutist royal oligarchies that are at the furtherest possible pole from "democracy" or "free elections."

(2) Saddam Hussein is a very bad man, the "Butcher of Baghdad." Absolutely, but he was just as much a butcher only the other day when he was our gallant ally against the terrible threat posed to the Gulf by the fanatical Shiites of Iran. The fanatical Shiites are still there, by the way, but they—as well as the Dictator of Syria, Hafez Assad, the Butcher of Hama—seem to have been magically transformed into our gallant allies against Saddam Hussein.

(3) But someday (three but more likely ten years) Saddam Hussein may acquire nuclear weapons. So what? The U.S. has nuclear weapons galore, the result of its late Cold War with the U.S.S.R., which also has a lot of nuclear weapons, and had them during the decades that they were our Implacable Enemy. So why is there far more hysteria now against Saddam than there ever was against the Soviet Union? Besides, Israel has had nuclear weapons for a long time, and India and Pakistan are at the point of war over Kashmir, and they each have nuclear arms. So why don't we worry about them?

The appeal to high principle is not going to succeed as a coherent explanation for the American intervention. Many observers, therefore, have zeroed in on economics as the explanation.

(4) The Oil War. Saddam, by invading Kuwait and threatening the rest of Arabia, poses the danger, as one media person put it, of being "king of the world's oil." But the oil explanation has invariably been posed as the U.S. defending the American consumer against an astronomical raising of oil prices by Iraq.

Again, however, there are many problems with the Oil Price explanation. The same Establishment that now worries about higher oil prices as a "threat to the American way of life," treated OPEC's quadrupling of oil prices in the early 1970s when we were far more dependent on Gulf oil than we are now, with calm and fortitude. Why was there no U.S. invasion of Saudi Arabia then to lower the price of oil? If there is so much concern for the consumer, why do so many politicians long to slap a huge 50 cents a gallon tax on the price gasoline?

Indeed, it is clear that the power of OPEC, like all cartels, is strictly limited by consumer demand, and that its power to raise the price of oil is far less than in the 1970s. Best estimates are that Saddam Hussein, even conquering the entire Gulf, could not raise the oil price above $25 a barrel. But the U.S., by its embargo, blockade, and continuing threats of war, has already managed to raise the price of crude to $40 a barrel!

In fact, it would be more plausible to suppose that the aim of the massive Bush intervention has been to raise the price of oil, not to lower it. And considering Mr. Bush's vice presidential visit to Saudi Arabia specifically to urge them to raise prices, his long-time connections with Texas oil and with Big Oil generally, as well as Texas's slump in recent years, this hunch begins to look all too credible.

But the likeliest explanation for the Bush intervention has not been raised at all. This view focuses not on the price of oil, but on its supply, and specifically on the profits to be made from that supply. For surely, as Joe Sobran has emphasized, Saddam does not intend to control oil in order to destroy either its supply or the world's customers whom he hopes will purchase that oil.

The Rockefeller interest and other Western Big Oil companies have had intimate ties with the absolute royalties of Kuwait and Saudi Arabia ever since the 1930s. During that decade and World War II, King Ibn Saud of Saudi Arabia granted a monopoly concession on all oil under his domain to the Rockefeller-controlled Aramco, while the $30 million in royalty payments for the concession was paid by the U.S. taxpayer.

The Rockefeller-influenced U.S. Export-Import Bank obligingly paid another $25 million to Ibn Saud to construct a pleasure railroad from his main palace, and President Roosevelt made a secret appropriation out of war funds of $165 million to Aramco for pipeline construction across Saudi Arabia. Furthermore, the U.S. Army was obligingly assigned to build an airfield and military base at Dhahran, near the Aramco Oilfields, after which the multi-million dollar base was turned over, gratis, to Ibn Saud.

It is true that Aramco was gradually "nationalized" by the Saudi monarchy during the 1970s, but that amounts merely to a shift in the terms of this cozy partnership: over half of Saudi oil is still turned over to the old Aramco consortium as management corporation for sale to the outside world. Plus Rockefeller's Mobil Oil, in addition to being a key part of Aramco, is engaged in two huge joint ventures with the Saudi government: an oil refinery and a petrochemical complex costing more than $1 billion each.

Oil pipelines and refineries have to be constructed, and Standard Oil of California (now Chevron), part of Aramco, brought in its longtime associate, Bechtel, from the beginning in Saudi Arabia to perform construction. The well-connected Bechtel (which has provided cabinet secretaries George Schultz and Casper Weinberger to the federal government) is now busily building Jubail, a new $20 billion industrial city on the Persian Gulf, as well as several other large projects in Saudi Arabia.

As for Kuwait, its emir granted a monopoly oil concession to Kuwait Oil Co., a partnership of Gulf Oil and British Petroleum, in the 1930s, and by now Kuwait's immensely wealthy ruling Sabah family owns a large chunk of British Petroleum, and also keeps enormous and most welcome deposits at Rockefeller-oriented Chase Manhattan and Citibank.

Iraq, on the other hand, has long been a rogue oil country, in the sense of being outside the Rockefeller-Wall Street ambit. Thus, when the crisis struck on August 2, the big Wall Street banks, including Chase and Citibank, told reporters that they had virtually no loans outstanding, nor deposits owed, to Iraq.

Hence, it may well be that Mr. Bush's war is an oil war all right, but not in the sense of a heroic battle on behalf of cheap oil for the American consumer. George Bush, before he ascended to the vice presidency, was a member of the executive committee of David Rockefeller's powerful Trilateral Commission. Mr. Bush's own oil exploration company, Zapata, was funded by the Rockefeller family. So this Oil War may instead be a less-than-noble effort on behalf of Rockefeller control of Middle East. ▶

98
A TRIP TO POLAND

In March 1986, I spent a fascinating week at a conference at a hotel in Mrogowo, in the lake country of northern Poland (formerly East Prussia). The conference, a broad-ranging symposium on "Economics and Social Change," was hosted by the Institute of Sociology at the University of Warsaw, and sponsored by a group of English conservative and free-market scholars.

Even though economically, as one of the Western participants noted, Poland is a "giant slum," its countryside, small towns, and cities in evident and grim decay, this gallant nation is intellectually the freest in the Eastern bloc. There is no other country in the Soviet orbit at which a conference of this sort could possibly be held.

The only restriction was that the announced titles of the papers had to be ideologically neutral. But, once the conference ran that particular gauntlet, and the meeting was approved by the authorities, anyone could—and did—say whatever they wished. (In my case, I bowdlerized the title of my paper, "Concepts of the Role of Intellectuals in Social Change Towards Laissez-Faire," by discreetly omitting the last three words, although the actual content of the talk remained the same.)

The first paper of the meeting was delivered by Professor Antony Flew, a distinguished English philosopher, who likes nothing better than to deliver—with intelligence and wit—zingers at the Left. Flew pulled no punches, pointing out the

---

First published in June 1986.

importance and necessity of property rights and the free market. The fascinating thing was that no Polish eyebrow was raised, and no Polish scholar reacted in horror. Quite the contrary. And it was enormously inspiring to see every one of the 20-odd Polish scholars denouncing the government, even though it was obvious to every one of us that there was a government agent listening intently to the proceedings. (The agent—the travel guide and director of the trip—was obviously highly intelligent, and aware of what was going on.)

The Poles ranged from libertarian to middle-of-the-road to dissident Marxist, but it was markedly evident that not one of them had any use whatsoever for the Communist regime. In addition to being opposed to Communism, none of the Polish scholars at the meeting had much use for *any* government. One told me, "of course, any act of government is done for the power and wealth of the government officials, and not for the public interest, common good, general welfare, or any other reasons offered."

"Yes," I said, "but the government's propaganda always says that they perform these actions for the common good, etc." The Polish professor looked at me quizzically: "Who believes government propaganda?" I replied that, "unfortunately, in the United States, many people believe government propaganda." He was incredulous.

The Polish scholars all knew English very well, a virtue that unfortunately we Westerners couldn't begin to reciprocate. Nevertheless, a real camaraderie developed. One amusing culture gap was the Polish waiters in our hotel (what passes for a "luxury hotel" in Poland is roughly equivalent to a low-end interstate motel in the U.S.) having to deal with the "kids" of the conference, two young English scholars who are insistent vegetarians. Poland is a land with a very high meat consumption per capita (the Communists never collectivized agriculture), but where meat is now rationed, and it was beyond the comprehension of the Polish waiters that two young privileged Westerners would keep calling for "more vegetables" while turning down top-grade beef and pork. Fortunately, there was always a Polish professor nearby who could serve as interpreter for these out-landish requests.

The most moving moment of the meeting came at the banquet on the final night, when the English sociologist who directed the conference, after thanking our Polish hosts, raised a glass and offered a heartfelt toast to "a free, sovereign, and Catholic Poland." Every one of us understood his intent, and everyone in that room, Protestants and unbelievers included, raised a glass and drank with fervor. Including the government agent. ▶

99
PERU AND THE FREE MARKET

He had been widely touted by the American media as the savior of Peru from hyperinflation and from the dangers posed by the current socialistic Garcia regime as well as the fanatical Maoist-type guerrillas who call themselves "The Shining Path." Mario Vargas Llosa, tall, aristocratic, eminent avant-garde novelist and ex-leftist, was running for president of Peru.

Vargas Llosa, trumpeted by the media, was a non-politician bound for inevitable victory on his free-market program. In the April presidential balloting, however, which Vargas was expected to sweep in a landslide forecast by the public opinion polls, the bubble burst. An unknown presidential candidate, Alberto Fujimori, operating with virtually no money out of a storefront in Lima, rose from a negligible amount of previous polls into a virtual tie with Vargas Llosa for first place. Fujimori may now win the runoff. What exactly happened on the road to the Peruvian free-market paradise?

Vargas Llosa had been converted to the free market by the remarkable economist, Hernando de Soto, whose best-selling work, *The Other Path*, not only called for a free market, but

First published in July 1990.

advocated a genuine "people's" free market based on private entrepreneurs, in contrast to Peru's (and other Latin American countries') unfortunate experiences with state capitalism that fosters privileged contractors and monopolists. In the early part of last year's presidential campaign, de Soto was one of Vargas's key campaign advisors. But de Soto soon broke with Vargas, denouncing him for selling out to the very state capitalism that de Soto had spent so many years denouncing.

Vargas's shift was the beginning of his troubles. His state-capitalist policies aggravated the fact that Vargas Llosa is one of the wealthy, white minority of European descent—the Criollos (approximately 2.8 million out of a largely Indian and mixed-Indian Peruvian population of 20 million)—who are the landlords and state capitalists of Peru and who are therefore cordially detested by the rest of the population. While Vargas Llosa surrounded himself with wealthy Criollos, he was visibly uneasy on the stump in Indian districts.

Vargas sealed his doom when he embraced the "free-market," "anti-inflationist" policies of the new Brazilian president, Fernando Collor de Mello. His "free-market shock treatment" for the Brazilian economy has been widely heralded as a salutary if radical "strong-man" technique of ending that country's accelerating inflation.

De Mello's policy may well be a "shock treatment," but it goes far beyond any shock administered by a free market. While there are some decontrol and privatization planks in the de Mello program, most of the shock is blatantly statist: including a massive increase in taxes, and, in particular, a Draconian deflationary program that freezes for many months everyone's bank account, thereby suddenly contracting the Brazilian money supply by 80 percent.

Austrian economists have often been accused of being grim "deflationists" for wanting to allow insolvent fractional reserve banks (including S & Ls) to go bankrupt without a bailout. But this contraction is nothing compared to de Mello's arbitrary deflation of 80 percent. Far from being free market, the Brazilian policy amounts to first engaging in a massive printing of money, then spending this newly-created money, driving up prices drastically, and then proclaiming a cure by confiscating the largest part of that money. In short, the Brazilian government has delivered to the country's economy a massive and lethal one-two punch. On his promising to Peru the same treatment as de Mello had just given Brazil, it is no wonder that the Peruvian voters turned from Vargas in droves. In the meanwhile, Fujimori came up fast on the outside. A member of the small but highly respected Japanese-Peruvian community of 55,000 Fujimori found himself embraced by the country's Indians as a fellow ethnic oppressed by the hated ruling Criollo elite.

The first Japanese were imported into Peru at the end of the nineteenth century to work as slaves on the coastal sugar plantations. The Japanese, however, rebelled within weeks, and moved to Lima, where they are now located. Fujimori's parents emigrated to Lima in the mid-1930s where his father, along with other Japanese, created hundreds of successful small businesses.

After Pearl Harbor, the U.S. government pressured Peru to go to war with Japan, to confiscate Japanese-owned businesses, including the elder Fujimori's tire repair shop, and to ship almost 1,500 Japanese to internment in the U.S. Hence, the Peruvian Indians' embrace of Fujimori as a fellow non-white rising up against the Criollos. The fact that Fujimori's immigrant mother does not speak Spanish works in his favor with the Inca masses, who don't speak Spanish either; Spanish is the language of Vargas Llosa and the Criollo conquerors.

Fujimori, by running a non-moneyed, grass-roots campaign, tapped this favorable sentiment. Moreover, his campaign slogan: "Work, Honesty, Technology," though a bit vague, resonated with the three key precepts of Inca law: don't be lazy, don't steal, don't lie. Fujimori also promised the Peruvians something far more concrete: that he would encourage massive private Japanese investment. As I write, the race is a toss-up. If Vargas loses, it will be because he deserves it. ◗

100
A GOLD STANDARD FOR RUSSIA?

In their eagerness to desocialize in 1989, the Soviets called in Western economists and political scientists—trying to imbibe wisdom from the fount of capitalism. In this search for answers, the host of American and European Marxist academics were conspicuous by their absence. Having suffered under socialism for generations, the Soviets and East Europeans have had it up to here with Marxism; they hardly need instruction from starry-eyed Western naifs who have never been obliged to live under their Marxist ideal.

One of the most fascinating exchanges with visiting Western firemen took place in an interview in Moscow between a representative of the Soviet Gosbank (the approximate equivalent of Russia's Central Bank) and Wayne Angell, a governor of the Federal Reserve Bank in the U.S. The interview, to be published in the Soviet newspaper *Izvestia*, was excerpted in the *Wall Street Journal*.

The man from Gosbank was astounded to hear Mr. Angell strongly recommend an immediate return of Soviet Russia to the gold standard. It would, furthermore, not be a phony supply-side gold standard, but a genuine one. As Angell stated, "the first thing your government should do is define your monetary unit of account, the ruble, in terms of a fixed weight of gold and make it convertible at that weight to Soviet citizens, as well as to the rest of the world."

Not that the Gosbank man was unfamiliar with the gold standard; it was just that he had imbibed conventional Western wisdom that the gold standard only be restored at some indistinct point in the far future, after all other economic ills had been neatly solved. Why, the Soviet financial expert asked Angell, should the gold standard be restored *first*?

First published in January 1990.

Wayne Angell proceeded to a cogent explanation of the importance of a prompt return to gold. The ruble, he pointed out, is shot; it has no credibility anywhere. It has been systematically depreciated, inflated, and grossly overvalued by the Soviet authorities. Therefore, mark or even dollar convertibility is not enough for the ruble. To gain credibility, to become a truly hard money, Angell explained, the ruble must become what Angell, with remarkable candor, referred to as "honest money."

"It is my belief," Angell continued, "that without an honest money, Soviet citizens cannot be expected to respond to the reforms," whereas a "gold-backed ruble would be seen as an honest money at home and would immediately trade as a convertible currency internationally."

With the ruble backed solidly by gold, the dread problem of the inflationary "ruble overhang" would wither away. The Soviet public is anxious to get rid of ever-depreciating rubles as soon as consumer goods become available. But under a gold standard, the demand for rubles would greatly strengthen, and Soviets could wait to trade them for more consumer goods or Western products. More goods would be produced as Soviet workers and producers become eager to sell goods and services for newly worthwhile rubles.

Without gold, however, Angell warned that the Soviet reform program might well collapse under the blows of rampant inflation and a progressively disintegrating ruble.

The man from Gosbank was quick with the crucial question. If the gold standard is so vital, why don't the United States and other Western countries adopt it? Angell's reply was fascinating in its implications: that the dollar and other Western currencies "have at least a history of gold convertibility" which enabled them to continue through the Bretton Woods system and launch the present system of fluctuating fiat currencies.

What, then, is Mr. Angell really saying? What is he really telling the Soviet central banker? He is saying that the United States and other Western governments have been able to get away with imposing what he concedes to be *dishonest* money because of the remnants of association these currencies have had with gold.

In contrast to the ruble, the dollar, the mark, etc., have still retained much of their credibility; in short, their governments are still able to con their publics, whereas the Soviet government is no longer able to do so. Hence, the Soviets must return to gold, whereas Western governments don't yet need to follow suit. *They* can still get away with dishonest money.

It would have been instructive to ask Mr. Angell about the myriad of Third World countries, particularly in Latin America, who have been suffering from severe currency deterioration and hyperinflation. Aren't those currencies in nearly as bad shape as the ruble, and couldn't those countries use a prompt return to gold? And perhaps even we in the West don't have to be doomed to wait until we too are suffering from hyperinflation before we can enjoy the great benefits of an honest, stable, non-inflatable, money? ▶

101
SHOULD WE BAIL OUT GORBY?

The debate over whether or to what extent we should bail out Gorby ($10 billion? $50 billion? $100 billion? Over how many years?) has almost universally been couched in false and misleading terms. The underlying concept seems to be that the United States government has, through some divine edict, become the wise and benign parent of the Soviet Union, which, in its turn, has for most of its career been a wild and unruly kid, but a kid that is now maturing and showing signs of taking its place as a responsible member of the family. It is supposed to be

---

First published in August 1991.

up to the parent, engaged in a behavioristic reward/punishment form of raising said kid, to mete out a reward/punishment scheme so as to reward improvement and to punish (by rewarding less—it's a very progressive form of child-rearing) any regression back to the wild-kid state. And in tune with modern mores, the "rewards" are exclusively monetary; that is, to put a candid face on it, we are engaged in a process of bribing the kid to be good.

And so the debate, within the circle of "parents" of the Soviet Union which all Americans have willy-nilly become, runs along these lines: Gorby did wonderfully, and freed Eastern Europe and began to free the Soviet Union; for this he should be rewarded copiously. On the other hand, Gorby slipped back for a while, and began to play with those bad companions the despotic Black Colonels, for which he should be punished (by withholding bribes); but recently, Gorby has gotten better.

In addition to the nuanced complications of trying to figure out to what extent to reward Gorby and to what extent to withhold the rewards, there is an extra complication, due to the fact that Gorby and the USSR are, after all, not one and the same. If we reward Gorby heavily, will it discourage the more advanced reformers such as Yeltsin, or will it push Gorby more in their direction? On the other hand, if we punish Gorby, will this lead to the dread Black Colonels—the real despots—taking over, or will Yeltsin and the liberals take over instead? The U.S. Establishment, which worships the status quo ("stability") almost above all things, at least in foreign affairs, and fears change like the head of Medusa, of course plumps for Gorby all the way.

Within this debate, too, everyone, even the most enthusiastic bailout advocates, recognize that the U.S. budget is limited, and that therefore there has to be some restraint upon the total handout.

The result of all these complexities is that, as in most other areas of American life, our seemingly vibrant democracy appears to be engaged in free and vigorous debate, but is really only parsing relatively trivial nuances within a basic, unargued, and implicitly assumed, paradigm: the U.S. as parent trying to find the precise formula for correcting previously unruly offspring. Unfortunately, the basic paradigm never gets discussed, and desperately needs airing and criticism.

There are many fundamental flaws with this universally held paradigm. First, no one appointed us as parents of the Soviet Union. To be more specific, the United States, as rich and powerful as it is, is not God; its resources are strictly limited and, over recent years, have experienced ever narrower limits.

Even if we wanted to and set out to do so, it is not in our power to cure all the ills of the world.

There is no way we can stop or reverse the volcanoes, heal the sick, or resurrect the dead. It is not just that we are not responsible for Third World (or Second World) poverty; there is nothing we can do about it, except bankrupting and impoverishing ourselves. We can only serve as a beacon-light on how to get out of the mire. For the United States and Western Europe did not become relatively rich and prosperous by accident or by a trick of nature; we lifted ourselves by our bootstraps out of the nasty, brutish, and short lives common to mankind.

We—or more precisely our ancestors—did it by devotion to property rights and the rule of law, and by providing the institutional means for a free and developing economy to flourish. The best indeed the only thing we can do for the impoverished Second and Third Worlds—is to tell them: look, here is how we became prosperous: by defending the rights of private property and free exchange, by allowing people to save and invest and keep their earnings. If you want to prosper, follow our forefathers: privatize and deregulate. Get your government off your backs and out of your lives.

If we adopt this new (or rather, return to the original U.S.) paradigm, the whole question of bailing out Gorby looks very different. U.S. government aid can only be a reward for Gorby and the rest of the neo-Communist *nomenklatura*. Regardless of rhetoric, such aid can only strengthen the State in the Soviet Union and therefore diminish and cripple the only hope for Russia and the other republics: the nascent and struggling private sector. Aid to Gorby, therefore, may be a reward for Gorby and his friends; but it is necessarily and ineluctably a harsh punishment for the peoples of the Soviet Union, because it can only delay and cripple their return, or advance, to a free economy.

To paraphrase a famous statement of Dos Passos ("all right, we are two nations"): every country is really two nations, not one. From one nation—the people interacting voluntarily, in families, churches, science, culture, and the market economy—all blessings flow. The "second nation"—the State—produces nothing; it acts as a parasitic blight upon the first, productive nation: taxing, looting, inflating, controlling, propagandizing, murdering. In the Soviet Union and other Communist countries, the State grew so wildly as to virtually swallow up the first nation, and the parasite ended up virtually destroying its host. The Soviet people need a U.S. bailout of its own State apparatus like it needs—to use an old New York expression—a hole in the head, and quite literally. And while the American public, one hopes, resists the notion of foisting upon the Soviet Union more of what has brought it to its current sorry state, we might even turn our attention away from foreign woes and tyrannies, and focus again upon our own beloved State here at home.

But then there is the seeming clincher in rebuttal: if we don't bail out Gorby, won't worse people come to power in the USSR? Well, who knows? In the first place, it is not given to us to decide the fate of the Soviet Union; that, after all, is up to the Soviets themselves. Again, the United States is not God. In the second place, since the future is uncertain, a post-Gorby Soviet Union could be better or worse. So if we can't predict the consequences, shouldn't we, for once, do what is right? Or is that too arcane a concept these days? ▶

102
WELCOMING THE VIETNAMESE

From its inception America was largely the land of the free, but there were a few exceptions. One was the blatant subsidies to the politically powerful maritime industry. Trying to protect what has long been a chronically inefficient industry from international competition, one of the initial actions of the first American Congress in 1789 was to pass the Jones Act, which protected both maritime owners and their top employees. The Jones Act provided that vessels of five or more tons in American waters had to be owned by U.S. citizens, and that only citizens could serve as masters or pilots of such vessels.

Times have changed, and whatever national security considerations that might have required a fleet of private boats ready to assist the U. S. Navy, have long since disappeared. The Jones Act had long ago become a dead letter, but let a law remain on the books, and it can always be trotted out to be used as a club for protectionism. And that is what has happened with the Jones Act.

Unfortunately, the latest victims of the Jones Act are Vietnamese immigrants who were welcomed as refugees from Communism, and who have proved to be thrifty, hard-working, and productive residents of the United States, working toward their citizenship. Unfortunately, too productive as fishermen for some of their inefficient Anglo competitors. In the early 1980s, Texas shrimpers attempted, by use of violence, to put Vietnamese-American competitors out of business.

The latest outrage against Vietnamese-American fishermen has occurred in California, mainly in San Francisco, where Vietnamese-Americans, legal residents of the U.S., have pooled their resources to purchase boats, and have been engaged in

---

First published in February 1990.

successful fishing of kingfish and hagfish for the past decade. In recent months, in response to complaints by Anglo competitors, the Coast Guard has been cracking down on the Vietnamese, citing the long-forgotten and long unenforced provisions of the Jones Act.

While the Vietnamese-Americans have been willing to pay the $500 fine per citation to keep earning their livelihood, the Coast Guard now threatens to confiscate their boat-registration documents and thereby put them out of business. The fact that these are peaceful, legal, permanent residents makes all the more ridiculous the U.S. government's contention that they "present a clear and present threat to the national security."

Dennis W. Hayashi of the Asian Law Caucus, who is an attorney for the Vietnamese fishermen, notes that all of them "are working toward citizenship. They were welcomed as political refugees. It is noxious to me that because they have not yet sworn allegiance to America there is an implication that they are untrustworthy."

In the best tradition of Marie Antoinette's "let them eat cake," the government replies that the Vietnamese are free to work on boats under five tons which would operate closer to shore. The problem is that the Vietnamese concentrate on fish that cater to Asian restaurants and fish shops, and that such kingfish and hagfish have to be caught in gill nets. So why not use gill nets in small boats closer to shore? Because here, in a classic governmental Catch-22 situation, our old friends the environmentalists have already been at work.

Seven years ago the environmentalists persuaded California to outlaw the use of gill netting in less than 60 feet of water. Why? Because these nets were, willy-nilly, ensnaring migratory birds and marine mammals in their meshes. So, once again, the environmentalists, speaking for the interests of all conceivable species as *against* man, have won out against their proclaimed enemies, human beings.

And so, seeking freedom and freedom of enterprise as victims of collectivism, the Vietnamese have been trapped by the

U.S. government as pawns of inefficient competitors on the one hand and anti-human environmentalists on the other. The Vietnamese-Americans are seeking justice in American courts, however, and perhaps they will obtain it. ▶

The End of Collectivism

103

THE COLLAPSE OF SOCIALISM

In 1988, we were living through the most significant and exciting event of the twentieth century: nothing less than the collapse of socialism.

Before the rise of the new idea of socialism in the mid and late nineteenth century, the great struggle of social and political philosophy was crystal-clear. On one side was the exciting and liberating idea of classical liberalism, emerging since the seventeenth century: of free trade and free markets, individual liberty, separation of Church and State, minimal government, and international peace. This was the movement that ushered in and championed the Industrial Revolution, which, for the first time in human history, created an economy geared to the desires of and abundance for the great mass of consumers.

On the other side were the forces of Tory statism, of the Old Order of Throne and Altar, of feudalism, absolutism, and mercantilism, of special privileges and cartels granted by Big Government, of war, and impoverishment for the mass of their subjects.

In the field of ideas, and in action and in institutions, the classical liberals were rapidly on the way to winning this battle.

First published in October 1988.

The world had come to realize that freedom, and the growth of industry and standards of living for all, must go hand in hand.

Then, in the nineteenth century, the onward march of freedom and classical liberalism was derailed by the growth of a new idea: socialism. Rather than rejecting industrialism and the welfare of the masses of people as the Tories had done, socialists professed that they could and would do far better by the masses and bring about "genuine freedom" by creating a State more coercive and totalitarian than the Tories had ever contemplated. Through "scientific" central planning, socialism could and would usher in a world of freedom and superabundance for all.

The twentieth century put this triumphant idealism into practice, and so our century became the Age of Socialism. Half the world became fully and consistently socialist, and the other half came fairly close to that ideal. And now, after decades of calling themselves the wave of the future, and deriding all their opponents as hopelessly "reactionary" (i.e., not in tune with modern thinking), "paleolithic," and "Neanderthal," socialism, throughout the world, has been rapidly packing it in. For that is what *glasnost* and *perestroika* amount to.

Ludwig von Mises, at the dawn of the Socialist Century, warned, in a famous article, that socialism simply could not work: that it could not run an industrial economy, and could not even satisfy the goals of the central planners themselves, much less of the mass of consumers in whose name they speak. For decades Mises was derided, and discredited, and various mathematical models were worked out in alleged "refutation" of his lucid and elegant demonstration.

And now, in the leading socialist countries throughout the world: in Soviet Russia, in Hungary, in China, in Yugoslavia, governments are rushing to abandon socialism. Decentralization, markets, profit and loss tests, allowing inefficient firms to go bankrupt, all are being adopted. And why are the socialist countries willing to go through this enormous and truly revolutionary upheaval? Because they agree that Mises was right, after all, that socialism doesn't work, and that only desocialized free markets can run a modern economy.

Some are even willing to give up some political power, allow greater criticism, secret ballots and elections, and even, as in Soviet Estonia, to allow a one-and-one half party system, because they are implicitly conceding that Mises was right: that you can't have economic freedom and private property without intellectual and political freedom, that you can't have *perestroika* without *glasnost*.

It is truly inspiring to see how freedom exerts its own "domino effect." Country after socialist country has been trying to top each other to see how far and how fast each one can go down the road of freedom and desocialization.

But much of this gripping drama has been concealed from the American public because, for the last 40 years, our opinion-molders have told us that the *only* enemy is Communism. Our leaders have shifted the focus away from socialism itself to a variant that is different only because it is more militant and consistent.

This has enabled modern liberals, who share many of the same statist ideas, to separate *competing* groups of socialists from the horrors of socialism in action. Thus, Trotskyites, Social Democrats, democratic socialists, or whatever, are able to pass themselves off as anti-Communist good guys, while the blame for the Gulag or Cambodian genocide is removed from socialism itself.

Now it is clear that none of this will wash. The enemy of freedom, of prosperity, of truly rational economics is socialism period, and not only one specific group of socialists.

As even the "socialist bloc" begins to throw in the towel, there are virtually no Russians or Chinese or Hungarians or Yugoslavs left who have any use for socialism. The only genuine socialists these days are intellectuals in the West who are enjoying a comfortable and even luxurious living within the supposed bastions of capitalism. ▶

104

THE FREEDOM REVOLUTION

It is truly sobering these days to turn from a contemplation of American politics to world affairs. Among the hot issues in the United States has been the piteous complaint about the "martyrdom" of Jim Wright, Tony Coelho, and John Tower to the insidious advance of "excessive" ethics. If we tighten up ethics and crack down on graft and conflict of interest, the cry goes, how will we attract good people into government? The short answer, of course, is that we will indeed attract fewer crooks and grafters, but one wonders why this is something to complain about.

And then in the midst of this petty argle-bargle at home comes truly amazing, wrenching, and soul-stirring news from abroad. For we are privileged to be living in the midst of a "revolutionary moment" in world history. History usually proceeds at a glacial pace, so glacial that often no institutional or political changes seem to be occurring at all. And then, wham! A piling up of a large number of other minor grievances and tensions reaches a certain point, and there is an explosion of radical social change. Changes begin to occur at so rapid a pace that old markets quickly dissolve. Social and political life shifts with blinding speed from stagnation to escalation and volatility. This is what it must have been like living through the French Revolution.

I refer, of course, to the accelerating, revolutionary implosion of socialism-communism throughout the world. That is, to the freedom revolution. Political positions of leading actors change radically, almost from month to month. In Poland, General Jaruzelski, only a few years ago the hated symbol of repression, threatens to resign unless his colleagues in the communist government accede to free elections and to the pact with Solidarity.

First published in August 1989.

On the other hand, in China, Deng Hsiao-ping, the architect of market reform ten years ago, became the mass murderer of unarmed Chinese people because he refuses to add personal and political freedom to economic reform, to add *glasnost* to this *perestroika*.

Every day there is news that inspires and amazes. In Poland, the sweep by Solidarity of every contested race, and the defeat of unopposed Communist leaders by the simple, democratic device—unfortunately unavailable here—of crossing their names off the ballot. In Russia, they publish Solzhenitsyn, and a member of the elected Congress of Deputies gets on nationwide TV and denounces the KGB in the harshest possible terms—to a standing ovation. The KGB leader humbly promises to shape up.

In the Baltic states, not only are *all* groups, from top Communists down-calling for independence from Soviet Russia, but also the Estonians come out for a free market, strictly limited government, and private property rights. In Hungary, numerous political parties spring up, most of them angrily rejecting the very concept of socialism.

In the "socialist bloc" covering virtually half the world, there are no socialists left. What all groups are trying to do is to dismantle socialism and government controls as rapidly as possible; even the ruling elites certainly in Poland and Hungary—are trying to desocialize with as little pain to themselves as possible. In Hungary, for example, the ruling *nomenklatura* is trying to arrange desocialization so that *they* will emerge as among the leading capitalists on the old principle of "if you can't beat 'em, join 'em."

We are also seeing the complete vindication of the point that Hayek shook the world with in *The Road to Serfdom*. Writing during World War II when socialism seemed inevitable everywhere, Hayek warned that, in the long run, political and economic freedom go hand in hand. In particular, that "democratic socialism" is a contradiction in terms. A socialist economy will inevitably be dictatorial.

It is clear now to everyone that political and economic freedom are inseparable. The Chinese tragedy has come about because the ruling elite thought that they could enjoy the benefits of economic freedom while depriving its citizens of freedom of speech or press or political assembly. The terrible massacre of June 4th at Tiananmen Square stemmed from the desire by Deng and his associates to flout that contradiction, to have their cake and eat it too.

The unarmed Chinese masses in Beijing met their fate because they made the great mistake of trusting their government. They kept repeating again and again: "The People's Army cannot fire on the people." They ached for freedom, but they still remained seduced by the Communist congame that the "government is the people." Every Chinese has now had the terrible lesson of the blood of thousands of brave young innocents engraved in their hearts: "The government is *never* the people," even if it calls itself "the people's government."

It has been reported that when the tanks of the butchers of the notorious 27th Army entered Tiananmen Square and crushed the Statue of Liberty, that a hundred unarmed students locked arms, faced the tanks, and sang the "Internationale" as the tanks sprayed them with bullets, and, as they fell, they were succeeded by another hundred who did the same thing, and met the same fate.

Western leftists, however, cannot take any comfort from the contents of the song. For the "Internationale" is a stirring call for the oppressed masses to rise up against the tyrants of the ruling elite. The famous first stanza, which is all the students were undoubtedly able to sing, holds a crucial warning for the Chinese or for any other Communist elite that refuses to get out of the way of the freedom movement now shaking the socialist world:

Arise, ye prisoners of starvation!
Arise, ye wretched of the earth,
For justice thunders condemnation,

A better world's in birth.
No more tradition's chains shall bind us,
Arise, ye slaves; no more in thrall!
The earth shall rise on new foundations,
We have been naught, we shall be all.

Who can doubt, any more, that "justice thunders condemnation" of Deng and Mao and Pol Pot and Stalin and all the rest? And that the "new foundations" and "the better world in birth" is freedom? ▶

105
HOW TO DESOCIALIZE?

Everyone in Soviet Russia and Eastern Europe wants to desocialize. They are convinced that socialism doesn't work, and are anxious to get, as quickly as possible, to a society of private property and a market economy. As Mieczyslaw Wilczek, Poland's leading private entrepreneur, and Communist minister of industry before the recent elections, put it: "There haven't been Communists in Poland for a long time. Nobody wants to hear about Marx and Lenin any more."

In addition to coming out solidly for private ownership and denouncing unions, Wilczek attacked the concept of equality. He notes that some people are angry because he recently urged people to get rich. "And what was I to propose? That they get poorer perhaps?" And *he* was rejected by the Polish voters for being too attached to the Communist Party!

East Europeans are eager for models and for the West to instruct them on how to speed up the process. How *do* they desocialize? Unfortunately, innumerable conservative institutions

---

First published in September 1989.

and scholars have studied East European Communism in the past 40 years, but precious few have pondered how to put desocialization into effect. Lots of discussion of game theory and throw weights, but little for East European desocializers to latch onto.

As one Hungarian recently put it, "There are many books in the West about the difficulties of seizing power, but no one talks about how to *give up* power." The problem is that one of the axioms of conservatism has been that once a country goes Communist, the process is irreversible, and the country enters a black hole, never to be recovered. But what if, as has indeed happened, the citizens, even the ruling elite, are sick of communism and socialism because they clearly don't work?

So how can communist governments and their opposition desocialize? Some steps are obvious: legalize all black markets, including currency (and make each currency freely convertible at market rates), remove all price and production controls, drastically cut taxes, etc. But what to do about State enterprises and agencies, which are, after all, the bulk of activity in communist countries?

The easy answer—sell them, either on contract or at auction—won't work here. For where will the money come from to buy virtually all enterprises from the government? And how can we ever say that the government *deserves* to collect virtually all the money in the realm by such a process. Telling individual managers to set their own prices is also not good enough; for the crucial step, acknowledged in Eastern Europe, is to transform State property into private property. So, some people and groups will have to be *given* that property? Who, and why?

As Professor Paul Craig Roberts stated recently in a fascinating speech in Moscow to the USSR Academy of Sciences, there is only one way to convey government property into private hands. Ironically enough, by far the best path is to follow the old Marxist slogan: "All land to the peasants (including agricultural workers) and "all factories to the workers! . . . Returning" the State property to descendants of those expropriated in 1917

would be impracticable, since few of them exist or can be identified, and certainly the *industries* could be returned to no one,
since they (in contrast to the land) were created by the Communist regime.

But there is one big political and economic problem: what to
do with the existing ruling elite, the *nomenklatura*? As the Polish opposition journalist Kostek Gebert recently put the
choice" "You either kill them off, or you buy them off." Admittedly, killing off the old despotic ruling elites would be emo-
tionally satisfying, but it is clear that the people on the spot, in
Poland and Hungary, and soon in Russia, prefer the more
peaceful buying them off to pursuing justice at the price of a
bloody civil war. And it is also clear that this is precisely what
the *nomenklatura* want. They want free markets and private
ownership, but they of course want to make sure that the transition period assures them of coming out very handsomely in at
least the initial distribution of capital. They want to start capitalism as affluent private entrepreneurs.

Interestingly, Paul Craig Roberts, whom no one could ever
accuse of being soft on communism or socialism, also recom-
mends the more peaceful course: "Historically in these trans-
formations ruling classes have had to be accommodated or overthrown. I would recommend that the Communist Party be
accommodated." In practice what this means is that "ownership
of the state factories should be divided between the ruling class
and the factory workers, and stock certificates issued." His solution makes a great deal of sense.

Alternatively, Roberts says that a national lottery could
determine the ownership of the means of production, since
whoever initial owners may be, an economy of private property
will be far more efficient, and "resources will eventually find
their way into the most efficient and productive hands." But the
trouble here is that Roberts ignores the hunger for justice
among most people, and particularly among victims of communism. A lottery distribution would be so flagrantly unjust that
the ensuing private property system might never recover from

this initial blow. Furthermore, it does make a great deal of difference to everyone where they come out in such a lottery; most people in the real world cannot afford and do not wish to take such an Olympian view.

In any case, Roberts has performed an important service in helping launch the discussion. It is about time that Western economists start tackling the crucial question of desocialization. Perhaps they might thereby help to advance one of the most welcome and exciting developments of the twentieth century. ▶

106
A RADICAL PRESCRIPTION FOR
THE SOCIALIST BLOC

It is generally agreed, both inside and outside Eastern Europe, that the only cure for their intensifying and grinding poverty is to abandon socialism and central planning, and to adopt private property rights and a free-market economy. But a critical problem is that Western conventional wisdom counsels going slowly, "phasing-in" freedom, rather than taking the always-reviled path of radical and comprehensive social change.

Gradualism, and piecemeal change, is always held up as the sober, practical, responsible, and compassionate path of reform, avoiding the sudden shocks, painful dislocations, and unemployment brought on by radical change.

In this, as in so many areas, however, the conventional wisdom is wrong. It is becoming ever clearer to East Europeans that the only practical and realistic path, the only path toward reform that truly works and works quickly, is the total abolition of socialism and statism across the board.

First published in March 1990.

For one thing, as we have seen in the Soviet Union, gradual reform provides a convenient excuse to the vested interests, monopolists, and inefficient sluggards who are the beneficiaries of socialism, to change nothing at all. Combine this resistance with the standard bureaucratic inertia endemic under socialism, and meaningful change is reduced to mere rhetoric and lip service.

But more fundamentally, since the market economy is an intricate, interconnected latticework, a seamless web, keeping some controls and not others creates more dislocations, and perpetuates them indefinitely.

A striking case is the Soviet Union. The reformers wish to abolish all price controls, but they worry that this course, amidst an already inflationary environment, would greatly aggravate inflation. Unfortunately, the East Europeans, in their eagerness to absorb procapitalist literature, have imbibed Western economic fallacies that focus on price increases as "inflation" rather than on the monetary expansion which causes the increased prices.

In Soviet Russia and in Poland, the governments have been pouring an enormous number of rubles and zlotys into circulation, which has increased price levels. In both countries, severe price controls have disguised the price inflation, and have also created massive shortages of goods. As in most other examples of price control, the authorities then tried to assuage consumers by imposing especially severe price controls on consumer necessities, such as soap, meat, citrus fruit, or fuel. As an inevitable result, these valued items end up in particularly short supply.

If the governments went cold turkey and abolished all the controls, there would indeed be a large one-shot rise in most prices, particularly in consumer goods suffering most from the scarcity imposed by controls. But this would only be a one-shot increase, and not of the continuing and accelerating kind characteristic of monetary expansion. And, furthermore, what consolation is it for a consumer to have the price of an item be cheap if he or she can't find it? Better to have a bar of soap cost ten rubles and be available than to cost two rubles and never appear. And, of course, the market price—say of ten rubles—is not at all arbitrary, but is determined by the demands of the consumers themselves.

Total decontrol eliminates dislocations and restrictions at one fell swoop, and gives the free market the scope to release people's energies, increase production enormously, and direct resources away from misallocations and toward the satisfaction of consumers. It should never be forgotten that the "miracle" of West German recovery from the economic depths after World War II occurred because Ludwig Erhard and the West Germans dismantled the entire structure of price and wage controls at once and overnight, on the glorious day of July 7, 1949.

In addition, the East European countries are starved for capital to develop their economy, and capital will only be supplied, whether by domestic savers or by foreign investors, when: (1) there is a genuine stock market, a market in shares of ownership titles to assets; and (2) the currency is genuinely convertible into hard currencies. Part of the immediate West German reform was to make the mark convertible into hard currencies.

If all price controls should be removed immediately, and currencies made convertible and a full-fledged stock market established, what then should be done about the massive state-owned sector in the socialist bloc? A vital question, since the overwhelming bulk of capital assets in the socialist countries are state-owned.

Many East Europeans now realize that it is hopeless to try to induce state enterprises to be efficient, or to pay attention to prices, costs, or profits. It is becoming clearer to everyone that Ludwig von Mises was right: only genuinely private firms, private owners of the means of production, can be truly responsive to profit-and-loss incentives. And moreover, the only genuine price system, reflecting costs and profit opportunities, arises from actual markets—from buying and selling by private owners of property.

Obviously, then, all state firms and operations should be privatized immediately—the sooner the better. But, unfortunately, many East Europeans committed to privatization are reluctant to push for this remedy because they complain that people don't have the money to purchase the mountain of capital assets, and that it seems almost impossible for the state to price such assets correctly.

Unfortunately, these free-marketeers are not thinking radically enough. Not only may private citizens under socialism not have the money to buy state assets, but there is a serious question about what the state is supposed to do with all the money, as well as the moral question of why the state deserves to amass this money from its long-suffering subjects.

The proper way to privatize is, once again, a radical one: allowing their present users to "homestead" these assets, for example, by granting prorata negotiable shares of ownership to workers in the various firms. After this one mighty stroke of universal privatization, prices of ownership shares on the market will fluctuate in accordance with the productivity and the success of the assets and the firms in question.

Critics of homesteading typically denounce such an idea as a "giveaway" of "windfall gains" to the recipients. But in fact, the homesteaders have already created or taken these resources and lifted them into production, and any ensuing gains (or losses) will be the result of their own productive and entrepreneurial actions. ▶

107
A SOCIALIST STOCK MARKET?

Even in the days before *perestroika*, socialism was never a monolith. Within the Communist countries, the spectrum of socialism ranged from the quasi-market, quasi-syndicalist

---

Previously unpublished.

system of Yugoslavia to the centralized totalitarianism of neighboring Albania. One time I asked Professor von Mises, the great expert on the economics of socialism, at what point on this spectrum of statism would he designate a country as "socialist" or not. At that time, I wasn't sure that any definite criterion existed to make that sort of clear-cut judgment.

And so I was pleasantly surprised at the clarity and decisiveness of Mises's answer. "A stock market," he answered promptly.

> A stock market is crucial to the existence of capitalism and private property. For it means that there is a functioning market in the exchange of private titles to the means of production. There can be no genuine private ownership of capital without a stock market: there can be no true socialism if such a market is allowed to exist.

And so it is particularly thrilling to see that in the headlong flight from central planning and socialism, several of the Communist countries are actually introducing, or preparing to introduce, a stock market. A prospect that would have been unthinkable only a few years ago! The process is already in its early stages in Communist China. And the Soviet Union is beginning to talk about introducing a stock market.

Stock markets already exist in several cities in China. So far, however, they are pitiful fledglings. Although the Communist leadership now allows the expansion of private firms and permits them to issue stock, only a few companies have issued stock and they are, so far, much more like bonds. Stock dividends are fixed very much like interest on bonds, and, more importantly, there is no free pricing system in these stock markets; instead, there is rigid price-fixing of the shares by the central government.

Even so these tiny stock markets are expanding, as state enterprises in China are selling off chunks of their shares to the public, while thousands of cooperatives are selling shares of ownership to their workers. Harry Harding of the Brookings

Institution comments that "the idea is to have enough public ownership so that they can say it's still socialist," while at the same time they "make the enterprises accountable to someone other than the state bureaucracy." Despite great reluctance, China and other Communist countries are anxious to induce productive savings from their citizens, and channel savings from jewelry and art, into capital investment.

Another motive propelling China, Soviet Russia, and other Communist countries into establishing stock markets is the desire to attract foreign investors. But it is obvious to all, including the Communist leaders, that to attract foreign funds, the ruble and other Communist currencies must be removed from their current absurd controls and overvaluations, and become freely convertible into dollars and other Western currencies. It will take the Communist governments quite a while to bite this bullet, but they are definitely moving in this direction.

As might be expected, the most radical advance toward free stock markets in the Communist countries has been in Hungary. A tiny stock market has been open in Budapest for some time, but on January 1, 1989, Hungary began to allow foreigners to invest in Hungarian stocks, even permitting foreigners to own up to 100 percent of a number of Hungarian firms, public and private. At first, these shares will be traded in the current tiny market, but within six months, Budapest is scheduled to open a functioning daily international stock exchange—the first in Eastern Europe since World War II.

This first real stock exchange will have from ten to twenty companies listed at its opening, and will, unfortunately, also come with all the attendant trappings of an American stock exchange—including insider trading rules and a Hungarian type of Securities and Exchange Commission. Learning too well from the West!

Particularly enthusiastic about the new development is Szigmond Jarai, deputy director of the Budapest Bank and chairman of the government committee supervising the establishment of the daily stock exchange. Jarai declared that "the stock market is the heart of an effective economy. . . . We need to reduce our bureaucracy and free up entrepreneurs," he added, sounding, as the *New York Times* commented, "more like a Wall Street free-market enthusiast than an official of a Communist government."

More freedom is coming soon. The Hungarian Parliament is considering a tax reform that would allow foreign equity investors to pay no Hungarian tax on either dividends or capital gains, and laws are being prepared allowing both Hungarians and foreign joint ventures to operate as stockbrokers. In addition, the way forward has been paved by the fact that Hungary already has in place the only bond market in Eastern Europe, as well as a system of bankruptcy laws so that insolvent firms can be forced out of business.

There is, of course, a long way to go, even in Hungary. But plans are in the works to privatize large sectors of the Hungarian economy within the next two years, and there are increasing mutterings about making the Hungarian forint convertible into Western currencies. Even in benighted Poland, there are bills now in Parliament to allow private commercial banking, and to eliminate exchange controls over the Polish zloty. Not only is socialism cracking all over the world, but, using Mises's criterion, we might be able to throw our hats in the air very soon and proclaim that Hungary is no longer socialist. ▶

108
THE GLORIOUS POSTWAR WORLD

Every war in American history has been the occasion for a Great Leap Forward in the power of the State, a leap which, at best, could only be partly rolled back after the war.

First published in May 1991.

A conflict as seemingly minor as the War of 1812 took the Jacksonians three decades to wash out of American life; and freedom was never able to recover fully from the Civil War and the two World Wars. After the two world wars in particular, statists had a seemingly irresistible argument: America should use the wonder and the glory, the united martial spirit, the singleness of national purpose, to wage wars at home against a battery of domestic ills.

There are always problems aplenty at home against which to mobilize the national will: depression, poverty, injustice, what have you. And that mobilization necessarily means collectivism in action: increased federal power under the commander-in-chief.

After the full-fledged War Collectivism of the first World War, a collectivism that joined Big Business, Big Labor, statist intellectuals, and technocrats under the aegis of Big Government, the youthful planners of that collectivism: the Bernard Baruchs, Herbert Hoovers, and Franklin Roosevelts, spent the rest of their lengthy lives striving to recapture those delightful days, and to fasten them permanently upon peace-time America. The institutions and the rhetoric of wartime collectivism were recaptured during the Hoover and Roosevelt New Deals to "combat" the Great Depression, often with the same institutions and the same people running them.

Thus, Eugene Meyer's War Finance Corporation lending federal money to corporations, which had lingered on during the peacetime 1920s, was renamed the Reconstruction Finance Corporation and enlarged by Hoover in 1932, with the same Eugene Meyer happily running the show, starting from the self-same offices in Washington, D.C. And then, World War II brought back the collectivist planning of World War I. Baruch's War Industries Board was reconstituted as the War Production Board of World War II, and was resurrected once more under General Electric's Charles E. Wilson during the Korean conflict.

The War Labor Board, designed to privilege unions, set wages, and arbitrate disputes, inspired the National Labor Board in the early Roosevelt New Deal, to be succeeded by the

National Labor Relations Board under the Wagner Act and to be supplemented by a reprised War Labor Board during World War II.

Particularly dangerous for an acceleration of statism are successful wars; while Korea and Vietnam led to an intensification of State power, they did not generate the lifelong nostalgia, the eagerness to recapture the glory days, of a successful war. No American war has been quite as successful as the Gulf War, particularly if we take the kill ratio of enemy to American, or that kill ratio per day.

We would therefore expect a supercharged atmosphere of bringing the war home to domestic life. In a world where television seems to speed up public responses, that postwar domestic mobilization has already begun. This spirit of domestic war, appropriately enough, was launched by President Bush in his victory address before Congress on March 6, 1991:

> In the war just ended, there were clearcut objectives, timetables and, above all, an overriding imperative to achieve results. We must bring that same sense of self-discipline, that same sense of urgency, to the way we meet challenges here at home.

After summarizing some of his current domestic agenda, proposals for "reform and renewal" including "civil rights," highways, aviation, transportation, and a "crime package," and hailing the past year's "historic" Clean Air Act, his "landmark" Americans with Disabilities Act, and his Child Care Act as portents for the future, the president gave Congress a deadline: "If our forces could win the ground war in 100 hours, then surely the Congress can pass this legislation in 100 days."

The president then noted that in his State of the Union address, five weeks before, he had posed this question to Congress: "If we can selflessly confront evil for the sake of good in a land so far away, then surely we can make this land all that it should be." By their victory, the president told us, our troops "transformed a nation at home." The president concluded that "there is much that we must do at home and abroad." And we will do it.

Hold on to your hats, and to your wallets and purses, Mr. and Ms. America, here we go again! ▶

109
THE REVOLUTION COMES HOME

The election of 1994 was an unprecedented and smashing electoral expression of the popular revolution that had been building up for many months: a massive repudiation of President Clinton, the Clintonian Democratic Party, their persons and all of their works. It was a fitting followup to the string of revolutions against government and socialism in the former states and satellites of the Soviet Union. The anti-government revolution has come home at last. An intense and widescale loathing of President Clinton as a person fused with an ideological hatred of Washington D.C., the federal Leviathan, and centralized statism, to create a powerful and combustible combination in American politics. So massive was the repudiation that it even changed many state governments away from the Democrats and the Democratic ideology of government intervention in the lives and properties of Americans. Formerly effective attempts to alter the meaning of the elections by Clinton and media spin artists (e.g., that it was "anti-incumbent") were swept away as laughable by the patent facts of the electoral revolution.

After Leon Trotsky was sent into exile by Stalin, he wrote a bitter book famously entitled *The Revolution Betrayed*. In the case of the Bolshevik Revolution, it took about 15 years for Stalin's alleged betrayal of the Leninist Revolution to take place. (Actually, despite the fascination of Western intellectuals with

---

First published in January 1985.

the Stalin-Trotsky schism, it was far more an intra-Bolshevik personal and factional squabble than any sort of ideological betrayal.)

In the case of the magnificent free-market revolution of November 1994, however, the betrayal began to occur almost immediately. Indeed it was inevitable, being built into the structure of current American politics.

The basic problem is the lavishly over-praised "duopoly" two-party system, cemented in place by a combination of the single-district, winner-take-all procedure for legislatures, and the socialized ballot, adopted as a "progressive reform" in the 1890s. This reform permits the government to impose onerous restrictions on the public's access to the ballot, to the expression of its electoral will. Before the adoption of the socialized, or what used to be called "the Australian," ballot, voting was secret but was achieved by dropping a card supplied by one of the candidates into the box. There was no "ballot" to worry about.

Because of the two-party system, the only way that the electorate of 1994 could express its revolutionary desire to throw out the hated Democrats was to vote Republican. Unfortunately, the controlling elites of the Republican Party have long had views very similar to those of the Democrats, thus depriving the American public of any genuine philosophical choice.

The ideology common to the ruling elites of both parties is Welfarist, Corporatist Statism; whether it's called corporate "liberalism" or "conservatism" is largely a question of nuance and esthetics. Essentially, the corporate and media elites have long been engaging in a shell game in which the American public are the suckers. When the public is fed up with one party, the elites offer up an alleged alternative that only turns out to be more of the same.

All is not hopeless however. The inner-tension with the system comes from the very fact that the public has been led to *think* there is a genuine choice, and that there are strong ideological differences between the two parties. As result, the rank-and-file, both among the voting public and among the respective party activists, tend to have clashing ideologies and to pour forth severely contrasting rhetoric.

The rank-and-file, as well as party militants, tend to believe the rhetoric and to take it seriously. And while the American public, especially the conservatives, tend to be satisfied with the rhetoric of their political leaders and not to bother with the reality of their deeds, they are also more likely now to turn their attention to what is really going on, with the American public rising up angry against the ever-burgeoning Leviathan State fastened upon them by Washington, D.C.

By this time, conservatives at the grass-roots have caught on to Robert Dole, who is now well-known for his accommodationist devotion to ever higher taxes and spending. The real danger is Newt Gingrich, who has cultivated a firebrand rhetoric that has seduced the conservative masses into placing trust in Newt to lead their revolution.

Even rhetorically, Newt Gingrich is all too reminiscent of the erratic Clinton, blowing hot and cold, changing from day to day, one day calling for a revolution (what David Broder of the *Washington Post* recently called "the bad Newt"), alternating with pledges of "cooperation" with his alleged arch-enemy in the White House ("the good Newt"). The much-contested Gingrich "contract," for example, far from an expression of rollback of Big Government, is either trivial or phony. Let us go down some of the crucial aspects of the anti-central government revolution, and see how the Republican elites, including Gingrich, shape up.

Taxes. Forget the piddling and minor cuts in capital-gains taxes, the increase of the child deduction, etc. The crucial point is that Gingrich and the other leaders are committed to the disastrous Bush-Clinton-bipartisan (a dread word that itself signifies duopoly and sellout of principle) concept of *never reducing* total government revenue, so that any tax cuts anywhere must be compensated by tax increases (or "fee" increases) somewhere else. In particular, until drastic cuts in the monstrous income tax are at least *proposed*, let alone passed, by the Republican elites, the leadership's alleged embrace of small government will continue to be a fraud and a hoax.

Repeal the Brady Bill and gun control in general. Not a word by the leadership or in the "contract."

Repeal of affirmative action. Not a word.

Deregulation, i.e., repeal of OSHA, the Americans With Disabilities Act, the Clean Air Act, etc. Not a word.

Immigration control. On opposition to floods of illegal immigrants, immigration in general, or welfare for immigrants, not a word.

Abolition of foreign aid. Not only not a word, but the entire Republican leadership, including Gingrich, is deeply committed to an American foreign policy of global intervention, economic and military.

Withdrawal from the UN, IMF, World Bank, etc. Ditto, since the entire leadership is committed to a continuation of the global interventionist foreign policy both parties have pursued since World War II.

Gatt and WTO. In this crucial drive toward managed world trade, with the public, insofar as they know anything about it, solidly against it, Gingrich, Dole, and the entire Republican Establishment are fervently for it, and heedless of the public's opposition. The exception is Jesse Helms, who has begun to rediscover his Old Right roots.

Government spending. No real cuts advocated by the elites; instead, the contract pledges increased military spending in a world where the Soviet threat has disappeared. Again the public's desire for a foreign policy strictly in the national interest is thwarted.

Abolition of the Federal Reserve. Ha!

Abolition of the Department of Education, Energy, etc. Ha!

Instead, the Republican elite serve up hoaxes such as the Balanced Budget Amendment, and *increasing* Executive power over

Congress with the line-item veto. There will be no real devolution of power to the states, or restoring the 10th amendment.

So why isn't the situation hopeless? Because of angry antigovernment fervor at the grass roots. Because a lot of the new Republican Congressmen were not thought to have a chance of winning, and therefore were not stifled in their political cradles by the party elites. A lot of these freshmen backbenchers reflect the Hard Right sentiments of their constituency.

If the public is alert and keeps up the pressure on the weak-kneed and unprincipled party elites, they might be drummed into and kept in line. Furthermore, the revolution is a polarized reaction to the advent of Clinton and the Clintonian movement. What the professionally "bipartisan" elite wants above all is almost identical major parties.

The elites dumped Bush for Clinton in '92 because they thought that Clinton was a safe and centrist "New Democrat." Instead, Bill, and especially Hillary, turned out to be Hard Left ideologues who pushed the entire political conflict in America many leagues leftward, too far for the centrist Social Democrats who want the political dialogue confined to such "moderate" Democrats as Al From and Al Gore in perpetual dialogue with "moderate" Republicans like George Bush and Bob Dole. Clinton's sharp move leftward upset the applecart and created a gap within which an antigovernment populism could develop and flourish.

Clinton's move leftward polarized American political opinion, and generated a massive reaction in the opposite direction. Genuine libertarians and conservatives must keep up and intensify the pressure from below on the Republican leadership, give heart to the backbenchers, and threaten to walk out and sit home should the leadership follow its instincts and betray Republican principles to the Democrats.

The peoples' revolution is not a one-shot proposition; it is an ongoing process, of which the grand sweep of November 1994 was a notable instance. The new populist revolution is multi-pronged, and necessarily takes place both inside and out-side the machinery of elections.

Note the war for whatever is left of the soul of Slick Willie since the election. The Republocrat elites are pleading with Clinton to move toward the center and fuse a coalition with "moderate" Republicans. The main hope for liberty and small government paradoxically, is for Clinton to follow Hillary and the ideologues and go Left instead, appealing to his core con-stituency, and polarizing and mobilizing a still more intense and massive populist reaction against his rule. If that happens, Clin-ton will be left with Jesse Jackson and ACT-UP, while anti-tax, anti-regulation, antigovernment populism rises up and topples his rule. ▸

110
THE TROUBLE WITH THE QUICK FIX

If conservatives and free-market economists are supposed to have one dominant virtue, it is a thoughtful awareness of the indirect and not just the immediate consequences of a public policy. In the spirit of Henry Hazlitt's "Broken Window Fal-lacy," they are supposed to bring a "look before we leap" atti-tude into political life.

Instead, in recent years, friends and colleagues who should know better have been increasingly running after some Quick Fix or some flashy gimmick that will magically solve our prob-lems and bring no ill consequences in its wake. Unfortunately, they seem to have forgotten the basic Misesian Law of Govern-ment: that government actions, even and perhaps especially Quick Fixes, are apt to get us into a worse mess than we are in already.

First published in May 1994.

The basic flaw of the Quick Fix is to focus on one aspect of a problem, often the most politically catchy part, to the neglect of other important issues. Thus, the school voucher scheme focuses on the horrors of the public school to the neglect of such broader and more important questions as tax-supported education and government control of all schools, public and private; opposition to welfare concentrates on taxpayers paying people to be idle, to the neglect of the broader question of tax-payer subsidy period, whether recipients are idle or not.

And we have mainly free-market economists to thank for the disastrous "Tax Reform Act" of 1986, which, in a Jacobin pursuit of equality and "fairness," closed the tax "loopholes" so successfully as to crush the housing market. In addition, and totally neglected, tax reform helped hasten the current Clinton health monstrosity by virtually eliminating deductions of uninsured medical payments from one's income tax, thereby creating the Problem of the Medically Uninsured.

The current Quick Fix craze of free-market economists was the late, unlamented Balanced Budget Amendment (BBA). It seems that every couple of years there is a Silly Season in Congress when this amendment pops up. Not only that; each successive incarnation of the BBA is worse than its predecessor. Pursuing an hysterical desire to pass any amendment, the limit on increasing taxes is progressively weakened. In the latest Simon amendment, a mere majority of Congress could "solve the problem of deficits" by increasing taxes.

The unwisely narrow focus of the BBA is, of course, on "the deficit," as if the deficit is the root of all fiscal evil and must be stamped out by Any Means Necessary. But the broader and more important problem of Big Government is not the deficit; it is not even, as Milton Friedman has long emphasized, total government spending; it is government action period, which fiscally means all three interlocking items: deficits, government spending, and taxation. Big Government is a swollen, ever-expanding and parasitic entity crushing the productive economy, the "private sector"; and the focus must be on rolling back, as much and as "drastically" as possible, all three of these facets of the government budget.

Looking at the BBA, then, the first obviously unfortunate consequence of focusing solely on the deficit is that it might well, and indeed would lead to drastic increases in taxation, and would do nothing about curbing government spending. The one fiscal thing worse than a deficit is higher taxes; imposing a BBA and raising taxes in order to combat deficits is akin to curing a patient of bronchitis by shooting him in the chest.

There are many other things terribly wrong with a BBA. It can be overridden at any time by only a three-fifths vote of Congress; it ignores the fact that an increasing number of spending items can be and are simply placed "off budget" and would therefore not be subject to any limits; and it ignores the off-budget federal government spending of mandates on states or private firms, which can be conveniently chalked up to their budgets but not to the federal government.

Moreover, the BBA is a total hoax; for it would not balance the budget at all. Ever since the mid-1970s, the federal budget process has focused not on the actual budget for any given year, but on estimated budgets over the next several years. The BBA would mandate a balance, not of the actual federal budget, but of Congressional estimates of next year's budget. And as any fool knows, it is all too easy to estimate anything you want, and to manipulate assumptions to get the desired result. Traditionally, government has always underestimated the expense of its future actions, and overestimated its revenue.

Thus a BBA would not only increase the crippling tax burden on the American people; it would also perpetrate a cruel hoax on a public that want deficits ended and who would embrace an amendment that only gives the appearance, and not the reality, of ending the deficit. In short, a BBA would aid Big Government by relaxing public opposition to its expansion—which might, after all, be the point of the whole thing.

There is a final, and totally neglected point that was emphasized by the leading opponent of the BBA, the much-maligned

Old Mr. Pork Barrel, Senator Robert Byrd (D-WV). Pork Barreler or not, Senator Byrd was eloquent in stressing a vital constitutional issue: that Congress must retain its one vital power, the power of the purse. A BBA would take that power away from Congress, which for all its sins is at least accountable to the voting public, and put it into the hands of federal judges, an unelected, unaccountable, and unremovable body of oligarchs who have long been engaging in runaway expansion of their own power.

As Senator Byrd put it in his opposition to the BBA, "The power of the purse belongs to the people. . . . It is vested in the branch that represents the people, elected by the people. Judges are not elected by the people."

And speaking of Quick Fixes, there is a veritable nightmare coming down the pike. Libertarians have long pushed privatization of government activities, but, as all too often happens, even a good thing like privatization has suffered from becoming a fetish, a cherished object of an ideological movement, to the neglect of broader and more important considerations. Thus, we have seen in the former Soviet Union that a lot depends on the extent and the form of "privatization"; for example should we really cheer when the Communist managerial elite of the old steel, copper, etc. monopolies, suddenly become the "private" owners of these uneconomic complexes?

Coming closer to home, we now find that our beloved Internal Revenue Service, backed by the Clinton administration, would like to engage in some privatization. It turns out it would be more efficient for the Treasury Department to contract out, to privatize, its collection of back taxes by bringing in private collection agencies to do the job. Hey, do we really want to make income tax collection more efficient by privatizing some or all of the tax agencies?

Do we really want our lives and records combed through, our door broken down, by the peremptory orders of IBM or McDonald's "tax police"? Anyone who knows history will know that the most hated institution in pre-modern Europe was that of the "tax farmers." The king used to get a lot of money quickly and save himself the costs of a giant bureaucracy by selling the right, or privilege, to collect taxes to some private firm, or "tax farmer." Can you imagine how intensely and bitterly the tax farmers, who lacked the cloak of sovereignty or legitimacy, were hated by the people?

There are those who believe that the worse the despotism the better, in order to provoke a revolutionary backlash among the public. Well, privatizing tax collection might just do it. ▶

Our Intellectual Debts

111
WILLIAM HAROLD HUTT: 1899–1988

On June 19, William Harold Hutt, one of the most productive and creative economists of this century, died in Irving,
Texas, at the age of 89. Born in London, Hutt served in the
Royal Flying Corps in World War I, and then went to the London School of Economics, where he studied under the great
free-market and hard-money economist Edwin Cannan. Hutt
was graduated in 1924, and spent several years in publishing.

His first important scholarly publication remains virtually
unknown today: an excellent and penetrating annotated bibliography, *The Philosophy of Individualism: A Bibliography*, which
he wrote, aided by the eminent laissez-faire liberal Francis W.
Hirst. The book was published anonymously by the Individual-
ist Bookshop of London in 1927. *The Philosophy of Individualism*
served, 30 years later, as the core of Henry Hazlitt's annotated
bibliography, *The Free Man's Library* (Van Nostrand, 1956).

From 1928 to 1965, Hutt taught economics at the University of Cape Town in South Africa. In his mid-60s, he came to
the United States, taught at several universities, and then settled
at the University of Dallas in 1971, where he taught for ten

First published in September 1988.

years, until the age of 82, an inspiration to a legion of students and colleagues. He continued to be an emeritus professor at Dallas until his death.

The shameful neglect of Hutt's great contributions can be attributed to two main factors: (1) the fact that he taught in the intellectual backwater of South Africa, far from the great intellectual controversies in the profession; and (2) that he stood like a rock against the major fashions of our time, in particular interventionism, Keynesianism, and the general enthusiasm for labor unions.

Hutt's first great contribution to economics was his concise and lucid *The Theory of Collective Bargaining* (P.S. King, 1930), which remains to this day the best book on the theory of wage determination. In this book, Hutt criticized many of the classical economists, and showed conclusively that unions cannot increase general wage rates, and that particular wage increases can only come at the expense of a dislocation of labor and a fall in wage rates of other workers. Ludwig von Mises wrote in the preface to the first American edition of Hutt's book:

> Professor Hutt's brilliant essay is not merely a contribution to the history of economic thought. It is rather a critical analysis of the arguments advanced by economists from Adam Smith down and by the spokesmen of the unions in favor of the thesis that unionism can raise wage rates above the market value without harm to anybody else than the exploiters.

In addition to his notable work in the theory of labor, Professor Hutt wrote two brilliant works in applied labor economics, i.e., labor history. His was the outstanding essay in the remarkable volume edited by F.A. Hayek, *Capitalism and the Historians* (University of Chicago, 1954). Here Hutt discussed the Factory Acts restricting child labor in early nineteenth-century Britain, demonstrating that these acts were based on mendacious testimony, and that the condition of children had been greatly improved by the Industrial Revolution.

In 1964, furthermore, the Institute of Economic Affairs in London published Hutt's innovative work, *The Economics of the Colour Bar*, in which he demonstrated that, contrary to myth, the South African system of *apartheid* was originated not by rural Afrikaners, but by Anglo unions, anxious to suppress the competition of Africans who were rising into the ranks of the foremen and skilled craftsmen. Indeed, he showed that industrial apartheid was imposed by a successful general strike in 1922 led by William H. Andrews, head of the Communist Party of South Africa under the slogan "Whites Unite and Fight for a Workers' World"! For his opposition to *apartheid* and advocacy of a free labor market, Professor Hutt's South African passport was withdrawn by the Department of Interior, in 1955, but was returned after criticism was raised in Parliament.

In his further scholarly work on trade unions after World War II, Hutt emphasized the crucial empirical fact about labor unions: that they rest on the use and the threat of violence, particularly against replacement workers during strikes (universally smeared in the supposedly objective news media as "scabs"). If Professor Hutt sometimes went too far and advocated outlawing unions as monopolistic *per se*, as well as removing their enormous governmental privileges and licenses to commit violence, he was at least far closer to the mark than the Chicago School, who persist in regarding unions as legitimate if sometimes inefficient employment agencies hired by workers.

William Hutt's other notable area of contribution was his defense of hard money and the free market's tendency to full employment, and his brilliant and superb critiques of Keynesian economics. In particular, we might cite his noteworthy *The Theory of Idle Resources* (Jonathan Cape, 1939) where he showed that Keynesian idle resources—unemployment and "excess capacity"— were simply cases of capacity withheld from the market by resource-owners, and not the result of insufficient market demand. Capacity can be withheld, furthermore, either because of government restrictionism holding up prices or wage rates, or because of expectations that restrictionist or inflationist policies will soon raise market prices.

In 1963, Hutt published a comprehensive if difficult critique of *Keynesianism, Keynesianism, Retrospect and Prospect* (Regnery, 1963), which, among other riches, contains the best criticism of the spurious "acceleration principle" ever written. A decade and a half later, a revision entitled *The Keynesian Episode, A Reassessment* (Liberty Press, 1979), which turned out to be largely a new book, presented a more easily accessible and updated critique of Keynesian doctrine.

Finally, one of Hutt's great contributions to the history and the clarity of economic thought was his correctly titled *A Rehabilitation of Say's Law* (University Press, 1974), which rescued that great critic of underspending notions from Keynes's deliberate misrepresentation in *The General Theory* as well as from Say's inconstant friends in the economics profession.

While he was not a full-fledged Austrian, Professor Hutt's methodology and analysis were very close to the Austrians, and he rightly considered himself a close sympathizer and supporter of the modern Austrian revival. Certainly he was closer to Misesian economics than the nominally "Austrian" nihilism of the later Professor Lachmann and his younger followers. But above all, Bill Hutt shall be remembered and honored for the unflagging kindliness and cheerfulness of his personality. All who came into contact with Bill Hutt admired and loved him, and all of us are poorer for his passing. ▸

112
FRIEDRICH AUGUST VON HAYEK: 1899–1992

The death of F.A. Hayek at the age of 92 marks the end of an era, the Mises-Hayek era. Converted from Fabian socialism by Ludwig von Mises's devastating critique, *Socialism,* in the early 1920s, Hayek took his place as the greatest of the

First published in June 1992.

glittering generation of economists and social scientists who became followers of Mises in the Vienna of the 1920s, and who took part in Mises's famed weekly *privatseminar* held in his office at the Chamber of Commerce. In particular, Hayek elaborated Mises's brilliant business cycle theory, which demonstrated that boom-bust cycles are caused, not by mysterious defects inherent in industrial capitalism, but by the unfortunate inflationary bank credit expansion propelled by central banks. Mises founded the Austrian Institute for Business Cycle Research in 1927, and named Hayek as its first director.

Hayek proceeded to develop and expand Mises's cycle theory, first in a book of the late 1920s, *Monetary Theory and the Trade Cycle*. He was brought over to the London School of Economics in 1931 by an influential English Misesian, Lionel Robbins. Hayek gave a series of lectures on cycle theory that took the world of English economics by storm, and were published quickly in English as *Prices and Production*.

Remaining at a permanent post at the London School, Hayek soon converted the leading young English economists to the Misesian-Austrian view of capital and business cycles, including such later renowned Keynesians as John R. Hicks, Abba Lerner, Nicholas Kaldor, and Kenneth E. Boulding. Indeed, in two lengthy review essays in 1931–32 of Keynes's widely trumpeted magnum opus, the two-volume *Treatise on Money*, Hayek was able to demolish that work and to send Keynes back to the drawing-board to concoct another economic "revolution."

One of the reasons for the swift diffusion of Misesian views in England in the 1930s was that Mises had predicted the Great Depression, and that his business cycle theory provided an explanation for that harrowing event of the 1930s. Unfortunately, when Keynes came back with his later model, the *General Theory* in 1936, his brand new "revolution" swept the boards, swamping economic opinion, and converting or dragging along almost all the former Misesians in its wake.

England was then the prestigious center of world economic thought, and Keynes had behind him the eminence of Cambridge University, as well as his own stature in the intellectual community. Add to this Keynes's personal charm, and the fact that his allegedly revolutionary theory put the imprimatur of "economic science" behind statism and massive increases of government spending, and Keynesianism proved irresistible. Of all the Misesians who had been nurtured in Vienna and London, by the end of the 1930s only Mises and Hayek were left, as indomitable champions of the free market, and opponents of statism and deficit spending.

In later years Hayek conceded that the worst mistake of his life was to fail to write the sort of devastating refutation of the *General Theory* that he had done for the *Treatise*, but he had concluded that there was no point in doing so, since Keynes changed his mind so often. Unfortunately, this time there was no demolition by Hayek to force him to do so.

If the business cycle theory was swamped by the Keynesian model, so too was the Mises-Hayek critiques of socialism, which Hayek had also brought to London, and to which he had contributed in the 1930s. But this line of argument had been brought to an end, in the late 1930s, when most economists came to believe that socialist governments could easily engage in economic calculation by simply ordering their managers to act as if they were participating in a real market for resources and capital goods.

During World War II, at a low point in the fortunes of human freedom and Austrian economics, in the midst of an era when it seemed that socialism and communism would inevitably triumph, Hayek published *The Road to Serfdom* (1944). It linked the statism of communism, social democracy, and fascism, and demonstrated that, just as people who are best suited for any given occupations will rise to the top in those pursuits, so under statism, "the worst" would inevitably rise to the top. Thanks to promotion efforts funded by J. Howard Pew of the then Pew-owned Sun Oil Company, *The Road to Serfdom* became extraordinarily influential in American intellectual and academic life.

In 1974, perhaps not coincidentally the year after his mentor Ludwig von Mises died, F.A. Hayek received the Nobel Prize. The first free-market economist to receive that honor, Hayek was accorded the prize explicitly for his elaboration of Misesian business cycle theory in the 1920s and '30s. Since both Mises and Hayek had by that time dropped down the Orwellian memory hole of the economics profession, many economists were sent scurrying to find out who this person Hayek might be, thus helping give rise to a renaissance of the Austrian School.

Hayek's receipt of the Nobel at this time was deeply ironic, since after World War II his ideas began to diverge increasingly from those of Mises and thus acquire acclaim from latter-day Hayekians who are scarcely familiar with the work which had made Hayek eminent to begin with. To the extent that Hayek remained interested in cycle theory, he began to engage in shifting and contradictory deviations from the Misesian paradigm—ranging from calling for price-level stabilization, in direct contrast to his warning about the inflationary consequences of such measures during the 1920s; to blaming unions instead of bank credit for price inflation; to concocting bizarre schemes for individuals and banks to issue their own newly named currency.

Increasingly, Hayek's interests shifted from economics to social and political philosophy. But here his approach differed strikingly from Mises's ventures into broader realms. Mises entire lifework is virtually a seamless web, a mighty architectonic, a system in which he added to and enriched monetary and cycle theory by wider economic political and social theories. But Hayek, instead of providing a more elaborate and developed system, kept changing his focus and viewpoint in a contradictory and muddled fashion. His major problem, and his major divergence from Mises, is that Hayek, instead of analyzing man as a rational, conscious, and purposive being, considered man to be irrational, acting virtually unconsciously and unknowingly.

Since Hayek was radically scornful of human reason, he could not, like John Locke or the Scholastics, elaborate a libertarian system of personal and property rights based on the insights of human reason into natural law. Nor could he, like Mises, emphasize man's rational insight into the vital importance of laissez-faire for the flourishing and even survival of the human race, or of foregoing any coercive intervention into the vast and interdependent network of the free-market economy.

Instead, Hayek had to fall back on the importance of blindly obeying whatever social rules happened to have "evolved," and his only feeble argument against intervention was that the government was even more irrational, and was even more ignorant, than individuals in the market economy.

It is sad commentary on academia and on intellectual life these days that Hayek's thought, possibly because of its very muddle, inconsistency, and contradictions, should have attracted far more scholarly dissertations than Mises's consistency and clarity. In the long run, however, it will be all too obvious that Mises has left us a grand intellectual and scientific system for the ages whereas Hayek's lasting contribution will boil down to what was acknowledged by the Nobel committee—his elaboration of Misesian cycle theory. In addition, Hayek must always be honored for having the courage to stand shoulder to shoulder with his mentor, in the dark days of the interwar and postwar years, against the twin evils of socialism and Keynesianism. ▶

113
V. ORVAL WATTS: 1898–1993

V. Orval Watts, one of the leading free-market economists of the World War II and post-war eras, died on March 30 this

First published in July 1993.

year. When I first met him, in the winter of 1947, he was a leading economist at the Foundation for Economic Education (FEE), the only free-market organization and think-tank of that era. He was a pleasantly sardonic man in his late forties. Born in 1898 in Manitoba, Vernon Orval Willard Watts was graduated from the University of Manitoba in 1918, and went on to earn a master's and a doctor's degree in economics from Harvard University in its nobler, pre-Keynesian era.

After teaching economics at various colleges, Orval was hired by Leonard Read in 1939 to be the economist for the Los Angeles Chamber of Commerce, of which Leonard was executive director. Watts thereby became the first full-time economist to be employed by a chamber of commerce in the United States.

Leonard Read had built up the Los Angeles Chamber into the largest municipal business organization in the world, and Read himself had been converted to the libertarian, free-market creed by a remarkable constituent of the Chamber: William C. Mullendore, head of the Southern California Edison Corporation.

During World War II, Read, assisted by Watts, lent his remarkable organizing talents to making the Los Angeles Chamber a beacon of freedom in an increasingly collectivist world. When Read took the bold step of moving to Irvington-on-Hudson in New York to set up FEE in 1946, he took Orval with him as his economic adviser.

During World War II, Orval published his book *Do We Want Free Enterprise?* (1944). In his FEE years, he published several books, as well as writing numerous articles for free-market publications. His books included *Away From Freedom* (1952), a critique of Keynesianism; his pungent critique of unions, *Union Monopoly* (1954), and his perceptive attack on the United Nations, *United Nations: Planned Tyranny* (1955). He also served as economic counsel to Southern California Edison and several other companies in the Los Angeles area.

In 1963, at an age (65) when most men are thinking seriously of retirement, Orval resumed his teaching career, moving to the recently established Northwood University (then Northwood Institute), a free-market center of learning in Midland, Michigan.

Orval, bless him, served as director of economic education and chairman of the Division of Social Studies at Northwood for 21 years, until he retired in 1984 at the age of 86. While at Northwood, he published an excellent anthology of free market vs. government intervention articles, *Free Markets or Famine?* (1967), as well as his final book *Politics vs. Prosperity* (1976).

Orval Watts died in Palm Springs, California, this March, having just turned 95. He is survived by his wife Carolyn, a son, three daughters, nine grandchildren, and two great-grandchildren.

We can see in the present world how vitally important history is for the values and self-definition of a family, a movement, or a nation. As a result, history has become a veritable cockpit of contending factions. Any movement that has no sense of its own history, that fails to acknowledge its own leaders and heroes, is not going to amount to very much, nor does it deserve a better fate. ▶

114
LUDWIG VON MISES: 1881–1973

For those of us who have loved as well as revered Ludwig von Mises, words cannot express our great sense of loss: of this gracious, brilliant and wonderful man; this man of unblemished integrity; this courageous and lifelong fighter for human freedom; this all-encompassing scholar; this noble inspiration to us all. And above all this gentle and charming friend, this man who

---

First published in *Human Events*, October 20, 1973, p. 7

brought to the rest of us the living embodiment of the culture and the charm of pre-World War I Vienna.

For Mises's death takes away from us not only a deeply revered friend and mentor, but it tolls the bell for the end of an era: the last living mark of that nobler, freer and far more civilized era of pre-1914 Europe.

Mises's friends and students will know instinctively what I mean: for when I think of Ludwig Mises I think first of all of those landmark occasions when I had the privilege of afternoon tea at the Mises's: in a small apartment that virtually breathed the atmosphere of a long lost and far more civilized era. The graciousness of Mises's devoted wife Margit; the precious volumes that were the remains of a superb home library destroyed by the Nazis; but above all Mises himself, spinning in his inimitable way anecdotes of Old Vienna, tales of scholars past and present brilliant insights into economics, politics and social theory, and astute comments on the current scene.

Readers of Mises's majestic, formidable and uncompromising works must have been often surprised to meet him in person. Perhaps they had formed the image of Ludwig Mises as cold, severe, austere, the logical scholar repelled by lesser mortals, bitter at the follies around him and at the long trail of wrongs and insults that he had suffered.

They couldn't have been more wrong; for what they met was a mind of genius blended harmoniously with a personality of great sweetness and benevolence. Not once has any of us heard a harsh or bitter word escape from Mises's lips. Unfailingly gentle and courteous, Ludwig Mises was always there to encourage even the slightest signs of productivity or intelligence in his friends and students; always there for warmth as well as for the mastery of logic and reason that his works have long proclaimed him.

And always there as an inspiration and as a constant star. For what a life this man lived! Ludwig Mises died soon after his 92nd birthday, and until near the end he led his life very much in the world, pouring forth a mighty stream of great and immortal works, a fountainhead of energy and productivity as he taught continually at a university until the age of 87, as he flew tirelessly around the world to give papers and lectures on behalf of the free market and of sound economic science—a mighty structure of coherence and logic to which he contributed so much of his own creation.

Ludwig Mises's steadfastness and courage in the face of treatment that would have shattered lesser men, was a never-ending wonder to us all. Once the literal toast of both the economics profession and of the world's leaders, Mises was to find, at the very height of his powers, his world shattered and betrayed. For as the world rushed headlong into the fallacies and evils of Keynesianism and statism, Mises's great insights and contributions were neglected and scorned, and the large majority of his eminent and formerly devoted students decided to bend with the new breeze.

But shamefully neglected though he was, coming to America to a second-rate post and deprived of the opportunity to gather the best students, Ludwig Mises never once complained or wavered. He simply hewed to his great purpose, to carve out and elaborate the mighty structure of economics and social science that he alone had had the genius to see as a coherent whole; and to stand four-square for the individualism and the freedom that he realized was required if the human race was to survive and prosper. He was indeed a constant star that could not be deflected one iota from the body of truth which he was the first to see and to present to those who would only listen.

And despite the odds, slowly but surely some of us began to gather around him, to learn and listen and derive sustenance from the glow of his person and his work. And in the last few years, as the ideas of liberty and the free market have begun to revive with increasing swiftness in America, his name and his ideas began to strike chords in us all and his greatness to become known to a new generation.

Optimistic as he always was, I am confident that Mises was heartened by these signs of a new awakening of freedom and of the sound economics which he had carved out and which was for so long forgotten. We could not, alas, recapture the spirit and the breadth and the erudition; the ineffable grace of Old Vienna. But I fervently hope that we were able to sweeten his days by at least a little.

Of all the marvelous anecdotes that Mises used to tell I remember this one the most clearly, and perhaps it will convey a little of the wit and the spirit of Ludwig von Mises. Walking down the streets of Vienna with his friend, the great German philosopher Max Scheler, Scheler turned to Mises and asked, with some exasperation: "What is there in the climate of Vienna that breeds all these logical positivists [the dominant school of modern philosophy that Mises combatted all his life]?" With his characteristic shrug, Mises gently replied: "Well, after all, there are several million people living in Vienna, and among these there are only about a dozen logical positivists."

But oh, Mises, now you are gone, and we have lost our guide, our Nestor, our friend. How will we carry on without you? But we have to carry on, because anything less would be a shameful betrayal of all that you have taught us, by the example of your noble life as much as by your immortal works. Bless you, Ludwig von Mises, and our deepest love goes with you. ❯

115
MARGIT VON MISES: 1890–1993

Margit von Mises died on June 25, just a week short of her 103rd birthday. While physically frail the last few years, Margit remained mentally alert until a few months before her death. Indeed, such a conventional phrase as "mentally alert" scarcely begins to describe Margit: down nearly to the end, she was sharp as a tack, vitally interested in the world and in

First published in September 1993.

everyone around her. It was impossible to put anything over on her, as people often try to do with the elderly. Indeed, since the death of her husband Ludwig von Mises 20 years ago, one had the impression she could out think and outsmart everyone with whom she came into contact.

After the death of her beloved Lu, Margit swung into action, to become an indefatigable one-woman "Mises industry." She dug up unpublished manuscripts of Lu's, had them translated and edited, and supervised their publication. She also supervised reprints and translations of Mises's published work. She was chairman of the Ludwig von Mises Institute. And she was fervent in pressing the cause of her late husband, as well as the ideas of freedom and free markets to which he had devoted his life. She refused to let any slighting or denigration of Mises by his genuine or less-than-genuine admirers or disciples go unremarked or go unchastised.

Margit's greatest achievement in the Mises industry was her wonderful memoir of her life together with Lu, a touching and romantic, as well as dramatic, story, on which she embarked after Lu's death in 1973, and which she published three years later (*My Years with Ludwig von Mises*, Arlington House 1976; CFE 1984). It is notable that, unlike necessarily stiff and formal biographies from outside observers, the memory of both Lu and Margit will be kept eternally alive in this lovely valentine to a devoted marriage.

It is a blessing that Margit was able to spend her last days and months in her beloved apartment in Manhattan's Upper West Side where she and Lu had lived since 1942. It was a cozy and elegant flat, filled with mementos, and, in recent decades, with a marvelous bust of Mises sculpted by a lady who became a family friend. For all friends of the Miseses, it is an apartment arousing memories of charming conversations, being plied with tasty sandwiches and cakes at tea parties, and of visits with Lu in his study.

Margit was a remarkable woman, who inspired great devotion in friends, neighbors, doctors, and nurses alike. For Margit, her physician, a distinguished cardiologist, thought nothing of making repeated house calls; indeed even her dentist, whom she went to for half-century, made house calls replete with drilling equipment. But although Margit was mostly bedridden the last couple of years, she had been hardier than most people around her. Like most Viennese, the Miseses were inveterate walkers and mountain-climbers; into her nineties, Margit could out-walk (or out-sprint!) people a half or a third her age. Indeed, at Margit's memorial service, her granddaughter talked with wonder about Margit's rapid walks that virtually put the grand-daughter ("used to buses") under the table.

One time, Margit was telling me that someone had asked her if there was anything in common between Lu, her first husband Ferdinand Sereny, and other men she had admired. "They were all elegant," she said. And elegance is a term that springs to mind about Lu, Margit, and other products of the courtly and marvelous age of Vienna before World War I. It applies to Lu, whom Margit says in her memoir would never allow himself to be caught without his jacket, even in the hottest and muggiest weather. And to Margit herself, an actress in her youth, who when I first met her in the 1950s, was so stunningly beautiful that I was convinced that Mises had married a child bride.

Margit von Mises was the last of the Austrians, the last vestige of Old Vienna. And now Hayek is gone, and Margit is gone, and gone is that apartment on West End Avenue that held so many memories, and that held together and fostered so many of the luminaries of the Misesian movement: Larry and Bertha Fertig, Harry and Frances Hazlitt, J.B. and Ruth Matthews, Philip Cortney, Alfred and Ilse Schütz. It is vital that we keep faith with them, and honor their lives, lest they and their work and their cause be forgotten.

Margit and Ludwig von Mises were a magnificent team. In contemplating their lives, all the fuss about "family values" and "feminism" seems absurdly banal. Those who knew Margit know that she was one of the strongest-minded women they have ever met. And yet, despite or perhaps because of that fact, Margit was unsurpassed in devotion to Mises the person in life and in perpetuating his memory and his ideas after his death.

We live in an age where everyone seems to be bending to the latest wind, anxious to maintain his status as "politically correct." Lu and Margit were of a different and far nobler cloth and of a different age. They followed their own convictions and their own star without even a thought of compromise of principle, let alone of surrender. The death of Margit von Mises, yes even at age 102, leaves us all poorer and diminished in spirit. ❯

116
THE STORY OF THE MISES INSTITUTE

The Mises Institute comes at both economic scholarship and applied political philosophy from a very different perspective. It believes that "policy analysis" without principle is mere flim-flam and *ad-hoc*ery—murky political conclusions resting on foundations of sand. It also believes that policy analysis that does not rest on scholarly principles is scarcely worth the paper it is written on or the time and money devoted to it. In short, that the only worthwhile analysis of the contemporary political and economic scene rests consistently on firm scholarly principles.

On the other hand, the Mises Institute challenges the all-too-prevalent view that to be scholarly means never, ever to take an ideological position. On the contrary, to the Mises Institute, the very devotion to truth on which scholarship rests *necessarily* implies that truth must be pursued and applied wherever it may lead—including the realm of current affairs. Economic scholarship divorced from application is only emasculated intellectual

---

First published in May 1988.

game-playing, just as public policy analysis without scholarship is chaos cut off from principle.

And so we see the real point underlying the uniqueness of the Mises Institute's twin programs of scholarship and application: the artificial split between the two realms is healed at last. Scholarly principles are carried forward into the analysis of government and its machinations, just as contemporary political economy now rests on sound scholarly research. From first axioms to applications, both scholarship and applied economics are an integrated whole, at long last.

And now, too, we see the real point behind the title of the Mises Institute. It is no accident that the Institute is the only organization in the United States that honors Ludwig von Mises in its title. For Ludwig von Mises, in his life and in his work, exemplified as no other man the fusion, the integration, of scholarly principle and principled application. Mises, one of the greatest intellects and scholars of the twentieth century, scorned any notion that scholarship should remain content with abstract theorizing and never, ever apply its principles to public policy.

On the contrary, Mises always combined scholarship with policy conclusions. A man of high courage, a scholar with unusual integrity, Ludwig von Mises never knew any other way than pursuing truth to its ultimate conclusions, however unpopular or unpalatable. And, as a result, Ludwig von Mises was the greatest and most uncompromising champion of human freedom in the twentieth century.

It is no wonder, then, that the timorous and the venal habitually shy away from the very name of Ludwig von Mises. For Mises scorned all obstacles and temptations in the pursuit of truth and freedom. In raising the proud banner of Ludwig von Mises, the Mises Institute has indeed set up a standard to which the wise and honest can repair.

The Mises Institute is expanding and flourishing as never before. The *Review of Austrian Economics*, a high level journal in the theory and applications of Austrian economics, is also the *only* journal in the field. It serves to expand and develop the truths of Austrian economics. But it *also* nurtures Austrians, encourages new, young Austrians to read and write for the journal, and finds mature Austrians heretofore isolated and scattered in often lonely academic outposts, but who are now stimulated to write and submit articles.

These men and women now know that they are *not* isolated, that they are part of a large and growing nationwide and even international movement. Any of us who remember what it was like to find even *one* other person who agreed with our seemingly eccentric views in favor of freedom and the free market will appreciate what I mean, and how vitally important has been the growing role of the Mises Institute.

The Institute's comprehensive program in Austrian education also includes publishing and distributing working papers, books, and monographs, original and reprinted, and holding conferences on a variety of important economic topics, and later publishing the conference papers in book form. Its monthly policy letter, the *Free Market*, provides incisive commentary on the world of political economy from an Austrian perspective.

Furthermore, the Mises Institute now has its academic headquarters at Auburn University, where M.A. and Ph.D. degrees in economics are being granted. The Mises Institute also provides a large number of graduate fellowships, both resident at Auburn University, and non-resident to promising young graduate students throughout the country.

Last but emphatically not least, the Institute sponsors a phenomenally successful week-long summer conference in the Austrian School. This program, which features a remarkable faculty, has attracted the best young minds from the world over, and gained deserved recognition as the most rigorous and comprehensive program anywhere. Here, leading Austrian economists engage in intensive instruction and discussion with students in a lovely campus setting. Participants are literally the best, the brightest and the most eager budding Austrians. From there they go on to develop, graduate, and themselves teach as

Austrian scholars, or become businessmen or other opinion leaders imbued with the truth and the importance of Austrian and free-market economics.

In addition, the Institute is unique in that instructors avoid the usual academic practice of giving a lecture and quickly retiring from the scene; instead, their attendance at all the lectures encourages fellowship and an *esprit de corps* among faculty and students. These friendships and associations may be lifelong, and they are vital for building any sort of vibrant or cohesive long-run movement for Austrian economics and the free society.

The basic point of this glittering spectrum of activities is twofold: to advance the discipline, the expanding, integrated body of truth that is Austrian economics; and to build a flourishing movement of Austrian economists. No science, no discipline, develops in thin air, in the abstract; it must be nurtured and advanced by *people*, by individual men and women who talk to each other, write to and for each other, interact and help build the body of Austrian economics and the people who sustain it.

The remarkable achievement of the Mises Institute can only be understood in the context of what preceded it, and of the conditions it faced when it began in 1982. In 1974, leading Mises student F.A. Hayek won the Nobel Prize in economics, a startling change from previous Nobel awards, exclusively for mathematical Keynesians. 1974 was also the year after the death of the great modern Austrian theorist and champion of freedom, Ludwig von Mises. Hayek's prize sparked a veritable revival in this long-forgotten school of economic thought. For several years thereafter, annual scholarly week-long conferences gathered the leading Austrian economists of the day, as well as the brightest young students; and the papers delivered at these meetings became published volumes, reviving and advancing the Austrian approach. Austrian economics was being revived from 40 years of neglect imposed by the Keynesian Revolution—a revolution that sent the contrasting and once flourishing school of Austrian economics down the Orwellian memory hole.

In this burgeoning Austrian revival, there was one fixed point so obvious that it was virtually taken for granted: that the heart and soul of Austrianism was, is, and can only be Ludwig von Mises, this great creative mind who had launched, established and developed the twentieth-century Austrian School, and the man whose courage and devotion to unvarnished, uncompromised truth led him to be the outstanding battler for freedom and laissez-faire economics in our century. In his ideas, and in the glory of his personal example, Mises was an inspiration and a beaconlight for us all.

But then, in the midst of this flourishing development, something began to go wrong. After the last successful conference in the summer of 1976, the annual high-level seminars disappeared. Proposals to solidify and expand the success of the boom by launching a scholarly Austrian journal, were repeatedly rebuffed. The elementary instructional summer seminars continued, but their tone began to change. Increasingly, we began to hear disturbing news of an odious new line being spread: Mises, they whispered, had been "too dogmatic . . . too extreme," he "thought he knew the truth," he "alienated people."

Yes, of course, Mises was "dogmatic," i.e., he was totally devoted to truth and to freedom and free enterprise. Yes, indeed, Mises, even though the kindliest and most inspiring of men, "alienated people" all the time, that is, he systematically alienated collectivists, socialists, statists, and trimmers and opportunists of all stripes.

And of course such charges were nothing new. Mises had been hit with these smears all of his valiant and indomitable life. The terribly disturbing thing was that the people mouthing these canards all knew better: for they had all been seemingly dedicated Misesians before and during the "boom" period.

It soon became all too clear what game was afoot. Whether independently or in concert, the various people and groups involved in this shift had made a conscious critical decision: they had come to the conclusion they should have understood long before, that praxeology, Austrian economics, uncompromising laissez-faire were popular neither with politicians nor with the Establishment. Nor were these views very "respectable" among mainstream academics. The small knot of wealthy donors decided that the route to money and power lay elsewhere, while many young scholars decided that the road to academic tenure was through cozying up to attitudes popular in academia instead of maintaining a commitment to often despised truth.

But these trimmers did not wish to attack Mises or Austrianism directly; they knew that Ludwig von Mises was admired and literally beloved by a large number of businessmen and members of the intelligent public, and they did not want to alienate their existing or potential support. What to do? The same thing that was done by groups a century ago that captured the noble word "liberal" and twisted it to mean its opposite— statism and tyranny, instead of liberty. The same thing that was done when the meaning of the U.S. Constitution was changed from a document that *restricted* government power over the individual, to one that endorsed and legitimated such power. As the noted economic journalist Garet Garrett wrote about the New Deal: "Revolution within the form," keep the *name* Austrian, but change the *content* to its virtual opposite. Change the content from devotion to economic law and free markets, to a fuzzy nihilism, to a mushy acceptance of Mises's ancient foes: historicism, institutionalism, even Marxism and collectivism. All, no doubt, more "respectable" in many academic circles. And Mises? Instead of attacking him openly, ignore him, and once in a while intimate that Mises *really*, down deep, would have agreed with this new dispensation.

Into this miasma, into this blight, at the point when the ideas of Ludwig von Mises were about to be lost to history for the second and last time, and when the very name of "Austrian" had been captured from within by its opposite, there entered the fledgling Mises Institute.

The Ludwig von Mises Institute began in the fall of 1982 with only an idea; it had no sugar daddies, no endowments, no billionaires to help it make its way in the world. In fact, the powers-that-be in what was now the Austrian "Establishment" tried their very worst to see that the Mises Institute did not succeed.

The Mises Institute persisted, however, inspired by the light of truth and liberty, and gradually but surely we began to find friends and supporters who had a great love for Ludwig von Mises and the ideals and principles he fought for throughout his life. The Institute found that its hopes were justified: that there are indeed many more devoted champions of freedom and the free market in America. Our journal and conferences and centers and fellowships have flourished, and we were able to launch a scholarly but uncompromising assault on the nihilism and statism that had been sold to the unsuspecting world as "Austrian" economics.

The result of this struggle has been highly gratifying. Thousands of students are exposed to the Austrian School as a radical alternative to mainstream theory. For the light of truth has prevailed over duplicity. There are no longer any viable competitors for the name of Austrian. The free market again has principled and courageous champions. Justice, for once, has triumphed. Not only is the Austrian economic revival flourishing as never before, but it is now developing soundly within a genuine Austrian framework. Above all, Austrian economics is once again, as it ever shall be, Misesian. ▶

Postscript

117

THE NOVEMBER REVOLUTION . . .
AND WHAT TO DO ABOUT IT

In a famous lyric of a generation ago, Bob Dylan twitted the then-dominant "bourgeois" culture, "it doesn't take a weatherman to know the way the wind blows." Indeed, and the significance of this phrase today has nothing to do with the group of crazed Stalinist youth who once called themselves "the Weathermen." The phrase, in fact, is all too relevant to the present day.

It means this: you don't have to have to be a certified media pundit to understand the meaning of the glorious election of November 1994. In fact, it almost seems a requirement for a clear understanding of this election not to be a certified pundit. It certainly helps not to be a member of Clinton's cadre of professional spinners and spinsters.

The election was not a repudiation of "incumbents." Not when not a single Republican incumbent lost in any Congressional, Senate, or gubernatorial seat. The election was manifestly not simply "anti-Congress," as George Stephanopoulos said. Many governorships and state legislatures experienced

---

Murray Rothbard wrote this essay one week after the November 1994 election. It circulated privately as a Confidential Memo. It is first published in this book.

upheavals as well. The elections were not an expression of public anger that President Clinton's beloved goals were not being met fast enough by Congress, as Clinton himself claimed. All too many of his goals (in housing, labor, banking, and foreign policy, for example) were being realized through regulatory edict.

No, the meaning of the truly revolutionary election of 1994 is clear to anyone who has eyes to see and is willing to use them: it was a massive and unprecedented public repudiation of President Clinton, his person, his personnel, his ideologies and programs, and all of his works; plus a repudiation of Clinton's Democrat Party; and, most fundamentally, a rejection of the designs, current and proposed, of the Leviathan he heads.

In effect, the uprising of anti-Democrat and anti-Washington, D.C., sentiment throughout the country during 1994 found its expression at the polls in November in the only way feasible in the social context of a mass democracy: by a sweeping and unprecedented electoral revolution repudiating Democrats and electing Republicans. It was an event at least as significant for our future as those of 1985–1988 in the former Soviet Union and its satellites, which in retrospect revealed the internal crumbling of an empire.

But if the popular revolution constitutes a repudiation of Clinton and Clintonism, what is the ideology being repudiated, and what principles are being affirmed?

Again, it should be clear that what is being rejected is big government in general (its taxing, mandating, regulating, gun grabbing, and even its spending) and, in particular, its arrogant ambition to control the entire society from the political center. Voters and taxpayers are no longer persuaded of a supposed rationale for American-style central planning.

On the positive side, the public is vigorously and fervently affirming its desire to re-limit and de-centralize government; to increase individual and community liberty; to reduce taxes, mandates, and government intrusion; to return to the cultural and social mores of pre-1960s America, and perhaps much earlier than that.

WHAT ARE THE PROSPECTS?

Should we greet the November results with unalloyed joy? Partly, the answer is a matter of personal temperament, but there are guidelines that emerge from a realistic analysis of this new and exciting political development.

In the first place, conservatives and libertarians should be joyful at the intense and widespread revolutionary sentiment throughout the country, ranging from small but numerous grassroots outfits usually to moderate professionals and academics. The repudiation of the Democrats at the polls and the rapid translation of general popular sentiment into electoral action is indeed a cause for celebration.

But there are great problems and resistances ahead. It is vital that we prepare for them and be able to deal with them. Rolling back statism is not going to be easy. The Marxists used to point out, from long study of historical experience, that no ruling elite in history has ever voluntarily surrendered its power; or, more correctly, that a ruling elite has only been toppled when large sectors of that elite, for whatever reasons, have given up and decided that the system should be abandoned.

We need to study the lessons of the most recent collapse of a ruling elite and its monstrous statist system, the Soviet Union and its satellite Communist states. There is both good news and at least cautionary bad news in the history of this collapse and of its continuing aftermath. The overwhelmingly good news, of course, is the crumbling of the collectivist U.S.S.R., even though buttressed by systemic terror and mass murder.

Essentially, the Soviet Union imploded because it had lost the support, not only of the general public, but even of large sectors of the ruling elites themselves. The loss of support came, first, in the general loss of moral legitimacy, and of faith in Marxism, and then, out of recognition that the system wasn't working economically, even for much of the ruling Communist Party itself.

The bad news, while scarcely offsetting the good, came from the way in which the transition from Communism to freedom and free markets was bungled. Essentially there were two grave and interconnected errors. First, the reformers didn't move fast enough, worrying about social disruption, and not realizing that the faster the shift toward freedom and private ownership took place, the less would be the disturbances of the transition and the sooner economic and social recovery would take place.

Second, in attempting to be congenial statesmen, as opposed to counter-revolutionaries, the reformers not only failed to punish the Communist rulers with, at the least, the loss of their livelihoods, they left them in place, insuring that the ruling "ex"-Communist elite would be able to resist fundamental change.

In other words, except for the Czech Republic, where feisty free-market economist and Prime Minister Vaclav Klaus was able to drive through rapid change to a genuine free market, and, to some extent, in the Baltic states, the reformers were too nice, too eager for "reconciliation," too slow and cautious. The result was quasi-disastrous: for everyone gave lip service to the rhetoric of free markets and privatization, while in reality, as in Russia, prices were decontrolled while industry remained in monopoly government hands.

As former Soviet economist and Mises Institute senior fellow Yuri Maltsev first pointed out, it was as if the U.S. Post Office maintained its postal monopoly, while suddenly being allowed to charge $2 for a first-class stamp: the result would be impoverishment for the public, and more money into the coffers of the State. This is the reverse of a shift to free markets and private property.

Furthermore, when privatization finally did take place in Russia, too much of it was "privatization" into the hands of the old elites, which meant a system more like Communist rule flavored by "private" gangsterism, than any sort of free market. But, crucially, free markets and private enterprise took the blame among the bewildered Russian public.

BETRAYING THE REVOLUTION

The imminent problem facing the new American Revolution is all too similar: that, while using the inspiring rhetoric of freedom, tax-cuts, decentralization, individualism, and a roll back to small government, the Republican Party elites will be performing deeds in precisely the opposite direction. In that way, the fair rhetoric of freedom and small government will be used, to powerful and potentially disastrous effect, as a cover for cementing big government in place, and even for advancing us in the direction of collectivism.

This systematic betrayal was the precise meaning and function of the Reagan administration. So effective was Ronald Reagan as a rhetorician, though not a practitioner, of freedom and small government, that, to this day, most conservatives have still not cottoned on to the scam of the Reagan administration.

For the "Reagan Revolution" was precisely a taking of the revolutionary, free-market, and small government spirit of the 1970s, and the other anti-government vote of 1980, and turning it into its opposite, without the public or even the activists of that revolution realizing what was going on.

It was only the advent of George Bush, who continued the trend toward collectivism while virtually abandoning the Reaganite rhetoric, that finally awakened the conservative public. (Whether Ronald Reagan himself was aware of his role, or went along with it, is a matter for future biographers, and is irrelevant to the objective reality of what actually happened.)

Are we merely being "cynical" (the latest self-serving Clintonian term), or only basing our cautionary warnings on one historical episode? No, we are simply looking at the activity and function of the Republican elites since World War II.

Since World War II, and especially since the 1950s, the function of the Republican Party has been to be the "loyal . . . moderate," "bipartisan," pseudo-opposition to the collectivist and leftist program of the Democratic Party. Unlike the more apocalyptic and impatient Bolsheviks, the Mensheviks (or social democrats, or corporate liberals, or "responsible" liberals, or "responsible" conservatives, or neoconservatives—the labels change, but the reality remains the same) try to preserve an illusion of free choice for the American public, including a two-party system, and at least marginal freedom of speech and expression.

The goal of these "responsible" or "enlightened" moderates has been to participate in the march to statism, while replacing the older American ideals of free markets, private property, and limited government with cloudy and noisy rhetoric about the glories of "democracy," as opposed to the one-party dictatorship of the Soviet Union.

Indeed, "democracy" is so much the supposed overriding virtue that advancing "democracy" throughout the globe is now the sole justification for the "moderate," "bipartisan," Republicrat policy of global intervention, foreign aid, and trade mercantilism. Indeed, now that the collapse of the Soviet Union has eliminated the specter of a Soviet threat, what other excuse for such a policy remains?

While everyone is familiar with the bipartisan, monopoly-cartel foreign policy that has been dominant since World War II, again pursued under various excuses (the Soviet threat, reconstruction of Europe, "helping" the Third World, "free-trade," the global economy, "global democracy," and always an inchoate but pervasive fear of a "return to isolationism"), Americans are less familiar with the fact that the dominant Republican policy during this entire era has been bipartisan in domestic affairs as well.

If we look at the actual record and not the rhetoric, we will find that the function of the Democrat administrations (especially Roosevelt, Truman, and Johnson), has been to advance the march to collectivism by Great Leaps Forward, and in the name of "liberalism"; while the function of the Republicans has been, in the name of opposition or small government or "conservatism," to fail to roll back any of these "social gains," and indeed, to engage in more big-government collectivizing of their own (especially Eisenhower, Nixon, Reagan, and Bush). Indeed, it is arguable that Nixon did even more to advance big government than his earthy Texas predecessor.

The Illusion of Choice

Why bother with maintaining a farcical two-party system, and especially why bother with small-government rhetoric for the Republicans? In the first place, the maintenance of some democratic choice, however illusory, is vital for all varieties of social democrats. They have long realized that a one-party dictatorship can and probably will become cordially hated, for its real or perceived failures, and will eventually be overthrown, possibly along with its entire power structure.

Maintaining two parties means, on the other hand, that the public, growing weary of the evils of Democrat rule, can turn to out-of-power Republicans. And then, when they weary of the Republican alternative, they can turn once again to the eager Democrats waiting in the wings. And so, the ruling elites maintain a shell game, while the American public constitute the suckers, or the "marks" for the ruling con-artists.

The true nature of the Republican ruling elite was revealed when Barry Goldwater won the Republican nomination for President in 1964. Goldwater, or the ideologues and rank-and-file of his conservative movement, were, or at least seemed to be, genuinely radical, small government, and anti-Establishment, at least on domestic policy. The Goldwater nomination scared the Republican elites to such an extent that, led by Nelson Rockefeller, they openly supported Johnson for president.

The shock to the elites came from the fact that the "moderates," using their domination of the media, finance, and big corporations, had been able to control the delegates at every Republican presidential convention since 1940, often in defiance of the manifest will of the rank-and-file (e.g., Willkie over Taft in 1940, Dewey over Taft in 1944, Dewey over Bricker in 1948, Eisenhower over Taft in 1952). Such was their power that they did not, as usually happens with open party traitors, lose all their influence in the Republican Party thereafter.

It was the specter of the stunning loss of Goldwater that probably accounts for the eagerness of Ronald Reagan or his conservative movement, upon securing the nomination in 1980, to agree to what looks very much like a rigged deal (or what John Randolph of Roanoke once famously called a "corrupt bargain").

The deal was this: the Republican elites would support their party's presidential choice, and guarantee the Reaganauts the trappings and perquisites of power, in return for Reaganaut agreement not to try seriously to roll back the Leviathan State against which they had so effectively campaigned. And after 12 years of enjoyment of power and its perquisites in the executive branch, the Official Conservative movement seemed to forget whatever principles it had.

THE PARASITIC ELITE

So is our message unrelieved gloom? Is everything hopeless, are we all in the ineradicable grip of the ruling elite, and should we all just go home and forget the whole thing? Certainly not. Apart from the immorality of giving up, we have so far not mentioned the truly optimistic side of this equation. We can begin this way: even given the necessity of the elite maintaining two parties, why do they even have to indulge in radical rightist, small-government rhetoric?

After all, the disjunction between rhetoric and reality can become embarrassing, even aggravating, and can eventually lose the elites the support of the party rank-and-file, as well as the general public. So why indulge in the rhetoric at all? Goldwater supporter Phyllis Schlafly famously called for a "choice, not an echo"; but why does the Establishment allow radical choices, even in rhetoric?

The answer is that large sections of the public opposed the New Deal, as well as each of the advances to collectivism since then. The rhetoric is not empty for much of the public, and certainly not for most of the activists of the Republican Party. They seriously believe the anti-big-government ideology. Similarly, much of the rank-and-file, and certainly the activist Democrats, are more openly, more eagerly, collectivist than the Democrat elite, or the Demopublican elite, would desire.

Furthermore, since government interventionism doesn't work, since it is despotic, counter-productive, and destructive of the interests of the mass of the people, advancing collectivism will generate an increasingly hostile reaction among the public, what the media elites sneer at as a "backlash."

In particular, collectivist, social democratic rule destroys the prosperity, the freedom, and the cultural, social, and ethical principles and practices of the mass of the American people, working and middle classes alike. Rule by the statist elite is not benign or simply a matter of who happens to be in office: it is rule by a growing army of leeches and parasites battening off the income and wealth of hard-working Americans, destroying their property, corrupting their customs and institutions, sneering at their religion.

The ultimate result must be what happens whenever parasites multiply at the expense of a host: at first gradual descent into ruin, and then finally collapse. (And therefore, if anyone cares, destruction of the parasites themselves.)

Hence, the ruling elite lives chronically in what the Marxists would call an "inner contradiction": it thrives by imposing increasing misery and impoverishment upon the great majority of the American people.

The parasitic elite, even while ever increasing, has to comprise a minority of the population, otherwise the entire system would collapse very quickly. But the elite is ruling over, and demolishing, the very people, the very majority, who are supposed to keep these destructive elites perpetually in power by periodic exercise of their much-lauded "democratic" franchise. How do the elites get away with this, year after year, decade after decade, without suffering severe retribution at the polls?

THE RULING COALITION

A crucial means of establishing and maintaining this domination is by co-opting, by bringing within the ruling elite, the opinion-moulding classes in society. These opinion-moulders are the professional shapers of opinion: theorists, academics, journalists and other media movers and shakers, script writers and directors, writers, pundits, think-tankers, consultants, agitators, and social therapists. There are two essential roles for these assorted and proliferating technocrats and intellectuals: to weave apologies for the statist regime, and to help staff the interventionist bureaucracy and to plan the system.

The keys to any social or political movement are money, numbers, and ideas. The opinion-moulding classes, the technocrats and intellectuals supply the ideas, the propaganda, and the personnel to staff the new statist dispensation. The critical funding is supplied by figures in the power elite: various members of the wealthy or big business (usually corporate) classes. The very name "Rockefeller Republican" reflects this basic reality.

While big-business leaders and firms can be highly productive servants of consumers in a free-market economy, they are also, all too often, seekers after subsidies, contracts, privileges, or cartels furnished by big government. Often, too, business lobbyists and leaders are the sparkplugs for the statist, interventionist system.

What big businessmen get out of this unholy coalition on behalf of the super-state are subsidies and privileges from big government. What do intellectuals and opinion-moulders get out of it? An increasing number of cushy jobs in the bureaucracy, or in the government-subsidized sector, staffing the welfare-regulatory state, and apologizing for its policies, as well as propagandizing for them among the public. To put it bluntly, intellectuals, theorists, pundits, media elites, etc. get to live a life which they could not attain on the free market, but which they can gain at taxpayer expense—along with the social prestige that goes with the munificent grants and salaries.

This is not to deny that the intellectuals, therapists, media folk, *et al.*, may be "sincere" ideologues and believers in the glorious coming age of egalitarian collectivism. Many of them are driven by the ancient Christian heresy, updated to secularist and New Age versions, of themselves as a cadre of Saints imposing upon the country and the world a communistic Kingdom of God on Earth.

It is, in any event, difficult for an outsider to pronounce conclusively on anyone else's motivations. But it still cannot be a coincidence that the ideology of Left-liberal intellectuals coincides with their own vested economic interest in the money, jobs, and power that burgeoning collectivism brings them. In any case, any movement that so closely blends ideology and an economic interest in looting the public provides a powerful motivation indeed.

Thus, the pro-state coalition consists of those who receive, or expect to receive, government checks and privileges. So far, we have pinpointed big business, intellectuals, technocrats, and the bureaucracy. But numbers, voters, are needed as well, and in the burgeoning and expanding state of today, the above groups are supplemented by other more numerous favored recipients of government largess: welfare clients and, especially in the last several decades, members of various minority social groups who are defined by the elites as being among the "victims" and the "oppressed."

As more and more of the "oppressed" are discovered or invented by the Left, ever more of them receive subsidies, favorable regulations, and other badges of "victimhood" from the government. And as the "oppressed" expand in ever-widening circles, be they blacks, women, Hispanics, American Indians, the disabled, and on and on *ad infinitum*, the voting power of the Left is ever expanded, again at the expense of the American majority.

CONNING THE MAJORITY

Still, despite the growing number of receivers of government largess, the opinion-moulding elites must continue to perform their essential task of convincing or soft-soaping the oppressed majority into not realizing what is going on. The majority must be kept contented, and quiescent. Through control of the media, especially the national, "respectable" and respected media, the rulers attempt to persuade the deluded majority that all is well, that any voice except the "moderate" and "respectable" wings of both parties are dangerous "extremists" and loonies who must be shunned at all costs.

The ruling elite and the media try their best to keep the country's tack on a "moderate . . . vital center"—the "center," of course, drifting neatly leftward decade after decade. "Extremes" of both Right and Left should be shunned, in the view of the Establishment. Its attitudes toward both extremes, however, are very different.

The Right are reviled as crazed or evil reactionaries who want to go beyond the acceptable task of merely slowing down collectivist change. Instead, they actually want to "turn back the clock of history" and repeal or abolish big government. The Left, on the other hand, are more gently criticized as impatient and too radical, and who therefore would go too far too fast and provoke a dangerous counter-reaction from the ever-dangerous Right. The Left, in other words, is in danger of giving the show away.

THE ADVENT OF CLINTON

Things were going smoothly for the vital center until the election of 1992. America was going through one of its periodic revulsions from the party in power, Bush was increasingly disliked, and the power elite, from the Rockefellers and Wall Street to the neoconservative pundits who infest our press and our TV screens, decided that it was time for another change. They engaged in a blistering propaganda campaign against Bush for his tax increases (the same people ignored Reagan's tax increases) and excoriated him for selling out the voters' mandate for smaller government (at a Heritage Foundation event just before the election, for example, an employee carried a realistic and bloodied head of Bush around on a platter).

Even more crucially, the elites assured the rest of us that Bill Clinton was an acceptable Moderate, a "New Democrat," at worst a centrist who would only supply a nuanced difference from the centrist Republican Bush, and, at best, a person whom Washington and New York moderates and conservatives and Wall Street could work with.

But the ruling elite, whether Right-or Left-tinged, is neither omnipotent nor omniscient—they goof just like the rest of us. Instead of a moderate leftist, they got a driven, almost fanatical leftist administration, propelled by the president's almost maniacal energy, and the arrogant and self-righteous Hillary's scary blend of Hard Left ideology and implacable drive for power.

The rapid and all-encompassing Clintonian shift leftward upset the Establishment's apple cart. The sudden Hard Left move, blended with an unprecedented nationwide reaction of loathing for Clinton's persona and character, opened up a gap in the center, and provoked an intense and widespread public detestation of Clinton and of big government generally.

The public had been tipped over, and had had enough; it was fed up. An old friend reminds me that the Republicans could well have campaigned on the simple but highly effective slogan of their last great party victory of 1946: "Had Enough? Vote Republican!" In short, the right-wing populist, semi-libertarian, anti-big government revolution had been fully launched.

What is the ruling elite to do now? It has a difficult task on its hands—a task which those genuinely devoted to the free market must be sure to make impossible.

The ruling elite must do the following. First, it must make sure that, whatever their rhetoric, the Republican leadership in Congress (and its eventual presidential nominee) keep matters nicely centrist and "moderate," and, however they dress it up, maintain and even advance the big-government program.

Second, at least for the next two years, they must see to it that Clinton swings back to his earlier New Democrat trappings, and drops his Hard Left program. In this way, the newly triumphant centrists of both parties could engage once again in cozy collaboration, and the financial and media elites could sink back comfortably into their familiar smooth sailing, steadily advancing collectivistic groove.

THWARTING DEMOCRACY

It is no accident that both of these courses of action imply the thwarting of democracy and democratic choice. There is no doubt that the Democratic Party base leftists, minorities, teacher unions, etc.—as well the party militants and activists, are clamoring for the continuation and even acceleration of Clinton's Hard Left program.

On the other hand, the popular will, as expressed in the sweep of 1994, by the middle and working class majority, and certainly by the militants and activists of the Republican Party, is in favor of rolling back and toppling big government and the welfare state. Not only that, they are fed up, angry, and determined to do so: that is, they are in a revolutionary mood.

Have you noticed how the social democratic elites, though eternally yammering about the vital importance of "democracy," American and global, quickly turn sour on a democratic choice whenever it is something they don't like? How quick they then are to thwart the democratic will, by media smears, calumny and outright coercive suppression.

Since the ruling elite lives by fleecing and dominating the ruled, their economic interests must always be in opposition. But the fascinating feature of the American scene in recent decades has been the unprecedented conflict, the fundamental clash, between the ruling liberal/intellectual/business/bureaucratic elites on the one hand, and the mass of Americans on the other. The conflict is not just on taxes and subsidies, but across the board socially, culturally, morally, aesthetically, religiously.

In a penetrating article in the December 1994 *Harper's*, the late sociologist Christopher Lasch, presaging his imminent book, *The Revolt of the Elites*, points out how the American elites have been in fundamental revolt against virtually all the basic American values, customs, and traditions. Increasing realization of this clash by the American grass roots has fueled and accelerated the right-wing populist revolution, a revolution not only against Washington rule, taxes, and controls, but also against the entire panoply of attitudes and mores that the elite are trying to foist upon the recalcitrant American public. The public has finally caught on and is rising up angry.

Prop. 187: A Case Study

California's Proposition 187 provides a fascinating case study of the vital rift between the intellectual, business, and media elites, and the general public. There is the massive funding and propaganda the elites are willing to expend to thwart the desires of the people; the mobilizing of support by "oppressed" minorities; and finally, when all else fails, the willingness to wheel in the instruments of anti-democratic coercion to block, permanently if possible, the manifest will of the great majority of the American people. In short, "democracy" in action!

In recent years, a flood of immigrants, largely illegal, has been inundating California, some from Asia but mainly from Mexico and other Latin American countries. These immigrants have dominated and transformed much of the culture, proving unassimilable and swamping tax-supported facilities such as medical care, the welfare rolls, and the public schools. In consequence, former immigration official Harold Ezell helped frame a ballot initiative, Prop. 187, which simply called for the abolition of all taxpayer funding for illegal immigrants in California.

Prop. 187 provided a clear-cut choice, an up-or-down referendum on the total abolition of a welfare program for an entire class of people who also happen to be lawbreakers. If we are right in our assessment of the electorate, such an initiative should gain the support of not only every conservative and libertarian, but of every sane American. Surely, illegals shouldn't be able to leach off the taxpayer.

Support for Prop. 187 spread like wildfire, it got signatures galore, and it quickly spurted to a 2:1 lead in the polls, although its organized supporters were only a network of small, grass-roots groups that no one had ever heard of. But every single one of the prominent, massively funded elite groups not only opposed Prop. 187, but also smeared it unmercifully.

The *smearbund* included big media, big business, big unions, organized teachers, organized medicine, organized hospitals, social workers (the latter four groups of course benefitting from taxpayer funds channeled to them via the welfare-medical-public school support system), intellectuals, writers, academics, leftists, neoconservatives, etc. They denounced Prop. 187 grass-roots proponents as nativists, fascists, racists, xenophobes, Nazis, you name it, and even accused them of advocating poverty, starvation, and typhoid fever.

Joining in this richly-funded campaign of hysteria and smear was the entire official libertarian (or Left-libertarian) movement, including virtually every "free-market" and "libertarian" think tank except the Mises Institute. The Libertarian Party of California weighed in too, taking the remarkable step of fiercely opposing a popular measure that would eliminate taxpayer funding of illegals, and implausibly promising that if enough illegals came here, they would eventually rise up and slash the welfare state.

The once-consistently libertarian *Orange County Register* bitterly denounced Prop. 187 day after day, and vilified Orange County Republican Congressman Dana Rohrabacher, who had long been close to the *Register* and the libertarian movement, for favoring Prop. 187. These editorials provoked an unprecedented number of angry letters from the tax-paying readership.

For their part, the neoconservative and official libertarian think tanks joined the elite condemnation of Prop. 187. Working closely with Stephen Moore of the Cato Institute, Cesar Conda of the Alexis de Tocqueville Institution circulated a statement against the measure that was signed by individuals at the Heritage Foundation, the American Enterprise Institute, the Manhattan Institute, the Reason Foundation, and even the Competitive Enterprise Institute.

The *Wall Street Journal* denounced the initiative almost as savagely as did the Establishment liberal *Los Angeles Times*, while neoconservative presidential hopefuls Jack Kemp and Bill Bennett cut their own political throats by issuing a joint statement, from the center of the Leviathan, Washington, D.C., urging Californians to defeat the measure. This act was self-destructive because Governor Pete Wilson, leading the rest of the California Republican Party, saved his political bacon by climbing early onto Prop. 187, and riding the issue to come from far behind to crush leftist Kathleen Brown.

The case of the think tanks is a relatively easy puzzle to solve. The big foundations that make large grants to right-of-center organizations were emphatically against Prop. 187. Also having an influence was the desire for media plaudits and social acceptance in the D.C. hothouse, where one wrong answer leads to loss of respectability.

But the interesting question is why did Kemp and Bennett join in the campaign against Prop. 187, and why do they continue to denounce it even after it has passed? After all, they could have said nothing; not being Californians, they could have stayed out of the fray.

Reliable reports reveal that Kemp and Bennett were "persuaded" to take this foolhardy stand by the famed William Kristol, in dynastic and apostolic succession to his father Irving as godfather of the neoconservative movement.

It is intriguing to speculate on the means by which Kristol managed to work his persuasive wiles. Surely the inducement was not wholly intellectual; and surely Kemp and Bennett, especially in dealing with the godfather, have to keep their eye, not simply on their presidential ambitions, but also on the extremely lucrative and not very onerous institutional positions that they now enjoy.

In the meantime, as per the usual pattern, the ruling elites were able to mobilize the "oppressed" sectors of the public against Prop. 187, so that blacks and groups that have been and will continue to be heavily immigrant, such as Asians and Jews, voted in clear if modest majorities against the measure.

Voting overwhelmingly against Prop. 187, of course, were the Hispanics, who constitute the bulk of legal and illegal immigrants into that state, with many of the illegals voting illegally as well. Polarizing the situation further, Mexicans and other Hispanics demonstrated in large numbers, waving Mexican and other Latin American flags, brandishing signs in Spanish, and generally enraging white voters. Even the Mexican government weighed in, with the dictator Salinas and his successor Zedillo denouncing Prop. 187 as a "human rights violation."

After a massive October blitz by the media and the other elites, media polls pronounced that Prop. 187 had moved from 2:1 in favor to neck-and-neck, explaining that "once the public had had a chance to examine Prop. 187, they now realized," and blah blah. When the smoke had cleared on election night, however, it turned out that after all the money and all the propaganda, Prop. 187 had passed by just about . . . 2:1! In short, either the media polls had lied, or, more likely, the public, sensing the media hostility and the ideological and cultural clash, simply lied to the pollsters.

The final and most instructive single point about this saga is simply this: the elites, having lost abysmally despite their strenuous efforts, and having seen the democratic will go against them in no uncertain fashion, quickly turned to naked coercion. It took less than 24 hours after the election for a federal judge to take out what will be a multi-year injunction, blocking any operation of Prop. 187, until at some future date, the federal judiciary should rule it unconstitutional. And, in a couple of years, no doubt the federal judicial despots, headed by the Supreme Court, will so declare.

So Much for "Democracy"!

To liberals, neocons, official conservatives, and all elites, once the federal judiciary, in particular the venerated Supreme Court, speaks, everyone is supposed to shut up and swallow the result. But why? Because an independent judiciary and judicial review are supposed to be sacred, and supply wise checks and balances on other branches of government?

But this is the greatest con, the biggest liberal shell game, of all. For the whole point of the Constitution was to bind the central government with chains of steel, to keep it tightly and strictly limited, so as to safeguard the rights and powers of the states, local communities, and individual Americans.

In the early years of the American Republic, no political leader or statesman waited for the Supreme Court to interpret the Constitution; and the Court did not have the monopoly of interpreting the Constitution or of enforcing it. Unfortunately, in practice, the federal judiciary is not "independent" at all. It is appointed by the President, confirmed by the Senate, and is from the very beginning part of the federal government itself.

But, as John C. Calhoun wisely warned in 1850, once we allow the Supreme Court to be the monopoly interpreter of governmental—and therefore of its own—power, eventual despotism by the federal government and its kept judiciary becomes inevitable. And that is precisely what has happened. From being the instrument of binding down and severely limiting the power of the federal Leviathan, the Supreme Court and the rest of the judiciary have twisted and totally transformed the Constitution into a "living" instrument and thereby a crucial tool of its own despotic and virtually absolute power over the lives of every American citizen.

One of the highly popular measures among the American people these days is term limits for state and federal legislatures. But the tragedy of the movement is its misplaced focus. Liberals are right, for once, when they point out that the public can "limit" legislative terms on their own, as they did gloriously in the November 1994 elections, by exercising their democratic will and throwing the rascals out.

But of course liberals, like official conservatives, cleverly fail to focus on those areas of government that are in no way accountable to the American public, and who cannot be thrown out of office by democratic vote at the polls. It is these imperial, swollen, and tyrannical branches of government that desperately need term limits and that no one is doing anything about. Namely, the executive branch which, apart from the president himself by third-term limit, is locked permanently into civil service and who therefore cannot be kicked out by the voters; and, above all, the federal judges, who are there for fourteen years, or, in the case of the ruling Supreme Court oligarchy, fastened upon us for life.

What we really need is not term limits for elected politicians, but the abolition of the civil service (which only began in the 1880s) and its alleged "merit system" of technocratic and bureaucratic elites; and, above all, elimination of the despotic judiciary.

WHY DEMOCRACY ANYWAY?

Across the ideological spectrum, from leftist to liberal to neoconservative to official conservative, "democracy" has been treated as a shibboleth, as an ultimate moral absolute, virtually replacing all other moral principles including the Ten Commandments and the Sermon on the Mount. But despite this universal adherence, as Mises Institute senior fellow David Gordon has pointed out, "virtually no argument is ever offered to support the desirability of . . . democracy, and the little that is available seems distressingly weak." The overriding imperative of democracy is considered self-evident and sacred, apparently above discussion among mere mortals.

What, in fact, is so great about democracy? Democracy is scarcely a virtue in itself, much less an overriding one, and not nearly as important as liberty, property rights, a free market, or strictly limited government. Democracy is simply a process, a means of selecting government rulers and policies. It has but one virtue, but this can indeed be an important one: it provides a peaceful means for the triumph of the popular will.

Ballots, in the old phrase, can serve as a peaceful and non-disruptive "substitute for bullets." That is why it makes sense to exhort people who advocate a radical (in the sense of sharp, not necessarily leftist) change from the existing polity to "work within the system" to convince a majority of voters rather than to engage in violent revolution.

When the voters desire radical change, therefore, it becomes vitally important to reflect that change quickly and smoothly in political institutions; blockage of that desire subverts the democratic process itself, and polarizes the situation so as to threaten or even bring about violent conflict in society. If ballots are indeed to be a substitute for bullets, then the ballots have to be allowed to work and take rapid effect.

This is what makes the blockage of voter mandates such as Prop. 187 so dangerous and destructive. And yet, it is clear that the ruling elites, failing at the ballot box, are ready and eager to use anti-democratic means to suppress the desires of the voters.

Prop. 187 is only one example. Another is the Gatt treaty setting up a World Trade Organization to impose global mercantilism, which was overwhelmingly opposed by the voters. It was brought to a vote in a repudiated and lame-duck Congress, by politicians who, as Mises Institute President Lew Rockwell pointed out, were virtually wearing price tags around their necks.

No doubt that the federal judiciary would find nothing unconstitutional about this. But it is ready to manufacture all sorts of constitutional "rights" which appear nowhere in the

Constitution and are soundly opposed by the electorate. These include the right to an education, including the existence of well-funded public schools; the right of gays not to be discriminated against; civil rights, affirmative action, and on and on.

Here we need deal only with the famous *Roe v. Wade* decision, in which the Supreme Court manufactured a federal "right" to abortion; ever since the founding of the Constitution, matters such as these were always considered part of the jurisdiction of state governments and the police power. The federal government is only supposed to deal with foreign affairs and disputes between states.

As *Washington Times* columnist and Mises Institute adjunct scholar Samuel Francis has pointed out, the horror at anti-abortionists employing violence against abortion doctors and clinics is appropriate, but misses the crucial point: namely, that those who believe that abortion is murder and should be outlawed were told, like everyone else, to be peaceful and "work within" the democratic system. They did so, and persuaded voters and legislatures of a number of states to restrict or even outlaw abortion.

But all of this has been for nought, because the unelected, unaccountable, life-tenured Supreme Court has pronounced abortion a federal right, thereby bypassing every state legislature, and everyone is now supposed to roll over and play dead. But in that case, aren't such antidemocratic pronouncements of the Supreme Court despots an open invitation to violence?

In response to violence by a few anti-abortionists, the pro-abortion movement has come dangerously close to calling for suppression of free speech: since they claim that those who believe that abortion is murder are really responsible for the violence since they have created an ideological atmosphere, a "climate of hate," which sets the stage for violence. But the shoe, of course, is really on the other foot. The stage, the conditions for the violence, have been set, not by anti-abortion writers and theorists, but by the absolute tyrants on the

Supreme Court and those who weave apologetics for that absolute rule.

It was not always thus. The truly democratic spirit of the Old Republic was much better expressed in the famous words of President Andrew Jackson about the leading big-government man of that epoch: "Mr. Justice Marshall has made his decision; now let him enforce *it*."

What to Do About the Judiciary

An essential ingredient of a truly effective revolution is that something must be done about the tyrannical judiciary. It is not enough, though vital, to advocate other essential legislative measures to roll back and abolish big government and the welfare state. The federal judiciary must be defanged for any of these programs to work.

Assuming that public pressure and voting can gain working control of Congress, it must then proceed against the federal judiciary. How? Impeachment is much too slow and cumbersome a process, and can only be done judge by judge. A constitutional amendment, to be submitted by Congress or the required number of states, the favorite goal of the term limits and Prop. 187 movements, is better, but is also very slow and can be blocked by a minority of the people. The swiftest and most direct path would be for Congress to act, as it can without cumbersome amendments, to remove virtually the entire jurisdiction of the federal judiciary.

Thus, if it is so desired, Congress can repeal the various federal judiciary acts and pass a new one returning the federal courts to their original very narrow and limited jurisdiction. And while, within the Constitution, Congress has to pay each Supreme Court member his existing salary, it can, using its appropriation power, strip the judges of all staff, clerks, buildings, perquisites, etc.

Furthermore, the Constitution only mandates a Supreme Court; Congress can abolish the rest of the federal judiciary, including the district and appeals courts, and thereby effectively crush the power of the Supreme Court by leaving it alone to try to handle all the thousands of cases that come annually before the federal courts. In a war between Congress and the federal courts, Congress possesses all the trump cards.

HAS THE REVOLUTION ALREADY BEEN BETRAYED?

It took less than 24 hours for the great, peaceful, democratic, popular revolution against big government and all its works to be betrayed. Not just by the courts, but most strikingly by the leadership among Republican Congressmen and Senators now positioned to thwart the will of the new Republicans whom the public installed to carry out their wishes. The leadership was egged on by our old friend William Kristol, who, at every post-election speech, urged Republicans not to go on "kamikaze" or "suicide" missions against big government. Instead, he urged them to focus on institutional reforms, win symbolic victories against one or two programs, slowly build public support for new reforms, etc.

And what should be the goal of all this tinkering and maneuvering? The goal, as he told an Empower America audience, is for Republicans to win back the White House in 1996. To Kristol and his friends, power for its own sake is the sole end of politics. What about limited government, liberty, property, and the like? Those are fine ideas to feed the conservative masses, but they have no relevance to "governing."

While the rank-and-file of conservatives has long caught on to Bob "High Tax" Dole, the major and dangerous betrayer of the Revolution is Newt Gingrich, who often engages in fiery, revolutionary, rightist rhetoric while actually collaborating with and sidling up to the collectivist welfare state. In the eighties, his spending record was not especially conservative and, indeed, was below average for Republicans. Recall too that the major legislative victory of this self-proclaimed "free trader" was the imposition of trade sanctions on South Africa, which he and Jack Kemp worked so hard for.

Unfortunately, the conservative public is all too often taken in by mere rhetoric and fails to weigh the actual deeds of their political icons. So the danger is that Gingrich will succeed not only in betraying, but in conning the revolutionary public into thinking that they have already won and can shut up shop and go home. There are a few critical tests of whether Gingrich or his "contract" is really, in actual deed, keeping faith with the revolution or whether he, or the other Republican leaders, are betraying it.

Taxes. Are tax rates, especially income taxes, substantially reduced (and, as soon as possible, abolished)? More important, is total tax revenue substantially reduced? Unfortunately, all the Republican leaders, including Gingrich, are still firmly committed to the axiom underlying the disastrous Bush-Democrat budget agreement of 1990: that any cut in tax revenue anywhere must be "balanced" by increased taxes, or "fees," or "contributions," somewhere else. So, in addition to big tax cuts in income taxes, no new or increased taxes should be proposed in any other area.

Government Spending. There must be big cuts in federal government spending, and that means real cuts, "cut-cuts," and not "capping," cuts in the rate of growth of spending, cuts in projected increases, consolidations, spending transfers, and all the rest of the nonsense that has altered the meaning of the simple word "cut." So far, "revolutionary" Gingrich has only talked about capping some spending to allow "cost of living" increases and transferring spending responsibilities from one agency or level of government to another.

But do I mean, horrors! cuts in defense, cuts in Social Security, cuts in Medicare, and all the rest? Yes, yes, and yes. It would be simplest and most effective to pass, say, an immediate, mandated 30 percent federal spending cut, to take effect in the first year. The slash would override any existing entitlements, and the bureaucrats could work out their hysteria by deciding what should be cut within this 30 percent mandate.

Deregulation. Deregulation of business and of individuals should be massive and immediate. There is no conceivable worthy argument for gradualism or "phasing in" in this area. It goes without saying that all unfunded mandates to states or individuals should be abolished forthwith. All "civil rights," disabilities "rights," regulations, etc. should be abolished. The same goes for any ballot or campaign regulations, let alone "reforms." Regulations and controls on labor relations, including the Norris-LaGuardia anti-injunction act and the sainted National Labor Relations Act, should be abolished.

Privatization. A serious move should be made to privatize federal government operations, and if not, to turn them over to the states, or at least, to private competition. A clear example would be the losing, inefficient, backward Postal Service. Federal public lands is another excellent example. Divesting federal assets, in addition to being a great good in itself, and aiding the Western anti-federal land revolution, would also help lower government expenditures.

Cutting the Bureaucracy. Again, capping, or slowing the rate of increase, of government employees, doesn't make a cut. There must be massive reductions, including abolition of entire useless and counterproductive government agencies. As a good start, how about abolishing the Departments of Energy, Education, HUD, Health and Human Services, and Commerce? And that means abolishing their functions as well. Otherwise, in a typical bureaucratic trick, the same functions would be shuffled to other existing departments or agencies.

Racial Preferences and Gun Control. Every honest pollster has to admit that these two issues were crucially important in the election, especially among a segment of the white male population who had previously evinced little interest in politics. Any government that denies a person the right to defend himself against private and public intrusion, and also prevents students and workers from realizing gains from their own hard work and study, is not a morally legitimate government. Yet at the urging of the Republican elite, the party has said nothing on these two issues. Gingrich himself has pledged not to repeal the Brady Bill, and the subject of civil-rights socialism is still banned from public discussion. Republicans are well positioned to break the ban, but the leadership is not interested in doing so.

Ending Counterfeit Money. Money is the most important single feature of the economy, and one way in which the government finances its own deficits and creates perpetual inflation is through what is essentially the printing of counterfeit money. To end this critical and destructive feature of statism and government intervention, we must return to a sound, free-market money, which means a return to a gold-coin standard for the dollar and the abolition of another crucial despotic federal agency not subject to popular or Congressional control: the Federal Reserve System, by which the government cartelizes and subsidizes the banking system. Short of abolition of the Fed, its operations should be "capped" or frozen, that is, it should never be allowed to purchase more assets.

Foreign Intervention, Including Foreign Aid and International Bureaucracies. Here is yet another case where all the "respectable" ruling elites, be they bureaucrats, academics, think tanks, big media, big business, banks, etc. are in total and admitted conflict with the general public. Under cover of the alleged necessity for "bipartisanship," the elites have imposed intervention, foreign aid, internationally managed trade, and approaches to world economic and even political government, against the wishes of the great majority of the American public.

In every case, from the United Nations and the Marshall Plan to Nafta and Gatt, the Republican leadership has gone in lockstep with the Democrats. As a result, Clinton was able to wheel in every ex-president, regardless of party, to agitate for each new measure of his. And at each step of the way, the president and the elites have threatened disaster to the world if each step is even delayed. And so far they have gotten away with it, despite the wishes of the public.

Using the above checklist, and sticking to these guidelines, every reader can easily decide for himself whether Gingrich, Dole, *et al.* have betrayed, or have cleaved to, the popular anti-big government, anti-Washington revolution. Forget such unenforceable diversions and gimmicks as the balanced-budget amendment, changing committee names, imposing new laws on Congress, or such relative trivia as the capital-gains tax cut, and look to real tax cuts, really balanced budgets, repealed regulations, and eliminated agencies.

The clearest test of whether the revolution has already been betrayed is to look at the truly outrageous action of Gingrich and Dole in betraying not only the popular revolution, but even their own recent victory. For they have scrambled, not only to pass the Clinton-Bush Gatt/WTO, but also to defy their own voters by agreeing to rush it through a totally discredited, Democrat-run, lame-duck Congress. The usual media outlets were strangely silent on the views of the American public, but an independent poll showed that 75 percent of the people opposed what as essentially a criminal procedure.

The disgusting spectacle of the defeated and discredited Tom Foley presiding over the shoving through of Gatt, with the help of Gingrich and Dole, and with the aid of the unconstitutional "fast track," was too much to bear. Foley is now lounging at home on the $123,804 pension he is "entitled" to for his years of government "service." Even after we kick them out of office, we can't stop these leeches from voting for global government schemes and sucking the blood of the taxpayer!

In this shocking and abject surrender to the Executive, Congress agreed to cut its own throat by depriving itself (and all its constituents) of the power to discuss and amend this monstrous treaty and even to collude in calling it an "agreement," so they can violate the clear constitutional requirement for a two-thirds vote of the Senate.

The elites can generally count on liberals to support big-government legislation like Gatt, Nafta, and the rest of the mercantilist-managerial apparatus of global economic control. But we must not forget, as the *Wall Street Journal* bragged the day of the Senate vote, that "The House GOP has now provided the bulk of votes for Bill Clinton's two notable achievements—Nafta and Gatt."

The rank and file is not at fault for these travesties of multinational statism. Many decent Republicans, including the others from Gingrich's state, voted against the treaty. But Gingrich will now use his power to punish such dissenters, and the incident will not be the last plunge taken by the Republican leadership into the politics of betrayal.

What Should Be Done?

The above assessment does not mean that there is no hope, that nothing can be done. On the contrary, what can and must be done is to mobilize the radical and revolutionary sentiment among the people. We need to translate the public's deeply held views into continuing pressure upon the government, especially on the Senators and Congressmen they have recently elected.

Among the freshman Congressmen, in particular, there are many genuine rightists and populists who sincerely burn to roll back big government, and who are not beholden to the Gingriches and the Rockefellers of the Republican Establishment. The voters and their organizations, aided by the truly conservative members of Congress, could keep pressuring the political elites to start putting into effect, instead of blocking, the will of the very voters that put them into power. If not, they can be swept away.

But nothing can be done without education. It is the crucially important task of conservative or libertarian intellectuals, think tanks, and opinion leaders such as the Mises Institute, to educate the public, businessmen, students, academics, journalists, and politicians about the true nature of what is going on, and about the vicious nature of the bipartisan ruling elites.

We must remember that the elites are a minority of the population; they have gotten away with their deceit and their misinformation because they have been in effective control of the institutional (media, intellectuals, etc.) channels that mould public opinion.

Most of the public have already come to a healthy suspicion and distrust of all the elites, and of their tendency to deceive and betray. But this mood of healthy distrust is not enough; the public and the worthy people in the media, academia, and politics, also have to understand what is really going on. In particular, they have to realize what measures would fulfill the popular will and carry through its desired revolution; what measures could only divert and scuttle the revolution against big government; and why and how the ruling opinion moulders have been deceiving them.

The Mises Institute, small as it is, is uniquely positioned to lead this education revolution. It is not beholden to government grants, big corporate interests, or even to the large foundations. That means it cannot be dictated to. Though relatively poor in overall resources, the Mises Institute possesses the most important assets of all: clarity of purpose and independence.

In the 12 years of its existence, Lew Rockwell carefully guarded these two assets, relying entirely on the financial support of principled individuals and unconnected businesses, and he has done this to the astonishment and anger of Left-liberals, official conservatives, and the legions of politico-think-tankers and Left-intellectuals on the make.

In all these tasks, the Mises Institute has already been extraordinarily effective. Standing virtually alone, and with severely limited resources, the Mises Institute has had a remarkably strong ideological impact. Just one example: the Mises Institute was first in print back in January with a sweeping denunciation of the World Trade Organization that not only exposed the present attempt to impose global trade management, but also delved into its history, tracing the WTO back through the 1970s, the 1940s, and even back to Woodrow Wilson's "World Trade Tribunal."

That article, along with the rest of the Mises Institute's work, defined the debate on the Right, Left, and center. Even one day before the House vote, an Associated Press story, in its section providing historical perspective, plagiarized from the Mises Institute virtually word for word.

The Institute didn't win—although it gave Clinton and his allies in the Republican Party plenty of trouble—but it did mobilize the American people and make sure that the revolution against big government will continue and intensify. And at its intellectual head will be the Institute.

By simply entering the public and intellectual debate from a principled and consistent libertarian and free-market perspective, the Mises Institute has already exposed the lies of that multitude of statists, would-be world planners, neo-Keynesian economists, left-over Marxists, and pretenders who dare to use such glorious words as "liberty . . . free markets," and "free trade" to connive at the exact opposite.

The word "liberal" was stolen from us by the social democrats a long time ago. Now we are in danger of these other words being filched from us as well. Only light from those dedicated to the truth can dispel this fog.

The Mises Institute has already been exerting the greatest ideological and political leverage per person and per dollar of any organization in this country. Any increase in its resources will be multiplied beyond measure in degree of impact.

Those who stress the importance of ideas in society and politics tend to concentrate solely on the long-run, on future generations. All that is true and important and must never be forgotten. But ideas are not only for the ages; they are vitally important in the here-and-now.

In times of revolutionary ferment in particular, social and political change tends to be sudden and swift. The elections of

November 1994 are only one striking example. The Mises Institute has a unique and glorious opportunity to make its ideas—of liberty, of free markets, of private property—count right now, and to help take back our glorious America from those who have betrayed its soul and its spirit. ◗

Index